Rent FAQ

Rent
FAQ

All That's Left to Know About Broadway's Blaze of Glory

Tom Rowan

APPLAUSE
THEATRE & CINEMA BOOKS
An Imprint of Hal Leonard LLC

Published in 2017 by Applause Theatre & Cinema Books
An Imprint of Hal Leonard LLC
7777 West Bluemound Road
Milwaukee, WI 53213

Trade Book Division Editorial Offices
33 Plymouth St., Montclair, NJ 07042

All images are from the author's collection unless otherwise noted.

All quotations from RENT® by Jonathan Larson are courtesy of the Larson family, Skeeziks, LLC

Every reasonable effort has been made to contact copyright holders and secure permission. Omissions can be remedied in future editions.

The FAQ series was conceived by Robert Rodriguez and developed with Stuart Shea.

Printed in the United States of America

Book design by Snow Creative

Library of Congress Cataloging-in-Publication Data is available upon request.

ISBN: 978-1-4950-5145-6

www.applausebooks.com

For my brother, Richard Rowan

Contents

Acknowledgments   ix

Preface   xi

Introduction   xvii

1 "One Song to Leave Behind": Jonathan Larson, Creator of *Rent*   1

2 "That Doesn't Remind Us of 'Musetta's Waltz'": The Opera That Inspired a Musical   20

3 "The Beauty of a Studio": From Conception to Workshop   42

4 "Our Benefactors on This Christmas Eve": The Producers and the Creative Team   59

5 "Who I Was Meant to Be": The Cast of Characters   67

6 "To Days of Inspiration": The Original Off-Broadway Production   83

7 "Being an Us for Once": The Original Cast   100

8 "How Did We Get Here?": A Synopsis of the Story of *Rent*   119

9 "Wanna Hit the Street?": *Rent* Makes It to Broadway   142

10 "Making Something Out of Nothing": The Designers and What They Brought to *Rent*   159

11 "Who's Heading Out of Town?": *Rent* on Tour   171

12 "Another Time—Another Place": *Rent* Crosses the Pond   187

13 "Adventure, Tedium, No Family, Boring Locations": *Rent* and Its Journey to Film   196

14 "But He's Got Great Footage": The Movie   213

15 "Seasons of Love": The Long Broadway Run and the Closing Performance   227

16 "Ginsberg, Dylan, Cunningham, and Cage": *Rent* Cultural Literacy   242

17 "Don't Look Back or You May Drown": The Return of *Rent* to Off-Broadway   282

18 "It'd Be Another Play": *tick, tick . . . BOOM!*   292

19 "I Escape and Ape Content": Spoofs and Imitations   300

20 "For Someone Who Longs for a Community of His Own": The Larson Legacy   305

21 "Anywhere You Could Possibly Go After New York": *Rent* in a Town Near You   310

Appendix One: *Rent* Timeline   351
Appendix Two: Cast List (with All Replacements) for Original
    Broadway Production, 1996–2008   353
Appendix Three: Opening Cast Lists for Touring and International
    Productions, 1996–1998   355
Appendix Four: Opening Cast Lists for Tours and Revivals, 2001–2016   357

Bibliography   359
Index   367

Acknowledgments

Billy Aronson
David Auburn
Blake Burba
Jonathan Burkhart
Paul Clay
Jerry Dalia
Tonya Dixon
Graham Duff
Drew Michael Gardner
Michael Greif
Victoria Leacock Hoffman
Jacqueline Hubbard
Ben Jay
Tamara Jenkins
Bob Johnson
Meghan Kastenholz
Marybeth Keating
Megan Kern
Bethany Knox
Al Larson
Julie Larson
Sandra Lee
Kerry Long
Joan Marcus

Kevin McCollum
Anne Dailey Meyer
Jonathan Mills
Nicola Murphy
James C. Nicola
Jason Niedle
Matthew O'Grady
Adam Pascal
Nina Pratt
Anthony Rapp
Carol Rosegg
David Roth
Richard Rowan
Daphne Rubin-Vega
Charlie Siedenburg
Jonathan Silverstein
Diane Smith-Sadak
Tracie Thoms
John Tomasicchio
Rob Urbinati
Adam Webster
Micah White
Anthony Wright
Marlies Yearby

Preface

I was living in Denver when I first heard about *Rent* but starting to think, tentatively, about moving to New York. So I was keeping close track of the city's theater scene with the help of the now long-gone but fondly remembered magazine *TheaterWeek* (and its successor *In Theater*). I was a lifelong musical theater aficionado and also, since college, a devoted opera lover, so when I read in the magazine about a new rock musical inspired by Puccini's *La bohème*, I was immediately intrigued. I followed news and reviews of the downtown show with great interest, as well as sorrow over the tragically timed death of its young creator.

This was during a time in my life when I was taking annual trips to New York to spend a week or so visiting my brother Richard, an actor in the city, and a few of my old college friends who had moved there—and of course seeing shows every night. By the time I started planning my 1996 trip, *Rent* had moved to Broadway and become a national sensation. Though limited finances meant I generally made my decisions about which shows to see based largely on what was available for half price at the TKTS booth in Times Square, that year I knew I absolutely had to see *Rent*, so I called Ticketmaster from Denver and paid full price for a decent orchestra seat. (It was worth it.)

I was fortunate enough to see the entire, inimitable original cast—not a single understudy on at that matinee—and I knew at the time that that was something I'd be talking about for years. (I didn't know until I started working on this book, however, that my Playbill from that day could now be worth around a hundred dollars! Don't worry, I'm keeping it.)

I was excited by the energy of the show, the beauty of the music (especially "Seasons of Love"), and the commitment of the cast. I had already lost several friends and colleagues to AIDS and was impressed to see that crisis addressed in a musical. But the number that hit me the most on that first visit was "What You Own," as I was at that point unsure about so many aspects of my future. Would I ever get the guts to leave Colorado and pursue my dream of a directing career in Manhattan? If so, would I myself become a starving bohemian artist? Could I handle that? (I had been delaying the decision to move to the city because of my perception that it was unaffordable, and *Rent* did little to allay that fear!) The great song, soaringly vocalized by Anthony Rapp and Adam Pascal, struck me with its immediacy: we were indeed facing the "end of the millennium," and it was scary. Would the world's computers all crash as people were predicting? Would there be any place left to pursue our dreams, or would financial exigencies crush us? Jonathan Larson had struck a chord for our generation.

I came home to Denver and told my friends, including my coworkers at the Tattered Cover Book Store, all about it. "You've actually seen *Rent?* Wow! What's it like?" they asked me. One of those coworkers, Mark Barnhouse, was also my roommate at the time; I lived in the spare bedroom of a condo he owned in Denver's Capitol Hill neighborhood. (Like Roger, I had a roommate named Mark!) Though not a "theatre person," as Joanne would have put it, Mark loved musicals and particularly the work of Stephen Sondheim. He collected every possible recording of every possible Sondheim song, and he had a similar devotion to Bob Dylan. So as that combination might suggest, he of course fell in love with the score to *Rent.* We got the CD and played it all summer, learning the songs by heart. We watched the cast perform at the Tony Awards and win Best Musical (I taped it on Mark's VCR!), as well as an episode of the *Charlie Rose Show* where that excellent interviewer spoke with the show's director, Michael Greif; producer, Kevin McCollum; and three of the cast members. It even included excerpts of "One Song Glory" and "Out Tonight"! I taped that, too, watched it a bunch of times, and showed it to my parents. My enthusiasm knew no bounds.

My mother in fact *was* a "theatre person," an actress, and during those last years in Denver we worked together on several plays. I wanted to share my growing enthusiasm for *Rent* with her, so when the national tour (the "Angel Company") came to town, I had my one day as a Renthead, spending a whole, very cold winter day sitting on the concrete in the outdoor Galleria of the Denver Center for the Performing Arts waiting for discounted tickets. That was of course the beginning of the "rush ticket" phenomenon, which the producers of *Rent* originated, and the touring companies were following the procedure established by the Broadway show. In Denver, getting there around nine o'clock in the morning proved early enough; I of course brought a book to read, though I can't remember what it was. I should have brought a blanket or pillow to sit on; my legs and my behind were frozen stiff by the end of the afternoon when I finally bought the tickets. My mom drove down to the theater to pick me up and took me out to a nice dinner in a warm restaurant before we went back to the Center to watch the show in the ultra-modern Buell Theatre. It lost something in that pristine environment: it didn't have the advantage of the downtown grunge club décor devised for New York's Nederlander Theatre; the sound team hadn't quite mastered the Buell's acoustics; and some of the touring cast members didn't demonstrate the same commitment the originals had to making sure we heard every word of

Jonathan Larson's lyrics. My mom was over seventy at the time, so her hearing wasn't the greatest anyway, and I felt a little let down by the fact that I was sure she was missing a lot of the words and much of the story. Nevertheless, even though *Rent* wasn't about her generation in any way, she knew a special musical when she saw it; afterward she said, "That really is a superb show." The long sit on the cold ground had been worth it.

I saw the Broadway production for the second time in the fall of 1998, when a directing fellowship with the Drama League got me to New York for four glorious months. (Thank you, Drama League!) It was just after Thanksgiving, and I had just started working on the first play I ever directed in the city (a revival of Richard Greenberg's one-act "The Author's Voice") when I found I had a night off and decided to head over to the Nederlander Theatre and try my luck for rush tickets. By that time the long lines had sensibly been replaced by a lottery system; no more waiting all day. There was a big crowd that afternoon, all atwitter with the usual anticipation and excitement. It was the first time I'd ever tried the lottery, so I wasn't expecting to win, but I was pleasantly surprised to run into G. R. Johnson—the young actor whom I had just cast as the lead in the Greenberg play—who was also waiting to see if he could get a ticket. (He was looking forward to auditioning for the role of Mark and wanted a refresher.) When both of our names were called, I took it as a positive omen for our show, my career, and life in New York in general! I called my old friend Scott McKinstry, with whom I had run a small Shakespeare company in Denver years earlier; he had already moved to New York but had never seen *Rent*, so I offered him my extra ticket and we saw the show together. Of course he loved it.

For the next several years I was living at 43rd Street and Eighth Avenue, just a couple of blocks from the Nederlander, which is on 41st between Broadway and Eighth. As I worked various jobs and directed and wrote plays, I loved having the opportunity to see *Rent* occasionally. As the years passed, the crowds at the six o'clock lottery drawing diminished in size somewhat; often close to half of the people trying for tickets would get in, and I had good luck on numerous occasions. One of the fun parts was being able to call a friend a few minutes after six and say, "Guess what, I just won the *Rent* lottery; do you want to see the show tonight?" There was one time I couldn't find anyone who was free on such short notice, so I sold the second ticket to a woman who was waiting for cancellations when I got back to the theater; after that I would occasionally go to the show by myself, but it was always more fun to share it with someone.

Part of the fun was seeing what different actors brought to it. Some of the roles are notoriously tough to cast, and the replacements had their ups and downs. But from seeing the show on Broadway seven or eight times over the years, even with memories of the originals, there are some specific characterizations that remain particularly vivid memories:

Marcy Harriell, the second Mimi, a petite spitfire who exuded such ferociously exuberant energy in "Out Tonight" that she defied anyone to call her cute.

Trey Ellett, who gave a deceptively low-key performance as Mark, commanding attention with smarts and subtle humor.

Natalie Venetia Belcon, later to create the role of "Gary Coleman" in *Avenue Q*, who was an especially glamorous, classy Joanne.

Jaime Lee Kirchner, the best dancer who ever played Mimi, stunningly beautiful and achingly convincing as a drug-addicted teen.

Will Chase, a real actor who found lots of layers in Roger and proved that a "Broadway voice" could rock persuasively.

(And of course any other fan of the show could and would come up with a different list.)

Even the less successful replacements usually had something. I remember one time when I commented on an understudy who gave a particularly woeful performance as Roger; the friend I saw the show with that evening responded: "You're absolutely right; he's really bad. But I liked him!"

A special excitement radiated from the Nederlander in 2008 when both Adam Pascal and Anthony Rapp returned to their original roles as Roger and Mark for a limited run. I was lucky enough to win the lottery one night early in their engagement, and I then went back and managed to get standing room for their last performance—a sentimental occasion, as most in the audience at that point assumed it would be the last time the two of them would ever do the show. It felt like a rock concert when they first walked out onstage: how often does a Broadway musical get a standing ovation not just at the end but *at the beginning*? But I will never forget the way Anthony Rapp handled that. A lesser actor could easily have treated that night as a victory lap, surfing the waves of the audience's excitement as they cheered and screamed for all their favorite moments. But there was no way Anthony was going to let that show devolve into a party; the musical itself and everything it meant was more important than that. He stood absolutely still on the stage and stared us down until the house was quiet and then, with impeccable seriousness and simplicity, began to tell the story of *Rent*. From the first word he made it clear that he felt honored to have the chance to tell that story one more time, and responsible for taking care of it; he accepted the energy coming at him from the house but through honesty and purity of intent transformed it into real attention, and took us on the journey he needed to take us on: a rich and full experience of the play. Adam and the rest of the cast followed suit, and you can be sure the audience heard every word; the standing ovation at the *end* of the show had been earned—not just by who these guys were and their place in the show's history, but by what they did that very special night. It remains one of my most cherished theatrical memories.

Because I have loved *Rent* for so long, the opportunity to research and write this book has been an unexpected privilege. It's been exciting to meet some of the amazing artists who worked on the show and talk to them one-on-one about their experiences. In some cases I was shy about requesting interviews; after twenty years, would any of them be tired of being asked about *Rent*? But there was no hint of that from anybody; the experience was so important in all of their lives that they still light up when they talk about it. Family members and close friends of Jonathan Larson have also been wonderfully generous, helpful, and very open in sharing painful recollections as well as joyful ones. I hope I have been able to honor them, and their memories, in telling the story of this uniquely gifted artist and the inspiring musical that has meant so much to so many people.

Introduction

The musical play is considered one of the few distinctly American art forms. New musicals have appeared on Broadway every year for the past century, through good times and bad, and the genre has continued to develop, keeping pace (or not) with changing cultural mores and evolving tastes in music. In the middle of the last century, the Broadway musical was central to American culture, giving expression to themes and ideas and dreams deeply rooted in the national psyche. If you didn't live close enough to New York to see the latest hits on Broadway, you saw them on tour or at the movies or heard the songs on the radio or on TV. Shows like *Oklahoma!*, *South Pacific*, *Guys and Dolls*, *The Music Man*, and *West Side Story* became part of our national mythology, fed our sense of who we were, and provided much of the soundtrack to our lives. And then something happened.

As America moved into the sixties and seventies, the culture started to splinter. The "generation gap" divided parents, who grew up on the American Songbook, from their kids, who were rebelling and embracing new kinds of music. The Vietnam War and Watergate shook American's faith in the integrity of the nation. Times Square and the Broadway Theater District fell on hard times; drug dealers and porn shops and prostitutes competed with theaters for attention, and the area no longer felt safe for families. TV, film, and sporting events replaced theater at the center of American cultural life, and Broadway tickets became too expensive for many people to afford. Exciting or innovative new musicals like *Cabaret*, *A Chorus Line*, or *Sweeney Todd* occasionally appeared, but they were few and far between, replaced by revivals, or retro confections that seemed like revivals, and then by the megamusicals or pop operas of the eighties, most of which were imports from London. People took to referring to theater as "the fabulous invalid," even predicting the death of Broadway, or joked about musical theater having become the exclusive province of gay men, wealthy tourists, and senior citizens. What was once relevant had become nostalgia, even camp.

Enter Jonathan Larson, born in 1960. He was very clear about what he wanted to do. He was determined to change the face of American musical theatre, and he would do it by bringing it to his own generation, the "MTV generation." He was going to revivify the Broadway show by writing musicals that told stories through genuine rock music. How well did he succeed?

Larson was by no means the first person who had tried to merge the traditions of musical theater with the world of rock and roll. But the history of rock musicals prior to the mid-nineties had been a spotty one. Rock music, or a version of it, made an appearance on Broadway as early as the year of Larson's birth, in the squeaky clean *Bye Bye Birdie*. That essentially traditional, old-fashioned musical comedy took a light-hearted look at the impact that early rock and roll was having on American culture. Inspired by the frenzy into which teenagers all over the country exploded when Elvis Presley was drafted into the military in 1957, songwriters Charles Strouse and Lee Adams gave Conrad Birdie (their Presley stand-in) songs like "One Last Kiss" and "Honestly Sincere," which approximated Presley's rockin' style but did so in a tongue-in-cheek fashion, more as a spoof of rock and roll than a genuine contribution to the genre.

It wasn't until the late sixties that a show with an authentic rock ethos made a splash. The legendary *Hair*, with book and lyrics by James Rado and Gerome Ragni and music by Galt MacDermot, was billed as "an American tribal love rock musical"; it opened Joseph Papp's Public Theater in 1967 and, in a very different production with a revised book and a different director, made it to Broadway the next year. With its barely comprehensible plot and an undisciplined, freewheeling aesthetic, *Hair*, especially in its Broadway incarnation, made little attempt to follow the rules or observe the conventions of musical theater. But MacDermot's gorgeous score managed to charm even audiences who thought they didn't like rock music, and people flocked to the high-energy show as a relatively user-friendly way to experience a taste of the counterculture. Free love, ethnic and sexual diversity, and drug use were all zestfully celebrated in a musical that also expressed that generation's very real outrage over the war in Vietnam. Jonathan Larson loved it, and often cited it as a forebear of *Rent*, which he intended as "a *Hair* for the nineties." As Charles Isherwood pointed out in a 2007 *New York Times* article: "*Hair* was one of the last Broadway musicals to saturate the culture as shows from the golden age once regularly did." But though *Hair* was a phenomenon and spawned hit songs, it didn't really usher in a new movement in the theater; its hippies were enjoyed as rather exotic guests on Broadway, not hailed as the wave of the future. And though MacDermot had one more hit with the musical version of Shakespeare's *Two Gentlemen of Verona*, his other attempts to follow up the success of his first musical flopped. (Anybody remember *Dude* or *Via Galactica?*)

Though both musical theater and rock music are considered distinctly American art forms, the next big rock musical to hit Broadway was a British import. Lyricist Tim Rice and composer Andrew Lloyd Webber both thrilled and shocked theatergoers with *Jesus Christ Superstar*, a 1971 staging of their 1970 concept album. And if audiences at the time wondered what could possibly be weirder than a rock musical based on the life of Christ, the answer was obvious: *two* rock musicals based on the life of Christ. Stephen Schwartz's kinder and gentler take on the subject, *Godspell*, opened at around the same time Off-Broadway. Both musicals made it to the screen in 1973, and both were major influences on Larson as well. He saw *Superstar* on Broadway and listened to the album until he could play the whole score on the piano, and in college he got the role of Jesus in *Godspell*. Yet neither show, successful as they were, ushered in a new era. Nearly fifty years later, both Lloyd Webber and Schwartz are, impressively, still at work, but both composers have seemed to drift further away from their rock roots with each successive show. Lloyd Webber became the king of the British pop operatic spectacle (a genre Larson deplored) in the eighties; his record-smashing *The Phantom of the Opera* acknowledges Puccini's music as an influence, but Lloyd Webber used this influence in an utterly different way from how Larson used it in *Rent*. For his part, Schwartz followed *Godspell* up with a big Broadway hit, the stylish *Pippin*, in 1972, but he eventually decamped for Hollywood and Disney. He did return to Broadway with the megahit *Wicked* in 2003; call it a rock musical if you really want to.

So where were the young songwriters bringing Broadway into the future through rock and roll? The monster hit *Grease* (1972) used imitation fifties rock to evoke a middle-aged audience's nostalgia for high school. *The Rocky Horror Show* (1974), a so-bad-it's-good British import, flopped on Broadway but became a perennial cult hit as a film; designed to poke fun at fifties and sixties B-movies, it too had a retro slant (though its freewheeling take on alternative sexualities was ahead of its time). Tom Eyen and Henry Krieger's *Dreamgirls* (1981), in a dazzling production by the director Michael Bennett, was a black musical written by white men; it used imitation Motown and R&B to tell the story of a sixties girl group modeled on the Supremes. But isn't rock supposed to be the music of the young, challenging the establishment and changing the rules? The fact that even rock musicals were looking backward rather than forward says a lot about the state Broadway was in at the time.

After *Dreamgirls*, the major rock musical contender of the eighties was the always-problematic *Chess*, which, like *Superstar*, began life as a hit record. The first stage version was a mixed success in London, but the production was troubled; director Bennett withdrew midway into the process (no one knew he had AIDS) and was replaced by Trevor Nunn. Nunn reshaped the show for Broadway with the playwright Richard Nelson, and it flopped there in 1988. A collaboration between Rice and the songwriters of the Swedish rock group ABBA, the show used an international championship chess match as a metaphor for relations between the USSR and the West—but the Cold War was ending at the time, so *Chess* was dated before it even opened. Though the script didn't quite work, some critics hailed the music, perhaps justly, as the best rock score yet written for a musical. (They would most likely agree that, eight years later, *Rent* stole that title.)

So the rock musical still hadn't really taken hold of Broadway by the beginning of the nineties. There were a couple of interesting entries in the years leading up to *Rent*, however. Another British example, *The Who's Tommy*, which had started as a record album way back in 1969, actually predated *Superstar*; it had been the first piece to call itself a rock opera. Having thrilled fans for years as a concert and a movie, it finally made it to Broadway in 1993, but the visually dynamic production by the director Des McAnuff capped it with a family-values ending that was probably the furthest thing from what the creators had in mind. (The irony was not lost on Larson.) And in what was a particularly odd coincidence, the last original rock musical to become a major hit prior to *Rent* was, like *Rent*, also an adaptation of a Puccini opera! Written by Claude-Michel Schönberg and Alain Boublil, the French songwriters responsible for the earlier megahit *Les Misérables*, *Miss Saigon* transplants the story of Puccini's *Madama Butterfly* to the era of the Vietnam War. It opened in London in 1989 and on Broadway in 1991, when *Rent* was in its earliest developmental stages; given the timeline, there's no way either show could have been influenced by the other.

To be sure, there were other rock musicals that played Broadway between *Hair* and the advent of *Rent*, and some notable Off-Broadway entries as well. But there were always problems, and the most successful attempts were a generation old by the time Larson came around. To a teenager in the nineties, seventies rock could sound almost as dated as Rodgers and Hammerstein. Larson felt no one was writing musicals that really spoke to the people of his generation in their own musical language, and he was right. There was a niche waiting to be filled.

Why is it so hard to tell a story onstage through rock music? The perceptive musical theater historian Ethan Mordden, in his book *The Happiest Corpse I've Ever Seen*, summed up the dilemma as well as anyone: "Rock has not worked artistically for musicals because the percussive sound, driven by The Beat, makes characterization impossible." Other authorities, including

Stephen Sondheim, have expressed it in similar terms. The structure of a rock song is repetitious, driving the same phrases home again and again but generally not changing or moving forward; a musical theater song, on the other hand, has to tell a story: something has to happen, someone has to change. For this to occur you have to be able to understand the lyrics, and it can be extremely difficult to make that possible when there's a rock band playing. Even the original production of *Rent* took most of its Off-Broadway run to solve the sound balance problems, and theater groups that revive the show today are often taken by surprise at how much of a challenge that is.

Even if you have the perfect sound system, however, it's rare to find a rock musician who can write a theater song. But Larson was, as his friends sometimes put it, "a Broadway baby" as much as he was a rock and roller. He had loved musicals since childhood and had been mentored by no less a light than Sondheim. He understood the different song genres that need to be in a musical. There's the obligatory "I Want" song, where a leading character gets things started by telling the audience exactly what he or she wants from life. *Rent* actually has two of these—"One Song Glory" and "Out Tonight"—and they are both great examples. Then there's the "List Song," which not every musical has, but they sure can help. (Think of "You're the Top" from *Anything Goes* or "My Favorite Things" from *The Sound of Music*.) Both of *Rent*'s most iconic numbers—"La Vie Bohème" and "Seasons of Love"—fall into this category. The score includes character songs and comedy numbers, too. Most importantly, there are songs that tell a story, songs where characters change each other and come out at the end in a different place from where they started. Both James Nicola and Kevin McCollum (two of *Rent*'s original producers) have said that what really sold them on the score was the duet "Light My Candle": a genuine rock love song that is also a complete dramatic scene. Just as impressively, Larson constructed complex ensemble numbers for numerous voices, as ingenious as the ensembles in a Mozart or Donizetti opera, and what previous rock show could boast musical conversations to compare with "You'll See" or "Happy New Year"? It's not only a beautiful score but a truly sophisticated one.

Yet it's not just the music that made *Rent* the show that spoke to a generation. Larson had his finger on issues that his peers were passionately concerned about. Economic inequality, homelessness, gentrification, the plight of the artist in society, drug addiction, and above all the AIDS crisis were unusually serious, provocative, and timely subjects to find in a Broadway musical. Though *Rent* has sometimes been criticized for oversimplifying or romanticizing some of these issues, it didn't flinch from tackling them or from putting them onstage in ways that were both evocative and provocative. It engaged with the zeitgeist in a way musicals just weren't doing, and became a national sensation in the process—and then an international one. *Rent* gave voice to LGBT characters and marginalized populations. It celebrated individuality and diversity and gave disempowered young people a chance to see themselves onstage; many have said it saved their lives.

And yet there's more. To truly understand the impact of *Rent* and its unique appeal to audiences, it's useful to look at the opera that inspired it in the first place: Giacomo Puccini's 1896 classic *La bohème*. Initially dismissed by many critics, *La bohème* has become, at least in this country, by far the most popular opera in the repertoire. What makes it so special? Yes, the music is beautiful, and yes, the story is tragic and moving; the same can be said of many operas by Puccini and others. But most Italian operas of that time are relentlessly serious in tone. A tragic story was meant to be told in music of nobility and grandeur, and the line between tragedy and comedy was generally not crossed. *La bohème*, however, breaks that rule. It ends sadly, but it's full of comedy and humor. There are practical jokes, comedic anecdotes, and funny characters. Even in their poverty, the bohemian friends find humor and joy in their day-to-day lives: up to and including the last scene, right before Musetta enters with the dying Mimì, the friends are cavorting playfully, laughing and dancing and celebrating life. Perhaps that's why the opera is so much more beloved than any other. Because in reality, life is neither farcically comic nor relentlessly tragic; it's both at the same time. By mixing joy and humor into the pathos, Puccini and his librettists made an opera that feels like real life. And Jonathan Larson's musical does the same thing. A show about people struggling with poverty and homelessness and AIDS sounds like a daunting prospect, yet *Rent* is suffused with laughter and joy.

When the musical's script was still being developed, and Larson was struggling with an overly diffuse and confusing plot, James Nicola suggested that he come up with one sentence that encapsulated what the show was about. It took him a long time to boil it down, but the sentence he finally came up with was this: "*Rent* is about a community celebrating life, in the face of death and AIDS, at the turn of the century." That sense of celebration, of finding joy even within impossible circumstances, is what gives the show its lasting power. That it moves us as much as ever today, seventeen years after the turn of the millennium, when AIDS is no longer a death sentence and the world has changed in so many ways, proves that the show Larson wrote is bigger than even he thought it was.

When you ask people who knew Jonathan Larson, or who were involved in the creation of *Rent*, if there's anything they specifically want to say about the show, many of them have the same answer. They say that what makes them most angry is the suggestion, sometimes propounded by insensitive souls, that the musical only became a hit because of Larson's death. And they are right to be angry. Maybe the show could have run a year or two on that, but it ran on Broadway for twelve years and continues to thrill audiences all over the world. And a big reason for the long run was that, far more than most musicals, it got repeat customers, people who fell in love with the show and came back to see it again and again. That's not because of publicity, or curiosity about a tragic real-life story; that's because the show truly entertains people, and moves us, and changes us. When the show was about to close on Broadway, one of the cast members said that doing *Rent* makes you a better human being. Nine years later, the musical still helps us understand community, still teaches us how to celebrate life, and to value others and honor their creativity. We need it today more than ever.

But what of the *future* of rock musicals? How much did Larson really change the face of the musical theater? Though we can only imagine what other shows he himself might have written if he had lived, it is certain that his legacy has made a big difference. The yearly grants given by the foundation that bears his name support new young musical theater writers, providing them with the time and resources to create new work. And though Broadway is still home to lots of revivals, jukebox shows, and traditional musicals both new and old, there is a new generation of playwrights and songwriters honoring Larson's legacy by telling serious stories through contemporary music. All of them cite *Rent* as an inspiration. They include Tom Kitt and Brian Yorkey (*Next to Normal*), Benj Pasek and Justin Paul (*Dear Evan Hansen*), and of course Lin-Manuel Miranda (*In the Heights* and *Hamilton*).

In 2014, when he was preparing to play Jon (the character very closely based on Jonathan Larson) in a concert presentation of *tick, tick . . . BOOM!* at City Center, Miranda wrote an appreciation of Larson for the *New York Times*. He had first seen *Rent* on Broadway at age seventeen, and he revealed that it was the reason he had started writing musicals. It was the first show he'd seen that had a cast diverse enough to reflect the city around him, and he saw himself in it. It rocked his world, changed his life, and opened up a universe of possibility regarding what could be accomplished in the musical theater. He wrote:

> The characters were worried about the things I worried about: finding a community, being an artist, surviving in New York . . . Jonathan, if you can hear me, you fulfilled every promise and then some. We continue to perform your work, and when we do, someone else's life is changed. Someone else has permission to tell their story because you told yours. Someone else has permission to dream as big as you did. Someone else will struggle to do his best with the time they have. Someone else will try to find the right words to thank you, thank you, thank you.

"One Song to Leave Behind"

Jonathan Larson, Creator of *Rent*

J onathan Larson was born in Mount Vernon, New York, on February 4, 1960, the son of Allan Larson, a direct marketing executive, and his wife Nanette. Soon afterward the family moved to White Plains, a suburban community about thirty-five miles north of New York City in Westchester County, because they felt it would be a great place to raise a family. Jonathan's older sister Julie has recalled their formative years as an idyllic, *Leave It to Beaver*-type childhood. Though it was a fairly conservative community, the Larsons were always a politically liberal family; Al and Nan voted for George McGovern in the 1972 presidential election even though it seemed like all of their neighbors were for Nixon. Still, they were socially active and had a warm circle of close friends.

Jonathan was surrounded by music from a very young age. His father Al recalled a day when he was changing little Jonathan's diaper and the boy started singing "Yellow Bird" (a song he would later reference in the lyrics to *tick, tick . . . BOOM!*). Al Larson enjoyed listening to the live radio broadcasts from the Metropolitan Opera, and since *La bohème*—the eventual source material for the plot of *Rent*—was one of the most popular pieces in that company's repertoire, Jonathan would most certainly have heard the music from it early on. (According to Al, the first time Jonathan saw *La bohème* staged was when he was about eight years old; the family happened to see a puppet version of the opera in a Swedish restaurant in Chicago!)

The Larsons also had an affinity for folk music, from Paul Robeson to the Weavers and Pete Seeger, and young Jonathan loved to listen to rock and roll. His favorite artists included the Beatles, Billy Joel, Elton John, and the Who.

He developed a love for musical theater early on as well. His parents collected cast albums, which Jonathan and Julie listened to avidly, and White Plains is a quick train ride away from Manhattan, so the family came into the city periodically to see Broadway shows. The first one Jonathan saw, according to Nan, was *1776*, a hit that ran from 1969 to 1972; the now-classic *Fiddler on the Roof* soon followed. The Larsons also saw *Hair* and *Jesus Christ Superstar*, both of which left lasting impressions on Jonathan. When he got a little older he became a devotee of the works of Stephen Sondheim, especially *Sweeney Todd*; he was always drawn to shows that had something to say, rather than being just escapist entertainment.

School Days

Even as a young child, Jonathan was clearly a creative spirit. He and Julie, along with some friends, put on *The Wizard of Oz* in the backyard. Julie recalls that, when given a routine assignment like a book report, Jonathan would often find an unusually creative way to fulfill it—like making a film or turning it into a play. In fact, a play he wrote in the third grade was staged by his class, and a photo from it made the local newspaper.

Though he only studied piano formally for a couple of years, Jonathan sang in the school choirs and played in the band and orchestra: first trumpet and then, because he was tall, he was encouraged to take on the tuba as well. His music reading skills at that point were limited, but he had such an intuitive ear that he was able to get by, improvising within the structure of the song. Throughout high school, he got parts in all of the school plays and musicals, including *West Side Story* and *Gypsy*, and took part in community theater as well. If his personality was pleasantly unassuming, even slightly gawky in daily life, he evinced a genuine charisma and star presence when he hit the stage. His family, always supportive, encouraged him to pursue his dreams and came to believe he had the talent for a career as a professional actor.

Around sixth or seventh grade, Jonathan became best friends with a boy named Matthew O'Grady. He would take Matthew into the city to see musicals when they didn't have school—though O'Grady didn't always share Larson's enthusiasm for Sondheim's works. In the summers they went to camp together or to the beaches on Long Island. O'Grady knew he was gay from a very early age, but he kept it a secret in high school; at that time teenagers seldom talked openly about such things. The only friend he trusted enough to come out to was Jonathan, who proved very supportive. The early empathy Larson developed for gay people would play an important part, years later, in the creation of *Rent*.

College Years

When the time came to apply to colleges, Jonathan chose Adelphi University in Garden City, New York, which awarded him a four-year, full tuition scholarship to the BFA acting program. He quickly emerged as the school's leading actor, playing a wide range of parts from Malvolio in Shakespeare's *Twelfth Night* to Lucky in *Moonchildren*. He also wrote songs for cabaret shows presented in the cafeteria. These presentations, of which the school put on four per year, were often political in nature, dealing with social issues in a satirical style reminiscent of *Saturday Night Live*. From those early experiences, Jonathan took a certain Brechtian/cabaret sensibility, and a commitment to using live theater as a force for social change, that would inform his future work, up to and including *Rent*.

As Larson later told interviewer John Istel of *American Theatre*: "Adelphi was a lousy place to go to school in the sense that it's in suburbia and that's where I grew up. But it was run by a disciple of Robert Brustein's named Jacques Burdick, who basically made an undergraduate version of the Yale Drama School. And I was mature enough coming out of high school to appreciate it." Burdick recognized the young man's musical talent and became something of a mentor, asking Jonathan to compose the score for a play he was writing called *Libro de Buen Amor*, based on the work of a medieval Spanish poet. Another musical Jonathan wrote while still in school was the revue *Sacrimmoralinority*, a Brechtian satire on the Moral Majority. A collaboration with another student named David Glenn Armstrong, it was produced at Adelphi in the winter of 1981.

It was in college that Jonathan met someone who was to become one of his most significant friends and one of the staunchest and most resourceful supporters of his work: Victoria Leacock (now Victoria Leacock Hoffman). She was a freshman in the theater department when he was a senior and met him when she showed up to work tech for a production of *Godspell* in which he was playing Jesus. In the introduction she wrote for the published version of the libretto to *Rent*, she reveals that Larson was her first love. They dated for four months; Leacock ascribed the breakup to an argument they had over the movie *Pennies from Heaven*: he liked it, while she thought it was mean spirited. But as she says, "What we found so special in each other didn't change; it went right into being a really serious friendship." After they both moved to New York, she would work tirelessly to get his musicals out into the world, producing and publicizing readings and showcases at various venues.

Pursuing Dreams in the Real World

Following his graduation, Jonathan got a job in summer stock, working at the Barn Theatre in Augusta, Michigan, where he played piano and earned his Equity card. One of the actresses in the company was the future Broadway star Marin Mazzie; she and Jonathan became good friends.

Armed with his union card, Larson moved to New York City. With another friend from the Barn Theatre, the actor/songwriter Scott Burkell, Larson and Mazzie formed a trio act they called J. Glitz; the three of them performed around town at open mics and cabarets like Panache and Don't Tell Mama. As Burkell recently told James Sanford of the *Lansing City Pulse*, "Our opening number—without a hint of irony—was a medley of 'Fame,' 'Downtown' and

Jonathan Larson.   *Photo courtesy of the Larson family*

'On Broadway.'" (In 2010, Burkell was guest director for a production of *Rent* at Michigan State University.)

In New York Larson auditioned for many shows, both plays and musicals, but found that casting directors didn't know what to do with him: he was a leading man in a character actor's body. Before long he put acting on the back burner—to the dismay of his family, who missed seeing him in plays. He had decided his real calling was writing songs, and he wanted to devote his time to that.

He took a succession of survival jobs, including working as a waiter at Hamburger Harry's in the theater district, before settling in at the Moondance Diner in Soho; like many early diners, it was housed in an actual renovated railroad car. He would work there as a waiter for almost ten years; for part of that time, one of his coworkers was a young man named Jesse L. Martin, who would one day create the role of Tom Collins in *Rent*. Popular with customers and coworkers, Jonathan eventually established a schedule at the diner whereby he worked only Fridays, Saturdays, and Sundays—the best days for tips—leaving the rest of the week free for writing, which he pursued with great discipline, usually working eight hours a day on his music. This was the eighties, the era when Broadway was dominated by spectacular pop operas imported from Britain: *Cats*, *Les Misérables*, *The Phantom of the Opera*, etc. Not a fan of that type of work, Larson conceived of a personal mission to change the face of the American musical theater, and he wanted to do it by combining his love for Broadway with his passion for rock music, bridging the two worlds and creating musicals for the MTV generation.

An Inspiring Mentor

One source of encouragement was the legendary Stephen Sondheim, the greatest musical theater composer and lyricist of his generation. Jonathan had been inspired by the master's work since childhood, and viewed him as the epitome of what a musical theater writer should be. (He reportedly had long late-night talks with a college friend about "why Sondheim is god and Jerry Herman the enemy.") He was still at Adelphi when he first wrote to his idol, and during his years in New York he would periodically send Sondheim manuscripts he was working on for feedback. Though their styles were very different, Sondheim recognized the young man's talent and became a faithful supporter, often writing letters of recommendation when Larson applied for grants. Jonathan also got the opportunity to do an observership, shadowing Sondheim and observing his creative process during rehearsals for the master's musical *Into the Woods* (1987). On Sondheim's recommendation, Larson joined the American Society of Composers, Authors and Publishers (ASCAP) and took part in the organization's musical theater workshop. Though he later described it as being similar to a twelve-step program for songwriters, it was valuable because it gave him the opportunity to play his songs for top professionals in the musical theater community.

The Bohemian Life

During this period, Larson's own lifestyle was perilously close to that of the characters in *Rent*, though he lived on the west edge of downtown and not in Alphabet City. He found a fifth-floor loft at 508 Greenwich Street; the neighborhood was not quite part of the West Village nor officially in either SoHo or Tribeca, so he and his friends made up their own name for it: "Assho." He initially shared the apartment with a visual artist named Ann Egan and had numerous roommates move in and out over the years, including James Clunie and Greg Beals (brother of Jennifer Beals of *Flashdance* fame and later a writer for *Newsweek*). The other tenants were Jonathan's two pet cats, Finster and Lucy—who later gave their names to the Larson family's music publishing entity.

Several of Jonathan's closest friends during these years were pursuing careers in filmmaking, including Victoria Leacock, by then living in New York, as well as Eddie Rosenstein and Jonathan Burkhart. Facets of their personalities and their aspirations would one day inform the character of Mark Cohen, the budding filmmaker in *Rent*. Larson first met Burkhart in the summer of 1984 while working on Nantucket; he was looking for a roommate to share an apartment on the island, and Burkhart was waiting tables at the Opera House, a restaurant across the street from the Cargo Car, the bar where Larson played piano. Burkhart's family was from Nantucket but had moved away by that time, so he too was hunting for a place for the summer. The two Jonathans looked at several potential rentals together, but Burkhart was a little

Jonathan Larson and Victoria Leacock, circa 1991.
Photo courtesy of Victoria Leacock Hoffman

taken aback when Larson signed an agreement on one before checking with him—because he'd discovered it had one all-important amenity: a piano! Things worked out well, though; the two became fast friends and at the end of the summer Larson invited Burkhart to move into the Greenwich Street apartment.

Like Mark and Roger, they had an illegal wood-burning stove that they would sometimes use in the winter when there was no heat in the building. They also didn't have a working door buzzer, so, like Collins in the show, visitors would have to call upstairs from a pay phone and wait until Larson dropped down a set of keys from the window. (The leather pouch that held the keys—also immortalized in the stage directions to *Rent*—was a gift from Victoria Leacock.) Their bathtub was in the kitchen. But there were pluses, too, including a roof deck from which they could see the Hudson River. Although they lived precariously from paycheck to paycheck and sometimes didn't know where the next month's rent was coming from, it was a happy time. Jonathan was in New York City, pursuing his dreams. As his sister Julie put it in an interview for the film *No Day But Today: The Story of Rent*: "He had a really rich life. You never got a sense that he was lacking in anything in life, because he could truly make magic out of absolutely nothing." According to Matthew O'Grady: "How can you be happier than when you are pursuing what you want to do? He was living up to his ideals."

Writing New Musicals

It was a fertile time for Jonathan in terms of his own creativity and musical output, even if recognition seemed a long time coming. He and David Glenn Armstrong continued to work on their college musical, retitling it *Saved! - An Immoral Musical on the Moral Majority*. In 1992 it was produced at Rusty's Storefront Blitz, a showcase theater on 42nd Street with a seating capacity of about thirty; it was named after the theater's owner, Rusty Blitz, a sometime actor whose primary claim to fame was having played a gravedigger in the Mel Brooks movie *Young Frankenstein*. The show ran there for four weeks and won the writers their first official recognition: a writing award presented by ASCAP.

Larson collaborated with Seth Goldman on a show called *Mowgli*, an all-new adaptation of *The Jungle Book*, and began working on a very ambitious musical adaptation of George Orwell's *1984*. He devoted substantial time to this but ultimately was unable to persuade the Orwell estate to grant him the rights to the book. Still, he was inspired by the novel's dystopian vision and restructured his show around a new plot with similar themes.

Superbia

Leacock described this new work, now entitled *Superbia*, as "a futuristic allegory about bottom-line mentality in an orbiting studio where everyone lives on and for the camera." It also involved a *Romeo and Juliet*–type love story, with a score inspired by techno and new wave music. It took place in a brave new world founded by a rock star named Mick Knife and controlled by MBA (which stood in this case for "Master Babble Articulator"). There were two separate classes of citizens known as the Ins and the Outs. People who are familiar with the work have said it was ahead of its time and eerily prescient: Larson predicted several years in advance the advent of the "broadcast age," with human beings reduced to slaves of fashion, as tools of an all-encompassing media culture that has co-opted rock and roll. (Larson remained passionate about these themes: the notion of a mind-numbing, synthetic media culture cutting people off from the genuine experience of life survives in the "Cyberarts" and "Buzzline" plot threads of *Rent*.)

Jonathan envisioned *Superbia* on a large scale that would have made it expensive to produce, but he did get opportunities to develop it through ASCAP and the Dramatists Guild. The work-in-progress won several awards and a Richard Rodgers Development Grant; it was also given a workshop at Playwrights Horizons, one of New York's most prestigious nonprofit theaters focused on new plays and musicals (also the original home of Sondheim and James Lapine's *Sunday in the Park with George*). That workshop did not lead to offers of a full production. Leacock later said it had been a terrible presentation: Larson had not been able to get the right kind of rock band or the voices he wanted for some of the roles, and the theater pressured him to make changes in the script that he didn't agree with. She herself later produced a rock concert version of *Superbia* at the Village Gate, a famed cabaret theater in Greenwich Village, but after seven years of development there was still no full production in sight. Larson began to get discouraged, and his friends saw this reflected in successive drafts of the musical: the plot got darker and bleaker each time Larson revised it. As Burkhart recently put it, the show's tone "went from happy standard Broadway musical to thrashing rock and roll to nasty, angry cynicism." Ultimately Larson realized it was not going to happen, and focused his disappointment on a new project.

Boho Days

The new endeavor was *30/90*, an autobiographical musical so called because it was 1990 and Larson was facing his thirtieth birthday: a scary prospect for an artist who has not yet had a career breakthrough. The piece was a "rock monologue" about a frustrated composer struggling with life and work decisions, wondering if he's really cut out for the career he's chosen. If *Superbia* was too big and expensive to produce, Larson reasoned, he would counter with the smallest possible musical: he performed the new show himself as a solo piece, accompanying himself on piano and backed by a rock band—which was playfully dubbed "the Well Hungarians." The choice to do it as a one-man show was inspired by Larson's admiration for Eric Bogosian and Spalding Gray, both of whom had recently done solo shows in New York that he had admired.

Though, like *Superbia*, *30/90*—which was eventually retitled *Boho Days* and later *tick, tick . . . BOOM!*—failed to get Larson a commercial run, it was showcased for a couple of weekends at the Second Stage (then located uptown on Broadway and 76th Street). As she had done with *Superbia*, Victoria Leacock put together a production for the Village Gate, which she and Jonathan hoped would take off for an extended run. Though the musical itself didn't prove a career breakthrough, it did result in Jonathan's meeting a young man who would eventually change his life. The producer Jeffrey Seller, who saw the presentation at the Second Stage, followed up by writing the young composer/performer a letter, telling Larson he thought he was "amazing" and expressing his interest in working with him; Seller would eventually become one of the producers of *Rent*. (Several years after Larson's death, *tick, tick . . . BOOM!* would be adapted as a three-person musical and produced successfully Off-Broadway and around the country; see Chapter 18.)

Friends and Colleagues

The early versions of *Boho Days* contained lines about resisting the temptation to sell out and take work as a writer for hire on TV and film projects; like Mark in *Rent*, who turns down a lucrative offer to work on a tacky tabloid news show in order to focus on his own film, Larson was determined to spend his time on projects that were meaningful to him. Though he still wasn't having much luck getting his full musicals produced, he continued to work tirelessly toward his dream of bringing musical theater to the younger generation through rock music. He had the mantra "Make the familiar unfamiliar, and make the unfamiliar familiar" posted over his desk. His self-discipline was prodigious. Inspired by the classical composer Franz Shubert, a master of the art song, he determined to write a new song every day.

Larson's friends and roommates from that period remember him as very sociable but also extremely disciplined and devoted to his work. One of the few amenities he did have in his otherwise spartan life—and a rather rare one in New York City—was a car. Affectionately known as "Rusty," it was a green

Datsun 810 he had bought for a hundred dollars from a former girlfriend; it was old and in precarious condition, and Jonathan just as often got around town on his bike. Sometimes he and Burkhart would spontaneously drive out to the Hamptons and spend a day on the beach—though even on those days Larson made sure to take a pen and paper with him in case musical inspiration were to strike. He also loved going to parties with his friends, but he would usually be among the first to leave, generally because he wanted to get back home to whatever musical project he was working on.

One of the difficulties that Larson faced was the fact that rock music can only be appreciated when it's been fully realized in a sound studio. Unlike traditional show tunes, rock songs cannot adequately be demonstrated on a solo piano, so putting together demos that might help sell his shows was an ongoing challenge, financially as well as technologically. Larson initially composed on an outmoded 66-key Casio with severe limitations; it wasn't even equipped with the capability to sustain a tone. Burkhart took him to an electronics store on Canal Street and helped him pick out a much more advanced model with 78 keys, which was a major investment at the time. This

Jonathan Larson (left) and his friend Jonathan Burkhart relaxing together on a trip to the beach.   *Photo courtesy of Jonathan Burkhart*

lasted him several years; he used it in conjunction with a computer and a digital processor.

He met a music producer named Steve Skinner, who shared his interests in both popular music and theatre. Skinner had his own digital studio (though certainly not a "cyberstudio") where he and Larson would produce more sophisticated demo recordings of his songs and shows. Skinner had had a more formal musical education than Larson, and his inventive arrangements fleshed out Larson's musical ideas, adding depth and polish to his songs and contributing substantially to their effectiveness. Aware that Jonathan didn't have money, he was generous with his facilities and his time; the two enjoyed a very fruitful collaboration for over ten years, and to this day Skinner is credited for "musical arrangements" in the programs for productions of *Rent*.

In 1989 Burkhart, who was making decent money by that point, called Skinner for advice on equipment. He bought his friend Larson a state-of-the-art 88-key Yamaha keyboard that could simulate almost any sound. Larson adored it; this was the instrument on which the score for *Rent* would be composed.

The Peasant Feasts

In 1985, Larson and his roommate at the time, Ann Egan, hosted their first Peasant's Feast. A potluck dinner party held during the holiday season, this would become an annual event and a tradition dearly cherished in the memories of his friends and family. Larson sent out handmade invitations, sometimes printed with a carved potato. He and his roommates would transform the shabby apartment into something resembling a romantic bistro, the space lit by dozens of candles. A bedraggled little Christmas tree, inventively decorated, reminded people of the tree in *A Charlie Brown Christmas*. Though rundown, the loft was surprisingly spacious, and on these special occasions it would accommodate large groups of friends, family members, neighbors, artistic collaborators—and even people they had just met on the street and invited spontaneously. Traditional holiday turkey was generally served, along with a profusion of dishes contributed by the guests. There were impromptu readings and musical performances, and a great feeling of warmth and camaraderie. The extended family of friends that developed—supporting each other's creativity and individuality, celebrating life and reminding one another that they were all in it together—would eventually be reflected onstage by the close-knit community depicted in *Rent*. As O'Grady said, "He was writing about the love, the fun, the glory, the achievement in those communities. He saw the best of it; he wanted it to be documented. He wanted it to be known."

Other Projects

As Larson continued to spend his days writing music—and trying to get theaters and producers interested in his shows—some of his friends encouraged him to take more lucrative side jobs. O'Grady pushed him to submit songs for the Radio City Music Hall Christmas show; Rosenstein made connections that helped him get hired to write music for industrials; and Burkhart urged him to think about composing commercial jingles and scoring TV shows. If a job fell into his lap, Larson would usually take it, but he seldom pursued such opportunities on his own; he was consumed by his own ambitious creative projects and avoided commitments that might take precious time away from working on them. Friends estimated that he rarely if ever made over $20,000 in a year.

He did write some music for the long-running TV show *Sesame Street* as well as a pilot for a projected children's series called *Away We Go!* That project came about through a longtime regular customer at the Moondance Diner, who had the money to back a project. He asked Jonathan to pitch a children's video, and a week later Larson presented him with a concept and a budget. The show was a collaboration with Bob Golden; he and Larson each wrote four songs for it. Golden produced and Jonathan directed the thirty-minute video. One character was a puppet known as Newt the Newt; Larson later bemoaned the fact that the name took on other connotations when Newt Gingrich became a prominent political figure. (There is now a brief, humorous reference to Gingrich in the script of *Rent*; see Chapter 16.) *Away We Go!* was scheduled for a release in 1996, which would be the same year *Rent* opened. Copies of the rare videotape are considered collector's items.

In 1993, Larson was commissioned by Karen Butler, of Broadway Arts Theatre for Young Audiences, to write an original musical with the veteran lyricist/librettist Hal Hackady. Entitled *Blocks*, the show had a revue format and dealt with the challenges faced by inner city youth; it was written to tour public middle schools throughout New York City. The piece was presented at the Westbeth Community Performance Space in 1993 and revived at the York Theatre in 1995, after the workshop production of *Rent*. Actors who appeared in the show included *Rent* cast members Yassmin Alers, Rodney Hicks, and Anthony Rapp. In 1997, some of the songs Hackady and Larson wrote for *Blocks* were used in another musical, *I Make Me a Promise*, which was both performed and written by the kids of formerly homeless people living with HIV/AIDS. It was presented at the McGinn/Cazale Theatre in New York and in Washington, D.C.

The last major theatrical project Larson worked on before going into rehearsal for *Rent* was the musical *J.P. Morgan Saves the Nation*. Annie Hamburger, the artistic director of En Garde Arts—an experimental theater company known for putting on shows in non-theatrical, found spaces—had seen the 1994 workshop of *Rent*. Her company was developing a new show, described as an outdoor postmodern pageant, about the legendary American financier. The writer was Jeffrey M. Jones, and at first Dan Moses Schreier, who had collaborated with Jones on other projects, was set to write the music. When Schreier backed out, Hamburger asked Larson to come on board. The score he wrote for the piece, arranged by Steve Skinner, was eclectic, with influences ranging from the iconic American march composer John Philip Sousa to soul music and Seattle-style grunge. The production played in the summer of 1995 on the steps of the Federal Hall National Memorial on Wall Street. Though *New York Times* theater critic Ben Brantley had mixed feelings about the show, which he said "often seems like a revue put together by an earnest team of Marxist economics students," he was impressed with the score, adding, "Mr. Larson works adroitly in an assortment of musical pastiches, from ragtime to rap: his music-hall hymn to capitalist hunger, 'Appetite Annie,' winningly performed by Mr. Judy and the chorus, is charming."

Responding to an Epidemic

It was in 1989 that Ira Weitzman, of Playwrights Horizons, gave Larson's name to Billy Aronson, a young playwright who was looking for a collaborator to work with him on a musical modernization of the opera *La bohème*; this of course was the project that eventually evolved into *Rent*. Because the early development of the show is covered in Chapter 3, we will not go into it here. Suffice it to say that the idea kindled Larson's imagination and would become his primary creative focus for the rest of his life.

In an interview with John Estel for *American Theatre*, Larson talked about how he had put *Rent* aside for a while after the collaboration with Billy Aronson seemed to hit a wall—and the reasons he ultimately decided to go back to it. Chief among these was the AIDS crisis, and the way it was impacting the lives of so many of his friends. Matt O'Grady learned he was HIV positive, and Jonathan was the first person he told. Another friend and colleague, Gordon Rogers, who had been one of Victoria Leacock's best friends since childhood and was by this time a New York costume designer, was also diagnosed with the disease. Two of their other close friends, Ali Gertz and Pam Shaw—both beautiful, young heterosexual women—found out they had AIDS at around this time as well. It was becoming clear that the epidemic was not contained only within the gay community or the community of drug users: everyone they knew seemed to be at risk. Jonathan felt helpless in the face of the fear and grief all around him and angry at the government's apparent indifference to the escalating crisis. *Rent* gave him a vehicle to express all these feelings and a way to fight for his friends. In the completed script, three of the characters attending the Life Support meeting introduce themselves as Ali, Gordon, and Pam, in tribute to his friends, all of whom had passed away by the time the show opened. The script also invites actors doing productions of the musical to substitute the names of friends of theirs who were lost to the disease, but often the original names are still used. (Unlike those three, Matt O'Grady, who was first diagnosed with HIV almost thirty years ago, responded well to medication and never contracted full-blown AIDS; he is alive and healthy as of this writing.)

Love and Friendship

In the early days of *Rent*, shortly after Larson's death, many people mistakenly assumed that he himself had been gay and must have died of AIDS-related causes. Neither assumption was true. Starting in high school, Jonathan was almost always romantically involved with one girlfriend or another. Women considered him a very romantic, old-fashioned lover; he wrote tender notes and love letters that made them feel special. He was particularly drawn to dancers, at least two of whom he dated. One of them was a choreographer for whom he had written dance scores. He was seriously in love with her, but she left him for a woman she had secretly been seeing all along—a traumatic experience that inspired the Mark/Maureen/Joanne triangle in *Rent*. At the end of his life, he was seeing the actress Christina Haag, who had once been the girlfriend of John F. Kennedy Jr., and later wrote a book about their relationship, *Come to the Edge*. Jonathan's longest relationship was with Janet Charleston, also a dancer with whom he had collaborated. Quoted by Evelyn McDonnell and Katherine Silberger in the *Rent* coffee table book, Charleston said, "Part of Jonathan is in Angel—the romantic part, that belief in love in an idealistic way."

Indeed, family members recognize aspects of Jonathan in every character in the show, while friends see parts of their own personalities reflected. Jonathan Burkhart has said that he and Larson, sharing that rundown apartment while trying to get their artistic careers off the ground, were both Mark. (Filmmaker Burkhart had a 16 mm Bolex movie camera that he carried with him, shooting footage of the neighborhoods as he and Larson explored the city on their bikes; this was the same kind of camera Mark would carry in both the stage and film versions of *Rent*.) In a very real sense, Larson was also Roger, determined to write a truly great song that would be remembered. Indeed, Larson's own confidence in his talent and determination to change the world through his work can even be seen reflected in the character of Maureen. And Matt O'Grady, Larson's closest friend and one who did drag on some occasions, was proud to see himself in aspects of Angel. In an interview for the *Rent* coffee table book, he said, "My life may not be as long as I want it to be, but it's a really good life. Jonathan saw me evolving towards that . . . It's not about having HIV, it's about having a good life. It's about love. I'm so honored that he took all that and put it together."

Still, the colorfully bohemian world of the Lower East Side that Larson depicted in *Rent* was not precisely the world he and his closest friends inhabited; it was a world they knew but observed from a bit of an objective distance. Burkhart recalls that the two of them rarely hung out in the East Village, which at the time was too crowded and dirty; they tended to frequent bars and clubs near their own "Assho" neighborhood, which was on the far west side and much quieter. Neither of them was a particularly "good drinker," and though they enjoyed smoking pot to relax, Larson was otherwise not a drug user. They did, however, have several friends who were frequently strung out and struggled with heroin habits, so the addiction that plagues Mimi in *Rent* was something Larson had observed first-hand.

While Jonathan was working on *Rent*, his friends and family could tell that he was thrilled and excited. Though there were fears and frustrations along the way, he could feel his dreams

Jonathan with his parents, Al and Nan Larson, and his nephew, Matthew McCollum.

Photo courtesy of the Larson family

beginning to come true. He would often call up his sister or his friends on the phone to talk about how rehearsals were going or sing them songs he had just finished. He also sent Julie cassette tapes of himself singing the songs. These became lullabies for her two small sons, Matthew and Dylan, who adored the music. Their "Unky" Jonathan, famously great with children, was their favorite person in the world.

Final Days

As the day of the first rehearsal for *Rent* approached, and Jonathan knew he would finally be making some money from the piece, he took the major step of quitting his job at the Moondance Diner. He was finally starting to feel confident that writing musicals could be his livelihood. But because New York Theatre Workshop is a nonprofit theater, there wasn't money available to pay him a livable wage during the rehearsal process; this became a bone of some contention between him and the organization. He was still broke; Eddie Rosenstein bought him his groceries during the last week of his life. Ironically, he did receive a substantial check from the theater in the mail on the very day he died.

Nearly a year after Larson's death, Lawrence Van Gelder wrote an article for the *New York Times* detailing the medical crises and hospital visits that occurred during the final week of his life, compiled from details gathered from both the recollections of friends and a report that had just been released by the New York State Department of Health. It was on January 21, 1996, when *Rent* was in technical rehearsals, that Larson first began complaining of major chest pains. That day was a "ten out of twelve" for the cast: a day during tech week when Actors Equity Association allows an unusually long work day, with the cast permitted to rehearse for ten hours out of a twelve-hour period. When they came back from their dinner break to continue working through the show, Jonathan said he felt dizzy and added "my chest is killing me." He told one of the actors he thought he was having a heart attack and asked him to call 911; then he collapsed in the back of the theater. (He later told Jonathan Burkhart that as he lay on the floor waiting for the ambulance, he could hear the actors onstage singing the "dying in America" verse of "What You Own." He felt the irony—but did note that the sound system seemed to be working better.)

He was taken to Cabrini Medical Center on East 19th Street; the paramedics diagnosed him with pleuritic chest pain, meaning pain made worse by breathing. Very shortly after arriving, Jonathan was examined by two emergency room doctors, one of whom took an electrocardiogram. X-rays were also taken. One of the physicians recorded a note that read: "no cardiac

disease . . . just finished producing a play . . . increased stress." (The reference to the show wasn't much more accurate than the medical diagnosis
would turn out to be.) All in all, Jonathan spent just over three hours at the
hospital, accompanied by Burkhart. A doctor finally told them he suspected
food poisoning and decided to pump his stomach. They gave him Toradol (a
powerful pain medication) and told him to eat only bland food for the next
twenty-four hours and to come back to the emergency room if he had to. He
was sent home.

The next day, Monday, was a day off for the cast, so Jonathan didn't have
to go to the theater. He stayed home and Eddie Rosenstein looked after
him. Rosenstein later told *People* magazine that Jonathan had called Cabrini
Medical Center to ask for the results of the tests and find out whether they
had determined if he actually had food poisoning. He added: "They couldn't
find the results. But he was told they were sure if there was something wrong
he would have been notified." Jim Nicola, the theater's artistic director, spoke
to him on the phone and thought he sounded better. At some point that day,
a radiologist at Cabrini Medical Center looked over the chest X-rays from the
night before and noted them as normal.

On Tuesday, January 23, rehearsals for *Rent* resumed with another long
tech day; Jonathan stayed home. Around 11:00 that night, he had a fever and
was feeling bad enough to return to the emergency room. His roommate,
Brian Carmody, called Cabrini, and was was told by an attendant that they
wouldn't be able to access Larson's records from two nights prior. Instead of
going back there, Carmody took him to the ER at St. Vincent's Hospital in
the West Village; Burkhart came as well. A nurse asked Jonathan to rate his
level of chest pain on a scale of one to ten and he said a seven; a doctor finally
examined him shortly after midnight and ordered an electrocardiogram
and a chest X-ray, just as the staff at Cabrini had done two nights earlier.
Again, the X-rays were reviewed and found normal; the diagnosis was viral
syndrome. Jonathan's condition was listed as "improving," and once again
he was sent home.

Riding a taxi home in the middle of the night, he told Carmody he
wasn't feeling any better. On Wednesday morning, according to Van Gelder's
summary, a radiologist at St. Vincent's reviewed the X-rays from the night
before and made a note that said "Heart size is at upper limit of normal."
The cardiologist who interpreted the electrocardiogram noted a possible
"myocardial infarction," or heart attack. Nevertheless, the later investigation
found no evidence that either doctor had followed up or ever called Larson
to have him come back in.

The next night (Wednesday), he went to New York Theatre Workshop for
the final dress rehearsal, which was performed for an invited audience. It

was the only time he ever saw *Rent* with a house full of spectators. Although there were numerous technical issues still to be worked out, the run went well; audience response was strong and the energy in the theater was very positive. As Daphne Rubin-Vega (Mimi) recently recalled: "It was the first time we did the show without stopping. And with costumes. We were going and we were on. It was the first time it clicked for me." Looking back, the cast would take some comfort in the knowledge that Jonathan had experienced that and felt the audience's excitement.

One of the guests at the theater that night was Anthony Tommasini, opera and classical music critic for the *New York Times*. He had been working on what he thought was going to be an article about the hundredth birthday of *La bohème*; an editor had given him a tip about a new rock version in rehearsal downtown, and he was intrigued. (The fact that *Rent* was set to open almost exactly one hundred years after the opera it was based on sounds like a clever publicity stunt—but it was actually a total coincidence. Nobody at the theater had been aware of it.) As it turned out, Tommasini was so taken with the show, and with Larson, that he decided to focus his article on *Rent*. In all the hubbub following the rehearsal, the quietest place they could find to talk was the box office in the front of the theater. In that tiny room, Jonathan Larson gave his *New York Times* interview—something his friends knew he had long dreamed of doing. He answered Tommasini's questions about his childhood and college years, lamented the ongoing issues with the sound system—which was still making it hard to hear some of the lyrics—and spoke enthusiastically of how he had studied the opera, and the book it's based on, in creating the musical. Two quotes from the interview (which was not published until February 11, a couple of weeks after his death) are unbearably poignant in retrospect. He told Tommasini: "I'm happy to say that other commissions are coming up, and I think I may have a life as a composer." And he talked about how one of his friends with AIDS had inspired him, saying: "It's not how many years you live, but how you fulfill the time you spend here. That's sort of the point of the show."

When Tommasini and Larson finished their conversation at about ten minutes after midnight, director Michael Greif and the design and tech staff were still having a meeting in the theater, going over notes from the rehearsal. There was much to discuss, and Jonathan made plans to meet Greif and Nicola at nine o'clock the next morning for breakfast at Time Café. Then he went home and put on some water to boil for tea. At 3:30 a.m. on Thursday, January 25, 1996, Brian Carmody came home and found Jonathan lying dead on the floor of their kitchen. An autopsy was performed the next day, and the cause of death was officially listed as "aortic dissection due to cystic medial degeneration of unknown etiology."

Partly as a result of a feature on ABC's *Prime Time Live*, the New York State Health Department began an investigation into the treatment Larson had received at the two hospitals; the results were released in December of 1996. Although she acknowledged that an aortic aneurysm can be difficult to identify, especially when the patient is young and otherwise healthy, State Health Commissioner Barbara DeBuono said that neither hospital had performed a CAT scan or an MRI, which might have revealed the problem, nor did they even check Larson's blood pressure or vital signs before discharging him. She added that there was no good basis for the diagnosis of food poisoning; the pumping of his stomach might have aggravated his condition, and the Toradol, which masked his pain, might have prevented a more accurate diagnosis. Said DeBuono: "Had they moved aggressively toward diagnosis, there might have been treatment options available that could have saved his life . . . You're a team—we're not pointing a finger at one individual. We're saying to the hospitals, 'You could have done better.'" The hospitals conducted their own investigations and issued the opinion that their staffs had done nothing wrong. However, based on the state's evaluation, Cabrini Medical Center was fined $10,000 and St. Vincent's Hospital, $6,000. (Much later, the Larson family concluded that the aneurysm was probably the result of a rare condition called Marfan Syndrome, which often goes undiagnosed. In the years since, they have made it part of their mission to educate the public about the disease.)

Jonathan Larson's memorial service was held on Sunday, February 3, 1996. The original plan was to have it at New York Theatre Workshop, but when his friends realized how many people would want to be there, it was moved to the Minetta Lane, a much larger Off-Broadway theater in Greenwich Village. The cast of *Rent* sang four songs from the show. Many of Jonathan's friends spoke, sharing stories and introducing performances of songs from his various works. Afterward, some of them went together to eat at the restaurant next door to the theater, which was called La Bohème.

2

"That Doesn't Remind Us of 'Musetta's Waltz'"

The Opera That Inspired a Musical

Jonathan Larson based the plot of *Rent* on Puccini's beloved opera *La bohème*, but he had never seen a stage production of the opera when he began writing his adaptation. He and his family saw a puppet show version in Chicago when he was a child, and he certainly listened to the score, but he reportedly didn't see *La bohème* onstage until after he had written the first three songs of *Rent* with Billy Aronson. One of the people he sent the demo tape to was producer Robyn Goodman. Excited by his work, Goodman then took him to see a production of *La bohème* at the New York City Opera. And later, when Larson was struggling to clarify the story and work out the dramaturgical kinks in the script of *Rent*, Kevin McCollum thought it might be useful to return to the well of inspiration and took him to see the opera at the Met. Larson loved it and became excited about the idea of taking the cast of *Rent*, then in rehearsal, to the Met to see it as a group. Sadly they never got the chance.

This chapter examines Puccini's beautiful, romantic opera and the way Larson adapted it for his generation: what he changed, and what stayed very much the same.

Giacomo Puccini

The composer was born in Tuscany, Italy, in 1858. His father, grandfather, great-grandfather, and great-great-grandfather had all been church musicians and musical directors at the cathedral in their town of Lucca. Puccini graduated from the Pacini School of Music in that town at the age of twenty-two and then went on to the Milan Conservatory, where his teachers included Amilcare Ponchielli, composer of the classic opera *La gioconda*, and his roommate was Pietro Mascagni, who, like Puccini, would go on to become one of the foremost composers of the *verismo* school of Italian opera. The word "verismo" can be translated as "realism" and refers to a late nineteenth- and early twentieth-century type of opera characterized by melodramatic, often violent stories; the characters are real people, often of the middle or lower classes, as opposed to the kings, queens, knights, and ladies of earlier "romantic" operas. The music is bold and earthy, with sweeping, soaring melodies but without the vocal filigree and pyrotechnics of the earlier *bel canto* period; there is a continual musical texture with dialogue flowing seamlessly in and out of arias, as opposed to the once-traditional format of distinct musical "numbers" alternating with recitative. Puccini's operas do not always conform to all of these standard characteristics of *verismo*, but he is generally considered a pioneer of the genre and its most famous representative.

The composer's first two operas, *Le Villi* and *Edgar*, met with only moderate success and are rarely revived today. During the early years of his career he was often poverty-stricken, and on more than one occasion he had to pawn belongings in order to come up with funds for necessities like food and rent. (Sound familiar?) He later claimed that his personal experiences during this period contributed nearly as much to the later writing of *La bohème* as the Henri Murger novel on which the story is based. Fortunately, the great music publisher Giulio Ricordi took an early interest in Puccini's talent and, with commissions, helped support him through his early endeavors; his belief in the young composer paid off with *Manon Lescaut* (1893). Puccini had wanted to write the opera's libretto himself but was talked out of it. Several different librettists tried to collaborate with him but were discouraged by his constant demands for changes; the team who ultimately finished the job turned out to be Luigi Illica and Giuseppe Giacosa. They stayed with Puccini for his next three big successes, which included *La bohème*.

At that time, when the composition and production of new operas was a vital industry, it was not unusual for composers to compete for a property that lent itself to musical adaptation. Puccini came across this difficulty twice. The novel by the Abbé Prévost that he adapted as *Manon Lescaut* was also adapted at about the same time as *Manon*, an opera by the French composer Jules Massenet; it has been said, curiously, that Puccini tried to set different scenes from the novel to avoid stepping on Massenet's toes. And when it came to Henri Murger's book *Scènes de la vie de bohème*, rival composer Ruggero Leoncavallo claimed to have a prior claim on the property. But Puccini would not back off, and since the novel was in the public domain he didn't have to. Though many opera fans and critics still feel today that Massenet's *Manon* is even better than Puccini's, Puccini's *La bohème* was far more successful than Leoncavallo's version, which is hardly ever revived today. (Still, Leoncavallo too went on to attain a measure of operatic immortality for his *I pagliacci*, a classic of the *verismo* genre.)

After the success of *La bohème* (1896) and the highly dramatic *Tosca* (1900), Puccini suffered debilitating injuries in a car accident, which slowed down the completion of his next opera, *Madama Butterfly*. Based on a Broadway play by David Belasco, it tells the tragic story of a Japanese geisha who is married to, and later abandoned by, an American naval officer. (Like *La bohème*, it was later adapted as a rock musical: *Miss Saigon*, which changes the setting and updates the story to the time of the Vietnam War.) His next opera, *La fanciulla del West*, is known as "the first spaghetti western." Also based on an American play by Belasco (*The Girl of the Golden West*), it tells the story of a feisty barmaid in California gold rush territory and was the first opera to have its world premiere (1910) at the Metropolitan Opera House in New York City.

The composer's life was not without its share of scandal. In his youth he ran off with his piano student Elvira Gemignani, who was unhappily married to another man at the time. They ultimately married, but only after the birth of their son, Antonio, and the death of Elvira's first husband. Years later, Elvira accused Puccini of having an affair with their maid, Doria Manfredi. Though Puccini was known to have had extramarital flings with several prominent sopranos, his wife's suspicions in the case of Doria are believed to have been mistaken. The girl committed suicide, and Elvira was convicted of slander; her persecution of the innocent young woman was weighing on Puccini's mind when he created the character of Liù, the tragic slave girl in his final opera, *Turandot*. Based on an Italian play by Carlo Gozzi and set in a fantasy version of ancient China, this highly ambitious opera, with its implausible story, employs a huge chorus and extravagant sets. Its title role, written for a high dramatic soprano, is one of the most demanding vocal challenges in Italian opera; it has been theorized that Puccini, who was suffering from throat cancer at the time, felt compelled by his affliction to explore the limits of what a healthy voice could do. Like Jonathan Larson, Puccini never heard his final work premiered. He passed away in 1924 without having finished the opera's last scene; it was completed by composer Franco Alfano, working from Puccini's notes. *Turandot* was first performed in 1926 and has become a repertoire standard, thanks in no small part to the soaring aria "Nessun dorma," popularized by Luciano Pavarotti and now a favorite of tenors all over the world.

The Meaning of the Word

The title of Henri Murger's book *Scènes de la vie de bohème*, variously called a novel or a collection of interrelated short stories, can be translated as "Scenes of Bohemian Life" (though English translations are sometimes officially titled *Scenes from the Latin Quarter*). The book, which was the basis for Puccini's opera, helped popularize the word "bohème" (memorably used in *Rent*) or "bohemian."

"Bohemian" is defined by Merriam-Webster as "a person (as a writer or an artist) living an unconventional life usually in a colony with others." In the early nineteenth century, the word was first used that way in France. Colonies of impoverished artists moved into urban neighborhoods inhabited by the Romani, a wandering race that had originated in Northern India and for centuries lived an "off-the-grid" existence, moving nomadically throughout Europe and America. They have often colloquially been called "gypsies"; the French mistakenly thought they had come from Bohemia, which was an ancient name for the country that later became Czechoslovakia and is now the Czech Republic. The historically inaccurate name stuck and was transferred to the artist types who chose to live in that particular ghetto area and shared something of the outsider ethos of the Romani. Wikipedia elaborates on the definition: "Outsiders apart from conventional society and untroubled by its disapproval. The term carries a connotation of arcane enlightenment (the opposite of Philistines), and also carries a less frequently intended, pejorative connotation of carelessness about personal hygiene and marital fidelity." The East Village denizens of *Rent* are spiritual descendants not just of the Parisian artists and writers of Murger's and Puccini's works but of other communities of disaffected artists and free spirits, including the "Lost Generation" of Gertrude Stein's salons in 1920s Paris, the "Beat Generation" of 1950s New York, and the hippies and flower children of the 1960s. According to author and musical theater expert Jack Viertel: "'La Vie Bohème' paid tribute to *La Bohème*, but more directly to the spirit that sustains outsider communities, dreamers, slackers, and those who would rather be lost in a dangerous world than found in a conventional one."

Synopsis of the Opera

Act One

The story begins on a Christmas Eve in the 1830s. It's early evening in the Latin Quarter of Paris, in a small garret apartment shared by four artistic friends. When the curtain rises we meet two of them: Rodolfo, a poet, and Marcello, a painter. Marcello is working on a painting of the crossing of the Red Sea (a story from the Old Testament); Rodolfo sits looking out a window and laments that, though he can see a thousand chimneys sending smoke up into the Parisian sky, the little wood stove in the room is not keeping them warm, as they have no fuel to burn. Marcello says his hands are too cold to keep painting, and the heart of his girlfriend Musetta, who recently left him, is also frigid. He is not only cold but hungry, and he suggests breaking up an old chair in order to burn the wood. Rodolfo has a better idea: they can burn the first act of the manuscript of the play he's been working on! This provides enough heat for them to warm themselves and cheer each other up, if only for a moment.

Colline, their philosopher roommate, enters and throws a parcel of books down on the table; he had tried to pawn them for cash but was told it's not permissible on Christmas Eve. He sits down by the fire as Rodolfo burns the second and third acts of the play; they joke about the sparkling scenes and crackling dialogue as they watch the flames consume the pages.

The entire script has been burned and the room is getting cold again when some delivery boys unexpectedly enter with a supply of firewood, along with food, wine, and cigars. They are followed by the musician Schaunard, the fourth roommate, who tosses some coins into the room. Marcello, Rodolfo, and Colline enthusiastically unpack the provisions and set the table for a meal, scarcely paying attention as Schaunard tells the story of how he got the cash to pay for all the groceries: An English lord requested his services as a musician—not to teach lessons as he first thought, but to play his instrument incessantly in the hopes that the sound would cause the irritating parrot on the first floor of his building to drop dead. Schaunard says he played for three days without the desired effect, so he charmed a maid into giving him some parsley. He fed that to the bird, which died, and so he received his fee! But he takes the food away and clears off the table: these supplies are to be saved for Christmas Day, for tonight they must eat out and enjoy the charms of the ladies in the cafés of the Latin Quarter!

The four friends are about to indulge in a bit of wine before leaving when there is a knock at the door: it's Benoit, their dreaded landlord, come to collect the rent!—which of course they cannot afford to pay. Making a grand show of hospitality, the four friends insist that the old man sit down and have a drink; they toast to his health. Marcello playfully mentions having heard that a few nights earlier Benoit was observed at the notorious Parisian cabaret Mabille enjoying an amorous encounter with a beautiful woman; as the friends continue to ply the landlord with wine, getting him drunker and drunker, they flatter him with tales of his seduction of the woman, and he brags that it's all true. He remarks that he finds shapely girls more desirable than skinny women—such as his wife. Marcello feigns shock that a married man would seduce another woman; the other three join in on the joke and, pretending to be outraged by Benoit's immoral behavior, righteously kick him out of the apartment—without, of course, giving him any rent money.

The threat removed for the time being, Schaunard suggests they all leave for the Café Momus and generously divides the money he got from the Englishman among the four of them. Marcello shows Colline his face in a broken mirror and suggests he visit a barber, to which the philosopher agrees. Rodolfo says he needs five minutes to finish an article he is writing for a journal called *The Beaver*; the other three agree to wait for him downstairs and exit. But it's dark in the stairwell and Colline can be heard taking a tumble on the way down; nothing serious. Rodolfo sits down at the table, to write by the light of a single candle, and hears a knock at the door.

He asks who's there and, on hearing a woman's voice, gets a bit excited. It turns out the visitor is Mimì, a seamstress who lives in the building; her candle has gone out and she needs someone to light it for her. Rodolfo immediately invites her to come in. She politely declines at first, but he insists and she enters the room. She has a bad cough, and he is concerned because she looks pale; she says she's out of breath from climbing the stairs and suddenly faints, dropping both her candle and the key she's been carrying on the floor. Rodolfo sprinkles some water on her face, and she awakens; he helps her to a chair closer to the stove and offers her some wine. She says she's fine now and just needs him to light her candle; he does so and she leaves, but as soon as he goes back to trying to work on his article she reappears, having realized she's lost her key. The breeze in the hallway blows out her candle again, and Rodolfo invites her back inside, but as he moves to her his own candle is blown out, leaving them in darkness. They both kneel down and start moving around the floor, feeling for the key in the dark; he finds it but, not wanting to lose her company, puts it in his pocket without telling her. As they both grope along the floor their hands meet, and he takes her small one in his. He comments on how cold her hand is, and tells her it's too dark to find the key but at least they have the moonlight. He offers to tell her about himself and sings a romantic aria about the life of a poet; he may be poor in money but the words and ideas in his head make him rich in imaginings. He tells her two thieves—her eyes!—have come into his room and stolen his dreams, but replaced them with hope! He invites her to tell him about herself as well, and her aria directly follows his.

She says she is called Mimì, but she doesn't know why as her real name is Lucia. She makes her meager living embroidering flowers on fabric; the flowers represent springtime and love—her creations to her are like poetry, something he can understand. She lives alone, cooking her own meals and looking out her window at the sky, and she admits she doesn't always go to

Mass but instead prays to God on her own. Each year she looks forward to seeing and feeling the warmth of the first rays of springtime sun—a sentiment that she expresses in arching, yearning phrases that somehow suggest she can only hope to see another spring. She delights in the beauty and the scent of flowers but tells Rodolfo she regrets that the flowers she makes have no fragrance. That's all she can think of to tell him about herself; she apologizes for coming and being a nuisance in the night.

Downstairs Marcello, Colline, and Schaunard are getting tired of waiting; they call up to Rodolfo to hurry up, playfully taunting him for his laziness. He tells them he is with someone, sends them off to the café to save a table, and then turns back to Mimì. Seeing her face in the moonlight, he sings to her that she is as beautiful as a dream from which he would hope never to awaken. She melts at his words; they kiss. She tells him to go join his friends and then shyly asks if she might come along. He offers to stay in the garret with her instead, as it's freezing out. She says she'll be warm enough if they are together, and he offers her his arm. Admitting to each other that they have fallen in love, they leave the room together, and we hear the final rapturous phrases of their duet sung from offstage.

Act Two

This festive scene takes place a little later that night, outdoors in the Latin Quarter. We see the Café Momus and surrounding shops and vendors; the scene is full of townspeople, children, soldiers, and others all enjoying the sights and sounds of the holiday or trying to make last minute purchases. Mimì and Rodolfo stroll the square together as Colline and Schaunard consider what to buy and Marcello is jostled by the crowd. Patrons at the café call impatiently for coffee and drinks as shopkeepers and vendors hawk their wares. Rodolfo and Mimì find a milliner's shop where he buys her a pretty pink bonnet as a Christmas present. Colline buys a used coat and puts his books into its many pockets, Marcello tries to flirt with some of the girls in the crowd, and the musician Schaunard buys a horn and a pipe. These three reach the Café Momus and decide it's time for dinner, but it's too crowded inside so they bring a table out to the sidewalk. Rodolfo and Mimì are enjoying each other's company, but he has a moment of jealousy when he thinks she's looking at another man. He brings her to the table and introduces her to his friends; Colline and Schaunard, playfully trying to impress Mimì, respond in Latin.

Just then the toymaker Parpignol arrives ostentatiously on the scene with a cart full of merchandise to delight the children in the crowd. They beg their mothers to buy them toys; after much resistance some of the mothers give in, as the four bohemians peruse the menu and order delicacies they can't really afford. Marcello asks Mimì what Rodolfo bought for her and she sings a lovely, tender melody about the pink bonnet; Rodolfo must have read her heart, for it is something she has always wanted. Seeing that he's smitten, Colline and Schaunard tease Rodolfo a bit. Marcello admits that to him, love is bitter. Intending to get his mind off of his unhappy love life, the others prepare to drink a toast—but Marcello sees Musetta approaching and grumbles that he would prefer to drink poison.

The glamorous Musetta, elaborately dressed, makes a grand entrance, eliciting an admiring reaction from the crowd. She's followed by a pompous, elderly gentleman—her current beau, Alcindoro—but she maneuvers over to the table where the friends are seated and appears to be more interested in getting Marcello's attention. She treats Alcindoro like a servant and calls him "Lulu," as if he were her pet dog, and despite his grumbling over being cold, she insists that they sit at one of the outdoor tables. Mimì comments on Musetta's pretty clothes and asks who she is; Marcello says her nickname

A scene from Act Two of *La bohème* at the Metropolitan Opera House in New York City, circa 1995. Making a Christmas Eve toast at the Café Momus are Marcello (Dwayne Croft), Rodolfo (Marcello Giordani), Mimì (Hei-Kyung Hong), Schaunard (Eduardo Del Campo), and Colline (Stefano Palatchi). *Erika Davidson/courtesy of the Metropolitan Opera Archives*

is "Temptation," explaining that she changes lovers incessantly, eating their hearts in the process—which is why he himself no longer has a heart. Aware that Marcello is ignoring her and suspecting the others are laughing at her, Musetta begins to make a spectacle of herself: she complains to the waiter that her plate smells bad, then tosses it to the ground and breaks it. Puzzled, Alcindoro tries to get her to behave herself and orders dinner. Colline and Schaunard enjoy observing the comic spectacle of Musetta trying to get Marcello's attention—and Rodolfo mentions in an aside to Mimì that he would not forgive her if she were to behave so outrageously.

Mainly for Marcello's benefit, but to the delight of the other customers, Musetta begins to sing her famous Waltz song: a luscious, seductive aria in which she describes how she exults in the attention of all the passersby who ogle her as she walks down the street. Clearly singing to Marcello, she says she knows he's dying inside, though trying to hide his feelings. As she sings, the embarrassed Alcindoro tries vainly to control her, while Marcello attempts to ignore her. Rodolfo fills Mimì in on the background of Marcello and Musetta's affair, and Mimì tells him gently that she feels sorry for Musetta because it's so obvious that she's in love with Marcello, and yet it's an ungenerous kind of love. Colline, for his part, resolves to avoid love entirely and keep himself entertained with books and his pipe.

Realizing it's time to rid herself of Alcindoro, Musetta feigns a pain in her foot; she shrieks that her shoe is too tight and hands it to the old man, dispatching him to the shoemaker's shop down the street to get her another one. Finally unable to resist Musetta's charms, Marcello, reprising the melody of her own Waltz song, admits his heart is not dead after all; it is ready to reopen to her.

The waiter brings the bill but none of the friends has enough cash to pay it; Schaunard is astonished that they have so quickly gone through his money. A military band approaches, and the children in the crowd are immediately excited at the prospect of seeing the soldiers. Musetta tells the waiter to give the bills for both tables to the old gentleman who was with her. She is unable to walk out with the others because of her missing shoe, so Marcello and Colline lift her up and carry her out triumphantly on their shoulders, following the band. Schaunard joins the procession, playing on his new horn, and Mimì and Rodolfo, arm in arm, also begin to follow the parade. All cheer Musetta for saving the evening, and as the friends follow the festive procession out through the streets of the Latin Quarter, Alcindoro returns to his table, carrying the new pair of shoes he has just purchased for Musetta. When the waiter presents him with the bills for both tables, he looks at the amounts and collapses, defeated, into his chair.

Act Three

It is now the dead of winter, just before dawn on a February morning. The setting is the Barrière d'Enfer, a tollgate where customs officers monitor entrances into the city of Paris. We see the outside of a tavern at one side of the stage; an especially observant audience member might notice that the sign over the door is the painting of the Red Sea that Marcello was working on in Act One. Shouts, laughter, and the clinking of glasses can be heard from inside, suggesting that some rowdy revelers have been up all night; one of the voices is recognizable as Musetta's.

An officer comes out of the tavern with wine for his colleagues, who are trying to stay warm at a brazier. First a group of street sweepers is passed through the gate, then some milkmaids (who according to the libretto are riding donkeys), and finally a group of farm women are admitted into the city and exit up the street after paying their toll. (To be perfectly honest, this first part of the scene is usually performed in dim, predawn light, and the audience can seldom tell what is going on. But the music is atmospheric!)

The various venders and workers having gone off to begin their day, the scene is lonely and desolate as Mimì enters, looking around uncertainly for her destination. She leans on a tree and suffers a fit of coughing. She then asks the customs sergeant the way to a tavern where a painter has been working, and he points it out to her. A female server comes out of the building, and Mimì asks her to tell Marcello that she is here and needs to speak with him.

By now the sun has risen, but it's a dark, snowy day. A few people leave the tavern and head home; Marcello comes out after them and greets Mimì. He tells her that he and Musetta have been staying there for a month; he paints and she teaches singing to the guests, so the innkeeper doesn't charge them rent. He invites Mimì to come in out of the cold, but when he tells her Rodolfo is there she says she doesn't want to see him. Coughing again, she asks Marcello for help: she tells him she knows Rodolfo loves her, but he is so suspicious and jealous that it has become impossible for the two of them to live together. Marcello offers to awaken Rodolfo—he had shown up at the tavern shortly before dawn, after leaving Mimì in anger. Through the window, Marcello sees Rodolfo coming, but Mimì says she doesn't want him to see her. Marcello suggests she go home to avoid a public scene. She seems to leave but remains behind a corner of the building, listening.

Distraught, Rodolfo tells Marcello he's glad they are alone so they can talk. He wants to leave Mimì; he claims to be angry and jealous because she is a terrible coquette, flirting outrageously with various other men. Marcello

isn't convinced, so Rodolfo admits the truth: he loves Mimì more than anything, but he is afraid because she is so ill; he believes she is dying. The garret
is terribly cold and drafty, he cannot afford to keep her warm or take care
of her properly, and he fears that living in such conditions is destroying her
health.

Mimì, who hadn't fully realized her illness was that serious, is frightened
by what she has overheard. She coughs again, inadvertently revealing her
presence. Marcello is dismayed to learn she is still there and has heard their
conversation; Rodolfo embraces her and tries to make light of what he has
said. He invites her to go inside the tavern but she refuses. Marcello hears
Musetta laughing with a man inside; now he himself becomes jealous and
goes inside to see what's happening.

In an achingly lovely aria, Mimì bids farewell to Rodolfo. She says she will
go back to her own lonely room and her embroidery. She will send someone
to pick up her few belongings, but he may keep the pink bonnet he gave her
as a remembrance if he wishes. She hopes there will be no bitterness between
them. She and Rodolfo sing their farewells, remembering the arguments as
well as the kisses and the tenderness they shared; to be alone in the winter
will be hard indeed, but when spring comes each of them will have the sun
as a companion.

From inside the tavern we hear the sounds of breaking dishes—Marcello
and Musetta are throwing things at each other! They come flying out the door
in the midst of a fight. He accuses her of flirting with a customer who asked
her to dance; she reminds him that they aren't married, so he shouldn't
behave like a jealous husband—she requires her freedom. The scene develops
into a quartet: Musetta and Marcello's fight descends to name-calling as Mimì
and Rodolfo sing rapturously of the spring. Musetta stalks off in a huff and
Marcello slams into the tavern as Mimì and Rodolfo reaffirm their love and
promise to stay together until the return of the season of flowers.

Act Four

The last scene opens on the same tableau as the first—in the garret, with
Marcello at his easel and Rodolfo at the table—but it is daylight this time, and
the weather is warmer. The two are avoiding work by chatting. Rodolfo tells
Marcello he recently happened to run into Musetta on the streets of Paris; she
was in a luxurious carriage and dressed in velvet, clearly under the protection
of another rich gentleman. Marcello replies that he has seen Mimì as well,
in similar circumstances. Both men pretend not to care, then put down pen
and paintbrush and sing a melancholy duet about their lost loves, who are
still relentlessly haunting their memories. They mention they are hungry

The final scene of *La bohème* as seen at the Metropolitan Opera, circa 1992. Shown here are Colline (played by John Cheek), Marcello (Dwayne Croft), Musetta (Nancy Gustafson), Rodolfo (Luis Lima), and Mimì (Gabriela Benacková). *Erika Davidson/courtesy of the Metropolitan Opera Archives*

The corresponding scene in *Rent* as performed by the Harbor Lights Theater Company on Staten Island in 2015. From left: Roger (Travis Artz), Mimi (Emily Jeanne Phillips), Joanne (Madeline Fansler), and Maureen (Zuri Washington). *Bitten By A Zebra*

and haven't eaten in a while; Schaunard and Colline enter with food, but it's a much more meager meal than the one Schaunard supplied on Christmas Eve. Still, the four amuse themselves by pretending to have a lavish banquet. They joke about having been invited to a ball at the king's court, then clear aside the furniture so they can dance together like romantic couples. A mock fight erupts between Colline and Schaunard and they pretend to fight a duel, but the rambunctious merriment is interrupted by the sudden, surprising arrival of a highly agitated Musetta.

Musetta tells the men that she has brought Mimì with her, but the latter is very ill and has collapsed, unable to make it to the top of the stairs. Alarmed, Rodolfo runs to her and with Marcello's help carries her into the apartment. Colline and Schaunard quickly set up a cot for her, and Musetta brings a glass of water. Reviving, Mimì shyly asks Rodolfo if he wants her there; he reassures her: "Always, always."

Off to one side, Musetta tells the other three men that she has heard gossip that Mimì, fearing she was deathly ill, had fled the rich viscount she had been living with. Musetta searched for her until she found her, alone and dragging herself through the streets. Mimì said she wanted to die with Rodolfo, so Musetta brought her home.

Mimì looks around the familiar room and tells Rodolfo she feels happy to be there; Schaunard pulls Colline aside to say he thinks she has but half an hour to live. Coughing, Mimì says she is cold and longs for a muff to warm her hands. She greets the group of friends and tells Marcello that Musetta is very good; he says he knows, and takes Musetta's hand. Musetta removes her earrings and gives them to Marcello, instructing him to sell them to get medicine for Mimì, and to bring back a doctor. Realizing that the wish for a muff may be Mimì's last request, Musetta resolves to get one for her and leaves with Marcello.

Colline takes off his beloved overcoat—the one he got on Christmas Eve—and bids it farewell in a brief, tender aria; he has resolved to pawn it to get money to help Mimì. He asks Schaunard to go with him so that Mimì and Rodolfo can be alone together.

The two lovers share a tender scene as she lies on the cot. She tells him she wanted to be alone with him so she could tell him how much she still loves him. He says she is still beautiful, as beautiful as the dawn, but she says no—she is now like a sunset. He places the pink bonnet on her head, and, as they remember the innocence of the night they met and fell in love, they sing a duet that includes wisps of the melodies they sang in the first act. But she has another spasm of coughing, alarming Rodolfo—and Schaunard, who has just returned.

Musetta and Marcello have come back as well, with a muff and a vial of medicine. Marcello says the doctor has agreed to come. He lights a spirit lamp, and Musetta gives Mimì the muff. Mimì is delighted with the gift and thanks Rodolfo, thinking he got it for her; Musetta, declining to take credit for her good deed, graciously confirms this.

Rodolfo begins to weep, which concerns Mimì, but she tells him there's no need: she's better. Marcello tells Rodolfo the doctor will be there soon. As she heats up the medicine over the spirit lamp, Musetta prays to the Virgin Mary to spare Mimì's life.

Rodolfo tries to hang Musetta's shawl over the window to shade Mimì from the sunlight. While he is thus distracted, Schaunard checks on Mimì and quietly tells Marcello that she has died. Colline returns with the money he got for his coat and gives it to Musetta. As Musetta announces that the medicine is ready, Rodolfo sees the looks on Marcello's and Schaunard's faces and can tell that something is very wrong; Marcello embraces him and says "Courage!" Finally understanding what has happened, Rodolfo runs to the cot and falls to his knees beside Mimì's body, helplessly crying out her name as the curtain comes down.

Adapting a Classic

In getting to know *La bohème*, one starts to see what elements Jonathan Larson (who studied the original Murger novel as well as the opera) borrowed, which ones he kept the same, and what he changed—all of which can shed light on the story and themes of *Rent* and the process behind its creation. First off, we'll look at the characters.

Rodolfo/Roger

The tenor hero, a poet and playwright in Puccini's opera, becomes Larson's rock tenor heartthrob, the songwriter and former front man of a band who is mourning his lost love, April, and determined to write one great song before he succumbs to AIDS. In the opera, Mimì is the only character who is sick, so Rodolfo, though also a near-starving artist, doesn't have quite as much of a burden to carry as Roger. Both men, however, have issues with jealousy and problems with commitment.

Marcello/Mark

Puccini's baritone painter becomes Mark Cohen, the aspiring filmmaker who sets out to document the lives of his friends. As the opera and the musical open, both men have recently lost their girlfriends: Musetta having left Marcello before taking up with the elderly but wealthy Alcindoro, and Maureen having dumped Mark in favor of a lesbian relationship with Joanne. Only in the opera will the couple get back together; only in the musical does Mark take on the responsibilities of a narrator. When Marcello's painting of the Red Sea ends up being used as a sign over a tavern, he could be accused of "selling out" just as Mark almost does when he considers taking a job with *Buzzline*.

Mimì/Mimi

Though the name is the same (minus the accent mark), Larson's transformation of Puccini's modest, delicate seamstress into a fierce, sexually aggressive club dancer and drug addict can strike audiences as the most audacious departure from the original—and of course, Mimì's tuberculosis becomes Mimi's AIDS. It's important to point out, though, that Mimì is probably not quite as innocent as she initially appears to be; though her relationship with a rich viscount is only mentioned very briefly in the last scene, the character has been referred to as a "grisette," or a young woman who lives on the protection of a wealthy man in return for her romantic or sexual favors: not quite the same thing as a prostitute, but the implication is that perhaps Mimì has had more than one of these relationships (as, almost certainly, has Musetta). An impoverished, unmarried young woman had few other options for survival in those days. There's also a parallel here to Mimi's relationship with Benny in *Rent*, which involves him supporting her financially and offering to pay for her rehab. Jonathan Larson wanted his musical to be about hope, so his Mimi, unlike Puccini's, doesn't die at the end: that particular change has been much debated over the years and remains controversial.

Benoit/Benny

The names are close, and both men are landlords trying to collect the rent, but the similarities end there. Benoit is a silly old codger who is ridiculed and taken advantage of by the young friends and dispatched in one brief scene, never to be heard from again in the course of the opera, whereas Benny has much more complicated relationships with the other characters and plays an important role throughout the musical. His business goals and attitudes about the neighborhood and its homeless denizens are also important as they serve to draw focus to the perniciousness of gentrification, an issue that was important to Larson and integral to *Rent*'s themes.

Soprano Catherine Malfitano as Mimì in *La bohème* and Julia Santana as her rock counterpart in the Los Angeles company of *Rent*, 1997

Left photo from the collection of the author / right photo Joan Marcus

Colline/Collins

Puccini's basso philosopher shares a generous spirit and a certain bookish eccentricity—as well as a powerfully resonant voice—with Larson's computer-age philosopher, though it's hard to imagine him being as much of an activist. And of course, Colline and Schaunard are not ill in the opera, though in the musical they both have AIDS.

Schaunard/Angel

Since Angel, not Mimi, is the character who actually dies in *Rent*, it could be argued that Angel also inherited part of the Mimì role. But he shares his last name, with the spelling slightly changed, with Puccini's Schaunard, and both are musicians. (Angel is a percussionist, though he plays on a pickle tub rather than a real drum; Schaunard plays the violin.) Both have made some unexpected cash on Christmas Eve related to the deaths of animals, and both are generous in sharing it with their friends. Schaunard doesn't do drag (that we know of), but he does playfully pretend to be a girl and sing in falsetto in the "ball" scene of the last act. And of course, the romantic relationship between Collins and Angel is Larson's invention. Or is it? Neither Colline nor Schaunard seems to have a girlfriend, and they do spend a lot of time together . . .

Musetta/Maureen

Musetta's frivolous lifestyle doesn't include anything resembling Maureen's social activism. However, both divas make grand entrances and know how to play a crowd, and both are proud of their beauty and confident in their sexual prowess. When Musetta leaves Marcello and takes up with a wealthy old man, it's clearly for the financial benefits; Maureen's new love, Joanne—being a lawyer and from a prominent family—is also better off than most of the other characters in *Rent*, but there's no indication that Maureen is interested in her for her money, and the relationship is definitely emotional as well as sexual. In the last scene, Maureen's role in bringing Mimi back to the loft and taking care of her parallels Musetta very closely.

Alcindoro/Joanne

Not much of a correspondence here, except that both are the new partners of Musetta/Maureen after she leaves Marcello/Mark. But while Alcindoro, like Benoit (the two roles are often played by the same singer), is an old man who is taken advantage of and then forgotten after one brief scene, Joanne becomes a major character. In fact, in Act Two she sort of shares the Marcello role, since Mark never gets back with Maureen but Joanne does: the on again/off again relationship between the two women parallels Marcello and Musetta much more than Mark's relationship with Maureen does.

The Same Only Different

New York Times classical music critic Anthony Tommasini, who had interviewed Larson on the last night of his life and has remained a devotee of *Rent* ever since first seeing it at that evening's dress rehearsal, reflected on the parallels between the opera and the musical in a piece he published shortly before *Rent* closed on Broadway: "Mr. Larson also talked that night about his fascination with 'La Bohème,' which depicts a group of artists in the Latin Quarter of 1830s Paris who are quick to fall in love but shun emotional commitment in the face of poverty and disease. In Puccini's depiction of four wisecracking guys who share a ratty garret and spend one another's money, when they have any, Mr. Larson recognized himself and his friends, fledgling artists who held down makeshift jobs to support their work amid an urban scene of drugs, poverty and AIDS."

Though familiarity with *La bohème* is in no way a prerequisite for appreciating *Rent*, knowing the opera can make for a richer experience of the musical—and vice versa. Not only do the themes and big questions of the two works reflect off each other in provocative ways, but on a simpler level it can be fun spotting parallels both large and small—and noting the very major differences. For instance, the opening scenes of both works show the two pairs of leading men in their unheated apartments trying to stay warm. In the opera Rodolfo burns the manuscript of a play he's been working on in their wood stove; Marcello offers his painting of the Red Sea as well but Rodolfo tells him burning the painted canvas would stink up the room. In *Rent*, they burn both Mark's old screenplays (since he has just decided to shoot without a script) and posters of Roger's gigs at punk clubs. When Collins and Angel arrive, the list of provisions in the pickle tub closely parallels the array of groceries provided by Schaunard. "Firewood! Cigars! Wine!" is modernized to coffee (Bustelo), Marlboro cigarettes, bananas, cereal, and, yes, firewood.

One winking reference that's easy to miss: In "We're Okay," Joanne asks her lawyer colleague Steve what's happening with "the Murget case." Though spelled differently, when pronounced as a French name "Murget" sounds the same as "Murger"—the last name of the author of the book *La bohème* is based on.

The scenes between Mimì and Rodolfo/Mimi and Roger display the closest parallels, but the ways in which Larson twists and tweaks the Puccini originals are often telling. "Light My Candle" follows the scene of Mimì and Rodolfo's first meeting very closely, candle and all, but in the opera Mimì is shy and Rodolfo takes the lead in the flirtation, whereas in the musical Roger is wary and Mimi is the aggressor. The dropped key becomes a stash of heroin, but while Rodolfo conceals the key simply to keep Mimì in the room longer, Roger hides the harmful drugs in his pocket out of concern over the girl's addiction. In the opera, both characters sing major arias in that scene. The melody of Rodolfo's aria, *Che gelida manina*, is subtly echoed in Larson's music for "Light My Candle," and its opening line, in which Rodolfo notices how cold Mimì's hand is, gets mirrored by Roger's comment, "cold hands," toward the end of the song. The first line of Mimì's own aria, *Sì, mi chiamano Mimì*, translates directly into the modern Mimi's exit line: "They call me Mimi."

Though in the opera that first scene between the two characters progresses directly into a love duet, *O soave fanciulla*, the musical's Roger and Mimi take a lot longer to get to that point. But when their love song, "I Should Tell You," does finally arrive (late in Act One), it builds to a soaring, yearning melody that in its own way recalls Puccini's duet. And even though Larson's score is of a completely different idiom than Puccini's, it's also possible to hear the subtle influence of Mimì's tearful third-act farewell aria, *D'onde lieta uscì*, on the arching, keening lines of "Without You" and "Goodbye, Love."

Some of the changes Larson made are deeply ironic, pointing up the harsh ways in which the world had changed over the preceding century. Transforming Mimì from a humble seamstress to an S&M club dancer is the most obvious example (the former director of a major American opera company once stated in an interview that he hated "what they did to Mimì" in *Rent*), but the St. Mark's Place scene, in which drug dealers and homeless street vendors take the place of Puccini's merry shopkeepers and toymakers, also makes a powerful statement through contrast. Still, it's possible to hear in the music of Larson's "Christmas Bells" some of the same pulsing, anticipatory energy with which Puccini colored the opening bars of the Café Momus scene.

The great quartet in the third act of *La bohème*, in which Rodolfo and Mimì reconfirm their love while Marcello and Musetta are arguing, is a wonderful example of the "ensemble"—an operatic number in which several different characters are singing different musical lines, all at the same time, while advancing the story. This kind of complex composition is rarely attempted in musical theater, so it's worth noting that Larson pulled it off with remarkable dexterity in several songs, including "Christmas Bells," "Happy New Year," and "Goodbye, Love." This achievement is part of what qualifies *Rent*, though we've been referring to it here as a musical, as a genuine rock opera.

Some of the parallels pop up in surprising places. Musetta sings her famous Waltz song at the Café Momus, in a scene that corresponds to the Life Café scene in *Rent*, but the aria's lyrics—about walking down the street and attracting admiring stares—are mirrored closely not in that scene but much later, as the opening verse of "Take Me or Leave Me." And "Tango: Maureen" is another allusion to "Musetta's Waltz," each title linking the character's name with a popular dance form. The waltz is also directly referred to in the musical, its memorable melody played three times on guitar. (This brings up an intriguing stylistic point, as Mark identifies it as "Musetta's Waltz" in the dialogue. Normally, a classic work and its adaptation would be thought of as existing in parallel but separate universes, but in *Rent* the characters are clearly aware that the opera *La bohème* exists.)

The melody of that tenacious waltz echoes again in the final scenes of both works: in the love song "Your Eyes"—the "one great song" that Roger finally writes and sings for Mimi—and in *O Mimì, tu più non torni*—the duet that Rodolfo and Marcello sing at the beginning of the last act of the opera. The closest parallel to that duet in *Rent* would of course be "What You Own," Mark and Roger's bewailing of America's declining values at the turn of the millennium. But while Larson's duet begins in sarcasm and builds to encompass rage, soul-searching, and creative resolution, Puccini's is gentle, elegiac in tone, and melancholy. Nevertheless there are lyric parallels: Marcello and Rodolfo are expressing how constant thoughts of their lost loves have invaded their minds and make it impossible to do their work, while Mark and Roger, equally consumed by thoughts of Angel and Mimi, ultimately find in them renewed purpose and inspiration.

Recordings and Videos

Unlike hit Broadway musicals, which generally only get one or two cast albums and almost never more than a handful, the most popular operas get re-recorded every few years. There have been around thirty commercial audio recordings of *La bohème* issued since 1918, and that's not counting the dozens of live "pirate" versions long circulated by collectors. As the opera is relatively short, each of the complete versions fits on two CDs. Though opera fanatics love to collect and compare different casts (and sometimes go broke in the process), a newbie looking to listen to the opera for the first time may find the number of choices overwhelming; a few helpful hints follow.

The legendary Maestro Arturo Toscanini, considered one of the greatest conductors in history, led the world premiere of *La bohème* in 1896. Remarkably, he also conducted an NBC radio broadcast of it fifty years later; the recording was released by RCA. The set is an invaluable historical document, notable not just for Toscanini's interpretation but for the detailed acting of the great Puccini soprano Licia Albanese as Mimì. Still, most new listeners will want a more recent recording with better sound quality.

Luciano Pavarotti and Mirella Freni, who grew up together in Modena, Italy, virtually owned the roles of Rodolfo and Mimì for three decades on stages all over the world. Both singers were captured in their lush-voiced prime in a 1972 set for Decca/London under the legendary conductor Herbert von Karajan. It's a classic entry, though some listeners consider Karajan's unusually slow tempi to be a drawback. (Pavarotti, incidentally, became a devoted fan of *Rent* many years later; his fiancee, Nicoletta Mantovani, produced an Italian version of the show in 2000.)

Fans who prefer Plácido Domingo, Pavarotti's main rival for the title of Tenor of the Century, can hear him as Rodolfo on an RCA/BMG set, opposite the formidable Spanish soprano Montserrat Caballé under Maestro Georg Solti. This version won the Grammy Award for Best Opera Recording in 1974.

Broadway fans might be particularly curious about Leonard Bernstein's interpretation of the opera; he was a world-renowned opera and symphonic conductor as well as the composer of such musicals as *Candide* and *West Side Story*. Bernstein could have worked with the world's biggest stars and often did, but for the youth-oriented *La bohème* he chose instead to use fresh-voiced young American singers: the cast is led by Jerry Hadley, who also recorded the title role in *Candide* under Bernstein, as Rodolfo, with Angelina Réaux as Mimì; Barbara Daniels as Musetta; and future baritone star Thomas Hampson as Marcello. This 1988 set, released by Deutsche Grammophon, can be difficult to find.

In the new millennium, the production of studio recordings of operas has slowed down considerably, for a complex variety of reasons. These include the economic recession, an already saturated market, and the decline of the CD industry in general as more and more listeners get their music online. But at the same time, the selection of video versions has expanded dramatically in the last few years; this trend is due largely to the accessibility of digital technology and the advent of high definition simulcasts, most of which are taped for subsequent distribution on DVD.

So if you want to watch *La bohème* at home as well as listen to it, you have an array of excellent choices there as well. Most of these are recordings of stage performances, but there have also been at least three cinematic versions of the opera, the most recent of which (2008) features Anna Netrebko, probably the biggest soprano star in today's opera world, as Mimì, and Rolando Villazón, her frequent onstage partner at the time, as Rodolfo. Marcello and Schaunard are both played by actors lip-synching to the voices of prerecorded baritones. The film is by the Austrian director Robert Dornhelm, with orchestra conducted by Bertrand de Billy. It was released by Axiom Films; the DVD is available on the Kultur label.

For a traditional stage production, it would be hard to do better than Franco Zeffirelli's classic Metropolitan Opera version, which has been preserved on video twice with different casts. Premiered on December 14, 1981, this beloved production has been in the Met's repertory ever since (it's the one that Jonathan Larson saw) and has racked up more performances than any other production in the company's history. The lavish staging reproduces 1830s Paris in loving detail; the main criticism occasionally leveled at it is that the panoramic sets and huge crowd scenes can dwarf the leading singers, but of course this difficulty is minimized on camera, where close-ups focus the attention. The first release (1982) is taken from a PBS telecast and preserves the performances of the all-star opening season cast, including Teresa Stratas as an emotionally riveting Mimì, and Renata Scotto, a celebrated Mimì in her day, here making a late-career switch to Musetta. José Carreras and Richard Stilwell, both dashing young singers at the time, play Rodolfo and Marcello, with the great James Levine on the podium. The 2008 version, from the Met's popular Live in HD series, presents a different cast on the same sets, under the baton of Nicola Luisotti.

Musical theater audiences curious about film director Baz Luhrmann's production of *La bohème*, which was seen on Broadway during the 2002–03 season, can view his 1993 Australian Opera production—on which the Broadway version was closely based—on a video from London Records. Updating the setting to 1957 Paris with strikingly bold scenic designs, Luhrmann brings the relationships to life with a cast of attractive young Australian singers led by David Hobson and Cheryl Barker.

In an odd turn of fate, Luhrmann's Broadway production of *La bohème* was produced by Jeffrey Seller and Kevin McCollum, who had produced the original production of *Rent* six years earlier; both shows ran concurrently on Broadway. After the second preview performance of the opera, McCollum asked a young audience member outside the theater if he had liked it. The young man replied, "Yeah, but how were they allowed to rip off *Rent* like that?" McCollum thought to himself, "Aha! My job is done."

3

"The Beauty of a Studio"

From Conception to Workshop

T he initial idea that led to *Rent* originated with a playwright named Billy Aronson. It was 1989, and Aronson was a struggling young writer trying to get New York theaters and producers interested in his plays. He adored opera and the escape it offered from the hassles of life in the big city.

One particular night, Billy remembers, he went to the Metropolitan Opera House and saw *La bohème*. As he walked home afterward, from the splendor of Lincoln Center down fifteen blocks to his tiny apartment in Hell's Kitchen, he realized that the opera had made him feel different about life: He had connected with the story of struggling artists in Paris—particularly the image of the poet Rodolfo burning the manuscript of his play to heat his freezing garret—and he was inspired.

Aronson had been developing a relationship with Playwrights Horizons, an Off-Broadway theater that had done readings of his plays, so he went to Tim Sanford, the theater's literary manager (and later artistic director) and told him his idea: He wanted to adapt *La bohème* into a contemporary musical. Sanford referred him to Ira Weitzman, who was in charge of developing new musicals at the theater, and Weitzman thought it was a terrific idea. Aronson could write lyrics but he needed a composer, so Weitzman gave him the names and contacts of a couple of aspiring songwriters whose work he was familiar with and told him the first one he should call was Jonathan Larson.

A New Team

After an initial phone call, Aronson met Larson briefly to exchange work samples (scripts and tapes) in order to see if they connected with each other's work. By way of introduction Larson told him, "I write good FM rock";

Playwright Billy Aronson with Victoria Leacock at the inaugural event for the Jonathan Larson Foundation, 1997.   *Photo courtesy of Victoria Leacock Hoffman*

Aronson said Larson initially "made me think of Steely Dan and people like that." For his part, Larson said Billy reminded him of Woody Allen.

After reviewing and liking each other's materials, they met one evening on the rooftop of Larson's building on Greenwich Street, where they sat on beach chairs and talked, looking out over the Hudson River. Larson was immediately excited about the idea of a rock *La bohéme*. According to Aronson: "Right off the bat he said this could be the next *Hair*." Both men felt that the musical could respond to pressures that were being keenly felt in New York City at that time: the Republicans were in power, AIDS was coming into everyone's awareness, and life seemed to be all about money. With the controversial censorship of performance artists like Karen Finley and Tim Miller, even the National Endowment for the Arts, in Aronson's words, "made artists feel like we were the enemy."

Aronson was struck by the contrast between the romantic, lyrical beauty of *La bohéme* and the real world outside the opera house, which came to seem "noisy and mean" by comparison. He wanted to explore that dichotomy in the show. The two began working together, with Billy writing the book and lyrics and Jonathan the music. But neither of them was used to collaborating; Aronson later said that working on a musical with another person can be harder than trying to make a marriage work. To begin with, Aronson wasn't sure he loved the title Larson came up with, but Larson was committed to *Rent* as a title almost from the get-go. He loved the double meaning: not only was it the money the characters owed their landlord, it also meant "ripped open" or "torn apart."

The two had very different styles and aesthetics. Aronson is known for his unique, incisive sense of humor. When Weitzman had asked him initially what part of the city he wanted to set the musical in, he said the Upper West Side, though the idea of writing about a specific neighborhood wasn't what drew him to the piece. Larson's first suggestion was to move it downtown to the East Village and relate it to the recent Tompkins Square Park riots, where tensions between the police and the homeless people who lived in the park had come to a boil. He wanted to include characters struggling with drug addiction. Billy agreed to try this, but he lived on 51st Street and Ninth Avenue, a very different part of town, and though, as he said, "different drugs were sold on every floor of the building" at the time, he himself was not a druggie; he told Larson that writing about a heroin addict was not something for which he could draw from experience. Larson worried that Aronson was making the characters into yuppies, and criticized the first draft of the libretto as being too much like the then popular TV series *thirtysomething*. He was going for something edgier, so Aronson tried to inject anger into the piece; they wrote an early, rage-filled version of the opening number for the characters of Ralph (the name was shortly changed to Roger) and Mark. Working together, they also wrote "Santa Fe" and "I Should Tell You."

The Demo

With the help of Jonathan's friend Steve Skinner, and at a cost of about $600, the new team made a demo recording of the three songs to shop around. They put together a rather remarkable cast. "Santa Fe" was sung on the tape by Jon Cavaluzzo, an actor friend of Larson's who forged a unique career recording voiceovers for the audio tours played through headphones in dozens of museums; Larson told him he was writing the role of Tom Collins for him. "Rent" was performed on the demo by Larson himself and his close friend Roger Bart, who also sang "I Should Tell You" with Valarie Pettiford. Bart had already made his Broadway debut in *Big River* and would go on to great fame in *The Producers*. (Coincidentally, in 2016 he appeared in the Broadway musical *Disaster!* alongside Adam Pascal—the original demo Roger together with the man who originated the role onstage.) The glamorous Pettiford, who made her Broadway debut at age eighteen, had already been in four Broadway musicals, including *Sophisticated Ladies* and Bob Fosse's *Big Deal*; she has had a long career onstage and on television as a singer, dancer, and actress.

Weitzman and people at a couple of other theaters listened to the recording. Some of them were excited about the songs, but the book wasn't quite working, and the collaboration hadn't gelled. Aronson's writing style is spare and often ironic; he was interested in the position of artists in society circa 1990 and has said, "When artists are ambivalent about their lives and what they're doing it gets desperate and mean." He wanted to get the energy of that dynamic into the show, and added, "It's hard to express yourself romantically in these times." He was interested in exploring "this odd thing where people can't express themselves" and the broken rhythms that result from the attempt. That impulse remains very apparent in the lyrics to "I Should Tell You," but in general his notions were not clicking with Larson's music, which is powerfully direct and unabashedly emotional. The two found that they didn't know how to go forward—and at any rate no theater was expressing much interest in taking on the property. Not wanting to waste time on a project that didn't seem to be going anywhere, they decided to put *Rent* aside.

Going It Alone

Larson moved on to other projects, including his one-man musical *Boho Days*. But he remained haunted by the story of *La bohème*. He had lost several friends to AIDS, and in the fall of 1991 he learned that thee more close friends were sick. Struck powerfully by the parallel to Mimì's illness in *La bohéme*, he felt a more urgent connection to the work than ever before. He called Ira Weitzman and said he couldn't get the project out of his head.

Weitzman had misgivings; he thought it would be better if Larson had a collaborator. But since things hadn't worked out with Aronson, he advised Larson to call him and work out a deal that would allow him to continue working on the project by himself. Aronson agreed.

Larson sent the playwright a letter, dated October 4, 1991, promising that "if any such miracle as a production happens," Aronson would be credited for original concept and any lyrics of his that were still in the show. The letter also stipulated that at such time a more official agreement regarding compensation would be drafted.

(When Larson passed away so unexpectedly, no one yet knew just how much of a miracle the production would eventually turn out to be, and the promised agreement had not yet been drawn up. Aronson hired a lawyer who worked out the details with the Larson family just in time for the Broadway opening; though the terms are not public knowledge, the playwright has said his income from the show over the years has been a boon, and was helpful in putting his two children, Anna and Jake, through college.)

While working on the show, Larson would occasionally get in touch with Aronson, sending him some of the new material he was writing, asking for feedback, and keeping him updated on the progress of the production. According to Billy: "Shortly before the Off-Broadway opening I asked Jonathan what was left of my lyrics. He said the lyrics for 'Rent' were basically his, the lyrics for 'Santa Fe' were basically mine, and the lyrics for 'I Should Tell You' were half and half."

Billy Aronson has gone on to a successful career; his plays include *Light Years*, *The Art Room*, and *First Day of School*, and he has collaborated with composers on several children's musicals. He is a particular master of the one-act form. Many of his short works have been produced at the Ensemble Studio Theatre, where he is a member, and are available in a printed anthology, *Funny Shorts*, from Broadway Play Publishing. He has also enjoyed a parallel career writing for children's television, most recently the multiple-Emmy-winning PBS math series *Peg + Cat*, which he created with artist Jennifer Oxley. Aronson is executive producer of the animated show, for which he writes stories and many scripts. Though he had been ambivalent about some of Larson's ideas for *Rent* when they were trying to work together, he has said publicly that he has grown to love the finished show; he attended the opening night on Broadway and has enjoyed several other productions over the years.

New York Theatre Workshop

In 1979, a man named Stephen Graham started a foundation with the purpose of supporting playwrights. Graham, the son of legendary publisher Katharine Graham of the *Washington Post*, and a couple of his friends were interested in producing, but initially they did not want to start a theater with its own real estate; instead they created an organization with the flexibility to provide assistance and support to artists in various creative ways. In addition to identifying and cultivating new playwrights, they were interested in supporting the work of young directors, as at that time there were very few resources available for directors beginning their careers. They produced readings and workshops and in some cases provided support for full productions by other nonprofit theater companies.

As more and more artists came to them for assistance, Graham and his group realized they needed to define a more consistent structure, so Jean Passanante was hired as program director to administer the various projects; when the group incorporated as a theater under the name New York Theatre Workshop (NYTW) in 1983, Passanante was named as artistic director and Graham as executive director. Passanante, who has had a long and successful career as a television writer, moved on in 1988 and was succeeded as artistic director by James C. Nicola.

Nicola had begun his career as a director and had worked as a producing associate under Zelda Fichandler at Arena Stage, a prominent regional theater in Washington, D.C., and then as a casting coordinator under the legendary Joseph Papp at the Public Theater in New York. He considers Fichandler and Papp his "artistic parents" and was inspired by the examples they set: both were good directors, but their particular genius was for creating an environment where artists could thrive. At NYTW, Nicola put his own directing aside to focus on leadership. As he says, "Being an artistic leader of a theatre is in some ways its own discipline; it's an intense focus."

The company's first performance space was the Perry Street Theatre, a small Greenwich Village venue where they produced work from 1987 to 1992. It was when they were preparing to open their current space, the 198-seat New York Theatre Workshop on East Fourth Street, that Jonathan Larson first approached Nicola with his musical *Rent*.

The success of *Rent* was instrumental in raising the company's profile in New York and on the national and even international theater scenes; during its long Broadway run it also contributed substantially to the theater's finances. Now an acknowledged leader in the arts community with a particular interest in cultivating the work of diverse and underrepresented voices in the theater, NYTW is, as stated on the company's website, "both a laboratory for theatrical exploration and a producer of plays that expand the boundaries of theatrical form and address the critical issues of our times." The theater presents numerous readings and workshops of plays in progress every year, in addition to a mainstage season. Though the company is known for developing new works, there has also been a continuing focus on reimagined classics, from Greek drama to Shakespeare, Molière and Ibsen,

James C. Nicola, artistic director of New York Theatre Workshop, at a Peasant's Feast in Jonathan Larson's apartment.

Victoria Leacock Hoffman

and American masterpieces by Tennessee Williams and Lillian Hellman. NYTW has developed and produced the work of such major international artists as Tony Kushner, Caryl Churchill, Doug Wright, and the director Ivo van Hove, as well as countless young artists in the early stages of their careers. Besides *Rent*, productions originated at NYTW that have moved on to Broadway runs have included *Dirty Blonde*, *Peter and the Starcatcher*, and *Once*. In addition to their extended community of artists, known as the Usual Suspects, the theater has offered residencies to smaller ensemble theater companies, various fellowship programs for emerging artists of diverse backgrounds, and, in honor of the creator of *Rent*, the Jonathan Larson Lab, which "gives emerging and established theatre artists essential resources, a nurturing creative environment and an open canvas for exploring their ideas and developing their work."

A Theater on East Fourth Street

In the summer of 1992, New York Theatre Workshop was moving into its new space on East 4th Street between Second Avenue and the Bowery. While the building was still under renovation, Jonathan Larson rode by one day on his bicycle and took a look. It felt to him like the right place for *Rent*—both aesthetically, with its big stage, and geographically, as part of the East Village community. A few days later he biked back over and dropped off a draft of the musical.

The Reading

The theater's artistic director, Jim Nicola, read the script right away and listened to the demo recording. Though the material was rough, he was immediately interested. Nicola had always loved opera, even to the point of considering a singing career when he was younger, and the fact that *Rent* had been inspired by *La bohème* was very intriguing. And having just moved to the East Village, NYTW was looking to develop projects that spoke directly to the neighborhood; *Rent* seemed poised to do just that. Most importantly, Nicola could tell Larson was an extremely talented individual, and he decided the young artist was worth supporting. Soon Jonathan was made a member of the Usual Suspects, the theater's core group of artists, and Nicola offered to produce a reading of *Rent*.

This early version of the show was presented on June 17, 1993, on the same stage where *Rent* would open two and a half years later. It was directed by Christopher Grabowski, the theater's associate artistic director and literary manager. The cast comprised Beth Blankenship, James Bohanek, Angel

Caban, Jon Cavaluzzo, Bob Golden, Tony Hoylen, Bambi Jones, Clinton Leupp, David Levine, Rusty Magee, Joel Newsome, Nancy O'Connor, Karen Oberlin, Chiara Peacock, Anna Seckinger, and Robert Tate.

The young and ambitious producer Jeffrey Seller had been interested in Larson's work since seeing him perform *Boho Days* a couple of years earlier at the Second Stage. The two had stayed in touch, and Seller had heard enough about *Rent* that he was excited to see the reading, so he brought two colleagues, hoping he could persuade them to invest in a production. Unfortunately they did not share his enthusiasm: one of them left at intermission, and the other one stayed to the end but then said he didn't think the show could ever be made to work. Seller and Larson had a difficult conversation afterward. The producer told him the music was great but there just wasn't a story there yet. Larson was "stung by that," as Seller later put it, but the producer's belief in the young composer remained steadfast.

The next step was not immediately clear. The songs were terrific, but the general consensus was that the script was a mess. The show needed development, but Nicola did not feel the theater had the resources to devote to a workshop production, which for a musical can be very expensive. But Jonathan, who had been pouring his heart and soul into the musical for four years at that point, did not want to go back to the drawing board by himself; he needed collaborators and was eager for the energy of the rehearsal hall.

The cast of the first reading of *Rent* at NYTW, June 1993.

Photo courtesy of Victoria Leacock Hoffman

The Workshop Production

Larson thought of a possible solution. He was already familiar with the Richard Rodgers Awards for Musical Theatre, a program administered by the American Academy of Arts and Letters. Endowed in 1978 by Rodgers himself (the great American songwriter whose many classic musicals include *Oklahoma!*, *The King and I*, and *The Sound of Music*), the grant program is designed to facilitate development and various levels of production for musicals by new writers who have not yet established their careers. Larson had already won one for *Superbia*, which had helped finance the disappointing workshop of that show (see Chapter 1), but when he applied again in 1993 with an early draft of *Rent*, he was rejected. With the prospect of a workshop production at NYTW if the money could be raised, he decided to try again. The official rules of the Rodgers Awards prohibited resubmitting a work, but at Larson's request his mentor, Stephen Sondheim—who was head of the selection panel—agreed to make an exception in this case. The revised *Rent* was chosen as the recipient of the 1994 Richard Rodgers Development Award, a grant of $45,000 that made it possible for NYTW to go ahead with a full workshop production.

The first and most important decision Jim Nicola made at that point was the selection of the director. Michael Greif had a longstanding relationship with NYTW, and Nicola knew his work well. He told Barry Singer, author of the book *Ever After: The Last Years of Musical Theater and Beyond*, that he felt the show needed a director who was tough-minded as well as cool-headed, as a tonic to Larson's heart-on-sleeve passion and optimism. According to Nicola: "*Rent* was very fragile material at that time. It was so easy for it to become sentimental or hokey. I felt Michael had the right sort of dryness and sharpness to balance Jonathan's writing."

Larson knew the choice of a director was crucial, and he was initially concerned about Greif's lack of experience with musicals. But his friend Victoria Leacock reassured him that Greif would be the perfect choice; she had been impressed with his productions of *A Bright Room Called Day* and *Machinal* and felt his staging was innately musical.

The first time Michael Greif heard the score to *Rent* was on an airplane; he listened to the demo on a Walkman as he flew from California to New York. He was immediately excited. As he recalls: "I thought a lot of the songs were fantastic. I was drawn to the real exuberance of the characters. I loved that Jonathan was writing about people he loved who had HIV." For a 1996 interview in the *Los Angeles Times*, Greif told reporter Patrick Pacheco that he had also been drawn to the material because of the potential it offered to explore ways to bring a new, younger audience into the theater. He said: "Here was an opportunity to express things you generally don't find expressed in musical theater, yet it was a wonderful hybrid of some very operatic impulses, some very conventional musical theater impulses, and some not very conventional musical theater impulses, such as collage and nonrealistic storytelling. As I read on and listened, the doors of possibility opened."

The director was known to be strong on dramaturgy and structure; Nicola knew he could help Larson continue to develop the script. He also felt it was important for the musical to have a gay director, since Larson was a straight man writing about AIDS and about gay, lesbian, and bisexual characters; Greif's perspective could help ensure that the gay themes were handled with sensitivity. One of the director's chief dramaturgical contributions was emphasizing to Larson that, if Maureen was going to leave Mark for a woman, she shouldn't return to him at the end. Yes, Puccini's Musetta does end up going back to Marcello, but Larson had introduced a lesbian component into the story, and Maureen's relationship with Joanne needed to be handled with respect and not dismissed as a phase she was going through. Greif and Nicola spent a week with Larson in his apartment in the spring of 1994, combing through every beat of the script and score; they did more work on it that summer at Dartmouth College, where NYTW ran kind of a summer camp for the Usual Suspects. By the time they started rehearsals for the October workshop, the material had grown substantially, and Greif's input was a key part of that process.

Early Casting

NYTW hired Wendy Ettinger, a freelance casting director who had worked with the theater on other projects, to coordinate the auditions and casting process. Another major player in the development of the piece came onboard almost coincidentally. Tim Weil, who would become musical supervisor for the show, arranging the score and conducting the onstage band, first got involved when a staff member from NYTW called him to ask him to play piano for the auditions. They had called several pianists on their list and said he was the only one who called back! It was fortuitous, as he quickly became invaluable to the show.

Two performers who would become key players in the history of *Rent* also came on board at this early stage. Anthony Rapp, a professional performer since childhood, had managed to make his living as an actor for his first five years in New York (an impressive feat, as most young actors in the city would tell you). But at the time he was going through a lean spell and had recently taken his first day job—working at Starbucks. He was also sharing a crowded East Village apartment with his playwright brother and two other friends.

And as if those things didn't give him enough of a connection to the world of *Rent*, he went to his audition directly from a midtown memorial service for a friend who had recently passed away.

Daphne Rubin-Vega, the original Mimi, in *Rent*, 1996.   *Joan Marcus*

In his book *Without You*, Anthony recalls speeding downtown on his roller skates (then his preferred mode of travel) and entering NYTW for the first time. Like all the actors auditioning, he had been asked to prepare a contemporary rock or pop song; he sang "Losing My Religion," by R.E.M. (The choice may have been fortuitous, as Larson often described the characters' musical personalities in terms of famous musicians, and his early notes list Michael Stipe as a model for Mark.) Greif remembered Rapp from an audition for a recent production of Chekhov's *The Seagull*, and Larson knew his work from the film *Dazed and Confused*, which he said was one of his favorite movies. James Nicola has said that his audition didn't even feel like acting; Rapp simply was that character. He was called back on the spot; they handed him sheet music and a demo tape of the opening number (an earlier, angrier version of what we know today as the title song). He had a very successful callback and was promptly offered the pivotal role of Mark—a part he would play on and off over the next fifteen years.

Daphne Rubin-Vega didn't think she was interested in musical theater, which she considered "derivative." She was also already composing her own songs and wasn't sure she wanted to devote time to singing something she hadn't written. But in 1994 the girl group she had been touring with had broken up; she was making her living selling makeup at Patricia Field when her agent told her about the auditions for *Rent*. When she heard it was based on *La bohème*, she wasn't sure it sounded like something she would be able to relate to, but then she learned that this new version of Mimi was an S&M dancer and a junkie with AIDS, and she was intrigued. Someone had also told her that, for Mimi, they were looking for a combination of Gloria Estefan and Sinead O'Connor. Not knowing what to make of that, she decided to be herself; she sang "Roxanne" for her first audition. Jonathan Larson wasn't immediately sold. He told Greif and Nicola that she didn't have the kind of singing voice he had imagined for the character; the actress who was his first choice had toured as Maria in *West Side Story*. But before her callback, Rubin-Vega listened to a demo tape of a legit soprano singing the music and said to herself, "This song shouldn't be sung like that." She did her own thing with it, and Greif and Nicola were thrilled; she made the music come alive. They pushed Larson hard to reconsider. When the actress finally asked Larson directly what she needed to do to get the part, he said, "Just relax. And make me cry." She got it.

Rehearsals

Rehearsals for the workshop began in a small, stuffy rehearsal room in NYTW's office suite, located in the Times Square area of Midtown Manhattan.

In order to foster a sense of unity among the actors, Greif and Weil (now officially the musical director) decided to begin by teaching them the music to "Seasons of Love"—the song in which all the ensemble members as well as the principals took part as equals. On hearing, and singing, that beautiful melody and those simple, powerfully significant words for the first time, the company knew they were involved with something potentially very special.

After the first few days, rehearsals moved to a larger and more comfortable space: a room with a skylight, located on the top floor of the brownstone next door to NYTW. Greif wanted the cast to understand the world of the play, so he posted a collage of research material on a wall in the rehearsal studio: it included pictures of outdoor sculptures in the East Village (some of which would eventually help inspire the set for the full production), pictures and articles about Nirvana and other early nineties grunge bands, and so forth. With only two and a half weeks of rehearsal time available, Greif worked fast, often improvising staging in the rehearsal hall; he encouraged and welcomed ideas and suggestions from the cast. The characters, some of which had been only roughly sketched in, began to take on more dimensions in the hands of real actors. Larson was inspired by their voices to reshape some of the songs and write new ones as well.

Some of the performers brought to their roles interesting qualities that were very different from those of the actors who would eventually create them in the full production. Pat Briggs, who played Tom Collins, was in Rapp's words "a soulful white guy with a crazy rock voice"; Tom Waits was the musical inspiration. Sarah Knowlton, the respected stage actress who played Maureen, had a dry wit and great comic timing. She played the character as a pretentious downtown artiste with a coolly precise, ironic vocal delivery—a completely different approach from the raw, unleashed energy and brash sexiness that Idina Menzel would bring to it two years later. Roger was played by Tony Hoylen, who was something of a Bruce Springsteen sound-alike and who (like Adam Pascal, who would succeed him for the full production) was a singer-songwriter by trade. He also had a flourishing career in voiceovers; he was the "voice of VH-1" at the time and had worked with Larson on his children's TV pilot, *Away We Go!*

The workshop cast also included Shelley Dickinson as Joanne, Michael Potts as Benny, and Mark Setlock as Angel. The ensemble was comprised of Gilles Chiasson (who would eventually follow the show to Broadway), Deirdre Boddie-Henderson, Sheila Kay Davis, Erin Hill, John Lathan, and Jesse Sinclair Lenat.

The workshop had a minimal production budget, but costume designer Angela Wendt and lighting designer Blake Burba, who would stay with the show all the way to Broadway, first got involved at this point. Wendt did both scenery and costumes for that version—she dressed the cast on a shoestring budget, which was not out of keeping with the low-rent, thrift-store aesthetic of the characters—and Burba was inventive and unobtrusive, managing to devise an effective working design almost without interrupting the (extremely limited) rehearsal time for technical adjustments. There was no choreographer yet; Anthony Rapp was deputized to give a curtain speech before each performance, which informed the audience it was a work-in-progress and the final version would have dancing in it.

The Workshop Script

Comparing the script and the score of this 1994 version to the finished show we know today is fascinating. It sheds light on some of the thought processes behind the development of the musical.

The workshop version begins with a phone ringing and three messages left on Mark and Roger's answering machine (a device that would remain in the show, though used somewhat differently). The first one is from "Dave," Roger's boss at the bar where he's been working (we never hear about that job in the finished version); Dave fires him for missing too many shifts. A message from Mark's mother is similar to the one we know, but includes cutting him off from using (or abusing) his parents' bank account. And then there's a call from landlord Benny demanding cash. These messages are followed by "Splatter," an earlier version of what would become the famous title song. It's closer to what Larson originally wrote with Billy Aronson; the lyrics are desperate and bitterly angry, as Roger and Mark come up with numerous strategies for killing themselves due to inability to pay "last month's rent" (rather than "last year's"). Like much of the score, the number as arranged had a lean, raw sound: punkier and edgier than the revised version.

Quite a few of the songs were already in something close to their final forms—though in some cases there were individual lyrics that got changed or extra verses that were subsequently cut. These included "Today 4 U," "Santa Fe," "I'll Cover You" (both the initial duet and the funeral reprise), "Will I?" "Christmas Bells," "La Vie Bohème," "Seasons of Love," and "Contact."

"Out Tonight" was already there but in a very different position. Following "Seasons of Love" at the top of Act Two and set on Valentine's Day, it was staged with Daphne Rubin-Vega trying out and discarding various outfits, and included interspersed vignettes tracking the developments in the Mark/Maureen/Joanne triangle. Otherwise, much of the Mimi/Roger relationship was already in place, including "Light My Candle," "Another Day," "I Should Tell You," and "Goodbye, Love"—though "Without You" was sung by Maureen and Joanne.

Roger's solos, however, were different. There was a song called "Right Brain," which found the blocked songwriter trying to access the creative side of his psyche (and included some rather sexually explicit lyrics); the melody and some of the words would later find their way into the more powerful "One Song Glory." There was no "What You Own," but during his attempted escape to Santa Fe Roger had an emotional ballad called "Open Road," in which he agonized over having left Mimi. It followed another cut number, "Real Estate," in which Mark expressed his frustrations with America's money-obsessed culture and Benny tried to entice him to join him in the real estate business. (Amazingly, that song, written by 1994, includes the now-devastating lyric "Any fool can do it: Witness Donald Trump!") Roger's climactic love song "Your Eyes" had yet to be written: the emotion of Mimi's near-death scene was carried instead by an extended reprise of "I Should Tell You," resolving into the guitar rendition of "Musetta's Waltz." Mimi then woke up, recognizing the tune as "the theme from *Moonstruck*!"—the famous movie in which Cher and Nicholas Cage attend the opera.

Even without "Halloween" and "What You Own," Mark's character was largely in place—though the sung conversation between him and Roger leading into "Goodbye Love" had some significant differences. Whereas the final version is a bitter confrontation between the two friends, with Roger accusing Mark of living a lie and staying detached from life, in the workshop version Mark beats *himself* up for escaping into work, and Roger, as a supportive friend, attempts to shore him up by praising his talent; the song ends with a mutual "love you" rather than the rift that could only be repaired later.

"Over the Moon" was similar in outline to what we know today, but with less of the nursery rhyme imagery and less direct in its attacks on Benny. Instead, there were allusions to *Oedipus Rex* and digs at cable TV. The tone of the piece, delivered by Knowlton in a deadpan Laurie Anderson impersonation, was much more restrained; she accompanied herself on a cello.

With regard to characters, the biggest changes would come in the portrayals of Benny and Joanne, both of which were relatively small, underdeveloped roles in the workshop version. Benny had some music, later cut, that depicted him comedically as an almost operatic villain, complete with booming baritone voice. There was no "You'll See," and little indication of the layered, conflicted character he would later become. Joanne was largely undefined; there was no mention of the conflict with her parents or of her being a lawyer, no "We're Okay," and no "Take Me or Leave Me." She did have a duet with Maureen (and a reprise of it) called "Female to Female": the title uses the difficulty of connecting the ends of the sound system's electrical cables as a metaphor for their personal relationship.

In the spot where "Tango: Maureen" would later go, there was instead "You'll Get Over It," a cut duet for Mark and Maureen that had them flinging the title phrase at each other: she's sure he'll get over their breakup, and he suspects she'll get over being a lesbian. He asks her what it's like to be with a woman and begs her for another chance. The lesbian subplot would continue to be discussed and developed as the show moved forward.

Enter the Angels

The purpose of the workshop was as much to develop the script and score as it was to attract audiences and investors; rehearsals were held between the two weekends of performances, and even at that late juncture changes were made. The show had begun to generate buzz in the industry, and the final weekend of performances sold out. Once again, Jeffrey Seller attended, this time bringing along Kevin McCollum, his partner from The Booking Office, who had missed the earlier reading. McCollum said he found the first twenty-five minutes of the show confusing, but it all fell into place for him when Hoylen and Rubin-Vega sang "Light My Candle." The number not only worked as a beautiful pop-rock love duet, but it did what theater songs have to do and rock songs seldom can: it told a story about something real happening between two people. McCollum was sold by intermission; he pulled out his checkbook on the spot, and Jonathan Larson famously had to ask, "Do you want to see the second act?"

Nevertheless, the show was clearly unfinished. As was their usual procedure for a developmental workshop, NYTW handed out audience questionnaires at each performance. Comments on the questionnaires revealed that some people were confused or even irritated. Some found the show sentimental, and others wanted to know why they were supposed to care about the characters—why these self-absorbed kids couldn't "just get jobs!"

That's a question that sometimes comes up even today among people who just don't get *Rent*. Those of us who have sacrificed monetary comfort in order to chase our creative dreams understand it instinctively, as would anyone who really knows Jonathan Larson's own life story. But the head-scratching on the part of others can be understandable. As Michael Greif recently said, on first reading the script: "I was concerned that some of the characters were a little self-righteous, and I questioned their youthful assumptions that they should be guaranteed the privilege of pursuing their artistic goals. I had held plenty of day jobs, I came to learn that Jonathan had plenty of day jobs too. I still wish it were made clear in the script that Mark and Roger also had day jobs, and paid rent. Their latest economic problem was that with gentrification, they were being priced out of so many places to live."

Originally, of course, Larson had only planned on writing the music, to a book and lyrics by Billy Aronson. Now that Aronson was no longer involved, no one was really questioning Larson's obvious talent as a lyricist. But was he a playwright? At one point, James Nicola suggested bringing in a new collaborator to work on the book, but that was not something Jonathan wanted to hear.

Still, with the workshop behind them, Nicola wanted very much to move the project forward. He relished having his theater's capacities challenged by artists, and producing this rock musical would provide an opportunity for the company to stretch and grow. He felt Larson was the right artist for them to "hitch their destiny" to; he believed in the work. But a musical with a cast of fifteen is too expensive for an Off-Broadway theater with that small a seating capacity—even selling out every night, it would have lost money. They needed help financing it, and it needed to come from people who believed the show had a future beyond the nonprofit world. Nicola made a presentation to NYTW's board of directors, hoping they would come up with the needed capital. (If they had been able to finance the show on their own, without enhancement from commercial producers, the eventual financial benefit to the theater could have been much greater.) But as he recently recalled to journalist Rebecca Milzoff: "I failed to persuade them. I realize now that when you're making that kind of ask, you can't be hedging your bets. You can't say, 'I think it's going to be really good.' But I didn't have it in me to say, 'Get in on the ground floor! This is gonna be the best thing ever!'"

Fortunately, Seller and McCollum also believed fervently in Larson's work. At that point in their young careers as producers, the two of them could only come up with about half the amount that was needed to make it happen. But they found a third partner, a somewhat older and more experienced producer named Allan S. Gordon, who made up the difference; the three together put up $150,000, enabling NYTW to commit to a full Off-Broadway production of *Rent*. In return, McCollum, Seller, and Gordon obtained the commercial rights to the property, which meant they would have first refusal on moving it to a bigger theater if it was successful.

Its success would exceed their wildest expectations.

4

"Our Benefactors on This Christmas Eve"

The Producers and the Creative Team

In addition to the exemplary artistic director James C. Nicola and his staff at New York Theatre Workshop, the team that brought *Rent* to the stage was composed of producers and artists with vision, insight, and integrity. Most of them were very young at the time. They recognized Jonathan Larson's gifts when *Rent* was in its infancy, nurtured Larson in his artistic growth, and shepherded the musical to artistic maturity and commercial success.

Jeffrey Seller (Producer)

Seller, who as a young producer hitched his destiny to Jonathan Larson and made *Rent* possible, was adopted and raised in Oak Park, Michigan. Originally his family lived in the best part of town, and his father ran an industrial tool business passed down to him from his own father. But following a motorcycle accident that left him with brain damage, the elder Seller suffered from short-term memory malfunction. The family business went bankrupt, and Jeffrey's father eventually got a low-paying job as a process server while his mother worked at McDonald's. They moved into progressively cheaper homes in increasingly shabby sections of town, and Seller said the experience of being a Jewish kid in a downwardly mobile family, while their relatives were moving up the social ladder, enraged and frustrated him—but was also a big part of what motivated him toward his eventual success. His love for musical theater began when he saw a number from *Evita* on the Tony Awards telecast of 1980; he went to the library to listen to the cast album and ended up memorizing it. As a kid, he saved up for tickets to see touring musicals at the Fisher Theatre in Detroit. He told Michael Sokolove of the *New York Times Magazine*: "I remember working jobs after school, doing anything I could to see a show. I know the immense power of having that seat in the theater and seeing the magic happen. I know it because I was that kid." He attended the University of Michigan, where he dated Andrew Lippa, a composer he still works with; he and Kevin McCollum produced Lippa's Off-Broadway version of *The Wild Party*, and Seller recently directed Lippa's musical version of Jules Feiffer's novel *The Man in the Ceiling*, with a book by Feiffer himself, at the Bay Street Theatre. He also directed the new musical *Fly* at the Dallas Theater Center. Seller and Kevin McCollum were very young producers when they bet on *Rent*, and it made their careers; they continued to work together for many years. According to Sokolove: "Seller and McCollum would produce eight Broadway shows together, including *Rent* and *Avenue Q*. Almost all of them, Seller points out, were about 'young people asking themselves: Who am I? What am I going to do with my life? What is my purpose? Even *Avenue Q* was that, but it was done, brilliantly, with puppets.'" *Avenue Q* won Seller his second Tony Award for Best Musical in 2004; his third and fourth were for Lin-Manuel Miranda's *In the Heights* (2008) and the groundbreaking *Hamilton* (2016). Youth and ambition were also significant themes in *Hamilton*, which Seller, no longer partnering with McCollum, produced at the Public Theater and on Broadway; like *Rent*, it won a Pulitzer Prize and became the most talked about and influential musical in many years. Seller and his partner, the photographer Josh Lehrer, have two children.

Kevin McCollum (Producer)

McCollum spent his early years in Hawaii, where his mother worked for CBS. Both of his parents died when he was fourteen, after which he moved to Chicago and lived with relatives, some of whom were also in the television business. He studied Musical Theatre at the University of Cincinnati College-Conservatory of Music and began working as an actor in regional theater, playing such roles as Arpad in *She Loves Me*, Mordred in *Camelot*, and the title role in *Joseph and the Amazing Technicolor Dreamcoat*. Eventually growing bored with that, he went to the University of Southern California for a master's degree in film production and then moved to New York, where he started a company called The Booking Office, working with producers to sell their shows to different markets around the country. He started the company with Paul Blake, with whom he had previously worked at the Municipal Opera Company of St. Louis, and the first employee he hired was Jeffrey Seller. McCollum emphasizes that he has always viewed money as a means to an end rather than an end in itself, saying, "I was always looking for a way to use money as a way to work with my friends; a tool to make things out of nothing." The first theatrical venture he gave money to was a Chicago company, started by some of his friends, called Different Drummer; the first

New York production he raised funds for was David Mamet's Off-Broadway play *Oleanna* in 1992. His Broadway producing career began in the spring of 1994, when he juggled three projects: he was one of the producers of the revival of the classic 1955 musical *Damn Yankees*, which was a substantial hit; he was a producer of the New York production of the British play *The Rise of Little Voice*, which closed after nine performances; and his company The Booking Office was involved as associate producer of Anna Deavere Smith's acclaimed one-woman play *Twilight: Los Angeles, 1992*. Later that same year, the company produced Donald Margulies's play *What's Wrong with This Picture?* McCollum's next project was *Rent*. By this point he and Seller had started a second company called The Producing Office, though for a while they continued to book tours as well. Eventually, they shifted focus to concentrate on their own projects, but McCollum's successful approach to producing was conditioned by his experience in booking. As he says: "It's all about distribution. If you make it, make sure you know how you're distributing it." Following the huge success of *Rent*, McCollum and Seller produced a wide variety of new works, most of which were musicals. Many of them became hits; the team had a success ratio that would be the envy of most producers. Their Producing Office brought the 1896 Puccini opera *La Bohème* (the work whose plot inspired *Rent*) to Broadway, in a 2002 production directed by Baz Luhrmann. They moved the four-person musical *[title of show]*, which had started at the New York Musical Theatre Festival, to the Vineyard Theatre and then to Broadway; produced the musical *Avenue Q* (which also began at the Vineyard as a co-production with The New Group) on Broadway and then Off-Broadway at New World Stages; and produced *In the Heights*. They were part of a large group of producers who imported the 2002 revival of Noël Coward's classic comedy *Private Lives* to Broadway from London. They also produced the 2009 revival of the classic musical *West Side Story*, directed by the show's librettist, Arthur Laurents, and that same year McCollum was one of the producers of the Broadway revival of *Ragtime*; his wife, Lynnette Perry, had played Evelyn Nesbitt in the original production of that show. Their other projects included the Broadway run of Rajiv Joseph's play *Bengal Tiger at the Baghdad Zoo*, starring Robin Williams, as well as the short-lived musical version of *High Fidelity* and the 2008 and 2009 holiday runs of *Irving Berlin's White Christmas*. They also produced tours of *Stones in His Pockets* and *The Full Monty*. Seller and McCollum's last joint production was the Broadway musical *The Last Ship*, with a score by the rock star Sting, who also took over a role in the show during its brief run. McCollum then produced Robert Askins's play *Hand to God*, which had started at the seventy-four seat Ensemble Studio Theatre; he shepherded it through a larger Off-Broadway run for MCC Theater and then to Broadway, where it earned five Tony nominations. His other recent projects have included the musicals *Something Rotten!* and *Motown the Musical*. McCollum recently described his role in the creative process: "My job is to protect the environment so the artist can do his best work. I'm happy to be a bit of an editor and a good audience member. I want to create a room where people can do their best work, and I want them to have enough tools to do it. These include not only money but authenticity and honesty." In an interview with the Seattle alternative weekly *The Stranger*, he told theater critic Brendan Kiley: "I'm not a huge fan of turning movies into musicals; I'm not a fan of jukebox musicals. I care about finding and developing original material . . . Most people producing come from money—I didn't come from money, and there are only a handful of us like that. I wish I had more peers. I don't want to name names, but there are f ewer than 10 of us who are commercial producers who are not nonprofit who take a writer and grow a show."

Allan S. Gordon (Producer)

Gordon, the third member of the original producing team, was a graduate of Harvard Law School who had worked in law, investment banking, real estate, and venture capital, and through his investment banking firm Gordon, Haskett & Co. had utilized his earnings from these various endeavors to finance several film and live entertainment projects. Prior to *Rent*, events he co-produced included *Sammy Cahn in Person—Words and Music* and *The Real Live Brady Bunch*, which played in cities across America. Following the success of *Rent*, Gordon won further Tony Awards as producer of *Hairspray* (2003) and *Spamalot* (2005) and produced a Broadway revival of *Death of a Salesman*. He continued his relationship with the New York Theatre Workshop, where he eventually became vice-chairman of the board of trustees, and founded the Allan S. Gordon Foundation.

Michael Greif (Director)

Michael Greif was born in Brooklyn. He did his undergraduate work at Northwestern University in Evanston, Illinois, and then earned an MFA in Directing from the University of California in San Diego. At the school's affiliated regional theater, the La Jolla Playhouse, the young Greif assisted the theater's then artistic director, Des McAnuff, on the original production of *Big River*, the musical version of *Huckleberry Finn*, which gave him his only pre-*Rent* experience of working on a Broadway musical. He then spent several years in New York City. His relationship with New York Theatre Workshop began in 1984, when he was one of four young directors chosen for the company's New Director's Project; he and the other members of his group

(Lisa Peterson, Liz Diamond, and David Esbjornson) have all gone on to major careers. His NYTW directing credits before *Rent* included *Seventy Scenes of Halloween* by Jeffrey Jones. Greif was also an artistic associate at the New York Shakespeare Festival (the Public Theater) from 1989 to 1992. During that time at the Public, he directed works by leading American playwrights like Tony Kushner, Constance Congdon, and José Rivera, as well as revivals of Sophie Treadwell's *Machinal* and Shakespeare's *Pericles*. He made the rounds of some of the nation's best regional theatres in the late eighties and early nineties, directing for the Mark Taper Forum in Los Angeles, the Williamstown Theatre Festival in Massachusetts, Baltimore Center Stage, and the Trinity Repertory Company in Providence, Rhode Island. He first worked on Broadway in 1987 as assistant director to Walton Jones (who ran the directing program at UCSD) on a thriller by John Pielmeier (known primarily for *Agnes of God*) called *Sleight of Hand*, which ran for less than a week at the Cort Theatre. In 1995, he returned to the La Jolla Playhouse, having been chosen as its new artistic director; in his mid-thirties at the time, he was one of the youngest directors in America to head a major regional theater. His early projects there had included Randy Newman's modern musical adaptation of *Faust*. His work on *Rent* earned him a Tony nomination and the widest national and international recognition he had yet received; he became more identified with contemporary musical theater due to the show, though he has continued to direct new plays and classics just as frequently. He followed up *Rent* with the musical version of Jay McInerney's *Bright Lights, Big City* in 1998 (also for New York Theatre Workshop). That show developed something of a cult following and has occasionally been revived in small theaters, but it never transferred to a commercial run in New York. He received two more Tony nominations for Best Director of a Musical for *Grey Gardens* (2007) and *Next to Normal* (2009). Like *Rent*, these two projects were both developed and initially produced at nonprofit theaters before moving to Broadway: *Grey Gardens* opened in New York at Playwrights Horizons and *Next to Normal* played at both the Second Stage in New York and Arena Stage in Washington, D.C., before taking its final form on Broadway. That show, which was written by composer Tom Kitt and bookwriter/lyricist Brian Yorkey, was awarded the Pulitzer Prize for Drama—an award *Rent* had of course received fourteen years earlier—thus earning Greif the unique distinction of having developed and directed two musicals that went on to win that very prestigious honor. The busy director's next Broadway projects were lighter musicals: *Never Gonna Dance*, which had a new book by Jeffrey Hatcher tying together vintage songs by Jerome Kern, and *If/Then*, on which he was reunited with the writers of *Next to Normal* and his original *Rent* stars Idina Menzel and Anthony Rapp. He left his position at the La Jolla Playhouse

Rent director Michael Greif, center, with producers Kevin McCollum, left, and Jeffrey Seller.   *Bruce Glikas/Getty Images*

in 1999 and has continued to direct frequently Off-Broadway, focusing on new plays and classics. He directed the New York revival of Kushner's *Angels in America* for the Signature Theatre and the premiere of his *The Intelligent Homosexual's Guide to Capitalism and Socialism with a Key to the Scriptures* at the Guthrie Theatre and later at the Public. For the New York Shakespeare Festival, he has directed three outdoor summer Shakespeare in the Park productions since 2007: *Romeo and Juliet*, *The Winter's Tale*, and *The Tempest*. As of this writing, he has two high-profile new musicals on Broadway. *Dear Evan Hansen*, with a book by Steven Levenson and songs by the young team of Benj Pasek and Justin Paul, premiered to raves at the Second Stage in 2015 and was immediately scheduled for a Broadway transfer; it opened in late 2016 at the Music Box Theatre and earned Greif another Tony nomination for Best Director of a Musical. *War Paint*, a musical about the cosmetics industry, opened at Chicago's Goodman Theatre in 2016, with Broadway stars Patti LuPone and Christine Ebersole playing Helena Rubinstein and Elizabeth Arden. With a book by Doug Wright, music by Scott Frankel, and lyrics by Michael Korie, this new show reunites the creative team from *Grey Gardens* (which also starred Ebersole in a Tony-winning performance). It began performances in March 2017 at the Nederlander Theatre, where Greif's production of *Rent* had played for twelve years.

Tim Weil (Musical Director)

The multitalented Weil is a pianist/orchestrator/arranger/conductor and music director; he also writes music, with composition credits including the incidental music for the Broadway play *Sally Marr... and her escorts* (cowritten by and starring Joan Rivers) and the Dallas Theater Center's production of *A Christmas Carol*. He has worked on projects for the York Theatre, the New York Shakespeare Festival, Goodspeed at Chester, and Ford's Theatre. Since working on *Rent*, he has returned to Broadway as conductor and keyboardist for the Tom Stoppard play *Jumpers*, music director and conductor of *Shrek the Musical*, and arranger and orchestrator for *Lady Day at Emerson's Bar and Grill*, the play that starred Audra McDonald as Billie Holiday and was filmed for HBO. He was musical director of *South Pacific* at the Guthrie Theatre. On *Rent*, he was credited for "Music Supervision and Additional Arrangements" and had primary responsibility for the musical side of things, working closely with Jonathan Larson and Steve Skinner (Musical Arrangements) on the orchestration as well as coaching the singers and leading the onstage band. When he repeated as conductor and arranger for the film version of *Rent*, his wife, the well-known musical theater actress Randy Graff (*Les Misérables*, *City of Angels*) appeared on screen in the cameo role of Mrs. Cohen. For the original production of *Rent* on Broadway, Weil put together a tremendous group of sophisticated musicians who knew the history of rock and loved working in theater: they included Steve Mack on bass, Kenny Brescia on guitar, Jeff Potter on drums, Daniel A. Weiss on Keyboard 2 and Guitar 2, and Weil himself conducting and playing keyboard. Tim Weil has also served on the board of the Jonathan Larson Foundation.

Marlies Yearby (Choreographer)

Yearby performed professionally as a disco dancer in Oakland, California, when she was still a teenager. She entered San Jose State University as a Biological Studies major, but she took a dance class her first year and found that dance was what she wanted to focus on. She tried to stick with biology, though it wasn't her passion, in order to have a path to a sensible career or at least a safety net, but when her advisors saw that she was spending most of her time in dance classes, she realized it was time to change her major. In addition to her training at the university, she studied José Limon technique in San Francisco with Aaron Osborne. She was soon getting professional work as a dancer and choreographer, to the point where it was causing her to miss classes, so the college suggested she take some time off and focus on her dance career. She has toured nationally and internationally with Movin'

Spirits Dance Theater, a company she founded and of which she is the artistic director. The company has been commissioned by American Dance Festival, Harlem Stages, Kansas Lied Center for the Performing Arts, Jacob's Pillow, Lincoln Center, Performance Space 122, and the Tribeca Performing Arts Center, as well as the American Festival of Theatre and Dance in France. She has collaborated with numerous performance artists and playwrights, including Shay Youngblood and Laurie Carlos, and has had theater commissions from the American Music Theatre Festival in Pennsylvania, the Penumbra Theater in Minnesota, the National Black Arts Festival, and En Garde Arts. Yearby received a New York Dance Performance Bessie Award for her choreography for *Stained*, and she has been nominated for a Helen Hayes Award and a Joe A. Callaway Award. She had been self-producing her own work and was temporarily out of resources when she got a call asking her to submit a tape of her work for consideration for the choreography position on *Rent*; she took a chance and sent the tape, and the rest is history. The show was a different kind of project for her and one she embraced joyfully and wholeheartedly. Not identified with the world of traditional Broadway or musical theater dance, she is a modern/postmodern choreographer. Quoted in the *Rent* coffee table book, she said: "My work is interdisciplinary. I call it dance-based performance. . . . When I work with dancers and performers, the words and music become a landscape in which they can define their onstage personas or characters. The work is always telling someone's story." She was nominated for a Tony Award for her work on *Rent*, and her work was licensed for the film version, choreographed by Keith Young. She has worked with various companies of *Rent*, most recently the 2016 Twentieth Anniversary Tour.

5

"Who I Was Meant to Be"

The Cast of Characters

f you've always wanted to be in *Rent*, you probably know exactly which role you were born to play and have been singing his or her songs in the shower for ages. If you're new to the show, on the other hand, you may get a little confused about the relationships and the characters' backstories, given that a nearly through-sung score doesn't leave much opportunity for exposition. Either way, this chapter is your alphabetical guide to the characters in the show—both who they are in terms of the story and what they require, vocally and dramatically, from a performer. Break a leg at the auditions!

Angel Dumott Schunard

A character who has a particularly strong effect on audiences, Angel was originally played by Wilson Jermaine Heredia, the one actor in the cast who won Tony and Drama Desk Awards for his performance. Though some people have described the character as transgender, there's no indication that he is transitioning: he is a drag queen who performs and goes out to clubs and parties dressed as a woman, but he is comfortable with his identity as a gay man and also appears in male clothing at the beginning of the play (when we see him drumming for donations on the street) and again at the end. Like several of the other characters, Angel has AIDS, which he doesn't try to hide from anyone; he is the only one of the principals to die during the course of the play, and his death and funeral form a major sequence and turning point in Act Two. Unlike the typical image of the intimidating drag queen "with attitude," Angel is characterized first and foremost by kindness and generosity. (As *Rent* expert Victoria Leacock tells actors, "He's not a snap queen.") He is living on the edge of poverty but, when he receives a surprise thousand-dollar payment for orchestrating the death of Benny's wife's dog, he

David Merino as Angel in the Twentieth Anniversary Tour, 2016.   *Carol Rosegg/courtesy of Work Light Productions*

immediately uses some of it to buy groceries for the whole gang—as well as a coat to replace the one stolen from Tom Collins. The love between him and Collins, which blossoms so quickly in the first act, proves true and lasting. Until his illness takes over, Angel is full of high spirits, and he remains a force of goodwill and peace; on more than one occasion he tries to defuse conflict between other characters.

The name Angel can suggest that the character is a Latino, though his last name, with spelling slightly changed, comes straight from *La bohème*. Often the role has been cast that way, following the precedent set by Heredia, but there have also been black, Asian, and white Angels. It's a difficult role requiring a wide range of talents and skills. He generally sings in a high, light voice stylistically reminiscent of Prince or Michael Jackson; he needs to be able to open up and wail on the melismatic climax of "Contact." The actor should be comfortable and convincing in drag, but also boyishly appealing when in male attire, as he is when Collins first sees and is attracted to him. A sophisticated sense of rhythm and percussion skills come into play, as we first see him on the street drumming on a large plastic bucket (described as a "pickle tub") and he later does a fast, complex drumming routine with sticks on the tables during "Today 4 U." And on top of all that, he needs considerable dance ability. Heredia created a famous move (in "Today 4 U") where he jumps up onto a table while wearing platform shoes—which doesn't even seem like it should be possible. It has sometimes been omitted when a performer isn't up to it, but it's surprising how many of the Broadway Angels did it effectively. He needs to have a star presence and exude warmth and sweetness without being cloying or cute; Angel has had a tough life and knows he's very ill, so there is an edge and a strength underneath the light he shines on the play.

Benjamin Coffin III

Benny's name is adapted from that of Benoit, the landlord character in *La bohème*, but, other than the fact that each character shows up early in the first act demanding back rent, there is little similarity between the two. Benoit is an old man who is simply the bad guy—he is made a laughingstock and quickly dispensed with by the bohemian heroes—whereas Benny is an important player throughout the story of *Rent*, with complex motives and a tangled history with some of the other characters. His relationship with the struggling artists he is trying to evict is complicated by the fact that he used to be one of them, sharing the loft apartment that Roger and Mark still occupy. Benny also had a brief affair with Mimi, which Roger doesn't find out about until after he himself becomes involved with her. Benny's fortunes changed when he started dating Alison Grey, whom he has recently married: her family is referred to as "the Westport Greys," implying that they are a prominent and wealthy family from an affluent town in Connecticut. Alison's father is partnering with Benny in his business venture; they have bought the tenement and plan to evict all the tenants, as well as the homeless people who live on the lot next door, in order to build condominiums and a "cyberstudio." Though his values and ethics are decidedly different from those of the other characters, and other aspects of his behavior are morally questionable as well (he continues to fool around with Mimi, or at least says that he does, even after he marries Alison), Benny isn't a villain or a completely bad guy. He does offer to pay for Mimi's rehab, as well as Angel's funeral, which Collins doesn't have the money to cover. On some level he still values these people and hopes to remain their friend.

Casting-wise, the role has generally been played by African American actors, although, as with most of the roles, ethnicity is not specified in the script. This casting upends the usual stereotype of the rich white landlord oppressing economically disadvantaged tenants; it also underlines the sense that Benny is a social climber turning his back on his own world to satisfy his ambitions. (Westport is a famously white community.) As Benny seems to be something of a ladies' man, he is generally buff and good-looking, often sporting a very short buzz cut like the one Taye Diggs had when he originated the role. (At that time, Diggs hadn't yet adopted his now-famous shaved-head look.) Benny doesn't do as much singing as the other leads, but he needs a smooth, confident sound for "You'll See" and his part in "Happy New Year B"—the range is not extreme, so he can be either a baritone or a tenor. The role requires a solid actor with a certain charm and charisma, who can be slick and intimidating enough to pose a believable threat but who can also allow the audience to see the conflicted feelings underneath.

Joanne Jefferson

Joanne is an attorney, which would suggest that she is not suffering the same financial hardships as the rest of the group of friends. Also, given how long it takes to make it through law school, even if she only recently began practicing she is probably a bit older than most of the others. When we meet her, she has recently begun a romantic relationship with Maureen, which remains a rocky, on-again/off-again affair throughout the show. Though Maureen was previously involved with Mark and surprised her friends by taking up with a woman, there is no clear indication of how long Joanne has self-identified as a lesbian. In the movie, she is sometimes seen wearing neckties and men's suits, but her sartorial style in the stage version is generally more feminine. Her parents are not too pleased with her lifestyle, out of fear it could reflect badly on her mother's upcoming "confirmation hearings": an indication that the mother is probably a judge up for a federal appointment. Joanne's father seems to be involved with diplomacy in some way as well—he says Joanne could call the State Department for their holiday travel itinerary—but, as we meet her parents only briefly in phone calls, the details are left to the audience's imagination. Joanne is tough and no-nonsense, unafraid to back down from a confrontation, but good-hearted. She went to Harvard, one of the most competitive universities in the country. She prides herself on her self-discipline and organizational skills and may even be a bit compulsive: she says she makes lists in her sleep. The point she is making is that her personality is very different from that of the freewheeling, impulsive Maureen—and yet, as they say, opposites attract.

Though, like most of the characters, her ethnicity is not precisely defined in the script, Joanne has traditionally been played by African American actresses, starting with Shelley Dickinson in the workshop and then Fredi Walker in the original Off-Broadway/Broadway cast. (As we will see in Chapter 21, directors of regional revivals and school productions have very occasionally cast actresses of other ethnicities.) During the long Broadway run and on the tours, the character was played by an unusually wide variety of types; there were Joannes of many different shapes and sizes. The personality, the acting ability, and the voice are more important than the specific physical type. Joanne's one solo number, "We're Okay," is a fast-paced patter song in which she juggles multiple phone conversations; the actress needs to be deft and precise with text to put the lyrics across clearly there, and specific enough with the acting to keep the audience from getting confused about whom she's talking to. Her singing voice should be earthy and warm, with a certain maturity and the confidence to go toe to toe with Maureen in the belting contest of "Take Me or Leave Me." Joanne holds her own in a colorful bohemian world she doesn't really quite feel a part of. A solid professional and a caring friend, she provides a unique perspective that helps keep the play grounded.

Mark Cohen

Aspiring filmmaker Mark, originally played by Anthony Rapp, is in some ways the center of the musical. He introduces the first scene and provides occasional narration throughout the evening. He carries an old-fashioned movie camera and is often seen filming the other characters; he is understood to be shooting a film "without a script." His hope is that eventually it will be a documentary about his group of friends and their lives and struggles on the Lower East Side; ultimately he comes to focus primarily on Angel. In the last scene of the show and during the finale, he turns on a projector and the audience gets to see some of his footage; in a sense—though not absolutely literally—the whole show can be seen as Mark's movie.

Since his last name is Cohen and he is very specifically identified as coming from a Jewish family, the role is generally cast with a white actor. He seems to have a somewhat troubled relationship with his family; his mother is heard a couple of times leaving messages on his answering machine. Played for comic relief, these messages are generally loving and supportive, if embarrassingly overdemonstrative, yet Mark screens the calls and is never seen picking up the phone. He also has a line in the song "La Vie Bohème" about "of course" hating one's mother and father. He mentions having learned to tango at the Jewish Community Center in Scarsdale, an upscale suburban town north of New York City, so we know he probably comes from a family that is at least financially comfortable. Thus his continuing to live in near-poverty conditions on the Lower East Side is something of a rebellion; he has deliberately distanced himself from his family and identifies instead with a community of young artists challenging the status quo and insisting on living life on their own terms. His value system is challenged in the second act when he receives a lucrative offer to direct for the TV program *Buzzline*, described as a sleazy tabloid news show. Because the job seems like an opportunity to work in his chosen field and get paid well for doing it, as well as to make contacts that could lead to better things, his resistance to accepting it can be hard for some audiences to understand. But Mark is a young man still "coming into his own," struggling to articulate his values and his place in the world, and he feels impelled to do it alone, with integrity, and on his own terms.

Regarding casting requirements, Mark comes across as more clean-cut than the other characters; he usually wears glasses and has been described as "nerdy." Anthony Rapp's Mark was slight, blond, and boyish, and many of his successors in the role have shared at least some of these physical characteristics. A few of them sported somewhat longer or grungier hairstyles; some had a goofier, more "character" look. Many people have always felt that Mark is the autobiographical character in the musical, the one closest to Jonathan Larson himself—though of course Larson was a playwright/composer rather than a filmmaker, and by all accounts he had a loving relationship with his family. He had several close friends who actually were filmmakers, and traces of their personalities can be seen in the character as well. Still, Mark, like Jonathan, is the straight boy, the one who doesn't have HIV, the Jew from the suburbs, the smart one who observes and chronicles the lives of his friends, and some revivals have emphasized the parallels through casting and costuming. In any case, the actor should be able to dance the tango; he needs to be mercurial, quick on his feet, dexterous and physically expressive. Much of the body language of "La Vie Bohème" is left up to the individual actor, so he should be inventive, funny, and very comfortable in his body. It takes a performer of unusual energy and vibrant stage presence to lead that number where, even though Mark is the main soloist, there is so much colorful activity going on around him; some actors have been better than others at commanding the stage and connecting with the audience. Mark is articulate and very smart. He has most of the spoken lines in the show, and acting ability is paramount, but the vocal demands are also substantial. There are no range extremes, and unlike Roger he doesn't need to sound like a rock star, but he must be quick with patter, articulating the many lyrics of the fast-paced "La Vie Bohème" with effortless clarity. He also needs to be able to let loose and rock out on the title song and "What You Own," both of which call for sustained, impassioned singing. On the whole, the role requires great intelligence and warmth; Mark is the audience's guide through the world of the show, and we should see him as a friend.

Maureen Johnson

Maureen was previously in a relationship with Mark, and at the time they lived together. When she "dumped" Mark, Maureen moved out and started seeing Joanne; that seems to have been a surprise to the guys, but it's not absolutely clear whether this is her first lesbian relationship or she has a history of being bisexual. Either way, there's no sense that she's uncomfortable or unsure of herself in this new relationship—or in any aspect of her life: Maureen is nothing if not confident, even ego-driven. She is a "theater person" with ambitions to star in a movie directed by Mark, so we assume she has studied acting, but the only specific performance of hers that we learn anything about is the show she puts on in a vacant lot on Christmas Eve. She is protesting the gentrification of the block, led by Benny, who is forcing people out of their apartments (and wiping out a tent city of homeless people) in order to build a new cyberarts studio. We see her whole performance ("Over the Moon") in Act One; director Greif saw it as reminiscent of both Laurie Anderson and Diamanda Galas, two very different downtown performance artists of the period. In the second act, Maureen and Joanne's relationship continues to be a rocky one, with big fights and passionate reconciliations. Though we assume Maureen, like her friends, is a bohemian artist with very little money, she has a girlfriend with a good job, so she may not be suffering as much. She also doesn't seem to have any health issues (unlike so many of the other characters) and so, even if her work is fueled by righteous social indignation, she is a relatively carefree character, a source of high spirits and relentless energy throughout the show. This works as a contrast with the angst the others are experiencing. Even when she's angry or outraged, Maureen on some level is having a great time; she is a life force. According to Greif: "Maureen has a

Stephanie Genito makes her grand entrance as Maureen at the Ivoryton Playhouse, 2016.
Anne Hudson

very underdeveloped sense of who she is as a performer. She doesn't mature as a performer; she matures as a human being. She becomes a caring and compassionate person." In the last scene we see this new side of Maureen: her panic and concern over Mimi's condition are genuine, and, like Musetta, she takes on the responsibility for making sure that her friend is cared for.

In casting the role, voice is a primary consideration. Both of Maureen's big numbers need to be power-belted; she must be vocally fearless and ready to pull out all the stops. A raw rock voice can be effective—if she has the technique to sing eight shows a week without blowing it out. Since the character is a theater person, a musical theater sound is also not out of place, but only if it's a true belt as opposed to a "mix." The voice needs to be big and soulful and come from the gut. "Over the Moon" is tricky because in a way it's supposed to be bad; though it's done with affection, the writing evokes pretentious performance art to some degree. Still, the actress needs to play it with conviction and not appear to be making fun of it, or else the character ceases to be believable. After the first workshop production, the role was substantially rewritten to capitalize on Idina Menzel's unique personality and charisma. Like Menzel, Maureen must have an inventive sense of comic timing and the capacity to forge a rapport with the audience such that she can eventually get them to moo with her. Later, when she tells Joanne she has always turned heads on the street, it needs to be believable; she has to be sexy and, if not necessarily conventionally pretty, extremely striking. Her appeal comes partly from her boldness and brashness and total confidence in herself; she is supremely comfortable in her body and knows she looks good in the skintight Catwoman costume she wears to the New Year's Eve party. Though ethnicity is not specified in the script, the role is usually cast as Caucasian, but it works better if she's not too fresh faced and white-bread. Hailing from Hicksville (a town on Long Island), she's a New York girl with a hard edge and a certain funky, downtown glamour. As she herself puts it, she's a diva; it's a showy role that gives the performer a chance to strut everything she's got, and thus a part much coveted by actresses.

Mimi Marquez

Mimi lives in the same rundown building as Mark and Roger. She works as an exotic dancer at an establishment called the Cat Scratch Club, where her routines involve S&M imagery; Roger mentions that he has seen her being tied up there. Like several downtown venues of the period, it was probably also a rock club where punk bands like his performed. Mimi claims the job provides a living but still appears to be nearly destitute—probably because much of the money she makes goes to her drug dealer; she is struggling with

Alyssa V. Gomez as Mimi with Collin L. Howard as Benny. Ivoryton Playhouse, 2016.
Anne Hudson

a heroin habit. She is also taking AZT for HIV/AIDS, which she could have gotten either through sexual intercourse or shared needles, and, though she knows time is probably running out, she is passionately committed to living life to its fullest every day she has left. In addition to her rocky romance with Roger, she has been involved intermittently with Benny. In the second act, the drugs and illness catch up with her, and she finds herself living on the streets.

The role was originated by Daphne Rubin-Vega, who is of Panamanian descent. One of the few characters whose ethnicity is defined in the script, Mimi is definitely Latina; her mother speaks to her in Spanish, and she is reminded of home when she hears "Spanish babies" crying. This doesn't necessarily mean she is an immigrant; she could have grown up in a ghetto area like Spanish Harlem. Most people assume she is probably Puerto Rican, but this is not specified. Interestingly, few of the actresses who played the role on Broadway were actually Latina; most were light-skinned African American women. But diversity in casting is an ongoing conversation in theater circles, and opinions and standards continue to evolve. Today, more emphasis is placed on making sure minority performers are given the opportunity to play the roles specifically written for actors of their own ethnicities, so it's less likely that a non-Latina would be cast as Mimi in a major production—although it does still happen occasionally. The part is a tough one to cast in

Mimi, here played by Magdiel Cabral, tries to tempt Roger (Johnny Newcomb) with her stash in the 2015 production at the Edinburgh Festival Fringe.   *Rob Palin*

any case. Mimi is described as being nineteen but looking sixteen. She needs to have a body type that makes it believable she would be hired as an exotic dancer, and the combination of the drugs and her illness would probably make her even thinner; if the original costume designs are used, she has to be able to carry off those famous skintight blue vinyl pants. Though formal dance training isn't required, it helps; she should be very comfortable in her body and with her sexuality. The seductive moves in "Out Tonight" have to sizzle, and some of them are done on the railings of a high catwalk and steep stairway, so fear of heights could be an issue. She has to be a fantastic singer, as she has some of the biggest and most emotional numbers in the score; a genuine rock voice with some rough edges is usually preferred, though a Broadway belter type can be successful if she really understands the style. Some of the major Mimis ornamented the vocal lines with R&B-type embellishments, while others have sung them more straight, as written. As far as the acting is concerned, she needs a combination of little girl vulnerability and streetwise edge, and different performers have mixed these qualities in very different proportions. Rubin-Vega, with an authentic rock voice, brought enormous conviction and vulnerability to the songs; her Mimi was a scrappy alley cat with a playful sense of humor. Some of the early replacements brought a similar toughness to the role, but later casting has often tended to soften the edges and prettify the character to some degree, moving closer to Rosario Dawson's take on the role in the film version, or providing a touch of the sweeter, gentler original Mimì of *La bohème*. Still, there's no escaping the need for a ferocious charisma; it's a role like no other in musical theater. Mimi has to take over the stage like a rock star in "Out Tonight," make everyone in the audience fall in love with her, and then tear out our hearts in "Without You" and "Goodbye, Love." Both the pain and the joy in her voice have to be real and absolutely palpable.

Roger Davis

Roger is Mark's roommate and a singer/guitarist/songwriter, the former front man of a rock band, and a former junkie. Jonathan Larson told actor Adam Pascal that the character was a Kurt Cobain type, and he also thought of Eddie Vedder as a model; Pascal has said he saw him as more like Bruce Springsteen. Of course, Roger never attained that level of stardom as a musician, but there are few clues in the script to let us know just how successful he was. We're told he performed at CBGB, a major punk venue, but though top acts were featured there the club often presented unknown new bands as well. Somehow he managed to obtain a guitar valuable enough that, when he sells it in the second act, it nets him enough money to buy a car. When we meet him he is no longer pursuing his performing career but is struggling to write a song, determined to leave a great one behind when he dies; he is creatively blocked through most of the play. He has HIV; the script never reveals definitively whether he has full-blown AIDS, but director Michael Greif has said that he does. In the Broadway production, during "Without You," Roger was seen briefly visiting the hospital (represented by the table, covered by a white sheet, that Angel had previously occupied), thus indicating that he has begun suffering some symptoms. He learned he probably had the disease from a note his girlfriend, April, left for him before she killed herself. Roger admits to being a recovering drug addict, and either or both of them, living on the edge and as part of the volatile punk scene, could easily have been promiscuous; we have no way of knowing how they got the virus or which one of them was infected first. Through most of the first act, Roger seems traumatized and emotionally cut off, which is understandable given his medical status and the fact that he was probably the one who found April's body in the bathtub after she slit her wrists—quite an experience to recover from. Mark tells us Roger was in withdrawal for six months; he's now clean, but when he finally leaves the apartment it's a major event. Initially unable to conceive of having an affair with Mimi, he angrily rejects her advances; on

Roger (played by Justin Guarini, left) and Mark (Drew Gasparini) take a phone call from their landlord, Benny (played by Jeremy Gaston, seen at top). Surflight Theatre, 2011.
Jerry Dalia

learning that she too has HIV, he begins to open up, but their relationship continues to be a troubled one because of her drug addiction and his jealousy over her previous relationship with Benny. Though it's Tom Collins who fantasizes in Act One about leaving New York and moving to Santa Fe to open a restaurant, in Act Two Roger decides to do just that and leaves town, but he is haunted by images of Mimi and soon turns around and comes back.

Roger is historically the most difficult role in the show to cast. This is because it requires an unusually difficult combination of vocal, physical, and emotional attributes—and largely because Adam Pascal left an indelible impression that set the bar almost impossibly high for his successors. Pascal has one of the world's truly great voices, and it's inimitable. There's an authentic rock grittiness there, but it's also a big, open, powerful, and healthy sound, beautifully resonant and rich with emotion. The challenge is finding a performer who can sustain the right vocal and emotional balance. A throaty rock and roller could blow out his voice singing that score eight times a week (and it's happened), whereas a musical theater baritenor can sound too schooled and pristine. He also has to play the guitar onstage—though some of the Broadway and touring Rogers didn't learn how until after they got the role. Roger should also be a heartthrob; traditionally he is seen in the Life Café scene in a T-shirt with the sleeves cut off. (Pascal was working as a personal trainer when he was cast in the show.) He needs to register as a rugged, sexy, and straight leading man—while wearing black fingernail polish. Though the actors cast have generally appeared strapping and fit, he should be on the lean side due to his health problems and lack of funds; we get the idea he often has to be reminded to eat. The acting poses unusual challenges as well; he has to be sympathetic and avoid coming across as self-pitying. Some actors have overplayed the anger, but when Roger lashes out at Mimi and later at Mark, you need to feel the loneliness and the love behind it. Chemistry with the actress playing Mimi, even when they're fighting, is essential. All in all, it's a tall order. But when all of these (or even most of these) qualities come together, Roger is a haunting and unforgettable character.

Tom Collins

Tom Collins shares his name with a popular cocktail, though the coincidence is never pointed out in the script; he's the only character generally referred to by his last name rather than his first. At the beginning of the show, he hasn't seen the other characters for seven months, but we learn that he once shared the apartment with Roger and Mark. Figuring out Collins's precise backstory can be tricky; the lines in the libretto that provide clues are brief, few and far between: he is referred to as both a philosopher and a teacher of college-level computer science, which might lead one to wonder at first why he seems just as impoverished as his starving artist friends. But when he first enters the apartment, Mark introduces him to the audience as a "vagabond anarchist who ran naked through the Parthenon": a story we would love to hear more about but never do. He shortly explains that he was recently "expelled" from MIT (the Massachusetts Institute of Technology), which was presumably where he went when he moved out seven months ago. Since he also says he will soon be teaching at NYU (New York University), we can assume it was a graduate level program he was kicked out of—for his "theory of actual reality." We are left to wonder what this could possibly mean until Angel, during the "La Vie Bohème" number, provides a little more background, telling the audience that Collins's anarchistic exploits included the "reprogramming of the MIT virtual-reality equipment to self-destruct as it broadcasts the words 'Actual Reality—Act Up—Fight Aids.'" Some of the similar lines about the other characters' exploits in that song are facetious, but this one can probably be taken at face value and provides a more concrete explanation of why Collins got expelled. The overall sentiment there is in line with the theme of Maureen's performance piece, which the characters have just seen: reject artificial, computer-generated substitutes for experience, embrace genuine human emotion, and confront the real social problems the world at large has been ignoring! In the "Santa Fe" number, Collins says he is sick of grading papers and teaching students who would rather be watching TV, yet he has accepted a position at NYU, where he will soon begin teaching. In the last scene of the musical he reports having again used his highly advanced computer skills for heroically subversive purposes: this time programming an ATM machine at a Food Emporium to give free money to anyone with the code "A.N.G.E.L."

The great love that develops so quickly between Collins and Angel is a focal point of the play. The two meet shortly after Collins has been mugged;

Angel takes care of him, and they find themselves attracted to one another. Unlike Roger and Mimi, they immediately tell each other that they both have AIDS, so any obstacle that condition might have placed in the way of a relationship is removed right away. Their duet "I'll Cover You" is one of the sweetest and loveliest moments in the show, and Collins stays with Angel and takes care of him until he dies. (Though Collins also has the virus, he never shows any symptoms, and his condition has been described as nonprogressing.) The two share a tender, unconditional, and life-changing love that inspires not only the audience but also the other characters—and for some of them, it serves to emphasize the sad lack of those elements in their own relationships.

Therefore, in casting Collins, emotional openness and lack of self-consciousness about singing love songs to a drag queen are key qualities to look for. The character is generally presented as masculine and without any typically gay mannerisms, but the actor needs to be able to strike romantic sparks with a male partner; the chemistry with the actor playing Angel is vital. Collins has a generous heart and a self-deprecating, low-key sense of humor. He's a bit older than the other major characters but still likes to party and smoke pot; a wise free spirit. His grief over Angel's death anchors one of the most powerful scenes in the play; he has to be able to pull out the emotional and vocal stops there and take the audience with him. The voice is usually a deep, warm baritone, but he needs a high range as well for the musical climaxes, so a tenor is sometimes cast. Originally, Larson didn't specify ethnicity, but he said he wrote the role for his friend Jon Cavaluzzo, and in the 1994 workshop it was played by Pat Briggs—both white actors. But the script was still developing, and the creative team felt the character begin to come into focus when they started auditioning African American performers; Jesse L. Martin was cast and made the part his own, setting the pattern for future casting. As with most of the characters, the script still doesn't specify race, but it's difficult now to imagine a white actor being fully persuasive in the role, especially in the gospel-tinged reprise of "I'll Cover You."

The Ensemble

In addition to the eight principals listed above, *Rent* utilizes an ensemble of singer/actors who play all the small supporting and cameo roles and act as a singing and dancing chorus. In the original production, this group numbered four men and three women, each of whom played multiple roles, and most of them had understudy duties as well. In other productions, the number sometimes varies; especially when schools put on the show, the cast is often bigger, to give more students a chance to perform, and in those cases each person will play fewer roles. Though some of the characters they play are the parents of the leads, all the ensemble members tend to be in their twenties or early thirties. The idea is that they represent a group of young people playfully assuming various roles as part of telling a story; there is no attempt to create the illusion that they are the right age or type for every character, and in "Seasons of Love" they are seen basically as themselves. Many revivals follow the original breakdown, which is detailed below:

- Mark's mom and others (originated by Kristen Lee Kelly): White woman, a good dancer. This actress is generally the main understudy for Maureen, so casting is all about finding someone who can play that role.

- Christmas caroler, Mr. Jefferson, a pastor, and others (originated by Byron Utley): African American man, often tall. Needs a deep, impressive speaking voice to play stern authority figures and an expressive, rangy singing voice for the "Seasons of Love" solo. Often understudies Collins and sometimes Benny.

- Mrs. Jefferson, woman with bags, and others (originated by Gwen Stewart): African American woman with a big, powerful voice, a contralto/belt that also has a high extension up to C for the "Seasons of Love" solo. Warm, passionate gospel singer who can also play tough, strong older women. Sings in Spanish as Mimi's Mom in "Voice Mail # 5." Often understudies Joanne.

- Gordon, the man, Mr. Grey, and others (originated by Timothy Britten Parker): White man. A versatile actor, he has to take on the role of the dignified Mr. Grey, be a bit scary and intimidating as the drug dealer, and also be sensitive enough to play Gordon. Parker didn't understudy, but in the later casts the actor in this track generally covered Roger and sometimes Mark; ability to play one or both of those roles became the key consideration in casting.

- Steve, man with squeegee, a waiter, and others (originated by Gilles Chiasson): Usually a white male; sometimes Asian or Latino. As Steve in the Life Support group, this actor leads off the song "Will I?"—providing an especially memorable musical moment. He needs a beautiful, soaring tenor voice. Comedic skill and ability to establish a character with very few lines as the waiter is also helpful. This guy is usually younger-looking and not as tall as the actor in the Gordon track. If he's white, he understudies Mark and sometimes Roger; if Asian or Latino, he understudies Angel.

- Paul, a cop, and others (originated by Rodney Hicks): African American man, usually younger-looking than the guy in the Christmas caroler track, but has to have enough of an authoritative presence to lead the Life

Support group. Plays a flamboyantly gay character in the Life Café scene. Understudies Benny or Angel, sometimes Collins.

- Alexi Darling, Roger's mom, and others (originated by Aiko Nakasone): Usually an Asian American woman, this actress needs to have a distinct comic flair for Alexi's phone messages. Often small of stature, she is also the lead female dancer and the focal point of the "To dance" section of "La Vie Bohème." This was the one ensemble track that usually did not understudy anyone else in the Broadway company; on the national tours, she sometimes covered Mimi.

Professional companies of the show generally also include about five to seven swings, who cover the ensemble tracks as well as one or two principal roles each. On Broadway and on tour, three of them—wearing gas masks— also appeared onstage as cops in the St. Mark's Place scene—but don't tell anybody.

For the record, the swings in the original Broadway company were Yassmin Alers, Darius de Haas, Shelley Dickinson, David Driver, Mark Setlock, and Simone.

6

"To Days of Inspiration"

The Original Off-Broadway Production

O nce New York Theatre Workshop had committed to mounting a full production of *Rent*, Jonathan Larson quit, triumphantly, his longtime day job at the Moondance Diner. Not only was he beginning to feel confident that he would be making his living as a composer, but he needed to focus full-time on revising the script and the score. Because he had been working in isolation for so long on his various shows, trying in vain to get anyone interested in producing them, he had become something of a one-man band; he hadn't learned much about how to collaborate. With James Nicola, Michael Greif, and Tim Weil on one side and producers Jeffrey Seller, Kevin McCollum, and Allan S. Gordon on the other, he was surrounded by very smart and knowledgeable people who believed in *Rent* and were committed to doing anything they could to help it reach its potential—but it wasn't always easy for him to hear what they had to say.

Gradually he learned how to trust and to listen. For the most part, Nicola insisted that the producers give their notes to him, and then he would decide how to funnel the feedback to the artists, but sometimes a producer's critique of the evolving material got back to Larson directly, and this could be painful. At times he got angry or defensive. But to his credit, after he went away to think things over, he often realized his collaborators were onto something, and he would come back to the table with new material. Lynn M. Thomson, the dramaturg Nicola brought in, was instrumental in helping him flesh out the characters and clarify the structure of the story.

Larson agreed to Nicola's request to have a new draft ready to go by September of 1995, but got caught up in working on his last-minute commission for *J.P. Morgan Saves the Nation*. The team worried when the deadline came and went and the script was still unfinished. In October Larson brought in a new version with some strong new songs. It also had a new structure: the show started with Angel's funeral, and the rest of the story unfolded as a flashback. That felt like a step in the wrong direction to the team, but Larson didn't want to go back to the drawing board yet again, and casting was already underway. There were tense conversations and talk of postponing or even cancelling the production. That lit a fire under Jonathan, and he got back to work one more time and came up with a much-improved draft. Revisions would continue during the rehearsal process, but all parties agreed they were ready to get started.

Finding a Cast

Much thought and enormous care went into the casting for the Off-Broadway production of *Rent*. Nicola, Larson, and Greif had a strong sense of the kinds of performers they wanted for the show. It had to have a genuine sense of downtown street life; the cast would need to represent the world of avant-garde, struggling Lower East Side artists and rock musicians. They felt traditional "musical theater people" would in most cases come across as too trained and polished; the team wanted rougher edges, true individuality, and vivid, idiosyncratic personalities. This would mean looking outside the usual parameters of agent submissions and actors who would read the trades and come in to audition for an Off-Broadway play or musical; the casting director would have to be much more proactive and resourceful than usual. By the time all was said and done, the search for the perfect cast took more than four months.

The man chosen to take on the challenge was casting director Bernard Telsey. Telsey was born in 1960 (the same year as Jonathan Larson) and in 1981 graduated from New York University with a degree in Acting and Theatre Administration. Along with actor Robert LuPone, he cofounded Manhattan Class Company, an Off-Broadway theater group dedicated to developing new work. The company has grown steadily; now known as MCC Theater, it remains an important part of the New York theater community. While growing the company, Telsey also worked as an assistant at Simon & Kumin Casting and was subsequently hired as a casting director at Risa Bramon & Billy Hopkins Casting. In 1988 he opened his own office which, as Telsey + Company Casting, is known today as one of the best in the business, with countless Broadway and Off-Broadway shows, regional theater productions, and films to its credit. It was their work on *Rent* that really put them on the map and established their reputation as an office that could think outside the box. Telsey later said casting that show was the toughest challenge he had ever taken on; his contribution to its ultimate success cannot be overestimated.

Only three of the cast members from the 1994 workshop got the chance to repeat their roles in the full production: Daphne Rubin-Vega as Mimi, Anthony Rapp as Mark, and Gilles Chiasson, who played several roles as a member of the ensemble. (Mark Setlock and Shelley Dickinson, who played Angel and Joanne in the workshop, would come back on board later as understudies when the show moved to Broadway.)

Though Rapp was simply offered his role, Rubin-Vega had to audition again. Even during the workshop, Larson had been unsure whether she really had the right voice for the music he had written; when she asked him what she could do to ensure that she would get to continue in the role if it went to a full production, he told her to take voice lessons for a year. By that point she knew *Rent* was something very important and she was determined to hold onto her role; she took his advice and evidently found the right teacher. When she came in to audition for the 1996 version, she had been vocalizing every day and her voice was stronger than ever. Larson didn't need any more convincing; she was offered the role on the spot.

As Michael Greif later told Rebecca Milzoff of *New York* magazine, in many ways Rubin-Vega set the tone for what they were looking for: "If someone came in and showed us they were a vital, interesting, potentially authentic inhabitant of this world, that was more important than their experience." In search of undiscovered talent, Telsey and his associates went to shows at downtown rock clubs, open mic nights, and out-of-the-way experimental venues.

Tom Collins had originally been envisioned as a white character, either a Tom Waits or a Bruce Springsteen type. But when the team wasn't finding anyone they felt was perfect, someone suggested they start seeing "Marvin Gaye types." Bernie Telsey knew Jesse L. Martin's work; he sent him a demo of Larson singing some of the music and asked him to come in. Martin listened to the tape and didn't think it seemed like a fit; he later commented he thought Jonathan sounded like Kermit the Frog—which he made a point of saying he didn't mean disrespectfully! (He probably didn't know Larson had

Wilson Jermaine Heredia (Angel), Jesse L. Martin (Collins), and Anthony Rapp (Mark) perform "Santa Fe." Original cast, 1996.   *Joan Marcus*

actually written some songs for *Sesame Street*.) But Telsey persuaded him to go in; he sang "Amazing Grace" for the team, and their search for a Tom Collins was over.

The character Angel posed unique challenges. As Wilson Jermaine Heredia—who would end up winning a Tony Award for the role—told Vulture.com, he had never done drag before, but he had been a club kid and he knew that world: "I went into my audition in overalls, combat boots, and a goatee. I figured, *I'm not changing for an audition*." He sang "Amazing Grace"—coincidentally the same song Martin chose—and "Great Balls of Fire." He spun around and improvised dance moves, which helped convince Larson and Greif that he had the stuff to play the gender-bending role. They loved him, but he didn't hear anything for a week; when he called his agents, they said he had gotten the part but they had forgotten to tell him! Still, he nearly turned it down because he had just taken a new survival job (working the graveyard shift in a complaint center) and was reluctant to give up his health insurance for a limited Off-Broadway engagement.

Michael Greif recently said: "Angel wasn't originally conceived as Latino, nor was Collins conceived as African-American. I'm happy that we were all open to seeing a diverse group of actors for those roles, and especially happy that Wilson and Jesse won them, and set the template for those characters for future productions."

As with Martin, getting Taye Diggs to come in for the role of Benny also took persistence on Telsey's part. The actor had Broadway experience but was trying to focus on film and TV work, and didn't particularly want to do another musical, so he cancelled his first two appointments. When they called a third time, he finally went in, just to avoid antagonizing his agent, and sang a song from *Jesus Christ Superstar*. Greif and Larson felt he had the charisma to keep the character from becoming simply a villain; they wanted to make sure Benny had dimension and his own plausible point of view, and in Diggs they found a real actor who could deliver that.

Idina Menzel had been working on a singing career, performing at funky downtown clubs like The Bitter End with her band (to get an audience, she sometimes had to beg her friends to come) as well as frequent gigs singing at weddings. Her boyfriend at the time was working at an agency and secretly faxed her résumé to Telsey; she sang Bonnie Raitt's "Something to Talk About" for her audition. Later, she mentioned ironically that she had only gone in for *Rent* because she needed a way to pay hers, and January and February are traditionally the slowest time of year for weddings. So if the auditions had been a couple of months earlier or later, history might have turned out very differently! Actually, though, she might have gotten the part anyway, as Michael Greif had seen her at an audition the previous year for another project. He made a note to himself that if and when *Rent* went to a full production she would make a great Maureen—which of course is exactly what happened.

Of the principal roles, Roger took the longest to cast. When none of the Equity actors submitted by agents seemed right, Telsey's team hit the downtown clubs to find undiscovered rock singers. They also decided to have an open call, and about fifty guys showed up. One actor auditioned on the advice of an old friend—Menzel, who by then had been offered the role of Maureen. Adam Pascal had been fronting a rock band that had recently broken up. Menzel knew he had a terrific voice and didn't have much going on at the time; he wasn't pursuing acting, and since he had never auditioned for anything he didn't have a headshot, but she and her agent boyfriend urged him to give it a shot. (It turned out that Telsey and his assistant already had Pascal's name on their list, as he had been suggested by a rock and roll singing coach they had asked for recommendations.)

Telsey recalled that a lot of the hopefuls who showed up that day were Alice Cooper types, but Pascal was in the waiting area when the team walked in, and when they saw how handsome he was they literally prayed that he would be able to sing. He went in with his guitar and sang "Red Hill Mining Town," from the U2 album *The Joshua Tree*. The voice—as everyone now knows—was extraordinary, but casting someone that inexperienced would be a risk. Because Pascal was accustomed to performing with a rock band, the first challenge was getting him to sing with his eyes open. For a callback, Greif asked him to learn "Your Eyes," the love song from the last scene. He had him sing it directly to Telsey, imagining the casting director as the dying Mimi. According to Greif: "Adam was a strong performer. He had real truth and real emotional access when he sang, so it was just a matter of helping him bring that same kind of truth into the spoken dialogue."

Pascal went through two callbacks on consecutive days, but when they asked him to come back a third time, he nearly refused! He told a friend that he thought they had already seen enough and should be able to make up their minds. (To be fair, at that point all he or any of the auditioning performers knew was that they were trying out for a new, untried musical in a small, Off-Broadway theater, where the pay would be only three hundred dollars a week. No one had any idea that the show would very soon become the biggest Broadway sensation in twenty years.) The friend, who worked in the industry, explained to Pascal that this was just how the business worked; thankfully, he was able to persuade him to go in one more time, for the final callback that forever changed his life.

New Friends

Thrilled with the cast, Larson told his family that they were the most exciting group of people he had ever seen assembled, the sexiest and the most talented. Before rehearsals began, he invited the company to his ramshackle apartment for a special edition of his by-that-time traditional Peasant's Feast. The annual gatherings had always been for his friends and family; this one was for his new friends. In Anthony Rapp's book *Without You*, he quotes Jonathan's welcoming words to the cast: "I wrote this show about my life. About the lives of my friends. And some of my friends are gone. And I really miss them . . . I guess I just wanted to say that you all are going to bring my friends to life, and I wanted to thank you for that. I wanted to thank you all for being my new friends." He had welcomed them into his home and into his life, a rare and unusual thing for a writer to do, and it affected them profoundly. Michael Greif has said that forging a sense of trust and connection among the cast has always been an important part of his rehearsal process, but it was especially crucial for this show, which is really *about* friendship and the creation of a community. That Peasant Feast of December 18, 1995, was a defining moment in the history of *Rent*, and it set the tone for what was to follow.

Rehearsals

In a 2015 interview for Broadwayworld.com, Adam Pascal told Pat Cerasaro about getting to know Jonathan Larson: "He was a little reserved and kind of shy . . . He was incredibly sweet and incredibly passionate about this project and he was incredibly excited to have all of us involved. He was very confident in his own abilities, too . . . and, he was right. Everything that the show has accomplished in terms of its message, in terms of its place in the lexicon of musical theatre, in terms of its iconic status—he wanted all that and, in a way, envisioned all that, you know? Were he still to be around today, I can imagine him saying, 'See? I told you!'"

With the full cast in place, the rehearsal period was an exciting time. The actors hit it off and started to build a family, forging bonds that have lasted to this day. Pascal recently recalled how much he enjoyed the work, which was an entirely new experience for him. "It was so fun and exciting and exhilarating. Everything about it from the process to the people to the music and the material. It was all so exciting. I couldn't wait to come to work every day; I couldn't wait to be with those people and spend time with them and hopefully absorb some of their abilities." The others shared his sense of joy in the work; they credit Greif and musical director Tim Weil with setting the tone for an open, collaborative process.

New songs that hadn't been in the workshop version began to appear, and having a cast inspired some of Larson's best work. He told Anthony Rapp he wrote "Halloween" and "What You Own" with his voice in mind, and new material for Benny and Joanne gave those characters much more depth than they had had in the workshop.

There was some healthy sexual energy and playfulness in the rehearsal hall, which added sizzle to the work. Taye Diggs recalled that he checked out the women in the cast and was immediately attracted to both Rubin-Vega and Menzel. (As many people know, he and Menzel would eventually get married.) Rubin-Vega as Mimi and Pascal as Roger found a playful rapport in the relationship of their characters; she was charmed when he really kissed her in rehearsal, rather than indicating or faking it as more experienced actors sometimes do, and he described her as this "little firecracker of sexiness" with whom he looked forward to working every day. The chemistry paid off in scintillating performances of "Light My Candle," "Another Day," and "I Should Tell You."

Greif was an excellent leader whose contributions to the development of the show were incalculable. The show is almost through-sung, which limited opportunities for detailed character development in the text; the work Greif did with the actors provided a third dimension, a sense of real people with lives that extended beyond the immediate boundaries of the stories they were telling. As Anthony Rapp recently said of the director: "He was always about the most interesting, complicated way into the material. He wants to make sure that you're mining the depths and you're not just playing one thing or going for the easy way out. He likes texture and the space between people to be alive and complicated and rich." Rubin-Vega said "I loved Michael. I remember thinking I'll do anything he asks . . . I was so hungry and ravenous and curious and inspired."

Tim Weil was also a nurturing and inspiring presence in the room. As Greif remembers: "Tim is an amazing musical director who gets the best out of everybody and let me actually rehearse the musical as a play. I was able to rehearse it as a play because he had the musical elements so under control."

The choreographer, Marlies Yearby, was not a musical-comedy hoofer but came from the world of downtown contemporary dance and collaborative theater. She was particularly involved with helping Wilson Jermaine Heredia learn how to move like a woman, finding Angel in his body. She worked in that organic way with all the actors. As she explained it to Evelyn McDonnell and Katherine Silberger, editors of the *Rent* coffee table book, Broadway

Original ensemble members (from left) Rodney Hicks, Byron
Utley, Kristen Lee Kelly, Gwen Stewart, and Timothy Britten
Parker, portraying homeless people, sing "Christmas Bells."
Photo Joan Marcus/Carol Rosegg

dancers "tend to be slicker and more presentational. I ask people to be more
internal, to be inside breath, to have an easiness and naturalness in their
body." She was very successful with this, and most of the movement and dance
in the show has an improvisational quality, as if the actors are telling a story
spontaneously through their bodies.

This is in keeping with Greif's approach to the material. He didn't want
the show to look staged, and has said: "We tried to make it seem as if they were
'making something out of nothing,' and they were just throwing some things
around. We wanted it to feel as much like a play, as much like a concert, as
much like an improvised event as a musical." Particularly with the seven
actors who played the ensemble roles, there was no pretense of naturalism;
the audience was meant to be aware of them as young artists playfully taking
on various roles, some of which were close to themselves in age and personality, others not. Said Greif: "This is the group of people we're performing this
story with. A bunch of healthy young singers and dancers and actors who
variously portray an indigent community, a community whose life is in peril.
And then transform into a very youthful, exuberant community: members
of our principals' family of friends. You are aware of the roles they take on
throughout the evening."

The theater-as-rock-concert approach, along with the very real difficulty
of keeping the lyrics audible over the five-man rock band, led to one of the
most distinctive design choices the team made. Though most Broadway shows
carefully conceal their performers' body mics in wigs or costume pieces, all
the actors in *Rent* wore very visible microphone headsets. Though at least one
critic would complain that they made them look like telephone operators, the

mics became part of the show's aesthetic. And if one of them wasn't working, a crew member would come right out and give the actor a new one! For the same reason, there was little or no masking in the set design; the audience was meant to see the workings of putting on a show, stripped bare of illusion.

One of the final challenges during rehearsal involved fleshing out the lesbian relationship between Maureen and Joanne—not the easiest thing for a straight male writer to get inside of. Finally, inspired by the powerful, exciting voices of Idina Menzel and Fredi Walker, Larson wrote the duet "Take Me or Leave Me," an exuberantly sexy confrontation between two very different women who love each other. It would be the last major piece of music he wrote for the show.

Friends in Deed

About halfway through the rehearsal period, a guest speaker came in to talk with the cast. Cynthia O'Neal, informally known as Cy, was the director of Friends In Deed, an organization that provided support services and counseling, free of charge, to people who were facing life-threatening illnesses, as well as their families and friends. O'Neal had started the group with the famed director Mike Nichols, and Larson had discovered them when his close friend Matt O'Grady, after being diagnosed with HIV, invited him to one of their meetings; Jonathan was inspired and later worked with them as a volunteer.

The organization became the model for the group that in the show is called Life Support. In fact, at one of the meetings Larson attended he had heard a man with AIDS ask the question, "Will I lose my dignity?" Set to Larson's achingly beautiful melody, this would become one of the most memorable and haunting lines in the show. The refrain of "no other way, no day but today" was also influenced by Friends In Deed's philosophy. As O'Neal explained it (as quoted by McDonnell and Silberger): "The main precept of our work here is that the quality of your life is not based on circumstances. It's never outside of yourself. How you perceive life is entirely up to you. We do not view anything as a tragedy."

The government and society at large had been disgracefully slow to acknowledge the epidemic, as if AIDS were a dirty word. But Friends In Deed was nonjudgmental, providing a place for people to open up about their experiences rather than feeling ashamed. The condition of AIDS, they maintained, though it can be terribly difficult to cope with, does not have to be the defining factor of a person's life: love and friendship and feelings of self-worth are all still possible day by day. The idea that people are "living with, not dying from disease" became not only another important lyric in

Rent, but an overall way of looking at life that had a profound effect on the development of the musical.

In the program for the New York Theatre Workshop production, Larson included the following program note: "With this work, I celebrate my friends and the many others who continue to fulfill their dreams and live their lives in the shadow of AIDS. In these dangerous times, where it seems the world is ripping apart at the seams, we can all learn how to survive from those who stare death squarely in the face every day, and we should reach out to each other and bond as a community, rather than hide from the terrors of life."

The Final Dress Rehearsal

On the last night of his own life, Larson sat in the theater with a full house of invited guests for the final dress rehearsal of the show he had been working on for almost seven years. He cringed many times as the sound system, which he had described as the bane of his life, malfunctioned and obscured some of his lyrics; there were numerous glitches and technical issues, par for the course at that stage in the rehearsal process of a big musical. But it was clear the show was coming together, and the audience seemed genuinely excited.

Following the rehearsal, Larson did his interview with Anthony Tommasini of the *Times*, then poked his head in at the production meeting, where Greif was giving notes to the designers, to answer a few questions. It was the last time they ever saw him.

January 25, 1996

The painful details of Larson's trips to two emergency rooms over the previous days, and his death that night, were recounted in Chapter 1. Word of the tragedy spread quickly the next morning. NYTW's production manager, Sue White, was one of the first people to be informed by the police; she called Nicola at 7:30 in the morning. He was unable to get through to Michael Greif on the phone, so he went to the Time Café, where the two of them had planned to meet Jonathan at 9:30 a.m. to go over notes from the previous night; he had the painful task of telling Greif why Jonathan would not be showing up for the meeting. From there they went to the theater, where they began calling the actors.

The cast and production team gradually gathered at the theater. For a while they simply spent time together; they sat in a circle onstage, mostly quiet, sharing their disbelief, their shock and grief. Some of them talked, or cried, or held each other; some sat alone in the theater or took walks around the neighborhood. Many of Larson's friends, at a loss and needing to connect with someone, came down as well, and soon the theater was full of people. The staff and the Usual Suspects brought food for everyone and helped make the many necessary phone calls—which included calling the people who had purchased tickets for the show's first preview, scheduled for that night, and telling them it had been cancelled.

The huge question was what to do that evening at eight o'clock, when the preview had been scheduled to go up. What would be appropriate? What would be respectful? What would even be emotionally possible? Greif thought it was important that they at least run through the score; the best way to honor Jonathan and be with him would be to share his music, and they all felt sure that was what he would want. It was also important to consider what his family would want at that terribly difficult time; his parents, Al and Nan, had planned to attend that first preview and were already on a plane from their home in Albuquerque. While they were on a layover in Chicago, Al spoke to Larson's friend Jonathan Burkhart on the phone; Burkhart remembers him literally saying, "The show must go on."

The staff got on the phone and called as many friends and colleagues of Jonathan's as they could think of and invited them to come to the theater that night. After consulting with Nicola, Greif told the cast he thought the best way to approach the performance was to line up the three long tables on the stage and have the cast simply sit and sing through the show, with the band, but without props, costumes, lights, or staging. This was out of respect for the solemnity of the occasion, but also for practical reasons: they didn't want technical issues, lighting or costume problems—all of which were still being worked out at that stage in the process—to distract the cast or the audience. Quite simply, the evening needed to be about Jonathan's work, hearing his words and his music. Also, because the actors were grappling with such huge and unexpected emotions, just being able to sing would be a challenge; Greif was afraid they might hurt themselves if they were running around the stage, dancing, and trying to execute the intricate blocking. A simple sing-through of the score would give them, as well as the audience, room to breathe and space to mourn.

Toward the end of the afternoon, they rehearsed for about an hour and then took a dinner break. When they returned to the theater, some of them met Al and Nan Larson for the first time, in the lobby. Though shaken, the couple managed to greet the actors graciously. The seats in the small theater filled up quickly; soon there were people sitting in the aisles and on the steps and standing in the back.

Jim Nicola made a brief welcoming speech. He expressed the company's sorrow and their commitment to honoring Larson's memory by bringing his show to life every night in their theater.

The metal tables were equipped with glasses of water for each actor, and there were tissues and throat lozenges in case they needed them. None of the actors knew what to expect as they started to sing through the show; at times their throats threatened to close up, the emotion choking off the music, but they all managed to work through it and open themselves up to the beauty of the score. The audience listened intently, and even started laughing at the jokes. Given the circumstances, many of the songs and individual lines resonated more powerfully than ever before. Roger's determination to leave one great song behind "before I go" hit unbearably close to home, for both cast and audience, and Pascal's anguished singing rose to the occasion.

The unique energy and joy of Jonathan's songs, and the feverish response from the audience, gradually electrified the room, and soon it was all the actors could do to stay in their seats at the table. Anybody could see they were itching to get up and play the scenes for real. Toward the end of the first act, Anthony Rapp was the first to take the leap of faith. As he describes it in his book:

> By the time we got to "La Vie Boheme," it was clear that the time for sitting down was over, and as I began my opening verse, I climbed right up onto the table, just as I did in the show, and sang out to the crowd Jonathan's joyful valentine to all things bohemian. Soon, everybody else in the cast was joining me up on the tables, and we danced and spun and wailed our way through the song, its energy and drive overtaking us, its propulsive percolating beat sending us flying. As I led the group in our final "Viva la vie boheme!" I knew that there would be no going back to our seats when we came back from intermission. We'd have to get up and really do the show; its power was too great. And the audience seemed to agree, their cheers and applause enormous and full and overwhelming.

At intermission, Greif agreed there was no turning back. The show itself had taken over and they simply had to do the second act full out. Still no costumes, but they brought in lights and props and all the staging. Nearly every lyric seemed to take on an intensified significance as they moved from "Seasons of Love" through "Without You." When it came to Angel's funeral and the reprise of "I'll Cover You," the parallels to what they were really experiencing became almost unbearable. Jesse Martin told Milzoff that he held the final note of the song longer than he ever had before; he would have passed out if Adam Pascal hadn't held onto him to keep him standing. He added: "Honestly, it was then that I learned how Collins sings that song. I hate that it was Jonathan's death that got me there, but it did get me there."

As Greif later put it in a video interview for the film *No Day But Today*: "A lot of depth and a lot of complexity found itself that night." Having to sing the show in those circumstances taught the cast what it was really about. In "What You Own," Rapp and Pascal sang out, "For once the shadows gave way to light; for once I didn't disengage." The energy of Larson's message had indeed lit up the theater and forged a connection with the audience unlike anything any of them had experienced before. As Larson's friend Eddie Rosenstein put it, it was as if Jonathan "had written a manifesto about how to view this death, this tragedy. One last gift from Jonathan." It was a night when life and art merged completely. When the show ended, with the cascading repeated phrases "I die without you" and "no day but today," the audience rose in an ovation, cheers mixing with tears; the actors bowed and went backstage to put away their headsets and get their things, and when they came back out into the house they realized everyone was still sitting there in absolute silence. The cast joined them, equally silent, for a long, sustained moment, until finally a man's voice from the back of the house cried out, "Thank you, Jonathan Larson."

Mark and Roger (Anthony Rapp and Adam Pascal) answer the phone in the opening scene of the musical. Original cast, 1996.   *Joan Marcus*

Facing the Future

The postponed first official preview took place the next night, January 26. The news of Larson's untimely death, and its eerie resonance with the themes of the play, drew curious theatergoers down to the East Village, but it was word-of-mouth about the genuine beauty and power of the show itself that kept them coming. The official press opening was February 13, and the show got a rave review from Ben Brantley in the *New York Times*. That day the box office sold $40,000 worth of tickets. The run sold out immediately; originally announced to close on May 3, it was extended to April 1.

NYTW seats fewer than 200 people: audiences who were lucky enough to see *Rent* there still remember the emotional power the show had in that intimate space. It was fueled by the passion of a cast that had bonded through a joyous period of discovery in rehearsal and then, through shared catastrophe, had become a family. The loss of Jonathan made the message of the show resonate in their hearts more powerfully than ever, and their eagerness to communicate every word of his story was palpable.

The production team was equally concerned with ensuring that Larson's words would be understood, and they continued to grapple with the sound system. Sound designer Kurt Fischer, who was hired shortly after the opening, was instrumental in finessing the mix at NYTW and eventually in moving the show to Broadway successfully.

The downtown audiences were thrilled, but there was still work to be done. As with any new musical aiming for an uptown run, the assumption would have been that the show would continue to undergo revision throughout the preview period and even beyond. Larson himself had certainly known that it wasn't finished. And following the emotional performance on the twenty-fifth, Al Larson had told the actors, "Now we have to make this show a hit." The very real dilemma facing the creative team, the producers, and Jonathan's family was this: how could they continue to work on and refine the show without the involvement of the man who was its composer, lyricist, and bookwriter? The one thing they knew for sure was that he wouldn't have wanted them to stop working.

James Nicola set the ground rules: any changes to the script and score were to be the responsibility of a four-person team consisting of himself, Greif, Weil, and Thomson. He promised Larson's family that no adjustments would be made unless all four of those people came to consensus on the change, and the family agreed to this arrangement.

As quoted in the *Rent* coffee table book, Greif said: "I was operating with a more focused sense of urgency than perhaps I have in other situations, because I really wanted to succeed for him. We proceeded with a lot of knowledge of Jonathan's intentions and a lot of experience discussing and collaborating and arguing with him about various things, with a lot of consideration and care. Because Jonathan is not here to argue with, I need to include his argument in my argument."

As Weil told Michael Portantiere of *Playbill:* "With deference to his family and friends and the fragile dynamics of the situation, we were faced with the fact that we had to present the show in the best possible light. We knew we could do a certain amount of editing without betraying Jonathan's conception. And we took a look at earlier drafts of *Rent* so that, if something had to be added, we could use his own material. . . . There's been some internal cutting: verses of songs and parts of verses. We've mostly been concerned with adjusting flow, rhythm and tempo while maintaining the integrity of the musical structure."

In addition to tightening the first act, they took some of Larson's stage directions and transformed them into spoken narration for Mark, the storyteller. This included introductions of a couple of the characters, as well as what is now the very first speech in the show, Mark's description of the apartment. Some of this material had been included in the 1994 workshop and then cut; Greif felt that putting it back in helped clarify the story, and that if Larson had seen how well it worked in previews he would have agreed.

Though the producers (Seller, McCollum, and Gordon) generally trusted Nicola and Greif to steer the ship, there were times when they too made suggestions. As Greif recently recalled:

> I'm sure they (our commercial producers) were extremely invested and concerned with our progress, but what I remember most is that during the Off-Broadway rehearsal, they respected the primacy of the collaboration between Jim Nicola, artistic director of the NYTW, and the creative team. When it was determined that we were moving to Broadway, Jeffrey, Kevin, and Allan initiated discussions of changes to the script and score. A song, or more correctly, a song fragment called "Door/Wall" was cut. The action in "Door/Wall" (Roger's decision to leave the loft) was added to the end of "Will I." I thought, and still think, that it was a terrific suggestion.

Even as it is, many people close to *Rent* and close to Jonathan feel the show remains unfinished. To this day, they question what Larson might have changed or added if he had lived to continue working on the show through the preview period, and perhaps even the Off-Broadway run and on into previews on Broadway. Musical director Weil, who probably had a closer relationship to the score than anyone else, has wondered whether Larson might have rewritten "Your Eyes," or come up with a different song for that all-important climactic scene. Early in the first act, in "One Song Glory,"

Joanne and Maureen's duet, "Take Me or Leave Me," was the last song Larson wrote for the musical. He was inspired by the voices of original cast members Fredi Walker (left) and Idina Menzel.   *Joan Marcus*

Roger expresses his yearning and determination to write a truly great song before he succumbs to his illness; when he finally sings to Mimi "you were the song all along," we are meant to understand that "Your Eyes" is the culmination of that wish. But even Adam Pascal, who sang the song every night, has said he felt it was a little bit of a letdown. The irony is that "One Song Glory" itself *is* a truly great song, whereas "Your Eyes," though it would probably sound spectacular in any average musical, is not one of Larson's best.

In a real sense, though, the slightly rough-around-the-edges, unfinished nature of *Rent* is part of its strength, and probably even part of the reason for its success. For a "finish," like varnish on wooden furniture, even as it smooths the surface can obscure the genuine grain and texture of the piece. That this never happened with *Rent* is part of its appeal. As the show made its way uptown and became an enormous money-making machine—complete with expensive souvenirs, magazine cover stories, and a clothing line at Bloomingdale's—the production was accused by some of selling out, of being absorbed into the corporate, money-driven media culture it had been meant to repudiate. But of necessity the musical itself, fated to remain much as it was on its first night in a small theater on East 4th Street, stayed pure and innocent of such pernicious influences, whether real or imagined. It still feels like a group of smart, eager young iconoclasts from downtown taking over a space and telling their story in their own way, raw edges and all, with no interest in being part of a "well-made play" or a slick, polished Broadway musical. As Daphne Rubin-Vega told McDonnell and Silberger: "Part of what makes *Rent* beautiful is its roughness. It's just like living on the Lower East Side: there's a lot of shit going on. It's messy. Good."

By the time the reviews came out, there was no question in anyone's mind but that *Rent* was going to have a long life, and in a bigger venue. Seller and McCollum and Gordon were so eager to get Larson's message out into the world as quickly as they could, and to as many people as possible, that the move uptown was informally dubbed "Operation Desert Storm." The next chapter in the story of *Rent* was already being written.

"Being an Us for Once"

The Original Cast

The original cast of *Rent* was an extraordinary group of people: the result of an unusually wide and extensive search, led by casting director Bernard Telsey, to find young artists who understood the world of the musical and could bring it to life with honesty and authenticity. Their voices and personalities inspired Jonathan Larson as he fleshed out the characters and developed the script—and when they lost him midway through the process, they drew together in their determination to tell his story and convey his message with truth and integrity. Night after night and week after week, they thrilled and delighted audiences with their passionate voices and with the conviction and love they brought to the show. Even for those fans who never saw them onstage, their unique performances, as preserved on the cast album (and in the cases of six of them, in the film), will forever shape the way these characters are seen and perceived—and all of them would tell you that the show changed their lives profoundly as well. This chapter looks at these fifteen remarkable individuals, their careers up to the time they did *Rent*, and what they have done since.

Gilles Chiasson (Man with Squeegee, a Waiter, and Others)

Born in 1966, Chiasson was nearly thirty when *Rent* opened, making him one of the older cast members. Few would have guessed that, however, given his boyish good looks. He was one of the few in the cast who came from a traditional musical theater background, and his soaring tenor voice as "Steve" on the heartbreaking opening verse of "Will I?" provided one of the memorable cameos in the show. He also understudied both Roger and Mark, going on in both roles during his two years with the Broadway company. He was born in Michigan to French Canadian parents and received a BFA from the School of Music at the University of Michigan, home to one of the nation's biggest and best musical theater training programs. Shortly after graduation, he was cast as Marius in the national company of *Les Misérables*; he later went on tour again as Jinx in *Forever Plaid*. He was in an Off-Broadway musical called *Groundhog* at the Manhattan Theatre Club and appeared at major regional theaters in such shows as *Pippin* and *A Little Night Music*, as well as straight plays like Neil Simon's *Broadway Bound*. While still in his twenties he founded, with a group of his friends, the Adirondack Theatre Festival, a small but highly respected regional theater in upstate New York; he remains on the theater's advisory board to this day. Following his long run in *Rent*, Chiasson went on to perform in two Broadway musicals with scores by Frank Wildhorn—*The Scarlet Pimpernel* and *The Civil War*—and he received an Outer Critics Circle Award nomination for Best Supporting Actor in a Musical for his role as Corporal William McEwen in the latter show. He also appeared in the original musical *Fermat's Last Tango* at the York Theatre. He was probably the only cast member from *Rent* to go on to appear in a major production of the opera that was the original source for the musical's story, taking an ensemble part in director Baz Lurhmann's Broadway production of *La bohème* and then appearing in the same show in Los Angeles, an engagement that precipitated his decision to move to the West Coast and pursue a new career in the film industry. In 2005 he took a job as director of development for Moresco Productions, a post he held for five years, working on such TV shows as *The Black Donnellys* and *Crash* and developing scripts for feature films. From 2010 to 2012 he was producing director for the Reprise Theatre Company, an acclaimed Los Angeles theater group known for concert stagings of classic and obscure musicals, and he has more recently taken on co-producer duties on a number of films. Other creative endeavors have included performing as a guest vocalist with various symphony orchestras and recording a solo CD entitled *Slow Down*. He has also written a musical of his own, *Chrysalis*, which has had workshop productions in Houston and New York, including one at New York Theatre Workshop, the original home of *Rent*. Chiasson is married to the actress Sherri Parker Lee; they live in Los Angeles with their two children.

Taye Diggs (Benny)

Diggs grew up in Rochester, New York; his mother, Marcia, was an actress and teacher, and he developed an interest in performing early on. His real first name is Scott; as a child, he pronounced Scotty as "Scottay," and the resulting nickname stuck. He graduated from the School of the Arts, a progressive alternative public high school in Rochester, and then went to Syracuse University, where he earned a BFA in Musical Theatre. Early professional performing gigs included stints with two summer stock companies in New Hampshire and a show called *Sebastian's Caribbean Carnival* at Tokyo Disneyland. At age twenty-three, he made his Broadway debut in the Lincoln Center Theatre revival of Rodgers and Hammerstein's classic musical *Carousel*; he was a member of the ensemble and understudied film actor Fisher Stevens in the role of Jigger. Following his run in *Rent*, he appeared twice more onstage opposite his costar from that show, Idina Menzel: both were featured in Andrew Lippa's musical adaptation of *The Wild Party* at the Manhattan Theatre Club in 2000, and Diggs later took a turn as Fiyero, the love interest of Menzel's Elphaba, in the Broadway company of *Wicked*. (He was filling in for the role's creator, Norbert Leo Butz, who had also been in *Rent* on Broadway as an understudy and replacement Roger.) Diggs and Menzel got married in 2003. He appeared in the long-running Broadway revival of *Chicago* as a replacement in the role of the lawyer Billy Flynn, and also played the part of a bandleader in Rob Marshall's Oscar-winning film version of that show. His screen acting career took off quickly with television roles on *Guiding Light* and *Ally McBeal*; he made a splash in the theatrical film *How Stella Got Her Groove Back* and followed it up with other movies, including *Go*, *Wood*, *The Best Man*, and *Equilibrium*. Over a dozen more films have followed, including the 2005 movie of *Rent*; his most recent films include *Between Us*, *Baggage Claim*, and *The Best Man Holiday*, a 2013 sequel to the original 1999 *The Best Man*. TV appearances have included the title role in the series *Kevin Hill* (2004–05)—for which he won an NAACP Image Award for Outstanding Actor in a Drama Series—as well as numerous guest appearances, and recurring roles on *Will and Grace*, *The West Wing*, and *Rosewood*. He appeared on three episodes of the popular medical series *Grey's Anatomy* and then starred with Kate Walsh on a spinoff from that series, *Private Practice*, which ran from 2007 to 2013. Since 2014, he has been playing the role of Inspector Terry English on the TNT series *Murder in the First*. He is also a published author, having written two children's books entitled *Mixed Me!* and *Chocolate Me!* In 2015 he returned to Broadway, taking over the title role in *Hedwig and the Angry Inch*, the first Broadway production of John Cameron Mitchell and Stephen Trask's 1998 rock musical. The show had opened at the Belasco Theatre in 2014 starring Neil Patrick Harris, who was followed in the role by a succession of high profile actors: Andrew Rannells, Michael C. Hall, author Mitchell (who had created the role Off-Broadway in '98), Darren Criss, and finally Diggs, the first African American actor to play the part in a major production. In 2014 his marriage to Menzel ended in divorce; they have one son, born in 2009.

Wilson Jermaine Heredia (Angel)

The son of two immigrants from the Dominican Republic, Heredia grew up in Brooklyn. Prior to being cast in *Rent* he danced in and choreographed several rock videos. Early theater credits included *Popol Vuh* on tour and at Intar and Lincoln Center in New York, and *The New Americans*, a show about young immigrants put together by the director/writer/composer Elizabeth Swados (*Runaways*). The cast collaborated with Swados on writing the show, for which Heredia composed a song entitled "No Es Asi." Heredia was the most decorated member of *Rent*'s original cast, winning the Tony and Drama Desk Awards for Best Featured Actor in a Musical, as well as an Olivier Award nomination for the London production, but his career did not take off as quickly as might have been expected following his success in the show. In recent years, however, he has amassed a substantial number of film credits,

Wilson Jermaine Heredia, the original Angel, shown here performing "Today 4 U" in the movie of *Rent*.

including *Three Chris's*, *The Girl from the Naked Eye*, *Descent*, *Nailed*, *Johnny Was*, *Flawless*, and *On a Mission from God*, in addition to the movie of *Rent*. TV credits include appearances on *Without a Trace*, *Medium*, *Law and Order: Special Victims Unit*, and *Spin City*. He was a member of the ensemble cast of an original theater piece called *Tales from the Tunnel*, which premiered in the New York International Fringe Festival and was later remounted Off-Broadway. In 2011 he returned to Broadway as a replacement in the revival of *La Cage aux Folles*, taking over the role of Jacob from Robin De Jesús—who, as an understudy, had also played Angel in *Rent* on Broadway. Since moving to the San Francisco Bay Area, Heredia has done more musical theater, including playing Lancelot in a revival of *Camelot* at the San Francisco Playhouse. Recent TV credits include roles on *Banshee*, *Blindside*, and the YouTube series *My Gay Roommate*.

Rodney Hicks (Paul, a Cop, and Others)

Though only twenty-one years old when he was cast in *Rent*, Hicks had been performing professionally for years, beginning as a host and dancer on a TV show called *Dance Party USA* in his home town of Philadelphia. Before joining *Rent*, he had appeared in the musical *Bring in the Morning - A Wake-Up Call* with Lauryn Hill at New York's famed Apollo Theatre, and a tour of the pop opera *I Was Looking at the Ceiling and Then I Saw the Sky*, directed by the visionary and often controversial Peter Sellars. He had also played Simon in a revival tour of *Jesus Christ Superstar* and appeared Off-Broadway in *Lotto*, both at the Billie Holiday Theatre and at Lincoln Center. Early credits also included print modeling, industrial shows, commercials, and an appearance on the daytime drama *One Life to Live*. After his initial stint in *Rent*, in which he understudied Taye Diggs as Benny in addition to playing his own ensemble track, he did *Superstar* again, this time playing Peter in the 2000 Broadway revival. That same year he starred as Joe Bonaparte, a role famously originated by Sammy Davis Jr., in a revival of the musical version of *Golden Boy* at the Long Wharf Theatre in Connecticut. In 2006, he was in the cast of the Off-Broadway revival of *Jacques Brel is Alive and Well and Living in Paris*; he can be heard on the cast album of that production. Two years after that he returned to the Broadway company of *Rent*, this time playing the role of Benny, and stayed until the end of the run, making him one of only two original cast members to appear in the show's final performance on Broadway, now available on DVD. In 2010, Hicks returned to Broadway again in *The Scottsboro Boys*, a Kander and Ebb musical that had received very strong reviews and numerous awards for engagements at the Off-Broadway Vineyard Theatre and the Guthrie Theatre in Minneapolis but then surprisingly ran for less than two months on Broadway, where it nevertheless received several Tony nominations. He returned to the show for the 2012 production at the Philadelphia Theatre Company, this time playing the role of Haywood Patterson, which he had understudied on Broadway; he won the prestigious Barrymore Award for Outstanding Leading Male Actor in a Musical. That year he also gave an award-winning performance as Jim in the musical *Big River* at the Village Theatre in Issaquah, Washington. He also played Curly in the first professional production of the Rodgers and Hammerstein classic *Oklahoma!* to employ an all-African American cast, at Portland Center Stage in Oregon. That show was directed by the theater's artistic director, Chris Coleman, to whom Hicks is now married. His recent stage appearances have included the role of Martin Luther King Jr. in the Portland Center Stage production of *The Mountaintop* and other regional work, including the title role in *Othello*, as well as a return to Broadway in the 2017 musical *Come From Away*. TV credits have included guest appearances on *NYPD Blue*, *Law & Order: Criminal Intent*, *Hope & Faith*, *Grimm*, and *Leverage*, as well as the made-for-TV movie *Student Affairs*.

Kristen Lee Kelly (Mark's Mom, Alison, and Others)

Kelly came to *Rent* with a background as a serious stage actress; she had performed at regional theaters in such plays as *The Diary of Anne Frank*, *The Heidi Chronicles*, and *Oleanna*, a very demanding two-character drama by David Mamet. She had also appeared Off-Broadway at Ubu Repertory (in *The Apollo of Bellac*), the Watermark Theatre, and the Via Theatre, where she was a company member. She had played the role of Patricia Kennedy in the 1990 TV miniseries *The Kennedys of Massachusetts*. In addition to her own ensemble track in *Rent*, she understudied Idina Menzel as Maureen, and took over that role officially at the end of December 1997; she played it until September of the next year. In 1999 she appeared in *American Passenger*, a new play by Theron Albis, at the Kraine Theatre, a small venue located on East 4th Street, next door to *Rent*'s original home at the New York Theatre Workshop. She was featured in developmental readings of *Sugar Mountain*, a "rock concert musical" with a book by Stephen Belber and songs by Howard Schuman and Andy MacKay. Other Off-Broadway engagements included *Hedwig and the Angry Inch*, *After the Rain*, and *Love, Janis* (as Janis Joplin); she also took part in the first national tour of *The Vagina Monologues*. In 2000 she played a role in the film *Under Hellgate Bridge*, and she had guest roles on both *Law & Order: Criminal Intent* and *Law & Order: Special Victims Unit*. Kelly has returned to Broadway only once, as a swing in the 2000 revival of *The Rocky Horror Show*, a production in which her original *Rent* castmates

Daphne Rubin-Vega and Aiko Nakasone also appeared. In that show, she understudied both Alice Ripley as Janet Weiss and Joan Jett as Columbia. Jett, a noted rock singer, could not come to terms with the producers on a contract for the cast album, so Kelly is heard as Columbia on that release. On August 21, 2001, she replaced Jett in the production and played the role for the next month—until the show went on a hiatus in the wake of the terrorist attacks of September 11. It reopened in late October and played into the first week of January 2002. Kelly appeared in both *Mother Courage* and the world premiere of Ken Roht's *Echo's Hammer* at the Theatre at Boston Court in Pasadena, California, and currently lives in Los Angeles.

Jesse L. Martin (Tom Collins)

Martin already had two Broadway credits when he was cast in *Rent*: the first-ever Broadway production of Shakespeare's least popular play, *Timon of Athens* (1993), and a revival of Gogol's *The Government Inspector* (1994). Both were directed by Michael Langham and produced at the Lyceum Theatre by Tony Randall's National Actors Theatre. Martin was born in Rocky Mount, Virginia; he first met Jonathan Larson long before *Rent*, when the two of them were coworkers at the Moondance Diner. After studying theater at New York University, he toured with The Acting Company and appeared at major regional theaters like Arena Stage, the Cleveland Playhouse, and the Actors Theatre of Louisville, as well as Off-Broadway at the Manhattan Theatre Club and The Ensemble Studio Theatre. In the years since *Rent*, he has been one of the most visible of the original cast members, due largely to his long-running leading role as Detective Ed Green on the popular TV series *Law and Order*; he played the part from 1999 to 2008, except for a brief hiatus he requested to make the movie of *Rent*. (To make this possible, the show's writers devised a storyline that had his character wounded in the line of duty.) Though musical theater has not figured prominently in his career, he did record a role for the concept album of the musical *Bright Lights, Big City* and starred as Macheath in *The Threepenny Opera* at the Williamstown Theatre Festival in 2003. He also played the Ghost of Christmas Present in the 2004 TV movie version of *A Christmas Carol*, starring Kelsey Grammer. In 2010, he appeared in both summer offerings of the New York Shakespeare Festival's Shakespeare in the Park season, playing Polixenes in *The Winter's Tale* (reuniting him with *Rent* director Michael Greif) and Gratiano in *The Merchant of Venice*; the latter production, which starred Al Pacino, transferred to Broadway. Martin's film credits have included *Restaurant*, *Season of Youth*, *Peter and Vandy*, and *Puncture*. Among his many TV appearances, in addition to *Law and Order*, have been recurring roles on *Ally McBeal* and *Smash* (in which

Jesse L. Martin as Tom Collins in the film.

he played Scott Nichols, artistic director of the Manhattan Theatre Workshop—a fictitious theater clearly inspired by the New York Theatre Workshop, where *Rent* had premiered). He has had a long-term interest in the Motown singer Marvin Gaye, having worked on a one-man play about the artist in the nineties and subsequently been attached to play the role in two biopics; the first never materialized, but the second, entitled *Sexual Healing*, was still in preparation as of this writing. Most recently Martin has been playing the regular role of Detective Joe West on the TV series *The Flash*.

Idina Menzel (Maureen)

Though many of the then unknown performers who made up the original cast of *Rent* have gone on to continued success in the industry, twenty years after the premiere of the show the one who seems to have attained the most widespread celebrity is arguably Menzel. This is due primarily to her

Idina Menzel as Maureen in the movie of *Rent*.

triumphs in two blockbuster leading roles: Elphaba in the original Broadway cast of the Stephen Schwartz musical *Wicked*, and the voice of Elsa in Disney's phenomenally popular big-screen cartoon fairy tale *Frozen*. With their instant-classic, anthemic arias ("Defying Gravity" and "Let It Go," respectively) these roles secured Menzel's place as the quintessential belter of her generation, as well as an exemplar of "girl power," with legions of teen and preteen fans in addition to her adult followers. The singer/actress was born in 1971 and grew up in a Jewish family in Syosset, New York. At fifteen she was already working professionally as a singer, mainly at weddings and bar mitzvahs. Though she attended the Tisch School of the Arts at New York University, her bio in the original program for *Rent* listed no previous theater credits, identifying her only as a "singer/songwriter who performs with her own band throughout the New York City club circuit." She left *Rent* in July of 1997 and followed it up with *Still I Can't Be Still*, the first of several solo albums; she performed live concerts and took part in Lilith Fair before returning to musical theater in 2000 with Andrew Lippa's *The Wild Party* (Off-Broadway at the Manhattan Theatre Club). In that show she was again teamed with one of her original *Rent* castmates, Taye Diggs; the two were married in 2003 and have a son, Walker. Her next new musical was a stage adaptation of the film *Summer of 42*, presented regionally at the Goodspeed Opera House in Connecticut. In 2001 she played Sheila in the City Center Encores! concert presentation of *Hair* and then returned to Broadway, taking over the role of Amneris in the Disney/Elton John musical *Aida*. (Coincidentally, she was replacing Sherie Rene Scott, who had been her own first replacement in the Broadway cast of *Rent*.) Off-Broadway appearances include *The Vagina Monologues* and *See What I Wanna See*. In addition to the movie of *Rent*, her big-screen credits include *Kissing Jessica Stein*, *Ask the Dust*, and *Enchanted*; the most notable of her many TV appearances was the recurring role of Shelby Corcoran on *Glee* (2010–13). She has continued to concertize and record, and she starred in the 2008 London concert version of the musical *Chess*, in which her character was part of a romantic triangle with Josh Groban and her original *Rent* costar Adam Pascal. She was reunited with another *Rent* cohort, Anthony Rapp, as well as director Michael Greif for the Broadway musical *If/Then* in 2014—the year that marked her divorce from Diggs. Menzel received Tony nominations for *Rent* and *If/Then* and won for *Wicked*. She also performed Best Original Song nominee (and eventual winner) "Let It Go" at the 2014 Academy Awards ceremony, at which John Travolta mistakenly introduced her as "Adele Dazeem"—a much-joked-about gaffe that only added to her burgeoning celebrity. In 2016 she announced her engagement to actor Aaron Lohr, who had played the role of Gordon in the movie of *Rent*.

Aiko Nakasone (Alexi Darling, Roger's Mom, and Others)

The only Asian-American member of the original cast was also one of its most accomplished dancers; she was featured in the dance sequences, and she earned laughs for her role as the high-energy television producer Alexi Darling, who continually leaves importuning messages on Mark's answering machine. Nakasone had made her Broadway debut a year earlier in the first revival of *How to Succeed in Business Without Really Trying*, starring Matthew Broderick and Megan Mullally, a show on which she served as Dance Captain. She had also been in the casts of the national tours of *The Who's*

Tommy and *Starlight Express*. After her run in *Rent*, she was in the ensemble of the Broadway revival of *The Rocky Horror Show*, along with her *Rent* cast-mates Daphne Rubin-Vega (whom she also understudied as Magenta) and Kristen Lee Kelly. She was one of two Assistant Choreographers on the 1997 Broadway show *Dream*, a revue built around the lyrics of Johnny Mercer; the choreographer was Wayne Cilento, for whom she had danced in *How to Succeed* and *Tommy*. More recently, Nakasone has performed regionally in Steppenwolf Theatre productions of *after the quake* and *Kafka on the Shore*, both works adapted by director Frank Galati from books by the Japanese novelist Haruki Murakami. In 2001, Nakasone studied Bikram Yoga with its founder, Bikram Choudhury, in Beverly Hills; this led to a second career, and in association with Troy Myers, also a Broadway veteran, she has since opened successful Bikram Yoga centers in Brooklyn, downtown New York, and Pleasanton, California.

Timothy Britten Parker (Gordon, The Man, Mr. Grey)

Born in 1962, Timothy Britten Parker comes from a large theatrical family; he has three siblings and four half-siblings, many of them in show business. Like his best known sister, the actress Sarah Jessica Parker, Timothy (then known as Toby, which friends still call him) made his Broadway debut as a child actor: he appeared as an understudy in a revival of *The Innocents* (a theatrical adaptation of Henry James's novel *The Turn of the Screw*) and later as a member of the ensemble cast of *Runaways*, Elizabeth Swados's musical about runaway children and teens on the streets of America's cities. He performed in nearly fifty Off- and Off-Off-Broadway plays and musicals before joining *Rent*. A longtime close friend of Jonathan Larson, he had been in early readings of the show, as well as the workshop of Larson's *Superbia* at Playwrights Horizons in 1990. Following his run in *Rent* on Broadway, Parker has been almost continually involved with two roles to which he has returned frequently over a period of many years. He recurred periodically as a forensics technician on the long-running TV series *Law and Order* (appearing with *Rent* costar Jesse L. Martin) and, since 2001, has played the role of Doctor Dillamond in the hit musical *Wicked* all over the country: beginning with the First National Company in 2005, he has played multiple engagements in the part for over ten years, appearing with both national tours, the Chicago and Los Angeles companies, and as a replacement in the Broadway cast. He has also been seen in films including *Joey Breaker* and *Quiz Show* and has made guest appearances on numerous TV series. With a group of their friends, Parker and his brother, director/playwright Pippin Parker, were founders of the influential New York theater company Naked Angels.

Adam Pascal (Roger)

Pascal was born in the Bronx in 1970 and raised in Woodbury, a town on Long Island, by his mother and stepfather; Idina Menzel lived nearby and they were childhood friends. He attended the New York Institute of Technology and worked as a personal trainer while pursuing his interest in rock music. Famously, Pascal was in no way pursuing an acting career when he was persuaded to audition for *Rent*; his only acting experience had been during a brief stay at Stagedoor Manor (the prestigious theater camp in upstate New York that inspired the movie *Camp*), where as a pre-teen he performed in the comedy *A Thurber Carnival* and the musical *Cabaret*—playing a Nazi and singing "Tomorrow Belongs to Me." He has never pursued formal training in acting or voice. As a kid he was a fan of hard rock and heavy metal bands; he developed his voice by turning the stereo up high and singing at the top of his lungs along with singers like Ronnie James Dio, Freddie Mercury, and Steve Perry. (Don't try this at home; imitating that type of singer without a grounding in vocal technique and proper breath support could be a recipe for disaster. Somehow, though, Pascal had all the right instincts and figured out how to make his voice work on his own.) He played and sang in several bands with friends from school; the one that got the most attention was called Mute. In 1995, he was living on the Upper West Side of Manhattan; Mute had just broken up and he didn't have a lot going on, so he was open to suggestions when he learned, through Menzel, about the auditions for *Rent*. She knew they were having trouble finding a Roger and urged Pascal to go in; he had never been to an audition before. Pascal brought authenticity to the character of Roger, like himself a rock guitarist/singer/songwriter; Larson and Greif were drawn to his raw honesty as well as his good looks and warm, powerful voice, so they decided to take a chance on an untried actor. Their faith in him proved canny, and his moving performance in the role was rewarded with a Tony nomination and a Theatre World Award, as well as an Obie Award (administered by the Village Voice) for his work in the original Off-Broadway run. Still, when he left the show and attempted to pursue his new career as an actor, Pascal initially found his lack of training and technique were holding him back; he had numerous unsuccessful auditions for film and TV roles. His work on *Rent* had earned him a devoted following in musical theater circles, however, and though he had initially not intended to pursue a continuing Broadway career, he ended up coming back to the Main Stem as Radames, the male lead in the 2000 Disney production of Tim Rice and Elton John's rock musical version of *Aida*. Coincidentally, that show, like *Rent*, is based on a classic Italian opera, and Pascal was once again playing a rock version of an iconic operatic tenor role. He played opposite the Amneris of Sherie Rene Scott (who had also been the second Maureen in *Rent* on Broadway). She and her husband, Kurt Deutsch, had their own record label, Sh-K Boom Records, which specialized in cast albums and solo discs by Broadway performers; they were instrumental in relaunching Pascal's career as a rock musician and songwriter, this time for a wider audience, and produced his first solo album. More recently, he started his own label to produce *Blinding Light*, an album by his new band Larry and Me, which he formed with pianist Larry Edoff. Both in collaboration with Edoff and as a solo act with a small band, Pascal has enjoyed a successful career as a musician in smaller live venues as well as on recordings. His singing finally opened doors to roles in films, including *School of Rock*, *Temptation*, and *Falling Star*. He played a more serious acting role in *American Primitive* (also known as *Wild About Harry*) in addition, of course, to reprising Roger for the movie of *Rent*. Recent film projects have included *Punk Is Dead* and *Alleluia! The Devil's Carnival*. Still, his widest fame and recognition have continued to be in the realm of stage musicals; after *Aida*, he returned to Broadway several more times, for an encore engagement in *Rent* as well as taking over roles in the long-running revivals of two classic musicals by John Kander and Fred Ebb: *Cabaret* (playing the Emcee this time) and *Chicago* (in which he was one of a long and diverse parade of celebrities to take on the role of lawyer Billy Flynn). Pascal played Roger for the last time in a 2009–10 touring production of *Rent* with Anthony Rapp; the two had become fast friends over their years of doing the show together and have also performed a joint cabaret act. Following the tour, he took over the lead role of Huey in the Broadway musical *Memphis* when its originator, Chad Kimball, left the cast in 2011; he stayed with the show until it closed almost a year later. Pascal has also been much associated with the vocally and histrionically demanding role of Freddy Trumper in the musical *Chess*. He did not originate the part (the show dates from the eighties), but he has done it in two high-profile concert mountings, including a 2009 British version where he played opposite Menzel and Josh Groban; that performance was televised and is available on DVD. Other TV work includes episodes of *Cold Case* and *The Backyardigans*. Since 1998, Adam Pascal has been married to Cybele Chivian, a playwright. They have two sons (Lennon and Montgomery), and together they own Cybele's Free To Eat, a gluten- and allergen-free packaged foods company. After seeing the M. Night Shyamalan film *Unbreakable*, Pascal had a dream about it being made into a musical; following several unsuccessful attempts he was finally able to get Shyamalan to grant him the rights to the property. He initially wanted to develop it as a project for himself as a performer, but after the songwriters he approached turned it down he decided to write the score himself and has been working on it on and off for a couple of years. In 2016, Pascal returned to Broadway in two different shows. Early in the year, he starred in *Disaster!*, a short-lived musical by Seth Rudetsky and Jack Plotnick spoofing 1970s disaster flicks. He was then tapped to join the cast of the hit musical *Something Rotten!* as a rock-singing William Shakespeare, a part he played for the last few weeks of the Broadway run and then on tour.

Anthony Rapp (Mark)

Though only twenty-three when he was first cast in *Rent*, Anthony Rapp had the longest theater résumé of any of the principal players, having begun as a very busy child actor. He played parts like the title role in *Oliver!* (four times) and Tiny Tim in *A Christmas Carol*, making his professional debut before the age of ten in the Chicago production of *Evita*. Shortly thereafter he was cast opposite Michael York in *The Little Prince and the Aviator*, which unfortunately closed during previews on Broadway; at ten, he played Louis Leonowens in Yul Brynner's final national tour of *The King and I*. He also earned a scholarship to the prestigious Interlochen Arts Camp. Rapp's older brother is the playwright/director Adam Rapp. The family lived in Joliet, Illinois, and the boys' mother, Mary, was very supportive of young Anthony's career, often traveling with him for stage and film jobs. At fifteen, he appeared on Broadway in *Precious Sons*, winning an Outer Critics Circle Award; he went on to play Ben in the original Broadway production of John Guare's *Six Degrees of Separation*, later recreating the same role in the movie version. By the time *Rent* opened, he had also done the films *Adventures in Babysitting*, *Dazed and Confused*, *School Ties*, and *David Searching*, and had been in several Off-Broadway plays, including *Sophistry*, *The Destiny of Me*, and *Raised in Captivity*. In the months following the opening and sensational initial success of *Rent*, as he continued to perform the show eight times a week, Rapp found himself also dealing with his mother's illness and eventual death from cancer; he chronicled this tumultuous period of his life in his book *Without You: A Memoir of Love, Loss, and the Musical RENT*, published in 2006. He later adapted the book as a one-man show, which he has performed in various theatrical and cabaret settings both in America and abroad; a recording was issued on CD in 2012. The book and its theatrical version also dealt with his coming out; an interview in *Metro Weekly* had proclaimed him "one of the first openly gay men on Broadway," though Rapp said in a later interview that he preferred the term "queer." He played the title role in director Michael Mayer's 1999 Broadway production of *You're a Good Man, Charlie Brown* (the show that made Kristin Chenoweth a star) and toured as Seymour in *Little Shop of Horrors*. Still, *Rent* continued to come back into his life. He did a stint in one of the national touring companies, performing the show before family and friends in Chicago, and then went on to open the London production in 1998; he recreated the role of Mark in the film version in 2005. Along with Adam Pascal, he went back into the Broadway cast in July of 2007 and stayed for over two months; the two then reprised their roles yet again for a 2009 touring production, known as the Mark Company. Rapp also directed a production of the show in South Africa. He was assistant director (to Michael Greif) on Tom Kitt and Brian Yorkey's acclaimed musical *Next to Normal*, having previously played the doctor role in early showcase and workshop versions of the piece. Kitt and Yorkey subsequently wrote a role for him in their next Broadway show, *If/Then* (2014), which reunited him with both director Greif and his original *Rent* colleague Idina Menzel. Rapp's regional acting credits include his brother Adam's play *Nocturne* at the Berkeley Repertory Theatre. He has also appeared Off-Broadway in the Second Stage's revival of Richard Nelson's *Some Americans Abroad*. He played the title role in the rock musical *Hedwig and the Angry Inch* at the Brighton Fringe and, in 2015, returned to *Rent* once more as creative consultant to a version performed by a troupe of young American actors at the Edinburgh Festival Fringe (where he had also performed *Without You* three years earlier). He has appeared numerous times on television, including *The X-Files*, *Psych: The Musical*, and two different guest roles on *Law and Order: Special Victims Unit*. Film projects include *Road Trip*, *A Beautiful Mind*, *Blackbird*, *The Other Woman*, and several shorts. In 2015, he was one of the founders of BroadwayCon, an annual New York convention for fans of Broadway theater; the first annual installment featured a reunion of original cast members from *Rent*. Recent projects have included highly acclaimed cabaret engagements, both solo and in a joint act with Adam Pascal; they played an extended engagement at Feinstein's/54 Below in the fall of 2016.

Daphne Rubin-Vega (Mimi)

Rubin-Vega was born in 1969 in Panama City, Panama. After her parents' divorce, her mother moved with her children to New York; she remarried but died when Daphne was ten, and the girl was raised mainly by her stepfather, a writer. She recalled in an interview that her stepfather had season tickets to the Metropolitan Opera, so she had some familiarity with the Mimì of *La bohème* when she first heard about the very different version she would be auditioning for in *Rent*. Rubin-Vega was interested in acting—though not specifically musical theater—from an early age, and she also pursued a career as a singer, performing and recording with the band Pajama Party as early as 1989. She studied acting with the LAByrinth Theater Company and the noted New York teacher William Esper, and performed with the live comedy group

El Barrio USA, before being cast in *Rent*, which she joined first for the 1994 workshop production. She felt immediately that the show would be something important, and said: "I was so thrilled to be working on this project because I knew it was just so special. Because it reflected people who I identified with at the time. . . . I knew those people. I knew what that was. I grew up in the Village. I'd been around the block." For a 2011 *Playbill* interview, she told Jonathan Mandell that she was proud of the way *Rent* had attracted unusually diverse audiences to Broadway, saying, "We brought in both the blue hairs and the pink hairs." She was the first of the original cast members to depart the company, playing her last performance on April 5, 1997, before leaving to record an album and begin work on a film. She earned a Theatre World Award and a Tony nomination for her Mimi and followed up her success in the show with roles in several films, including *Flawless*, *Union Square*, and *Jack Goes Boating*, which was based on an Off-Broadway play she had done with Philip Seymour Hoffman. For her role in the film *Wild Things* with Kevin Bacon, she won the Blockbuster Award for Best Supporting Actress in a Suspense Thriller. She has also had success as a solo singer, landing songs on the dance music charts. Her first full-length album of original music, *Souvenir*, was recorded in 2001, but its release was derailed when her label, Mercury Records, was purchased by Seagram, which dropped the project; the CD eventually had a limited release for Broadway Cares. *Redemption Songs*, her second solo CD, came out in 2006 from Sh-K Boom Records. Her numerous TV appearances have included recurring roles on *Smash* and *Hustling*, and she has returned four times to Broadway. She played Magenta in the 2000 revival of *The Rocky Horror Show* and Conchita in Nilo Cruz's play *Anna in the Tropics*, which in 2003 earned her a second Tony nomination; like *Rent*, that play was also awarded the Pulitzer Prize for Drama, giving Rubin-Vega the rare distinction of having appeared in two works that earned that prestigious honor. The play's director, Emily Mann, also cast her as Stella in the 2012 Broadway revival of Tennessee Williams's classic *A Streetcar Named Desire*. (In that show, she got a bit of publicity after grabbing a cell phone away from a first-row audience member who was trying to take a picture of costar Blair Underwood; what is now thought of as pulling "a Patti LuPone" should perhaps more rightly be termed "a Rubin-Vega"!) Her other Broadway role was Fantine in the first (2006) revival of *Les Misérables*. In the spring of 2016, she appeared Off-Broadway at the Signature Theatre as Inez in the play *Daphne's Dive* by Quiara Alegría Hudes. As of this writing, she is working on *Miss You Like Hell*, a new musical by Hudes and Erin McKeown that premiered at the La Jolla Playhouse, and her own one-woman autobiographical show *FUQs: Frequently Unanswered Questions*. Rubin-Vega and her husband Tommy Costanzo live in New York's Chelsea neighborhood; they have one child.

Gwen Stewart (Mrs. Jefferson, Woman with Bags, and Others)

Although Stewart had substantial acting responsibilities in the show, playing Joanne's mother and the angry bag lady in the St. Mark's Place scene, it is for one of the "others" that she is most vividly remembered: the singer of the exhilarating, high-lying, Gospel-flavored female solo in "Seasons of Love." She has the distinction of being the only original cast member to appear in the same role in both the opening night and the closing performance on Broadway twelve years later, which was filmed. (Rodney Hicks was also in both performances but had switched from his original ensemble track to the role of Benny.) Before being cast in *Rent*, the actress/singer from Newark, New Jersey, had twice been a winner on *Showtime at the Apollo* and had done two other Broadway shows: *Starmites* in 1989 and the short-lived musical *Truly Blessed* the next year. She had also appeared Off-Broadway in *Suds*, a jukebox musical set in a laundromat and built around popular songs of the sixties. At regional theaters she had been in productions of *Ain't Misbehavin'* (in the Nell Carter role), *The Wiz* (playing Evillene, the Wicked Witch character), *Avenue X*, *Dreamgirls*, and *Abyssinia*, as well as the role of Alice in *Big River*, which she would later reprise in the 2003 Broadway revival. Stewart was the last person to join the original cast of *Rent*; though they had auditioned many people, Larson was insistent that the "Seasons" solo had to be "a showstopper," and wasn't willing to settle for anything less. Rehearsals had already begun when Stewart was scheduled for an audition with the team; it was a stormy day in Manhattan and she nearly decided to skip the appointment and turn around and go home. It was lucky that she didn't. She sang a gospel song called "He Looks Beyond My Faults," and sang scales with Tim Weil at the piano to demonstrate her (extensive) vocal range; Michael Greif asked if she would have any issues with playing a homeless woman, and she said she didn't as long as it was done tastefully and not to make fun of the character. By the time she got home there was a message on her machine offering her the role; she joined rehearsals the next day. Once the show had moved to Broadway, the cast was often called upon to do early morning interviews and TV performances. Stewart was living in New Jersey at the time, quite a commute from Times Square, and in the interest of getting enough rest and making sure not to be late for an early call, she took to occasionally sleeping on the floor of her dressing room. One morning David Santana, the hair and makeup consultant, showed up at the theater early and discovered her there; he informed her she was too important now to be doing that. From that point on the producers provided her with a hotel room whenever she needed it. In the fall of 1997, a year and a half into the run on Broadway, Stewart switched to the principal role of Joanne, taking over for Fredi Walker. However, when she later returned to the Broadway company on two separate occasions, it was to play her original track, which she reprised with the Mark Company on tour in 2009 and again at the Hollywood Bowl in 2010. Also on the West Coast, she played Sylvia in Musical Theatre West's production of *All Shook Up*, winning the L.A. Stage Alliance Ovation Award for Best Featured Actress in a Musical in 2008. Film credits include *Down to Earth* and *The Goods: Live Hard, Sell Hard*; she has also made guest appearances on numerous TV series including *Moesha*, *24*, *Charmed*, *Law and Order: Special Victims Unit*, and *True Blood*.

Byron Utley (Christmas Caroler, Mr. Jefferson, a Pastor, and Others)

With his deep, resonant voice, Byron Utley was most notable in the show as Joanne's stern father and as the male "Seasons of Love" soloist; he also understudied Tom Collins. Utley stayed in the Broadway company longer than any of the other original cast members. He had made his Broadway debut almost twenty years earlier, playing a sergeant and understudying Cleavant Derricks as Hud in the 1977 revival of *Hair*, directed by Tom O'Horgan, who had staged the first Broadway production. Two years later, he was seen as a dancer in Milos Forman's film version of that show. He subsequently returned to the Great White Way in the musicals *Reggae* and *Big Deal* and in *Death and the King's Horseman*, a play with music by the Nigerian playwright/director Wole Soyinka, presented at Lincoln Center. Utley has substantial regional theater acting credits including Shakespeare (the title role in *Othello*, Ross in *Macbeth*, and Puck in *A Midsummer Night's Dream*) at such venues as Hartford Stage, the Studio Arena Theatre, North Shore Music Theatre, and the Williamstown Theatre Festival. Film roles prior to *Rent* included appearances in *Wall Street*, *Awakenings*, *Night and the City*, and Spike Lee's *Malcolm X*. He has also made appearances on several TV series, including *Ghostwriter*, *Wonderworks*, *NYPD Blue*, and two episodes of *Law and Order*, and has performed internationally as a guest vocalist. Since his run in *Rent*, he has not returned to Broadway; his most recent film credits are *The Interpreter*, *Fair Game*, and the role of Frederick Douglass in *Freedom* (2014).

Fredi Walker-Browne (Joanne)

Born in 1962, Walker studied at New York University and made her Broadway debut in *Rent*. Other musical theater credits include productions of *The Buddy Holly Story* and *Little Shop of Horrors*, as well as the role of Rafiki in the national tour of Disney's blockbuster *The Lion King*. Before she did *Rent*, she was already starting to direct her own projects as well; she has focused on teaching and directing in recent years while making occasional returns to acting, including a guest appearance on *Law and Order* and, in 2012, a recurring role on the Showtime series *The Big C.* She has done numerous commercials and voiceovers and has modeled plus-size fashions for *Mode* magazine and Lane Bryant; she became a spokesperson for women's body issues and beauty, and was interviewed on the subject for *20/20.* Walker-Browne returned to NYU as a professional director, working with students in the Department of Dramatic Writing, and has completed several screenplays of her own. Other directing includes the Post Theatre Company production of *The Most Fabulous Story Ever Told.* She now teaches at the Music and Art Academy in Matawan and at her own studio in Neptune, New Jersey. For a Playbill.com interview on the occasion of the twentieth anniversary of *Rent,* she told Michael Gioia: "I carry and keep a picture of Jonathan everywhere I teach because I want him to see, and I want him to watch. I can only imagine what he'd be saying when the parents of people who were sleeping on the street bring me their kids to study. I'm like, 'This is crazy . . . That's why I put him there . . . because I want him to see it: 'Look what you did. Look what you gave us.' . . . I don't know what he would say, but I'm hoping that he loves it. I hope that he's seeing it all."

8

"How Did We Get Here?"

A Synopsis of the Story of *Rent*

T he plot of *Rent* involves interwoven storylines about eight different principal characters; though it's inspired by *La bohème*, it's more complex than the opera's story. With very little spoken dialogue, some of the exposition comes in songs where different characters are singing different things at the same time; important information can be difficult to hear. For these and other reasons, audience members often say they find the story confusing or hard to follow, at least the first one or two times they see the show.

To help with this, the *Playbill* for the Broadway production included a page with the heading "A note about the plot of *Rent*," which gave a brief summary of the backstory and the major events of Act One, followed by a two-sentence intro to Act Two. It was followed by a two-page spread entitled "RENT WHO'S WHO." This showed photos of the eight principal characters (actually nine photos, as there were two of Angel: one in and one out of drag) with lines connecting them and brief phrases defining the relationships and who was involved with whom. (The photos were frequently updated to reflect changes in the cast.)

For anyone who needs or is interested in a little more detail (well, okay, a lot more detail), the following synopsis, keyed to the titles of the musical numbers, is your guide to sorting out the relationships and following the plot strands of that very eventful Christmas Eve, and the year following. Descriptions of the staging refer to the original production, directed by Michael Greif.

Act One

The evening begins informally, without the traditional Broadway overture, rising curtain, or even a blackout. Members of the band and the crew are seen moving about the stage as the audience takes their seats, and the five musicians gradually take their positions under the raised platform on stage right. When the audience is mostly seated, the actors start to enter, beginning with Roger, who plugs his guitar into the onstage amp and works on setting levels for a moment before sitting down on one of the tables center stage. The other actors quickly come in from all sides, filling the stage; down center, Mark sets up his 16 mm movie camera and then, turning to the audience, begins to speak to us directly.

He tells us the story begins on Christmas Eve. (The official script does not specify the year. In the film it was moved back to 1988; the Off-Broadway revival had him say 1991.) He gives us the exact location: the corner of Avenue B and 11th Street; the loft where he and Roger live is the top floor of a building that used to house a music publishing factory. He explains how they are coping with the lack of heat and electricity and tells us there is a tent city of homeless people in the vacant lot next door before turning the camera on Roger and telling him to smile. It's nine o'clock in the evening.

Tune Up # 1

The first musical number begins with Mark expressing his plan to throw out his previous attempts at making a film and "shoot without a script." He tells us that Roger, a former drug addict, has just come through six months of withdrawal; not having played his guitar for a year, he is having trouble tuning it.

Voice Mail # 1

When their phone rings, Roger is relieved that an incoming call is saving him from having to answer Mark's questions and talk about himself on camera. They decide to screen the call and the answering machine picks up. (These were the days before most people had cell phones or voicemail.) The caller is Mark's mother, Mrs. Cohen; establishing a convention that will be used periodically throughout the evening, she is played by one of the young ensemble members, appearing in a spotlight on another part of the stage and speak/singing her message in a mode that suggests operatic recitative. Concerned about whether the machine is actually recording, she says she's calling to send the family's love and to say they will miss him the next day. It's a secular Jewish family; the word Christmas is never mentioned, but there is clearly a family celebration going on with Mark's sister Cindy and her kids in attendance. Mrs. Cohen refers to a hot plate she had sent Mark as a gift and then offers sympathy over Mark's having been "dumped" by his girlfriend Maureen—who has recently left him for a woman.

Tune Up # 2

Mark turns again to Roger and asks him speak to the camera and tell the "folks at home" what he's doing, but once again Roger is saved by the phone ringing. Tom Collins, one of their former roommates, is calling from the pay phone on the street corner downstairs. When they hear that it's Collins, Mark picks up and he and Roger hold the phone between their ears to talk to their old friend. Since their building doesn't have a working buzzer, the established routine is for a visitor to call, and then Mark will throw a set of keys out the window so the guest can let himself in. The keys are contained in a leather pouch, which Mark throws down; Collins catches it but sees two menacing figures approaching him on the street carrying clubs. He says he might be "detained" and then is mugged by the two men.

Mark and Roger are confused and can't tell what's happening, but they are immediately distracted by another phone call. This time it's Benjamin Coffin III, called Benny—another of their former roommates and now their landlord, who had let them go a year without paying rent but is now demanding it. He tells them he'll be there in a few minutes.

The threatened arrival of the landlord is the first direct clue that what we are watching may be a new version of the story of *La bohème*. For audiences who are familiar with the earlier work, Roger, who has gotten his guitar working, confirms it by playing a brief excerpt from Musetta's Waltz, one of the most famous tunes from the opera. But he doesn't get far before the electricity goes out: not surprising, since it comes through an extension cord snaking out the window to scavenge somebody else's power supply.

Rent

This crisis launches the two friends into the musical's title song. They sing of the near impossibility of generating creative work amidst the chaos of their lives: no money to pay rent, no electricity or heat, surrounded by homelessness, disease, and unbelievable headlines. Roger is also emotionally blocked and feels he can no longer write music. To get warm, they start shoving papers into their "illegal wood-burning stove" (often represented by a large metal trash can!). The papers they are burning are Mark's old screenplays and posters for Roger's past gigs in rock clubs.

As the guys wonder how they are going to pay the rent, lights come up on the payphone again and we meet Joanne, a young lawyer, who is trying to have a conversation with Maureen. Joanne has replaced Mark not only as Maureen's lover but also as her "production manager." She is trying without much success to set up the sound equipment for a show Maureen is planning to give later that night on the lot next door: a performance art piece protesting Benny's plan to evict the homeless people living on the lot. Though Joanne admits that she herself is not a "theatre person," she begs Maureen not to call Mark to help—but Maureen hangs up on her and does just that.

Nearby, we see a woozy Collins coping with the aftermath of his mugging and trying not to black out. Then another phone call: Benny is talking to his wife, Alison, a rich girl from Connecticut, expressing disappointment over the way Mark and Roger have turned on him. He says his plans will eventually benefit all of them and sings the refrain "Forces are gathering" as the various simultaneous scenes interweave and the music builds. The characters lament their inability to let go of past pain and make connections, and affirm their determination to continue the good fight in a world where "Everything is rent!" (A word that, significantly, also means ripped open or torn apart.)

You Okay, Honey?

On the street, a homeless man sings a little bit of a Christmas song, ending with a bleak joke. Angel is sitting on the Christmas tree sculpture on stage left, playing his drum—actually a plastic pickle tub turned upside down—presumably hoping for donations from passersby. Collins limps on, moaning, and Angel, who can tell he's been mugged, asks how he's doing and introduces himself. Collins says the thieves didn't get any cash (he didn't have any) but did take his coat—minus one sleeve that tore off, and which he is still wearing. Angel offers to help him out, get him a band-aid and a new coat, and take him out to eat, claiming he's got plenty of money; Collins takes a good look at the young man and is immediately attracted. Angel tells him he's going to a Life Support meeting at 9:30—for people with AIDS. Collins reveals that he too has the disease, so Angel insists that he come along, although Collins knows Mark and Roger are still expecting him. Angel says he's going to "change"—but we don't know yet how big a transformation this is going to entail—and the two go off together.

Tune Up # 3

Up in the loft, Mark tells Roger he's leaving to help with Maureen's equipment. He invites Roger to come to her show later that night, and to dinner, but Roger says he can't afford it. Mark reminds him to take his AZT: an AIDS medication. On his way out, he tells us that Roger's girlfriend, whose name was April, killed herself in their bathroom by slitting her wrists—after leaving him a note informing him she had the disease.

One Song Glory

Left alone, Roger fiddles with his guitar for a moment, then pensively puts it aside. He sings of his determination to write one truly great song before he succumbs to the disease, regretting the opportunities he wasted with his band, and the loss of his love. He wants to write a song about love and go out in a "blaze of glory." But he's interrupted by a knock at the door.

Light My Candle

Roger answers the door, thinking it's Mark returning to get something he forgot, but is surprised to see a beautiful young woman at the door. The power is still out and the girl, whose name is Mimi, needs a match to light her candle. Roger lights it for her and notices she is shivering; he tells her she reminds him of April. Wanting an excuse to spend more time with him, Mimi blows out the candle when he's not looking and asks him to light it again. After a moment of looking at each other, she leaves, but almost immediately knocks on the door again; she thinks she dropped her stash (of heroin) and asks him to help her look for it. They grope around on the dark floor and she flirts with him; he knows he's seen her before and she asks if he's ever been to a place called the Cat Scratch Club. He suddenly remembers seeing her perform there—dancing in handcuffs. He recognizes her shaking as a sign of addiction, and tells her he used to be a junkie as well. She blows the candle out and he lights it again; he finds her stash and pockets it, then playfully blows out her candle and tells her he's out of matches. He takes her cold hand in his, and she asks him to dance; they exchange names and she reaches behind him and pulls her drugs out of his back pocket, then flirtatiously runs out.

Voice Mail # 2

In Joanne and Maureen's apartment, the phone rings. Maureen, whom we can see only in silhouette upstage (her grand entrance is being saved for later) recites the outgoing message, which advertises her performance that night—entitled *Over the Moon*—and the party afterward at the Life Café. The callers are Joanne's high-powered parents, played by two of the ensemble actors. They leave her a message about their holiday plans, speak/singing how to get in touch with them if she needs to; her father also reminds her that her mother, a judge, is scheduled for "confirmation hearings" on January 10—so that is the deadline by which they expect Joanne to extract herself from her lesbian relationship. They instruct her on what to wear to the hearings before hanging up.

Today 4 U

There's a slight continuity issue in the storytelling here. When we last saw Mark, he was bidding Roger goodbye and leaving the loft to go to the lot to help with Maureen's sound system, and we will see him there shortly in an upcoming scene. But now we are back in the loft and Mark seems to be there with Roger as if he never left. (This is the result of some reordering of scenes that happened during the development of the show; director Michael Greif has explained that they justified it in rehearsal by deciding Mark had bumped into Collins on the way out the door and had then come back upstairs with him, but there's no clue to this in the script.) At any rate, Mark introduces us to Collins, who has finally made it to the apartment! He is carrying Angel's pickle tub/drum, now full of much-needed groceries they have bought for Mark and Roger. In a brief exchange of dialogue, we learn that the guys haven't seen Collins for seven months; he was at MIT (the Massachusetts

Mark, played by Chris McNiff, holds the pickle tub as Angel (Tyler Jent) sings "Today 4 U." Staples Players, 2011.   *Kerry Long*

Institute of Technology, a prestigious university), presumably working on a graduate degree, but was kicked out for his "theory of actual reality." (We will later learn that he rigged the school's virtual-reality equipment to blow up as part of an anti-AIDS demonstration urging students to "Act Up.") He tells them that he'll soon be teaching at New York University, and then introduces Angel, who makes a grand diva entrance: this is the first time we have seen him in drag.

Angel immediately launches into his big song (one of two numbers in the show for which the onstage band doesn't play; the heavily synthesized dance-club style accompaniment is prerecorded). He is waving twenty-dollar bills around, and the song explains how he got them: a rich lady saw him drumming on the street and hired him for a highly unusual assignment. She had been kept awake every night by her neighbor's barking dog: an Akita, named Evita. She offered Angel a thousand dollars to play his "drum" loudly and incessantly on the theory that this would cause Evita to bark herself to death—and he was so effective that the dog actually jumped out the apartment window, an apparent suicide. Any reservations the audience may have about the plausibility of this story are swept aside by Angel's virtuoso performance: singing up a storm, jumping up on the table and dancing with athletic abandon, and using his drumsticks to beat out a marvelously intricate percussion solo on everything in sight.

You'll See

Following the applause, Benny immediately shows up, and we hear him rudely shoo a homeless man off a Range Rover in front of the building. Mark quickly fills us in on his backstory: their former roommate, Benny now owns the building and the lot and is planning on developing it into a "cyberstudio." (In the brief synopsis printed in the Broadway program, we are told that he purchased them "with the help of his new wealthy father-in-law," but Mark's actual line in the script says he "bought the building and the lot next door from his father-in-law"—the word "from" suggesting that Mr. Grey already owned them. Does this mean Benny happened to meet his future wife because she was the daughter of his landlord? And if so, where did he get the money to buy the building? The interpretation that the two men bought the properties together, with Grey supplying capital to help facilitate his new son-in-law's business venture, seems most likely.) At any rate, Benny has come to collect a full year's rent, which he had previously told Mark and Roger they wouldn't have to pay, and they chide him for abandoning his community and his idealism. He dangles the prospect of the cyberarts studio, which he will make available to them for their own creative work, and promises to let them out of paying the rent on one condition: that they agree to persuade Maureen to cancel that night's performance—which he knows is a protest against his expulsion of the homeless people who live in the lot. Like the earlier "Light My Candle," this musical scene masterfully weaves dialogue and recitative into a melody that builds and surges. Benny leaves without knowing for sure whether Mark and Roger will take the bait. Collins and Angel invite them to come along to the Life Support meeting; Roger declines, and Mark says he still has to help Maureen save her show: Benny or no Benny, he clearly has no intention of asking her to cancel it. He leaves for the lot, and Collins and Angel head for the meeting, leaving a depressed Roger alone in the apartment.

Tango: Maureen

Mark shows up on the lot, where Joanne is still struggling to get the sound system operating. Dismayed that Maureen went against her wishes and called him for help, she tells him she doesn't need him because she already hired an engineer. But the woman is three hours late, so Joanne relents and asks him to stay.

As he works on the equipment, the two are uncomfortable being together, and yet in spite of themselves they start to commiserate, awkwardly at first, on the trials and tribulations of being in a relationship with the difficult Maureen. Mark lets Joanne know that Maureen cheated on him when they were together, which makes Joanne fear the same will happen again. They begin to tango together as they sing what turns into an old-school musical-comedy number about the power Maureen holds over them and the attraction they feel toward her despite the way she keeps them constantly dangling and on edge. By the time Mark has gotten the sound system up and running—and simultaneously shaken Joanne's confidence in her relationship—he feels much better, and she feels lousy.

Life Support

The scene shifts to the meeting of Life Support, a group for people living with HIV and AIDS. The leader, Paul (played by one of the ensemble members), welcomes Collins, Angel, and several others; Mark stumbles in late and awkwardly tries to tell them he doesn't have the virus and is just there to observe. The group starts to sing an affirmation about living one day at a time and not regretting anything, but one of them, named Gordon, challenges Paul, saying he actually does regret his low T-cell count. Still, as Paul helps him recognize, he feels better than he has all year and has lived three years longer than his doctors predicted; the group begins to sing "No Day But Today" as the scene shifts . . .

Out Tonight

In her apartment (suggested by a catwalk high above the stage), Mimi is getting dressed and primping for a night on the town. While dancing a sexy dance on the railings and the staircase, she sings a fierce song about looking for danger and adventure; we get a sense of what her performances at the Cat Scratch Club must be like as she descends the stairs toward Roger's apartment, belting all the way. She enters his apartment and aggressively begins to seduce him: moving his guitar out of the way, climbing up on his table, and flinging all his props and papers to the floor before kissing him hungrily.

Another Day

Feeling invaded, Roger angrily pushes Mimi away and tells her to leave. He says that if the time were different maybe they could have been together, but "the fire's out" and he can't handle her. (He also repeats to himself the refrain "I should tell you," but he can't bring himself to tell her the real reason he feels they shouldn't be together, which is that he has HIV.) Not one to be put off without a fight, Mimi insists on living for tonight, forgetting regret, letting go, and opening up to love; her plea melds with the "no day but today" credo of the support group, still onstage; their voices join hers as the song builds. But Roger continues to resist and lash out at her in counterpoint until she runs out.

Will I?

Roger, now alone, repeats his determination to write one great song. A young man (Steve) from the Life Support group begins a soaring new melody, plaintively asking "Will I lose my dignity?" and wondering if anyone will take care of him, or if maybe the disease is just a nightmare he will wake up from tomorrow. The rest of the ensemble, in four groups, repeats his lines in the form of a round, and the song builds to a heartbreakingly beautiful crescendo—until Roger grabs his coat and finally leaves the apartment.

On the Street

A trio of ensemble members playing street people starts to sing the same facetious little Christmas song we heard the homeless man begin earlier.

A "squeegeeman," who stands in the street cleaning people's car windshields in the hope of getting tips, is almost run over by an angry motorist. Three police officers, already in riot gear in anticipation of trouble at Maureen's show, happen by, and one of them uses his nightstick to poke and threaten a sleeping bag lady. Mark appears with his camera to film the guy, threatening only half playfully to share the footage with *Nightline*; the officers leave for the time being, but the homeless lady berates Mark for filming her. She accuses him of using her to assuage his guilt when he doesn't even have a dollar to give her. Angel tries to smooth things over, but the woman stalks off.

Santa Fe

Shaken by the ugliness of these street confrontations, Angel, Mark, and Collins fantasize about getting out of the city and moving to someplace much more pleasant—like Santa Fe, New Mexico, where they could open a restaurant. The easy, playful number has a flavor of R&B and soul—and one line borrowed from Burt Bacharach's "Do You Know the Way to San José?" It provides a brief, harmonious respite from the conflicts and hassles of city life, complete with street people singing and dancing in the background.

I'll Cover You

Mark leaves to head home, telling his friends he will try again to persuade Roger to join them for the evening's festivities. Left alone on the street, Collins and Angel confirm that they are together and sing a tender, fanciful love duet that includes a romantic dance. They promise to look out for each other and be there for each other no matter what.

We're Okay

Joanne is still at the pay phone; she does her one solo number, a complex patter song that finds her juggling three different phone calls. She's on her cell phone, catching up with Steve—another lawyer from her firm (and probably not the same Steve who was at the Life Support meeting)—about a couple of cases they have been working on, when Maureen calls on the pay phone to ask about props for the show. Still smarting a bit from her conversation with Mark, Joanne slips in a question for Maureen about how much she cheated on him when they were together. She then puts Steve on hold when another call comes in on her cell phone. It's her father, whose pager she called. In defiance of his earlier command to rid herself of Maureen, Joanne says she's going to bring her along to her mother's confirmation hearing. Maureen can hear her talking and reminds her to tell her parents that Newt Gingrich has a sister who is an open lesbian. Ending the calls with Steve and Dad, Joanne, who has kept her cool admirably up to this point, becomes alarmed when she hears that Maureen is with somebody: a woman named Jill—the sexy model who lives in the penthouse of their building. Assuring herself and the world that there is no cause for alarm, Joanne tells Maureen she's on her way home.

Christmas Bells

As it starts to snow, we find that the little choir of homeless people has increased in number to five. They ask passersby for change as they sing of how shut off they are from the Christmas festivities the rest of the world is enjoying—and the squeegeeman continues his work.

The scene shifts to St. Mark's Place in the East Village, a colorful and bustling bazaar-type setting where various vendors are hawking their wares in the open air. A woman shows Angel an assortment of used coats, and he tries to decide which one to buy for Collins, who has been coatless since his mugging earlier in the evening. Collins sings the praises of Angel's generosity and tells him he doesn't have to do it, but Angel still has plenty of cash on hand from his fee for doing away with the noisy dog.

Mark and Roger appear. Roger is telling Mark about his unfortunate encounter with Mimi, and starting to regret the way he treated her—when Mimi arrives on the scene. She is one of several people approaching a dealer—known simply as "The Man"—and hoping to score some drugs. Roger interrupts her and apologizes for his behavior, offering to make it up to her by inviting her to dinner. The Man threatens him but Roger, acknowledging that he himself is a former customer, stands up to the guy and moves away with Mimi.

Several overlapping conversations now go on all at once, some spoken and some sung. Roger introduces Mimi to Mark, who says he thinks they have met before. Collins and Angel are still browsing the various coats on sale—until Collins recognizes one of them as the coat that was stolen from him! Because the thief fortuitously brought them together, Angel prevails upon him not to make a big deal out of it; he buys him a nicer leather one instead—after successfully haggling with the crooked vendor to get the price down from twenty-five dollars to fifteen. Meanwhile Benny is again on the phone with Alison; he tells her his efforts to get Maureen's show cancelled have been unsuccessful, and is alarmed when she tells him her father (and Benny's lead investor) will be there. All the while two unique Christmas carols are being sung: the homeless people asking for donations, and the police looking forward to arrests. As the junkies continue to follow The Man around, the refrain "It's beginning to snow" takes on a double meaning, with the dealer using the word as a euphemism for cocaine or heroin.

Roger and Mark are telling Mimi about Maureen's upcoming performance when Maureen herself finally appears—a spectacular entrance on a motorcycle (usually suggested by a single headlight on a small cart wheeled on by a stagehand). She grandly asks Joanne, "Which way to the stage?"—and we know it's time for her show!

Over the Moon

We are now part of the audience for Maureen's show, presented on the vacant lot from which Benny is attempting to evict a tent city of homeless people. The show is done in a style that emulates, while also poking affectionate fun at, downtown performance art of the era. The solo performer is aided by a microphone and soundboard, which she controls herself (the "digital delay" Mark fixed for Joanne is used for some echoing reverb effects); she also provides live sound effects involving a drumstick and a cowbell. (Backup vocals are supplied live by the female ensemble members but may be interpreted as being prerecorded.)

Maureen relates the story of a dream she says she had the previous night. She was in a desert called "Cyberland"—this of course being a reference to the cyberstudio Benny wants to build on the property. It's a barren, lifeless place, with virtual reality having replaced nature. Maureen is thirsty; she asks a cow named Elsie for something to drink, and Elsie tells her producing milk is illegal here: only Diet Coke is allowed. If the narrative and imagery start to seem more and more nonsensical, that's intentional, as performance art can be confusingly abstract or deliberately obscure. It makes a little more sense if you remember that most of the imagery Maureen is using comes from a classic nursery rhyme, which goes: "Hey diddle diddle, the cat and the fiddle, / The cow jumped over the moon. / The little dog laughed to see such sport / And the dish ran way with the spoon." (And of course, the original rhyme is in itself nonsensical.) Here Benny is cast as the dog: a lapdog to his wealthy wife. The dish and the spoon are immigrants he evicts from his property; they then elope. Picking up on Benny's philosophy that "the only way out is up," Maureen chooses to take it literally. She sucks a refreshing drink of sweet milk directly from the imaginary cow's udder, then climbs onto the animal's back and they launch into space: the "over the moon" refrain becomes a call to activism, and Maureen gets the audience to "moo" along with her and take a "leap of faith" as the piece builds to its conclusion. Applause!

La Vie Bohème

The scene shifts immediately to the post-show dinner at the Life Café, where the whole gang (except Joanne, who is presumably taking down the sound equipment) is lined up waiting for a table. The nervous waiter doesn't want to let them in because there's an important customer in the restaurant and he can't afford having a large, rowdy group of bohemians who probably won't be able to pay for anything anyway. Coincidentally, the important customer turns out to be Mr. Grey, Benny's father-in-law; the two of them are already seated at a small table downstage right. Seeing that "the enemy" is there, Maureen is determined to stay. The whole group takes over a large table and orders drinks—to the waiter's dismay—and Benny toasts Maureen's show while subtly belittling it. Roger asks why Alison wasn't there, and Benny says it was because their dog just died. She was an Akita . . . and Collins, Angel, and Mark all guess the name: Evita.

It turns out that Benny knows Mimi. He says he's surprised to see her hanging out with this group of "slackers" and comments that Roger and Mark are not honoring the deal they made with him; they continually mock him even though he's doing his best to clean up the neighborhood. He compares it to Calcutta (a city in India famous for extreme poverty) and claims that Bohemia is dead.

This is all the cue Mark needs to launch into a comic number, acting out a funeral ceremony in honor of the late lamented Bohemia. The group backs him up with funeral chants sung in Latin, Greek, and Hebrew. He turns it into a toast and jumps up onto the table to sing the praises of the bohemian life (in approximate French: *la vie bohème*) in joyful defiance of the disapproval of Benny and Mr. Grey. The number celebrates individualism, innovation, and the friends' nonconformist, creative lifestyle.

Joanne enters briefly a couple of times to exchange dialogue with Maureen about the sound equipment, which leads to Maureen sexily slapping her behind and later kissing her. As Joanne exits, Maureen jokingly tells the shocked Mr. Grey that the two of them are sisters.

The friends order food and the song continues; the whole group gets in on the fun, toasting their favorite foods and drinks and all the things they love to do—including diverse sexual practices. They gleefully name many of their favorite forebears of alternative culture: activists, iconoclasts, radicals, and innovators in a plethora of creative fields (see Chapter 16 for background on all of these references) while dancing on the floor, on the chairs, and on the tables. An outraged Mr. Grey departs, and Benny calls the waiter to try to get the festive mayhem under control, but the waiter himself seems to have joined the partying group.

Though the celebration is now in full swing, with the characters jokingly announcing various impromptu performances to follow, a number of tensions are emerging. When Joanne enters for the third time, she sees Maureen playfully kissing Mark, which doesn't please her. Benny approaches Mimi and asks if Roger knows about the two of them; it seems they were involved with each other, but it ended three months ago, and she says there was nothing to it—though Benny still seems to want to talk.

Mimi, who was invited as Roger's date, pulls him aside and asks why he's ignoring her. He claims to be doing his best, but he wants to take it slow as he has "baggage" she doesn't know about. The "I should tell you" theme returns—until the scene is interrupted by several beepers going off to remind their owners to take their AZT. Collins and Angel are seen taking their pills, and Mimi's and Roger's beepers both sounded as well, so each of their secrets is finally out.

I Should Tell You

Now that they know the disease is no longer an obstacle to their being together, Mimi and Roger face each other and begin a tentative love duet. Though full of trepidations about embarking on a relationship, they resolve to trust their feelings and take a leap into the future together, repeating "Here goes" as they leave the stage.

La Vie Bohème B

An angry Joanne returns and tells Maureen she wants her out of the apartment by next week; Maureen doesn't understand why. Joanne goes on to say that Benny called the police: Mark and Roger's building has been padlocked, and the homeless people are rioting; the cops are trying to get them to leave the lot, but they are defiantly sitting on the ground—and mooing, as Maureen's performance inspired them to do! The young people continue to sing, dance, and celebrate in the café; Mark leads them in a final, rousing paean to nonconformity and creativity, and the first act ends as Roger and Mimi share a kiss outside in the snow.

Act Two

Seasons of Love

After the intermission, during which the stage crew and musicians can be seen moving about the stage preparing for the second act, all of the cast

"I Should Tell You": Emily Jeanne Phillips as Mimi and Travis Artz as Roger. Harbor Lights Theater Company, 2015. *Bitten By A Zebra*

members come back on from all directions and form a simple line across the front of the stage. They sing the musical's most beloved song, a humane anthem to celebrating every minute in the year and living fully and honestly, measuring your life in love. Two ensemble members, one female and one male, contribute gospel-inflected solos, and the woman's soaring high notes cap the number as the principals take their places for the beginning of Act Two—which will take us through the next year in the lives of these characters.

Happy New Year/Voice Mail # 3

It's almost midnight on New Year's Eve, exactly one week since the end of Act One. The front door to the building where Mark, Roger, and Mimi lived is still padlocked—and we don't know where they have been staying for the past week, although it's obvious that Mimi and Roger have been together, and happily so. As they try to pick the lock on the door, Mimi sings of her excitement at being with Roger and her plan to give up drugs and go back to school.

Mark enters and says, "That's for midnight"—Roger and Mimi have gotten an early start on the champagne. The friends are gathering for a "breaking-back-into-the-building party" when Maureen shows up with snacks. She is costumed as a "cat burglar," resembling Catwoman from *Batman*. She calls

"Happy New Year": Lyonel Reneau as Benny, Thomas Green as Angel, and Magdiel Cabral as Mimi in Uncompromising Artistry's production at the Edinburgh Fringe, 2015.   *Rob Palin*

Joanne on her cell phone and begs for forgiveness (a brief reprise of "We're Okay"), but Joanne must have been on her way there anyway because she appears almost immediately. She announces that her contacts at Legal Aid have told her the friends might have a legal right to stay in the building as squatters. But she has also brought a rope to help get into the apartment via the fire escape. She, Maureen, and Mark struggle with it as Mimi and Roger continue to sing about their happiness together and Collins and Angel arrive on the scene—dressed, respectively, as James Bond and Pussy Galore. Angel has brought a blowtorch to help with the break-in.

Up on the fire escape, Mark hears two messages being left on his machine inside and comments ironically on the fact that Benny had the power turned back on after evicting him and Roger. The first caller is Mark's mother, Mrs. Cohen, calling to wish him a Happy New Year and to congratulate him on the fact that the footage he shot of the Christmas Eve riot was shown on the TV news. The second is Alexi Darling, a producer from a sleazy newsmagazine show called *Buzzline* who was also impressed with the footage and is calling to offer Mark a lucrative network deal. Joanne thinks that accepting the job would be selling out, but Maureen is excited by the prospect of being on TV; taking credit for the film of the riot that her performance inspired, she suggests that they stage another protest/performance—starring herself, of course—which Mark can film.

Both methods for breaking into the apartment prove successful: when Angel finally breaks through with the blowtorch and the door falls in, we see Maureen, Joanne, and Mark right inside the door—they got in through the fire escape window.

The seven friends celebrate their success as it turns midnight—and as the New Year arrives, so does Benny. He is disappointed to see that they wrecked the door but claims he came to make peace and offers Roger a key to the apartment—after asking Mark to film the moment and his little speech. Roger accuses Benny of using them as a public relations opportunity; Maureen points out that he hasn't let the homeless people back on the lot. Benny claims it was Mimi who got him to change his mind and that they enjoyed a sexual encounter; she says he came on to her and then she kicked him out, but Roger isn't convinced. The conflict starts to escalate, and Angel attempts to make peace. Collins proposes a toast to friendship, but there is still unresolved tension, especially between Roger and Mimi. They finally apologize to each other, but as Roger leaves with the others Mimi lags behind. The Man appears and offers her a baggie of heroin; it becomes clear she is still using.

Take Me or Leave Me

In a brief bit of narration, Mark skips forward a month and a half to Valentine's Day. He says Collins and Angel are still together but he doesn't know where they are living; Roger has been spending most of his time at Mimi's although he is still jealous over her supposed relationship with Benny. Mark is alone, and Maureen and Joanne are working on a film together.

In Joanne's loft, we see her directing Maureen. They are rehearsing a new film to protest Benny's real estate project, and arguing about the script. They have been fighting a lot, and Joanne is angry because Maureen flirted with

Emily Goglia (left) played Maureen and Amber Mercomes was Joanne in the 2015 production at La Mirada; here they are shown singing "Take Me or Leave Me" in the second act.   *Jason Niedle*

another woman when they went to a club together. Maureen tells her there will always be other people competing for her attention; she has always turned heads on the street and always will, but that's the price to be paid for having a sexy girlfriend! Joanne counters that she's the organized, disciplined one, and Maureen shouldn't take her for granted; Maureen thinks she's overly controlling. The conflict escalates into a hot, rip-roaring duet as the two climb up onto the tables and chairs and belt out their differences and their expectations. By the end each of them threatens to leave—but for now they both sit down, spent.

Seasons of Love B

A brief reprise of the song, with new lyrics, moves us further along in the year.

Without You

This scene takes place in three different locations, usually represented by three "beds," which are in turn represented by the three big metal tables. Collins is at a hospital caring for Angel, whose condition is worsening very quickly. Joanne and Maureen are apart, at least temporarily. Roger and Mimi are technically together, but he is angry because she is almost never home. He thinks it's because she's spending time with Benny, but actually her drug addiction is taking over her life. The two sing of their loneliness as the three scenes switch places, playing "musical beds." Roger is briefly seen on the "hospital" bed, as he too is now experiencing symptoms of the virus. Joanne and Maureen reconcile by the end of the number; Angel is clearly near death.

Voice Mail # 4

By now it's been established that each scene of this act is going to be taking place on a holiday as we move through the year. It's now Labor Day Weekend. Calling from the Hamptons, Alexi Darling of *Buzzline* leaves another message on Mark's answering machine, teasingly urging him to sell his soul by signing a contract to work on the show—and not to be afraid of the money.

Contact

A complex fantasy sequence combining dance, spoken lines, and song finds all the characters plunging into deep, dark sexual places. As the number builds, the difference between unprotected contact and "latex" sex is emphasized. The characters are covered by a huge sheet to continue their various encounters as Angel, dressed in white, appears above them and sings "Take me, take me." (There are lines that reprise bits of "Today 4 U," and like that song this one is accompanied not by the band but by prerecorded dance music.) Angel surrenders himself up to love, to sex, and to death, as the three merge into one and consume him. Emerging from the sheet, the other characters have all experienced bad sex; they tell each other "It's over"—and for Angel it really is.

I'll Cover You: Reprise

In a church, the friends gather for Angel's memorial. One by one Mimi, Mark, and Maureen take the podium to eulogize Angel with memories of *her* humor, her kindness and generosity, her style and creativity, and the gift of her friendship. Then the grief-stricken Collins takes the stage and sings an intensely felt, mournful reprise of their love song; it gradually builds to a gospel-like power and expansiveness, with first Joanne and the "Seasons" soloist joining in and then the full ensemble weaving in a reprise of "Seasons of Love" as Collins pays tribute to his loss and the great love he and Angel shared.

Halloween

Outside, Mark calls Alexi on a pay phone and tells her assistant he's running late for their appointment but not to worry—he signed the contract and he will be there. Then he sings about the previous Christmas Eve: how could the coincidences and chance encounters of one night have changed all their lives so much? He is the chronicler, but will he be the one who ends up alone?

Goodbye, Love

The others come out of the church. Mimi has just found out that Roger has decided to leave the city and move to Santa Fe; he sold his guitar to pay for a car. He accuses her of two-timing him with Benny, that "yuppie scum," who in turn reminds Mimi that she told him she'd never speak to Roger again. Joanne tries to stop Maureen from interfering in their argument, so a fight between the two of them erupts as well, in overlapping recitative. Mimi and Joanne commiserate in unison: neither Roger nor Maureen can commit, and both long for a love like the one Angel had with Collins. Roger counters that Mimi is the one who was unfaithful—as a former addict himself, he points out that it's her lack of self-esteem that keeps her from finding real love.

Finally Collins steps in and halts the arguments: this is still Angel's funeral! Collins can't believe that Roger is leaving or that this close group of friends, who have come to feel like a family, is falling apart. Joanne and Maureen, moved by what Collins has said, suddenly reconcile, and fall into a deep kiss. The moment is almost ruined when Maureen accuses Joanne of biting her tongue—but thankfully they get past it.

Mimi walks toward Roger, wanting to say something, but when he turns away she leaves with Benny. Left alone with Roger, Mark urges him to stop running away for once and commit to Mimi. Roger counters by accusing Mark of hypocrisy: Mark is always preaching to others about being brave and open to feelings, and yet he himself stays detached, hiding in his work. Mark admits it's because he is the only one of their group who's not sick, and he can't bear the thought of losing his friends. He reminds Roger that Mimi still loves him: isn't Roger really afraid because he can see that Mimi is dying? As Roger is about to run out, he turns and sees that Mimi is standing there; she has heard everything. She sings an aching aria of goodbye; he overlaps with a brief reprise of his need to find one blaze of glory, and leaves.

Mimi needs help desperately; Mark says he knows of a rehab clinic. Mimi looks to Benny and he offers to pay for her to go there. She bids a final goodbye to love—and hello to disease—as she leaves the stage.

What You Own

Collins reemerges from the church, chased out by the angry pastor because he can't pay the bill for Angel's funeral. Benny offers to take care of it, so Collins feels obligated to tell him that Angel was responsible for the death of Benny's wife's Akita. Benny says he already knew that—and that he'd always hated the dog. The two ask Mark to go out for a drink with them; Mark says he can't because of his appointment with Alexi Darling, so the two go off without him.

Left alone, Mark imagines himself reporting tacky tabloid news stories on *Buzzline* and sings of what could become his new lifestyle: turning off his mind, swallowing the shame, and working a job he hates just for the money, because that's what Americans do at the end of the millennium.

Roger appears behind him and joins the song, though there's no indication that they are literally together; Roger may already be on the road to Santa Fe. The two face the same frustrations over needing to make a living but not wanting to sell out; both are haunted by their memories of last Christmas Eve, when Roger's connection to Mimi and the things Mark learned from Angel changed their lives. Roger realizes he finally knows what song he wants to write, and Mark, inspired by Angel's life and death, can suddenly see his film in his mind's eye; he calls Alexi and tells her he's not taking the job. The two young men are connected by the passionate drive to pursue their creative work—and their almost hopeless dreams of coming into their own in an empty, commercial world.

Voice Mail # 5

In overlapping answering machine messages, Joanne's father, Mark's mother, and Mimi's mother (in Spanish) ask their children where they are and plead with them to call home. So does Roger's mother, and in her message we learn that Roger has been sending her a confusing series of postcards about his move to Santa Fe: apparently he's now returned to New York and is starting a new band.

None of the kids pick up their phones . . .

Finale A

It's Christmas Eve again: exactly one year after the events of Act One. On the lot outside the building, the homeless people are again singing their ironic Christmas songs.

Up in the apartment, Mark has set up a projector (on a milk crate) to screen a rough cut of his film about Angel, now titled *Today 4 U: Proof Positive*. Both on the screen and in the room, Roger has his guitar again: he got it out of hock when he returned to town and sold the car. He has finally succeeded in finding his one great song, a love song for Mimi, and though he's been searching for her, he has no idea where she is. One of the scenes in the film shows Benny's wife Alison angrily pulling him off the lot; somehow she found out about his affair with Mimi, though they don't know who told her. Possibly Angel? (The implication is that she decided she didn't want her husband spending any more time in the neighborhood and therefore put the kibosh on the cyberstudio project—at least at that location—so Mark and Roger's building is no longer threatened.)

Collins arrives with both hands full of twenty-dollar bills, recalling Angel's similar entrance in the first act. He's come to help Roger and Mark out with some much-needed cash, which he has obtained through his latest computer hacking project: reprogramming an ATM machine at a grocery store to give money to anybody entering the letters A-N-G-E-L—a code he has provided to some of the homeless people of the neighborhood. The three guys sing a brief reprise of "Santa Fe"—until they are interrupted by Maureen's screams for help.

Maureen and Joanne have found a very ill Mimi huddled in the park; now homeless, she was freezing and begged to be taken to Roger's place. With the help of the guys, they bring her into the apartment and lay her down. Her condition seems so dire that Collins calls 911. While he's on hold, Mimi dazedly repeats lines from her previous encounters with Roger; she starts to tell him Benny didn't mean anything to her, and he tries to explain why he really left town. Mimi begins to lose consciousness as the two attempt to profess love to each other, but Roger rouses her to listen to the song he has finally been able to write for her.

Your Eyes

Accompanying himself on acoustic guitar, Roger sings the simple love song he has composed: He has been haunted by images of Mimi's eyes, both from the night they first met and the night he left her. He regrets letting her slip away before he had fully realized how important she was to him. He pleads with her to look into his eyes and see the truth of how much he has always loved her. As the song resolves into a final brief reprise of Musetta's Waltz, Mimi's head drops back lifelessly. Like Rodolfo in the opera, Roger wails out Mimi's name one last time as he holds her body.

Finale B

Miraculously, Mimi suddenly regains consciousness. She hasn't died after all! She says she "jumped over the moon," as in the story from Maureen's show. As the others realize her fever has broken, she describes her near-death experience of going through a tunnel toward a warm light—and meeting Angel, who told her to turn right around and go back to listen to Roger's song. Though there may not be much of a future, Mimi and Roger have at least another day together to affirm their love; all the friends are grateful to be together and share this precious moment of relief and joy.

As Mark's film plays on the wall, along with another film showing candid moments with each cast member, the whole ensemble sings a life-affirming choral finale that swells powerfully, weaving together reprises of "Will I?," "Without You," and "Another Day." As traditionally staged, the full cast, singing together, huddles in a tableau on and around the big metal table that served as Mimi's bed; at the very last moment, the actor who played Angel, simply dressed in jeans and a T-shirt, runs onstage to take his place beside them.

9

"Wanna Hit the Street?"

Rent Makes It to Broadway

T he New York Theatre Workshop production of *Rent* became a sensation, and uptown theater owners began competing for the transfer. Some people wondered, though, if the show really belonged on Broadway: with its distinctly alternative, antiestablishment ethos, would moving to the Great White Way be selling out? Would the people the show was about even be able to afford to see it there?

To preserve the downtown vibe, the producers briefly considered moving the show to a commercial Off-Broadway venue like the Variety Arts Theatre (a 499-seat space near Union Square) or the Minetta Lane (a 391-seat venue in Greenwich Village). There was also talk of obtaining an alternative space and transforming it into a club-like venue, but the expense of the renovations wasn't practical on an Off-Broadway budget. As Patrick Pacheco reported in an article for the *Los Angeles Times*, the show was considered something of a risk for Broadway, "with its very different demographics. After all, Broadway ticket buyers hardly seem to be hungering for a musical in which four of the seven leads are HIV-positive, the central romantic couple meets over a bag of heroin and vagrants snarl out Christmas carols."

In 2008, Jeffrey Seller looked back on the process of moving *Rent* to Broadway in an interview with Robert Simonson of Playbill.com: "After we opened Off-Broadway, many advisors, friends and colleagues recommended we not go to Broadway. The opinion of many was that that downtown crowd wouldn't come uptown to see the show and the uptown crowd wouldn't be interested in a downtown show. But Kevin [McCollum] and I felt it was our mission to go to Broadway. We felt that, if *Rent* can't be on Broadway, then the Broadway we grew up loving so much cannot accommodate us, that we can't work on Broadway. And we wanted to work on Broadway."

The Right Theater

After considering various Broadway houses and consulting with several of Larson's closest friends as well as his family and the creative team, the producers settled on the Nederlander Theatre at 208 W. 41st Street. Though at the time the Nederlander would probably have been considered about the least desirable theater for a new musical looking for a home on Broadway, for *Rent* it was singularly appropriate.

The well-publicized cleanup of Times Square and the Theater District was well underway in 1996, but the area south of 42nd Street was still a bit of a sketchy, sleazy neighborhood. And the theater itself was badly in need of refurbishing. It hadn't housed a substantial theatrical run since *Our Country's Good* five years earlier; the most recent tenants had been a brief run of the flop thriller *Solitary Confinement* in November of 1992 and a Jackson Browne concert engagement a year later.

Looking further back, though, the venue had an illustrious history. First opened in 1921 and run by the Shuberts, it had originally been called the National Theatre. The name changed to the Billy Rose Theatre when that legendary songwriter/impresario bought it in 1959. The Nederlander Organization (chief rivals to the Shuberts as Broadway producers/landlords) obtained the theater in 1979; it was briefly called the Trafalgar before they renamed it in honor of family patriarch David Tobias Nederlander. Over the years the theater often housed British imports and revivals of classics; stars who enjoyed appearing there included Walter Hampden, Judith Anderson, Maurice Evans, Noël Coward, Gertrude Lawrence, and Orson Welles. It was home to the original productions of several classic American plays, including *The Little Foxes* (1939), *Inherit the Wind* (1955), and *Who's Afraid of Virginia Woolf?* (1962). Historically, musicals were less frequent, and several that played the theater flopped; exceptions were the popular *Purlie* (1979) and *Lena Horne: The Lady and Her Music* (1981). The twelve-year run of *Rent* is the longest in the theater's history—and since then, musicals have been the norm.

When the theater was chosen for *Rent*, Anthony Rapp could see how appropriate it was. In his book he wrote: "We'd swoop in there and clean the joint up, breathing new life into it, the same way we were breathing new life into the world of musical theatre." According to Robert Viagas in the book *At This Theatre*:

> The Nederlander was a good choice for the anti-establishment *Rent*. Standing geographically apart from the rest of the Broadway theatre district on the far side of the pre-Disney Forty-second Street abutting the

The exterior of the Nederlander Theatre, redesigned for the Broadway run of *Rent*.   *Paul Clay*

(then) seedy Port Authority neighborhood, the site reflected a modicum of the grungy East Village atmosphere that the musical sought to capture onstage. To enhance the environmental staging, the inside of the theatre was redecorated to resemble a downtown club, complete with crumbling, sickly green paint and inlaid shards of mirror. The marquee used only the outline of the word "Rent" over bare fluorescent bulbs. Long after the gentrification decried in *Rent* had transformed the actual Alphabet City and brought it fatally upscale, a facsimile of the original was preserved at the Nederlander like a tattered fly in amber . . . Fans were encouraged to scrawl graffiti on the front of the theatre, and many of them left their names and personal messages to the cast—and to Larson's memory—on the green facade. For many theatregoers who were young during this period (and for many who were young at heart), the Nederlander was the magical place where *Rent* came alive each night. It was more than a theatre; it was a kind of shrine.

Breaking and Entering by Jonathan Burkhart

In 1992, riding our bikes to midtown with a sense of excited anticipation, Jonathan and I were on a mission to the New York Theatre Workshop. We were to track down Jim Nicola, the Artistic Director whose offices were located on 41st Street, just across the street from the Nederlander Theatre. Jonathan was delivering a draft of Rent for consideration. It was a very hot, very muggy August.

We turned onto 41st Street and saw tons of trash, crack heads, vagrants, and forlorn prostitutes patrolling the edges. The entire street smelled awful. The Workshop's offices were an elevator ride to the 9th floor. Jonathan was talking up the receptionist and I quickly got bored. I went down to keep an eye on our bikes.

Outside I was reading the faded posters at the Nederlander. Looking in the window, I saw it was dusty and very unused. Ten minutes went by before Jonathan made it down. As he crossed the street, I heard him launching into his usual speech about the decline of Broadway and how he had the answer to save it. "We need to start producing new musicals with rock 'n' roll and themes about current issues that will draw in younger crowds. And ticket prices should be comparable to CBGB's. It's time for a new audience, it's time for a rebirth." I had heard this many times before and each time he grew slightly more defiant in tone. He couldn't understand why Broadway theatre owners would let such grand venues go unused for long periods of time. He was always ready with a plan to mount a show. He just needed the space.

During his rant, I jiggled the door, tugged a bit, and it opened. Surprised, I slid in only an inch and looked around. He was freaking out while pushing me in, whisper yelling, "Go in, get in." We were in.

Before I go on, I'd like to take a moment here and get something off my chest. Jonathan and I broke into a lot of buildings. An astonishingly large amount. We didn't steal anything. The goal was to get to the roof. We wanted the view. And it was brilliant. We had it in us to get to the rooftop of every skyscraper we saw. It was a simple, cocky challenge that generally started by negotiating with either a doorman or someone's buzzer. A tone of conviction was all it took.

In the Nederlander, Jonathan had jumped on stage and started to clap. Loudly. Something he prided himself on. He had the loudest clap I'd ever heard. Always smacking his hands louder than anyone. It hurt my ears. He said again how he wished he could just have the theatre, for a little while, to play his music, and tell his stories. He was sure that somehow, some way, word would get out and everything would fall into place. Then he could stay in that theatre—any theatre—and the world of musical theatre would have its new voice. Our few minutes were up, and to be safe we needed to get out of there. Back down in SoHo, we spent the afternoon on his rooftop sweating and listening to the Mets play Cincinnati.

In 1996, when it was confirmed that *Rent* was moving to Broadway, I was invited to participate in the scout for potential theatres alongside the producers, Al Larson, Victoria Leacock and others. After scouting several theatres, we ended up at the Nederlander. It was a rainy, muggy day and once we walked into the theatre, I was overcome with emotion. I can remember being so choked up that I couldn't speak. But fortunately I didn't need to. In the theatre for only a minute, you could tell that everyone simultaneously had the same feeling. This was the place *Rent* should move to. The other details of that day are somewhat foggy, but I do remember turning to the security guard in the theatre in my emotionally wrecked state and confiding to him how I had had my first Broadway experience in this theatre and that Jonathan and I had broken in just a few years before. I felt we had bonded. He could not have cared less.

(A version of this essay appeared in the program book for the tenth anniversary concert performance of *Rent* on Broadway. Reprinted by permission of Jonathan Burkhart.)

The Pulitzer

If there was any continuing uncertainty about whether *Rent* would succeed on Broadway, it got an enormous vote of confidence while it was preparing to begin previews at the Nederlander. On April 9, 1996, it was announced that *Rent* was the winner of that year's Pulitzer Prize for Drama. The cast was onstage rehearsing when Kevin McCollum came into the theater to break the exciting news.

Intended to honor the highest standards in American drama, this very prestigious prize came with a certificate and a check for $3,000. It has been awarded almost every year since 1917, but there have been some years when no winner was chosen as the committee didn't find any play worthy. Usually it goes to a straight play, and *Rent* was only the seventh musical in history to receive the honor (there have since been two more).

Because the award to Larson was presented posthumously, there was bittersweet sentiment from all involved. Producer Jeffrey Seller told Robert Viagas of Playbill.com: "First and foremost this prize belongs to Jonathan Larson. We are continually gratified that so many people, both in and out of the theatre community, have expressed so much support and love for this incredible show. In a year that has brought some of the greatest highs and lows of our professional lives, this prize will go down as one of the highest highs yet."

Opening Night

The cast only had one day off between the closing night at New York Theatre Workshop and the start of rehearsals for Broadway. Previews began on April 16, and the official opening night was April 29, 1996.

Though the Broadway reviews hadn't yet been published, most of the major critics had seen the show downtown and reviewed it then; advance ticket sales were strong, and the company approached opening night feeling like they were in a hit. When they came out onstage to take their places, they were greeted by a standing ovation. Though standing ovations at curtain call have become so commonplace on Broadway that some people think they no longer really mean anything, for a musical to get one at the *beginning* of the show was almost unheard of (and it wasn't the last time this would happen at a performance of *Rent*). It proved not only that Michael Greif's conception of the show as something akin to a rock concert was successfully taking root, but that the cast was already building a fan base that worshipped and adored them as if they were in fact rock stars. Before the show on that opening night, Greif had spoken to Anthony Rapp about adding a brief statement to the top of Mark's opening monologue. When the audience had finally retaken their seats and quieted down, Anthony said, "We dedicate this performance, and every performance of *Rent*, to our friend Jonathan Larson." Another standing ovation followed.

Though celebrities had started coming to see the show at NYTW, the configuration of the building made it hard for them to come backstage, so the cast hadn't gotten to meet many of them. (Two exceptions were Danny DeVito and his wife Rhea Pearlman; they came on her birthday, and the cast sang to her after the show.) David Bowie and Billy Joel were among the notables who attended previews at the Nederlander. And the Broadway opening (along with the party afterward at Chelsea Piers) was truly a star-studded affair. Celebrities spotted included Brian Boitano, Christie Brinkley, George Clooney, Michael Feingold, Victor Garber, David Geffen, Jay Harnick, Isaac Mizrahi, Chaz Palminteri, Lola Pashalinski, Michelle Pfeiffer, Jeff Ross, Isabella Rosselini, Jim Simpson and Sigourney Weaver, Gloria Steinem, Jerry Stiller and Anne Meara, Patrick Swayze, and Barbara Walters!

The Reviews

Though a few of the established New York critics weren't quite ready to embrace such an unconventional show whole-heartedly, on the whole *Rent* received the kind of reviews producers dream about. And because it celebrated two opening nights in the course of two and a half months, there were two rounds of reviews to pull quotes from.

In his first review of *Rent*, following the Off-Broadway opening, Ben Brantley of the *New York Times* hailed the show as a landmark: "Sparked by a young, intensely vibrant cast directed by Michael Greif and sustained by a glittering, inventive score, the work finds a transfixing brightness in characters living in the shadow of AIDS. Puccini's ravishingly melancholy work seemed, like many operas of its time, to romance death; Mr. Larson's spirited score and lyrics defy it." He added that the show "restores spontaneity and depth of feeling to a discipline that sorely needs them. People who complain about the demise of the American musical have simply been looking in the wrong places."

When he re-reviewed the show two and a half months later on the occasion of its opening on Broadway, Brantley complained that it seemed like nobody had "thought rationally about reconceiving the show for a larger house." But he was steadfast in his admiration: "What makes 'Rent' so wonderful is not its hipness quotient, but its extraordinary spirit of hopeful defiance and humanity." He was also even more rapturous this time in his praise for the cast. "Adam Pascal . . . has an enhanced, effortless-seeming radiance that should quickly turn him into a matinee idol for a new generation. His shimmering sensuality is ideally complemented by the more shadowy eroticism of Daphne Rubin-Vega, whose Mimi gives off a transfixing blend of street swagger and mortal fragility. The couple's moonlit duet, 'Light My Candle,' and the recurring 'I Should Tell You' remain the show's romantic centerpieces."

The *Times* continued to cover the show in great detail, at one point even devoting most of a Sunday Arts & Leisure section to the production. On March 2, 1996, Frank Rich, the paper's former chief theater critic, published a piece on the show called "East Village Story." In keeping with his new position as an op-ed columnist, he focused on the musical's political implications while singing its praises: "*Rent* is all the critics say it is . . . It takes the very people whom politicians now turn into scapegoats for our woes: the multicultural, the multisexual, the homeless, the sick—and, without sentimentalizing them or turning them into ideological symbols or victims, lets them revel in their joy, their capacity for love . . . all in a ceaseless outpouring of melody."

Jeremy Gerard of *Variety* enthused that "'Rent' makes the musical theater joyously important again." Though he felt the second act was a bit "flabby," he summed up Larson's ethos as follows: "Larson had no wish to be an unknown, unsung artist. But, like the characters presented here, he was suspicious of compromise and contemptuous of those who sell out in an America, as one of the more blatant lyrics has it, where you are what you own. The show is all about taking chances, living on the edge, testing—best summed up in Mimi's riveting solo, 'Out Tonight,' a song that celebrates danger and which finds her thirsty for life and literally howling at the moon."

John Lahr, a particularly thoughtful and analytical critic and an elegant writer, was deeply affected by *Rent* and moved to go to Larson's memorial service, which he attended the week before his review of *Rent* at NYTW was published in *The New Yorker*. He pointed out the challenges of trying to use rock music to bring out the subtleties of characterization and opined: "'Rent' tells eight separate stories, but as a structure the through-sung musical can't support that kind of narrative overload. Inevitably, the theatrical shorthand of 'Rent' makes it wobble. What you get is a song cycle tricked out into a notional story whose events are not so much dramatized as indicated." Still, Lahr was moved by Larson's voice and achievement, which he described thus: "The aroma of 'Rent' may not be sweet, but it is also not sour. Larson's gift was for the elegiac, which celebrates both grief and gladness. He uncovers the poignance in his characters' panic—a manic quality that suits rock's electrified sound."

One of the few dissenting opinions was that of John Simon, the famously caustic reviewer from *New York* magazine. He found Larson's death "doubly sad when you consider that the gifted young man was groping his way to a unified personal style that this uneven, scattershot show does not yet achieve. For although *Rent* profits from the *Bohème* infrastructure, it is also hampered by it, as the author is obliged to think up clever parallels or disheveled variations that invite unfavorable comparison with the original. Still, even this partial success holds a genuine promise cut off from fulfillment."

John Istel, senior editor at *Stagebill* and an early champion of Larson's work, had interviewed him for the *Village Voice*. After Larson's death, Istel published two articles about him in *American Theatre* magazine. He disagreed with Rich's position that the show lacked sentimentality and wrote: "Larson was a severe romantic and a shameless sentimentalist. . . . His East Village Romantics are Rodgers and Hammerstein versions. . . . In the most notable departure from Puccini, Mimi rises up from her death bed, her fever broken, her recovery assured. Ah, the American musical ending! This is pure art, as in artifice, and Larson, so well-versed in the musical and structural material of the genre in which he worked, knew it." Still, Istel didn't consider romanticism necessarily a bad thing, and he recognized that the musical showed a very real social conscience and political vision, proving Larson was "deeply disturbed by a society that could become obsessed with an exclusionary notion of 'family values' while alienating itself from the fundamental human values of community, caring and love."

The Ad Campaign and the Album

Very early in the run at NYTW, David Geffen saw the show. Immediately excited, he contacted Jeffrey Seller and said he wanted to do the cast album with his newly formed DreamWorks Records. Robin Sloane, creative director for Geffen Records, then called Drew Hodges and suggested he go to see *Rent* right away.

Hodges was the founder of a small company called Spot Design that had spent the previous ten years doing design work mostly for television and recording industry clients—but he loved theater. He sent Seller and McCollum a proposal the day after he saw the show, and, though he originally thought they were being considered only for the album package, Spot Design soon took on the challenge of designing the musical's whole ad campaign and the distinctive graphics that branded it for the next twenty years. Their work was so successful that they were immediately hired for the Broadway revival of *Chicago* as well. Jeffrey Seller suggested to Hodges that he should consider starting a full-service ad agency, and the rest is history. The new entity, christened SpotCo, has become the leading creator of ad campaigns for Broadway shows; as of 2016 they had represented eight winners of the Pulitzer Prize and eight consecutive winners of the Tony Award for Best Musical.

Seller and McCollum didn't want the ads for *Rent* to use the word "musical": they wanted the audience to be able to decide for themselves what it was. Maybe it was a play, or an opera, or a concert, or something else entirely. The full-page ad in the *Times*, created with the help of an old-fashioned typewriter, had so much white space and so little information that it made people nervous; it also projected confidence. In his book *On Broadway: From Rent to*

The original cast album was issued both as a double-CD set (left) and a single-disc selection of highlights dubbed *The Best of Rent* (right).

Revolution, Hodges explained the famous block-letters title logo, designed by Naomi Mizusaki: "I have been told they resemble tenements, tombstones, and suitcases. . . . In fact, they are stencils bought from a hardware store that you use to write 'Post No Bills' (you can see the yellow paper peeking through). Then they were held together with black masking tape and spray-painted." Regarding the distinctive color-splashed photos of the cast members, McCollum wrote: "Drew led us to [photographer] Amy Guip, and it was from there that we created the 'Brady Bunch' checkerboard, to demonstrate how all these people were family. Amy was tinting negatives, which, in 1996, was a very new and fresh thing to do. It was clear Amy herself was an artist, and that this musical was going to be about artists."

Sloane was also quoted in Hodges's book: "I called Drew and said that given the music and the grittiness, the graphics should feel more like a Guns N' Roses record than a Broadway show." Broadway hits had been advertised in train stations for years, but *Rent* was the first show to put up panels inside subway cars.

The cast album was recorded on July 16 and 17, 1996. Shown here are Adam Pascal and Daphne Rubin-Vega arriving at one of the recording sessions.   *Victoria Leacock Hoffman*

The cast album was produced for DreamWorks by Arif Mardin; the co-producer was Jonathan Larson's longtime friend and collaborator Steve Skinner. It was issued on a double-CD, or two cassette tapes (remember this was the nineties); the set omits most spoken segments but presents the score virtually complete. It conveys much of the thrilling impact of the theatrical event and was instrumental in spreading excitement about the show around the country long before people got to see it on tour. The second CD concludes with a bonus track of the cast singing "Seasons of Love" with the great Stevie Wonder. The album was released on August 27, 1996, and went platinum—unheard of for a Broadway cast album at that time.

The Coffee Table Book

Another item of merchandise much cherished by fans is *Rent by Jonathan Larson*, a large-format hardcover book published by Rob Weisbach Books, a subdivision of William Morrow, in 1997. The volume includes the full book and lyrics of the musical, as well as a substantial introductory section by Evelyn McDonnell and Katherine Silberger that chronicles Larson's life as well as the development and creation of the show, primarily as oral history, through extensive quotes from family, friends, and colleagues. Lavishly illustrated with production photos as well as candids and rehearsal shots, the book is a vivid account of the creation of *Rent* and the various forces and passions that shaped it; informally knows as "the *Rent* coffee table book," it has been valuable in the preparation of the present volume. In keeping with the show's aesthetic, the cover was designed to look like the spine was held together with duct tape.

For readers looking for a more affordable version of the script, the complete book and lyrics were also published as a trade paperback by Applause Theatre & Cinema Books in 2008.

The PR Machine

During the early days of the run, the cast was called on constantly to do interviews and make special appearances. There were photo shoots for *Harper's Bazaar*, the *New York Times*, *Out*, *Rolling Stone*, *Time Out New York*, *Vanity Fair*, and *Vogue*. A sexy photo of Adam Pascal and Daphne Rubin-Vega appeared on the cover of *Newsweek*. Seldom does a Broadway show get that kind of national media attention. It was exhausting, but the actors were all young and thrilled to be in a great show. And they were always together; Rubin-Vega told Michael Gioia of Playbill.com that they were an "inseparable posse," adding: "We were like a graffiti bunch of kids in the Village just going, 'Hey everybody, go see *Rent*!'. . . I don't know where that energy f*cking came from, but we could hang out all night, get up the next day, do press, do this, do that, do the show, hang out all night, get up the next day, do this, do that all over again. It was fun!"

Still, underneath it all there was always the consciousness of loss. They were spreading Jonathan's Larson's story, which was important and needed to be shared, and as Anthony Rapp put it in the same article: "Jonathan is not here, so yes, we will do anything . . . I mean, I can't speak for everyone. That's how I felt. We need to have his story be told."

In a 2016 interview with the *MetroWest Daily News*, while he was on tour with *If/Then*, Anthony Rapp spoke to reporter R. Scott Reedy about the parallels between the success of *Rent* and the phenomenon of *Hamilton*, exactly twenty years later. Rapp had spoken to some of the members of the *Hamilton* cast about being in a hit show of that magnitude. He emphasized that it was important to honor the extraordinary experience they were having rather than looking too quickly for the next opportunity, adding that being part of the creation of *Rent* was an "enormous privilege." He continued: "Like 'Hamilton,' it deserved all the acclaim and attention it got. In the middle of all the noise, however, it is important to stay grounded so you can have the fullest possible experience with the show. With 'Rent,' so much of what we went through was tempered by Jonathan Larson not being there . . . We lost a friend and our show's creator was not with us to reap the rewards of success. The story is about living fully in all circumstances and facing head on whatever life throws at you, however, so the show really helped us."

Awards Season

In addition to the Pulitzer, *Rent* was a major winner at all the major New York theater awards ceremonies that year. It was voted Best Musical by the Drama Desk, the Drama League, the New York Drama Critics Circle, and the Outer Critics Circle. Since it had started Off-Broadway, it was also eligible for the Obie Awards and was honored with three: Jonathan Larson for his book, music, and lyrics; Michael Greif for direction; and the entire cast for their ensemble performance. Adam Pascal and Daphne Rubin-Vega both won Theatre World Awards, which recognize newcomers making significant debuts on New York stages.

But of course the most anticipation attended the Tony Awards. The nominations were announced just days after the Broadway opening, and the show got ten, including Jonathan Larson for both Best Book and Best Score of a Musical, Michael Greif for Best Director, and Marlies Yearby for Best Choreographer. Blake Burba was nominated for Best Lighting Design (the only member of the design team to get a nod), and there was one nomination in each of the four musical performance categories: Adam Pascal for Best Actor, Daphne Rubin-Vega for Best Actress, Wilson Jermaine Heredia for Best Featured Actor, and Idina Menzel for Best Featured Actress. And of course, the show itself was nominated for Best Musical.

The year 1996 was the fiftieth anniversary for the Tony Awards, which added to the attention and the festive atmosphere. But there was also some controversy surrounding the awards that year. The legendary Julie Andrews had made her long-awaited return to Broadway in the lavishly produced *Victor/Victoria*; she was nominated for Best Actress in a Musical but made a public statement declining the honor, to protest the fact that the show itself, written and directed by her husband Blake Edwards, had received no other nominations. *Bring in 'da Noise/Bring in 'da Funk*, an acclaimed, innovative musical tracing African-American history through original music and phenomenal tap dancing, was widely considered to be *Rent*'s only serious competition for the Best Musical award, and *Rent*, with its huge advance sales and the Pulitzer already in hand, was favored.

Televised as always on CBS, the awards ceremony was held on June 2 at the Majestic Theatre. Nathan Lane introduced the performance by the cast of *Rent* in a brief comic monologue, announcing it as a new version of *La bohème* "complete with sex, drugs and transvestites: all the things we know Puccini adored." The cast took the stage and performed a shortened version of "Seasons of Love," then backed up to the table and pulled off their coats as Anthony Rapp provided a couple sentences of narration to set the scene for a high energy "La Vie Bohème." The audience went wild.

The award for Best Book of a Musical was presented by Matthew Broderick and his wife, Sarah Jessica Parker, who proudly squeezed in the comment "My brother's in *Rent!*" It was won by Larson and accepted by his sister Julie. She thanked the theater community for embracing *Rent* and her brother, "and most of all our parents, who taught him everything about life and the theater and love."

For Best Score, the other nominees included the legendary team of Rodgers and Hammerstein—as their musical *State Fair*, written fifty years earlier as a film, had debuted on Broadway that season—as well as the composers of *Bring in 'da Noise/Bring in 'da Funk* and *Big: The Musical*, based on the popular movie. When Larson was announced as the winner, Julie Larson took the stage again to accept the award from Diahann Carroll. She spoke briefly and graciously on her brother's behalf, acknowledging that he had worked very hard for fifteen years to "become an overnight sensation," and that therefore the family wanted to share the award with other artists still working day jobs and struggling to break through: "Stay true to yourselves and to your dreams and know they can come true; this is for you."

When Andrew Lloyd Webber appeared at the end of the evening to present the award for Best Musical, he began with "the good news: this year, there are some nominations to read out." (His own *Sunset Boulevard*, the only new musical of the previous season, had won the award by default). When *Rent* was announced as the winner, the producers joyously went onstage to accept the award. (Jeffrey Seller's name was misspoken by the TV announcer as "Jerry Seller"—something that would be unlikely to happen ever again.) In turn they thanked Michael Greif, the company of *Rent*, the audiences, and Jonathan Larson.

Jonathan Larson's sister Julie (center) accepted his awards on his behalf at the fiftieth annual Tony Awards in 1996. She is shown here at the ceremony at the Majestic Theatre with close friend Matthew O'Grady and her mother, Nan Larson.   *Victoria Leacock Hoffman*

Rent's tally of four Tony Awards, while undeniably a major achievement, might seem surprisingly low given the magnitude of the critical and audience acclaim the show had inspired. Other musicals that engendered comparable excitement on Broadway have tended to "sweep": *A Chorus Line* won nine Tony Awards in 1976, *The Producers* won twelve (still a record) in 2001, and *Hamilton* scored eleven in 2016. But despite winning for Larson's work and being named Best Musical, *Rent* lost in most of the production and acting categories. Its fourth Tony went to Wilson Jermaine Heredia for his memorable performance as Angel. Still, it was crystal clear that Broadway and the theater community, along with the nation at large, had embraced *Rent*. The love affair, which would continue for the next twelve years, had only just begun.

Rush Tickets and the "Rentheads"

One of the most significant decisions the producers made when they moved *Rent* to the Nederlander was the initiation of rush tickets. Alert to expressed concerns that putting the show on Broadway was somehow tantamount to "selling out," and that the very people the show was about would not be able to afford tickets (the top price in those days was $67.50!), they reserved the first two rows of the center orchestra section (thirty-four seats in all) for sale at the box office on the day of the performance, at a price of just twenty dollars each. Though some Broadway shows in the past had offered rush tickets specifically for people with student IDs, this type of general rush was something new, and the innovation added to the growing hype around the show. Young people were so eager to see it that they began lining up hours in advance to make sure they would get in; lines began forming the night before—when the actors came out of the stage door after performances, they would see kids already camping out, waiting for tickets for the next night's show. On Fridays there would be two different lines: one for that evening's show and one for the next day's matinee. This was the beginning of the phenomenon known as the "Rentheads"—devoted fans who returned again and again, memorized the score, and saw themselves reflected in the story. In many cases, lifelong friendships were formed on the line, as fans who sometimes considered themselves misfits or outsiders discovered kindred spirits, united by their love of *Rent.*

As Michael Riedel wrote in the *New York Daily News* in 1997:

> [Each night] 15 to 20 people can be found huddled under sleeping bags and plastic wrap on the sidewalk in front of the theater. They share food, play cards, gossip about cast members and sing songs from the show. Watching over them is Nederlander security guard Bobby Redgrave [who] says the "Rent"-heads are usually well behaved. "I tell them if they don't do drugs and don't drink alcoholic beverages, we won't have any problems," he says. He can't stop them from having sex, though, and once had to turn a blind eye to a teenage couple inside a Coleman sleeping bag.

Riedel interviewed Michael McCarthy, a thirty-one-year old New Jersey resident who by that point had seen the show sixteen times and gave no sign of slowing down. He revealed that he had discontinued his $150/hour sessions with his therapist because he found *Rent,* at twenty dollars for a rush ticket, not only cheaper but more effective; he said the musical and its message gave him hope.

Ken Bloom, in his recent book *Show & Tell: The New Book of Broadway Anecdotes,* recounts an especially extreme example of fan devotion: "As you might know, fans sometimes record the show on their phones. *Rent* had one actor who covered a number of roles. One of the Rentheads had recorded a number of shows and in each of them the actor had played different parts. So the fan spliced the tapes together in such a way that it seemed that this one performer played the entire show, with himself in almost all the male parts."

Preferring to remain anonymous, a hardcore Renthead recently shared some of her reminiscences:

I went away to college in 1997 with no social skills and was definitely on the fringes. I had trouble finding my place at a huge state school. One of the people that I met at school told me about this musical she was excited about, which was of course *Rent*. I did not at first see it in NYC, but instead, flew home from my college for a weekend, and went to see the touring company in DC. We of course waited in line for rush tickets, and while I can't remember all of the details of who I met that first time or what we spoke about, I do know that for the first time since I had left high school, I was connecting with peers in an authentic and accepting way. It was addicting. I flew back the next weekend and did it again, and again, and again. I lost count when I hit one hundred, but all in all I saw the show well over one hundred times in different cities, including NYC, and of course part of it was about the show, but it was also about finding one's people. I remember seeing the show week after week, and thinking to myself "maybe this time will be the last time for a while," and then getting to the end of Act 1, "La Vie Bohème," and being so inspired and excited that I would start to think in my head "OK, well, what am I doing tomorrow, maybe I can see it then." There were several weekends that I saw three or four shows in a row, swapping off "line sitting" with a friend or going in with a friend who had an extra ticket.

We idolized the cast. Awkward stage door memories abound. I once had a cast member who would chat with us on occasion ask me if I wanted the rest of his ice cream cone as I waited in line. I said yes, and was thrilled to have it offered. In retrospect, I'm disgusted by this!

When I traveled to see the show, I found myself coming out of my shell in a way that I hadn't been able to before. I made fast friends, was invited to stay in people's dorm rooms overnight instead of hostels, had people I just met stay in my hotel room in Detroit for a closing show there. When I would come to NYC, I would see *Rent* twice in a three-day trip, and then take maybe one other show in. It was a gateway drug for a long-term love of musical theater, but I only slowly weaned myself onto other shows.

It truly opened my mind and set a foundation for liberal values. It introduced me to my first gay friends and opened up conversations about sexuality and tolerance. My two closest friends in my adult life are friends I made in the *Rent* line or bonded with in the *Rent* line.

Before long, the producers realized the large numbers of fans camping out overnight waiting for tickets had become a safety issue, especially in the still-dangerous neighborhood of West 41st Street. On occasion drug deals took place. But no one wanted to discontinue the rush tickets, so a new system was devised. In the late afternoon, any and all people who showed up at the theater could write their names on index cards, along with the number 1 or 2 to indicate how many tickets they wanted. All you had to do was arrive by six o'clock (earlier on matinee days), when they cut off entries. An announcer with a megaphone herded all the hopefuls onto the subway grate in front of the theater; the cards were shuffled and the names of the lucky winners were called out. Thanks to *Rent*, this type of lottery has been adopted by numerous other productions in the years since, and the systems continue to evolve; many shows today conduct them online or via apps. According to a Playbill. com article by Logan Culwell-Block: "Rush and lottery crowds generally end up being a gathering of like-minded people—a community of theatre fans. Enthusiasm for something is always more fun when its shared with others. Live theatre is sometimes accused of having diminishing mainstream cultural relevance, which makes these communities all the more important. *Rent*'s rush and lottery programs might just turn out to be its most important and enduring legacy to the industry. For producer Jeffrey Seller, it was his 'proudest moment.'"

10

"Making Something Out of Nothing"

The Designers and What They Brought to *Rent*

ent was not conceptualized or designed like a traditional Broadway musical. It was meant to have a spontaneous, improvisatory feel, as if a bunch of creative downtown artists had just taken over an empty space and were figuring out how to tell a story in their own way. And because the show began at an Off-Broadway theater with fewer than 200 seats, the initial budget was relatively limited. The collaborative challenge of bringing the unique world of *Rent* to life in visual terms fell to a trio of inventive, resourceful artists.

Paul Clay, Set Designer

"Paul Clay is a real artist," said *Rent* producer Kevin McCollum recently. The man who created the set for the landmark musical has varied and eclectic interests, and though he has enjoyed substantial success as a scenic and lighting designer, he has never focused on the theater world exclusively or pursued an orthodox career path. He hasn't followed up *Rent* with another Broadway gig, though there were offers; instead, his work over the past twenty years has embraced opera and performance art both in the United States and abroad as well as multimedia and an increasing focus on event design. As Clay himself puts it: "There are so many things I'm interested in that I haven't wanted to repeat myself." He has designed environments, projections, and installations for a wide variety of events internationally, including book and album launch parties, fashion shows for top designers, and projects for nightclubs, galleries, and museums. His designs have included holiday windows for Bloomingdale's and Saks Fifth Avenue and events for Tommy Hilfiger and Tiffany & Co., among many others.

Clay's formal academic training was not focused on theater; his degree from the University of Notre Dame is in anthropology, and the influence of that background could be felt in the rigor with which he endeavored to capture the cultural milieu of *Rent*'s setting as well as in his active engagement with the social and political themes of the piece and the issues it raised. He considers himself to be self-taught as a designer, and this process began at Notre Dame, where, since there wasn't a technical theater degree program, friends who were directing experimental theater pieces would often call on him to do their sets or lights.

After graduation, Clay moved to New York, where his early projects were collaborations with performance artists and experimental theater companies like Mabou Mines; he started out in lighting and video design and then added set design to the mix, sometimes doing all three on the same production. He worked with various playwrights at the Downtown Art Company, where, in 1991, he collaborated with Lora Nelson on a performance piece called *A Window on the Nether Sea*; Clay and Nelson cowrote and directed the production as well as worked together on the lighting and set designs, which involved the creative use of seven tons of onstage water. During those years Clay also worked as an electrician, a gaffer, and a visual advisor on several feature films. He received a career development grant from the Theatre

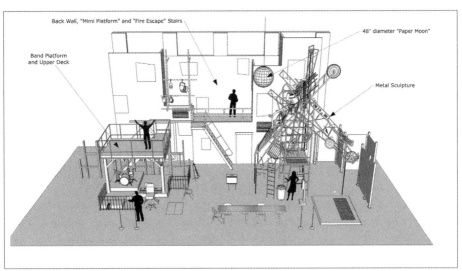

Set drawing by Paul Clay for the Broadway production at the Nederlander Theatre, 1996.

Courtesy of Paul Clay

Communications Group and the National Endowment for the Arts, which enabled him to travel nationally and internationally and study the work of artists he admired. He designed for contemporary dance companies and did sets and lights for new plays by experimental writer/directors like Susan Marshal, Eduardo Machado, and Tom Noonan. Venues included most of New York's most respected downtown alternative theaters, including P.S. 122, Soho Rep, HERE, Nada, and LaMaMa Experimental Theatre Club. More mainstream projects were the lighting design for Donald Margulies's play *The Model Apartment* at Primary Stages and set and lighting for Ellen McLaughlin's *Iphigenia and Other Daughters* for the Chautauqua Theatre Company. Clay's interest has always been in being part of the team creating a new work from scratch; when his NEA/TCG grant took him to an apprenticeship at the Arena Stage in Washington, D.C.—one of the nation's most prestigious regional theaters—he expressed dismay that they were reviving plays that had already been done on Broadway: what was the point of *that*?

Initially Clay turned down the offer to work on *Rent*; he felt he had no interest in musical theater as a form, and having read an early version of the script he was afraid that, if it wasn't done right, it could put out the wrong message politically. A committed member of the downtown artistic community, he had and has great respect for his fellow artists, and it was important to him that their world be depicted accurately and not mocked or made fun of; he was particularly concerned that Maureen's performance piece not turn into a spoof or a parody. Of course, his deeply rooted connection to the world of the play and his concern for portraying it with accuracy and integrity were major factors that made him perfect for the project. Nicola and Greif pursued him until he said yes.

The set for the original production of *Rent* was deceptively simple, suggesting an empty theater stripped down to its bare walls, but closer scrutiny reveals a wealth of painstakingly authentic detail. A key decision made early on was that, unlike most big musicals, there would be no set changes in *Rent*, no parade of separate settings designed to represent realistic locations. Instead, the idea was to use the architectural environment of the theater itself to create a versatile performance space, something like a warehouse or music club where it was possible to imagine a group of young performers coming in, setting up a few tables and chairs and sound equipment, and telling a story in a way that was more akin to an improvisation or a rock concert than a play. Clay used the whole large stage at NYTW, stripped down to the back wall, which was made of sheetrock. The catwalk at the far rear where Mimi appears to sing "Out Tonight," though constructed for the show, was inspired by architectural elements already in the theater. The stairs she descends were meant to look like a fire escape or a staircase in an abandoned loft space; like the rest of the set, Clay made sure they could evoke either interior or exterior locations. He had a friend who had a big paper lantern in her apartment, and he decided to use one like it to represent both a literal lighting fixture in Mark and Roger's loft and, for outdoor scenes, the moon itself.

Most of the locations were suggested by inventive use of three large, industrial metal tables, which could be pushed together or used individually in different configurations. (The crew took to calling them "the Frankenstein tables.") The idea for this originated with the Life Café scene and the notion of a group of young people so exuberant they are impelled to jump up onto the tables and dance; the end-to-end configuration of the three tables grew out of the religious imagery at the beginning of the song "La Vie Bohème," which suggests a "Last Supper" moment. The rest of the scene built from there, and Greif and his team decided to use the same tables to improvise everything else they needed to tell the story. Stood on end, one of them became the "door" to the padlocked building in "Happy New Year"; rearranged, all three became beds for "Without You." Some props, like the telephones, were realistic but not always used in literal ways. (Mark's mother is seen holding an answering machine while she leaves him a message.)

Rent deals with the lifestyles and politics of a very specific neighborhood, and from the beginning Clay turned to the Lower East Side and the art movements that flourished there in the eighties and early nineties for inspiration. Working within those established styles, he created his own art. At the time he had a studio in an old building across the street from New York Theatre Workshop; the rough, unfinished walls of that building became the model for how the bandstand on the set would eventually look. Jonathan Larson mentioned a specific sculpture by an artist named Eddie Boros that he had seen in a nearby community garden. Known as the "Tower of Toys," it was built from found pieces of wood and covered with stuffed animals and plastic toys. Boros worked on it over an extended period, and it eventually grew to a height of sixty-five feet; the sculpture attained some renown and was seen in the opening credits sequence of the TV cop series *NYPD Blue*. As Jerry Saltz described it in a piece for *New York* magazine: "It wasn't beautiful, but it was beautifully eccentric, part of a folk-art tradition put together from the detritus and wreckage of once-raggedy neighborhoods by individuals working on the edge of society." Clay, being an artist himself, didn't want to copy Boros's work too closely but instead used it as a starting point to inspire his own, which eventually led to the towering Christmas tree/totem pole sculpture that dominates the stage left side of the set for *Rent*. In designing it, he was inspired by the Rivington School, a downtown movement that began in the eighties and was known for large metallic sculptures welded together out of cast-off materials. According to Clay: "One of the main inspirations for what we refer to as the Rent Metal Sculpture was Linus Coraggio's fence on First Avenue. Also the 'Rivington Sculpture Garden,' originally constructed on Rivington Street near Forsyth Street, started by 'Cowboy' Ray Kelly, and also the very locally famous '2B' or 'The Garage,' at 2nd Street and Avenue B, an amazing mass sculpture on the site of an abandoned gas station."

There was a wealth of subtle detailing on the set to delight audiences alert enough to pay close attention. Inspired by East Village underground comics and the zine scene, Clay painted images of the housing wars, based on the work of local political cartoonists, in large format on the back wall of the set—but in such subtle colors that they didn't draw attention to themselves. Specific artists whose work he looked at were Eric Drooker, Peter Kuper, James Romberger, and Seth Tobocman. An East Village ceramic artist named Jim Power, who decorated streetlamp poles and other urban surfaces with broken plates and crockery, inspired the set's proscenium arch, a ceramic mosaic fashioned from a multitude of colored plates. (Custom fitted to the Nederlander stage, this element has usually been omitted from the slightly simplified sets for the touring companies.)

For the "Christmas Bells" sequence, very specifically set by Larson on St. Mark's Place, the designer quickly transformed the scene by flying in visual elements to suggest the merchandise sold in shops and by street vendors on that unique stretch of street. As Clay describes it:

> Visually I wanted this scene to mirror the energy and crazy punk and hippy quality of St. Marks Place of the time, as a kind of symbol of the East Village as capital of counter culture, and youth culture. All the look represents the Head shops, T Shirt Shops, and stores like Manic Panic, Mondo Kim's and Trash & Vaudeville. (Now on 7th Street, but on St. Mark's then.) At the same time I wanted to emphasize the crass commercial nature of the street and contrast this with deeper traditional holiday values. To do this I chose actual products from St. Mark's Place, and also made Duratrans Photos of them with transparent backgrounds, which evoked advertising for the products, and I also made Duratrans Negatives of the same, to suggest a kind of X-ray or deep examining of the meaning of these objects. What are they really? So the Christmas drop scenic element helps to make a big insane mashup celebration of all that is most crass and all that is most beautiful.

At the end of that scene, Maureen makes a diva-ish grand entrance on a motorcycle. The team initially joked about how that could have ended up like something out of *Cats* or *Miss Saigon*, with an elaborate, realistic motorcycle being lowered from the flies or rising up out of a trap door in the stage. Instead, in keeping with the improvisatory aesthetic, Clay and lighting designer Blake Burba provided a lone bright headlight on a rolling stand that a stagehand pushed onto the stage as Maureen simply walked on—with no apology or pretense of realism. Even when the show's eventual move to Broadway opened up options for a more spectacular effect, they stuck with the simplicity that had worked so well at NYTW; Clay knew that audiences respond well to being invited to use their imaginations.

Because he had substantial experience in visual design, Clay was also asked to handle the projections: the scenes from Mark's film that the audience eventually gets to see. Instead of video, he used actual film for this, beamed from the real old-fashioned projector Mark sets up in the last scene as well as an additional one attached to the balcony rail that projected images on the back wall. Rather than showing realistic scenes from the characters' lives, Greif wanted the film montage at the end of the show to give a sense of the performers as actors, to celebrate the work they had done bringing the musical to life. Clay hired a cinematographer named Tony Gerber, whose work he greatly admired, to shoot the actual footage; it turned into a bigger job than Gerber had bargained for when the show became a long-running Broadway hit, requiring him to return periodically to reshoot the film sequences with each successive replacement cast!

Clay's job grew larger than he could have imagined when *Rent* moved to Broadway. Though there was some reconfiguration of spacing to accommodate different sightlines, the original set was recreated quite faithfully on the stage of the Nederlander Theatre, since the producers didn't want to mess with what had worked so well downtown. But the theater itself hadn't been used in quite a while and had fallen into disrepair; it was clear that it would have to be substantially renovated and refurbished to house the hit musical, and Clay was given the assignment of designing a full environment for the show, including not only the house but the theater's marquee and exterior as well as the lobby, box office, and lounge areas. By that point Greif and the producers had so much confidence in him, based on his work on the set, that they never really considered asking anyone else to do the redesign of the theater. It had to be accomplished very quickly, and Clay, who loves taking on big projects, threw himself headlong into it. Jamie Leo, another downtown theater designer and artist, was hired to assist him and proved invaluable.

The exterior of the building was completely revamped, and the owner of the abandoned building next door gave permission for it to be decorated and worked into the design. An old neon sign with the world "HOTEL" on it was adapted to say "RENT." (Before the show closed, that building was rehabilitated and reopened as Hotel 41; it operates today under the name Hotel Shocard.)

At one point it seemed like the redesign might have to be aborted. One day while he was working, as Clay recalls, he was approached by a half dozen men in suits, smoking cigars—sent by the Nederlander Organization. One

Paul Clay's custom redesign of the Nederlander Theatre's lobby doors.   *Paul Clay*

of them said, "Kid, it's over," and told him to knock off work! He told them, very politely, that they weren't the people who had hired him, and if he was going to stop he needed to hear from those people. A tense meeting followed between the Nederlanders, who had become alarmed at how different their grand old theater was starting to look, and the show's producers. Fortunately the producers prevailed, but from that point on the theater owners provided a little more oversight, including assigning someone to pick out the carpeting (in the specified leopard-skin pattern), which had to be durable enough to withstand the traffic of a thousand pairs of feet every night.

The overall concept was to make the whole building look and feel like a downtown club space. Once again, Clay turned to friends and fellow artists from the East Village scene for inspiration and in some cases hired them to come in personally to contribute their unique specialties to the redesign of the space. He devised seven different treatments to refit the old wall sconces all over the theater and put different colored bulbs in each lamp of the main chandelier. He even stuck a light inside a grate for the air conditioning system "so it would cast weird lights on the wall." New lounge areas were designed and furnished. The large, ornate mirrors in the theater's lobby were smashed out of their frames; a graffiti artist was invited to decorate the frames and the surrounding molding, which remained. The team eventually curated an art show featuring works by East Village artists, which were displayed within the arches that had once held the mirrors. They must have chosen good pieces because one got stolen.

Angela Wendt, Costume Designer

Wendt designed both set and costumes for the minimally-budgeted workshop of *Rent* in 1994. With expanded resources, she was again onboard as costume designer for the full Off-Broadway production at New York Theatre Workshop and the move to Broadway; she was nominated for a 1996 Drama Desk Award for her work on the show. Fifteen years later, she was the only member of the original design team to work on the 2011 Off-Broadway revival at New World Stages.

Originally from Germany, Wendt trained in both costume and set design at Berlin's Hochschule der Kunste. Before *Rent*, she had worked with Greif on the New York Shakespeare Festival production of José Rivera's play *Marisol*. She has also designed productions of Shakespeare's *Twelfth Night* for Tennessee Rep; Aristophanes's *Lysistrata*, directed by Barry Edelstein; *The Great Pretenders* at the Juilliard School; and Martin Crimp's *Play with Repeats* for New York Stage and Film. No stranger to rock music, she came to *Rent* with experience designing for videos by such artists as Nina Hagen, LL Cool J, Maxy Priest, and Shabba Ranks. In the dance world, she designed productions for choreographers Molissa Fenley and Peggy Baher, and her film credits include the features *Childhood's End*, written and directed by Jeff Lipsky; *Love, Ludlow*, directed by Adrienne Weiss and starring Alicia Goranson; *Audition*, directed by Matt Herron; and Mako Kamitsuna's short film *Katya*.

Wendt has said that her favorite part of the designer's job is research. For *Rent*, she delved deeply into the world of the East Village in the 1990s: club culture and artists and street life, creative young people finding ways to express themselves through clothing despite having little or no money. Much of it was second nature because she herself had lived in a squat in the neighborhood when she first arrived from Germany. She looked at photos taken at legendary downtown nightlife venues like the Pyramid Club and Limelight. Other visual references included magazines like *Paper* and *ID*. Though she came in prepared with lots of ideas, she made a point of staying open and flexible until she got to know the actors, so she could choose clothes based on the choices they were making as they created their characters in the rehearsal room.

Pop culture phenomenon: Angela Wendt's costume designs for the show inspired a line of clothing, sold exclusively in a "*Rent* boutique" at Bloomingdale's. Store display, 1996.   *Victoria Leacock Hoffman*

As Wendt explained in a 2011 *New York Daily News* video feature: "Originally we really didn't want to be very costumey, but treat it like a concert. So instead of thinking fully costumed people, you think of East Village people appearing in a concert onstage." Michael Greif wanted the audience on some level to remain aware of the actors as performers, especially the seven ensemble members, who donned various costume pieces as they moved in and out of their different cameo roles; the base costume was determined more by who that actor really was than by any one of the characters he or she impersonated. Even with the leads, Wendt always made a point of finding out who the actor was, what they were comfortable in, and building from there. Daphne Rubin-Vega recently revealed that the clothes she wore in the show as Mimi were from her own closet. She was working at Patricia Field at the time, and the famous pants she wore for "Out Tonight," which were made of blue spandex vinyl, came from there. As she put it: "I knew those people; I knew what that was. I grew up in the Village; I'd been around the block . . . By the time *Rent* happened my closet was full of the right kinds of clothes." Wendt was able to make use of ideas the actors brought in, integrating them into a unified design.

The first time around, many of the clothes were bought, either new or from vintage or thrift shops. The stores Wendt scoured included Canal Jeans, Daffy's, Domsey's, Trash & Vaudeville, and the appropriately named Screaming Mimi's, as well as the clothes racks at the Salvation Army. For the 2011 revival, she also found useful items at chain stores that had come into existence in the years following the original production, like Forever 21, H&M, and Zara.

For both productions, Wendt and her crew built some of the clothes in her costume shop. One particular challenge was that, once the show became a hit and had to be reproduced for touring productions and replacement casts, unique items that had originally been thrift-shopped had to be recreated accurately and in multiples for the new actors and understudies.

In looking at photos of the early casts, it becomes clear that some of the costumes were not standardized until a year or so into the run. The famous blue and red sweater that Mark wears throughout the show was always part of the design, but Anthony Rapp originally also had a different red and gray shirt that he wore in some scenes. The familiar long-sleeved blue T-shirt with the multicolored sleeves and the skyline-and-moon illustration, which generations of Maureens have worn in "Over the Moon," was a later addition; Idina Menzel originally wore a collared pullover shirt with horizontal stripes. Even with the touring companies, Wendt enjoyed making small tweaks and changes each time she costumed a new cast. Occasional modifications were

Skyler Volpe shows off Mimi's famous blue vinyl pants; costume designed by Angela Wendt.
Twentieth Anniversary Tour, 2016. *Carol Rosegg*

made for specific replacement actors: one of the Mimis flipped the colors
on the iconic "Out Tonight" costume, wearing a blue top and black pants
rather than the other way around; this was presumably more flattering on
her particular figure.

The 2005 movie of *Rent* had its own costume designer, Aggie Guerard
Rodgers, but she closely reproduced Wendt's iconic looks for several of the
main characters, and for this Wendt was credited.

As *Rent* has made its rounds of regional, community, college, and high
school theaters, designers have often stayed close to the now-iconic looks
Wendt created for the original production. But the young characters all pride
themselves on being originals and breaking the mold; there is plenty of room
for invention when a new cast and a new designer approach the work.

Blake Burba, Lighting Designer

The young designer had an established relationship with New York Theatre Workshop when he was hired for *Rent*. He had been assistant lighting designer there on productions of Tony Kushner's *Slavs!* and Claudia Shear's *Blown Sideways Through Life* (which he also worked on at both the Cherry Lane Theatre in the West Village and the Coronet Theatre in Los Angeles), among others, and the lighting designer for Doug Wright's *Quills* and the 1994 workshop of *Rent*. He also did the lights for Squeezebox!, a legendary punk/drag party held on Friday nights at Don Hill's, a rock club located at 511 Greenwich street—right across the street from the building where Jonathan Larson lived. Burba designed for the opera and dance worlds as well. He was resident assistant lighting designer at Glimmerglass Opera and Opera Theatre of St. Louis, and he designed for the dance program *Triptych* at the Merce Cunningham Studio. (Cunningham is mentioned in the lyrics to "La Vie Bohème.") His other lighting design credits include *Too Many Clothes*, a one-woman piece by the writer/performer Linda Hill at The Kitchen in NYC. His design for *Rent* earned him a Tony nomination.

"Who's Heading Out of Town?"

Rent on Tour

Any hit Broadway musical is eventually going to spawn at least one national tour, but in the case of *Rent* the new companies began to spring up and multiply sooner, and in greater numbers, than is customary. This was because, following the death of Jonathan Larson, the producers of the show—Jeffrey Seller, Kevin McCollum, and Allan S. Gordon—became urgently, even zealously, committed to spreading his message as quickly and as widely as they could. As McCollum recently said, "We had to get Jonathan's words out there. It became a mission."

Out of a similar commitment to the late writer's work, and to ensure that the show maintained its integrity, Michael Greif stayed more hands-on with the replacement casts and touring companies than many directors (who often farm out such work to associates, stage managers, or assistants). He personally directed all the major American, Canadian, and British premiere companies up to and including the first non-Equity tour, plus the Broadway tour that went out in 2009.

Jonathan Larson's family, and especially his father Al, also remained closely involved. Just as Jonathan had done every year for his friends and family, and in 1995 for the original cast, they hosted Peasant's Feasts for most of the companies during their rehearsal periods, as a way of sharing their story, personalizing the experience, and giving the new casts, who had never had the opportunity to meet Jonathan, a sense of who he was and what his life was like. Some of Larson's closest friends have cohosted the Feasts as well; Victoria Leacock Hoffman did one as recently as the 2016 Twentieth Anniversary Tour.

Al and his wife Nan ended up seeing much of the world with the show, as they traveled the globe to meet foreign casts and see productions in various countries. In a Playbill.com interview, Al told Amy Asch that his involvement with caretaking the tours was a way of channeling his grief: "I was in a total funk for several years after Jon died, and—even though I hadn't the slightest idea of what I was doing—had this mad urge to make sure everyone understood that it was Jonnie's show, to be presented as if he was there keeping everyone on their toes. I don't think I fully appreciated that the show got into the blood of the people involved in it, and they didn't need my urging at all . . . It was pure luck for me that everyone indulged and included me and called me 'Pop.'" And indeed, the family's supportiveness became legendary among *Rent* cast and crew. As Greif told the *New York Times* in 2001: "They're wonderful ambassadors of good will, never intrusive, never demanding. . . . They come to let every company know that they matter, that Jonathan would be there if he could, and how meaningful it is to them that they succeed." Al and Nan became beloved surrogate parents to the family of *Rent* alumni that grew and grew, and many of them stay in touch to this day.

New Casts

If finding the brilliant original cast had been a unique challenge for Greif and the casting team led by Bernard Telsey, the assignment to round up several more complete companies to play the show in different cities—as well as replacements to jump into the Broadway company when the originals began to leave—must have looked daunting indeed. The difference, however, was that what had originally been an unknown new show in a small downtown theater was now the biggest sensation to hit Broadway in years. With a cast album, cover stories in national magazines, TV interviews, and so on, *Rent* had almost instantly become a topic of national conversation, a major presence on the pop culture landscape. Now every young person in the country with the ambition to be an actor, or a singer, or a rock star, or a performance artist—and many people who had never seriously thought about becoming any of those things but were inspired by the show to consider it—knew about *Rent*; they were reading the articles, buying the album, learning the songs, and trying to scrape together enough money to come to New York and see the show in person. Not only were they dying for it to come to their hometowns, but thousands were determined to do anything they could possibly do to get cast in it.

Because the casting directors were looking for genuine rock singers and edgy, alternative types, they knew it was important not to limit themselves to agent submissions and the usual New York audition community, so one of the first events scheduled was a huge open call, where absolutely anybody, regardless of experience level, could line up for a chance to be seen. It was held on Friday, July 12, 1996, at Musical Theatre Works, on the fifth floor of 440 Lafayette, across the street from the Public Theater in the East Village.

Between 2,000 and 3,000 (depending on whose count you believe) hopefuls lined up—starting as early as one o'clock in the morning. The line extended at least a quarter mile down Broadway. The casting call read: "raw singers who truly have a quality of street life, can move well, and have a good time onstage."

According to reporter Ralph Blumenthal, in an article that appeared the next day in the *New York Times*, two of the auditionees were "Sky Hall, a former commercial pilot and rock musician, and Charles Langley, a singer on cruise ships. Sleeping on a bedroll on the street didn't faze them, said Mr. Hall, amulets jangling from a necklace on an open chest. Like other performers, he said, 'We have enormous ego with low self esteem.'"

Patrick Pacheco covered the event for the *Los Angeles Times*, and Bernard Telsey told him: "Precisely because this show is about discovering unknown talent, we're only going to find out if someone is unknown and talented by doing these kinds of open calls. It becomes a very complicated process because few of the norms of casting apply."

There was not enough time, enough rooms, or enough personnel to hear everybody, so the casting team began with "typing"—a standard practice that means lining up a group of actors and deciding, based on their looks, who gets to stay and sing. Some people waited for five hours only to be dismissed after five seconds.

Heidi Marshall and Corry Ouellette, two of the casting directors from Telsey, were in charge of the room where the typing took place. They looked over résumés and asked the actors questions, including, "How do you describe your voice?" According to Blumenthal, "One singer replied: 'A cross between Madonna and Alanis Morissette.' If the look was right, a numbered ticket for an audition was awarded. The agent liked one genuine Lower East Sider, Mark Isreal. 'He's got a neat quality; he's authentic,' she said." On a break, she told Pacheco: "Even though I'm seeing a lot of very trained and qualified actors, they just don't have the right quality, the right rawness. It's a sexy, hot show, so if I see someone coming in here in a flowered dress, I think, 'Oh-oh, not the show, Miss.' Unless, of course, it's a man."

The casting notice specified sixteen bars of a rock, pop, or gospel song; anybody who came prepared only with a Broadway show tune was also sent home. But if a performer passed the typing, he or she was then sent into one of three different rooms to sing. One room was set aside for Equity members; some performers with Broadway experience, who in most situations could have expected to get an appointment through their agents, showed up for the open call. These included young Hunter Foster, who was on Broadway at the time, playing the role of Roger in the revival of *Grease*.

Original *Rent* cast member Rodney Hicks, who was still doing the show every night at the Nederlander, was there to help, calling out numbers and directing actors into the various rooms. He told Playbill.com that he wanted to be there to give the hopefuls someone friendly to talk to and help them not feel intimidated. Though pianists were provided, some people chose to accompany themselves on guitars—or, in one case, a "thumb piano" purchased on a recent trip to Tanzania.

Perhaps inspired (or confused) by the musical's title, there were also two individuals who joined the line at two o'clock in the morning and stayed most of the day, not to audition but to display a handmade banner demanding squatters' rights in the East Village and protesting the injustice of "rent slavery."

Those few singers who were fortunate enough to make it through the day without being eliminated could expect to be called in up to three more times for callbacks and "work sessions" with the casting directors. At that stage, they would be assigned specific characters and given music from the show to sing—and each time, the list would be further winnowed. It probably wouldn't be until their fourth or fifth session that, if they continued to show outstanding progress, they would finally get a chance to sing for Michael Greif.

Often there would also be a dance component. Choreographer Marlies Yearby worked with the performers on sections of "Santa Fe" and "Contact," exploring the concepts of "need, dissatisfaction, and desire." They also did an improvisation around "La Vie Bohème," so Yearby could see how they related to each other; she gave them popular dance styles of the period to work with. She has said she looked for actors who had "the ability to understand the body as a moving instrument, or an instrument to communicate with, and knew how to move from a place that is always saying something." According to Yearby, "It's always about the breath/body connection; learning how to breathe deep down in the pelvis—and this is something that was often learned in the course of the show."

As always with this show, authenticity and individuality were paramount; it was important that the singers not try to sound like someone else or imitate the cast album. "Be yourself" was the mantra of the day, because *Rent* is about truth and honesty. Still, the team considered it their mission to honor Jonathan Larson's work by finding people who could sing the score exactly as written; the policy was never to transpose a song into a different key.

As the years went by, Telsey's team continued to hold periodic auditions and turn over every possible rock in the hopes of finding untapped talent. After the first few years, Telsey staff member Bethany Knox became the lead casting director for the show, with the ongoing responsibility for finding a steady stream of new talent for Broadway and the road companies. Of course she stayed up on who was coming out of the top university and conservatory training programs like Carnegie Mellon and Juilliard, but she also kept tabs on experimental performance artists, downtown bands, and so forth. Knox and her associates frequented open mic nights and discovered people singing with wedding bands or on cruise ships. One of the best Mimis was first spotted as a backup dancer for Beyoncé; it turned out she could sing too! In contrast, at least one established Broadway star auditioned eight or more times and never got the show. But in keeping with the spirit of *Rent* itself, the casting directors adopted a "never say never" policy; though the competition was intense, they tried to be encouraging, and when someone was eliminated they would often say, "See you again in a year."

The Angel Tour

There's a tradition that touring companies of hit musicals are often named after individual characters in the shows to distinguish them from each other. The first national company of *Rent* was known as the "Angel Company," and the producers chose Boston for its opening engagement. As Jeffrey Seller told William Grimes of the *New York Times*: "'The heat of New York led us there. If you had to name the one city in the United States where people know the most about what's happening in New York, Boston is it."

The cast of the Angel Company, seen taking their curtain call at the Shubert Theatre in Boston on opening night, 1996.   *Victoria Leacock Hoffman*

The production opened on November 18, 1996, in Boston's Shubert Theatre, a venerable house that had hosted many a famous show on tour or in its pre-Broadway tryout. The Shubert was a new kind of venue for *Rent*, which until then had relied on the hip, downtown vibe of NYTW, and then the specially redesigned, funky nightclub ambience of the Nederlander, for authentic atmosphere. A large, elegant theater, the Shubert had just undergone an expensive renovation; its cream-and-gilt décor was decidedly upscale, and Paul Clay's gritty urban set design looked quite different in such posh quarters. To add to the opening night excitement, the audience had to cross a union picket line: the Association of Press Agents and Managers claimed they had no beef with the production of *Rent* specifically but were protesting against the venue's executives for hiring nonunion house managers.

Still, the opening was a ritzy affair with an air of celebration; a Hollywood-style spotlight was set up outside the theater and celebrities arrived in limos. Al, Nan, and Julie Larson were of course in attendance, as was movie star Molly Ringwald, who had been close to Jonathan Larson toward the end of his life. Broadway and TV legend Carol Burnett was there too; her daughter, the late Carrie Hamilton, was playing Maureen. And since the opening was scheduled on a Monday night, the entire Broadway cast of *Rent* had been brought up to Boston at the producers' expense to join the audience; they received a standing ovation from the crowd before the show started.

The much-publicized rush ticket policy was extended to Boston and the other cities on the subsequent tour: as in New York, seats in the first two rows were sold for twenty dollars apiece on the day of the show. It was reported that Boston audiences didn't start lining up quite as early as those in Manhattan; this may have been partly because there was also a section of the balcony at the Shubert with over 300 seats that were sold for a price not much higher: twenty-six dollars per ticket. Boston is known as the Athens of America due to the uniquely high number of colleges and universities in the area; students and other young people benefitted from the various affordable seats being offered, and they took the show to their hearts.

There had been some concern over whether a few of the references in the text were too New York-centric for an out-of-town audience to get. The line in the funeral scene about the Circle Line (a popular boat that takes passengers on a sight-seeing tour around the full perimeter of the island of Manhattan) didn't elicit the same reaction it got on Broadway. And one line was changed: Maureen was referred to by Mark as being from "Jersey," rather than "Hicksville" as in the original script. This was because while New Yorkers know that Hicksville is a town on Long Island, the producers were afraid out-of-towners, rather than recognizing it as that, would think of it as a slang term for a town where "hicks," or country bumpkins, live—and Maureen

C. C. Brown, center, was the first Tom Collins in the Angel company. Here he sings "Santa Fe" with cast replacements Christian Anderson (left, as Mark) and Shaun Earl (Angel), circa 1997.   *Joan Marcus*

Trey Ellett and Manley Pope, who played Mark and Roger in the Angel Company and later on Broadway, are shown here in the alley at the Nederlander Theatre, where cast members would meet their guests after the show.   *Gabe Palacio/Getty Images*

Johnson is emphatically not a country bumpkin. (That one minor text change is still made in touring productions of the show to this day.) But they needn't have worried about audiences getting the show. The opening night crowd was made up largely of devoted fans of the musical who cheered it to the rafters, but even after the VIPs were gone, Boston audiences adored it; the run there had originally been planned to last into January of 1997, but the demand for tickets was so intense that it was almost immediately extended to April. As Greif told the *Times*: "The situation transcends location. There are homeless people in every city, just as there are alienated, unhappy, angry, vibrant and feisty young people."

The cast also included Luther Creek as Mark, Simone (who went by only the single name) as Mimi, and Sean Keller as Roger. Like Adam Pascal, who originated the role, Keller was a singer-songwriter without much previous acting experience. Stephan Alexander, who played Angel, had a real Cinderella story: he had started out as an usher for the show at the Nederlander and then attended one of the open audition calls.

Malcolm Johnson, the theater critic for the *Hartford Courant*, thought that Greif had inspired the "new company with the same fervor communicated by the original cast." He went on, claiming: "In some ways, the new hands improve on their predecessors. In others, they fall short. . . . Sean Keller and Simone exhibit near-operatic chops. Simone (the ringletted daughter of Nina Simone) fails to deliver the sexy attitude and knockout high kicks of Daphne Rubin-Vega, but finds all the poignant poetry in 'Without You' with Keller. His Roger, with his chopped hair, looks more Alphabet City than Adam Pascal but cannot quite hit the last wrenching cry of 'Mimi.' Yet, on the road, even in a palace, 'Rent' strikes to the heart."

Markland Taylor of *Variety* wrote: "In what may be the musical's most difficult role, Carrie Hamilton (daughter of Carol Burnett and Joe Hamilton) makes bisexual sex-tease Maureen her own. She and Sylvia MacCalla's admirable lawyer Joanne tear into their lesbian love-hate duet, 'Take Me or Leave Me,' with unshakable confidence."

That first touring cast did not stay intact for long. Keller, who struggled with sustaining the demanding vocals eight times a week, was let go before the end of the Boston engagement; he was replaced by Manley Pope, a stage actor familiar to young television fans for his regular role on *Sweet Valley High*. Hamilton also did the show only in Boston; when the company moved on to St. Paul she was replaced as Maureen by Amy Spanger, who had been playing the Mark's Mom track in the ensemble. Luther Creek left the cast to take on the role of Roger in the Canadian tour, and Christian Anderson replaced him as Mark.

When the tour played Chicago, original cast member Anthony Rapp temporarily joined the company as Mark; he had grown up in Joliet, Illinois, and wanted to give his family and friends an opportunity to see him in the show close to home. To facilitate this, Anderson traded places with Rapp, thus getting the chance to play a brief stint with the Broadway company. The original Mimi, Daphne Rubin-Vega, also joined the touring cast briefly, playing the role in Los Angeles. Anderson was eventually switched to the role of Roger, and Trey Ellett came in as Mark. There were numerous further cast changes on the road, as the Angel Company continued to tour very successfully for over two years.

The Benny Tour

The second American touring company had an unusual launch. Because Michael Greif was at that time the artistic director of the La Jolla Playhouse in San Diego, California, it was decided to open the show there rather than in a commercial touring house. Although new musicals headed for Broadway are often developed in nonprofit theaters (more often today than they were in those days, thanks largely to the precedent set by NYTW and *Rent*), it is very unusual for a touring production of a show that is already a hit on Broadway to play such a venue; the involvement of Greif made it possible. The theater announced the show as the centerpiece of their fiftieth-anniversary season.

This tour is remembered as the one that featured a young Neil Patrick Harris, then known primarily for his role as a teenage doctor on the TV series *Doogie Howser, M.D.*, in the role of Mark. Another former teen television star, Wilson Cruz of *My So-Called Life*, played Angel. (These two TV "names," plus the tour's origins in California, led to the company being nicknamed by some fans as "the Hollywood Cast.") Sharon Brown, who had done a stint as Effie in *Dreamgirls* on Broadway, had the Mrs. Jefferson track ("Seasons of Love" soloist) in the ensemble, and D'Monroe crossed over from the Angel Company (where he had been playing the Paul track) to play Benny. Christian Mena and Julia Santana were Roger and Mimi.

A month before previews began on July 1, 1997, it was announced that the originally scheduled run of seventy performances was already standing room only. It was extended for two weeks (to September 14) but had to close at that point to move on to the Ahmanson Theatre in Los Angeles.

Charles Isherwood, who later became well known as a *New York Times* theater critic, was writing for *Variety* in those days; he published a review on July 15 of the company's opening at La Jolla and then reviewed them again at the Ahmanson two and a half months later. The first time around, he wrote: "As struggling filmmaker Mark, Harris—of 'Doogie Howser' fame—is fresh, earnest and energetic, and has a fine singing voice, too. Mena's voice is rich and resonant, and he has a sexy, brooding presence that adds texture to his role. (Their duet on the title tune is oddly homoerotic here.)" After seeing them in Los Angeles, he focused on the development of Harris's performance: "Neil Patrick Harris's charismatic turn as the narrator Mark no longer dominates the show. Perhaps it's the more somber edge he's bringing to the role, particularly in the opening number, or perhaps it's that we've recovered from the Doogie-Howser-singing-and-making-lewd-gestures thing. He's still terrific, but rather than seeming to host the party, he's joined it." Isherwood also alluded to something that would, as the years passed, become an ongoing theme in criticisms of the show: "With money rolling in, why does each company have to sport the exact same costumes—wouldn't it be more in keeping with the show's mean-streets ethos to have each bunch shop at a different thrift store?" As with any hit musical that sprouts numerous companies and replacement casts, finding a balance between recreating increasingly iconic images seen on Broadway versus allowing new actors to bring

Neil Patrick Harris as Mark in the Benny Company, 1997.   *Joan Marcus*

Jasmine Easler as Joanne and Katie LaMark as Maureen belt out "Take Me or Leave Me." Twentieth Anniversary U.S. Tour, 2016.
Carol Rosegg/courtesy Work Light Productions

themselves to the roles can become an ongoing challenge. With *Rent*, a musical essentially *about* individuality and nonconformity, the dilemma at times was foregrounded.

Initially there was some uncertainty about whether the show would prove to be "too New York" for Middle America; people questioned whether some of its themes and content might alienate audiences in more conservative parts of the country. But as the two touring companies continued to crisscross

America for the next couple of years, Larson's musical won the hearts of audiences in every city. As Jeffrey Seller told David Nightingale of the *Independent* in the days leading up to the opening in London: "In Dallas, Texas, which is the hotbed of what we might call conservative, right-wing assholes, we sold out. That wasn't because of the racial mix, HIV or the bohemianism. We win them over with heart. Ultimately, it's a story about young people trying to realize their version of the American Dream, and trying to figure out how to love and connect. Getting together and breaking up, we all know about that."

The Collins Tour

The third company was the Canadian tour, dubbed the "Collins Company." It began performances in December of 1997 at the 1,500-seat Royal Alexander Theatre in Toronto. The producers and casting directors expressed determination to find a new group of mostly unknown Canadian actors, but in the end four of the leads were from the States. Luther Creek, who had opened the Angel Company in Boston as Mark, was Roger this time around, playing opposite Krysten Cummings, an American singer who lived in London, as Mimi. Jai Rodriguez, who would soon find national fame as a TV personality on *Queer Eye for the Straight Guy*, first played Angel in this company; he would return to the role several times over the coming years, both on Broadway and regionally.

Mira Friedlander of *Variety* found the cast more effective individually than in their portrayal of the love relationships, adding: "Perhaps that's why Chad Richardson, as Mark, emerges as one of the production's anchors; without a love interest he is able to focus inward on character development while using all his energy to belt out the songs. By contrast, Krysten Cummings' Mimi, who has rubber limbs, is cute as a button and possesses a smoke-filled, raunchy voice, can't seem to raise much interest out of Roger (Luther Creek); he manages to look peaked and put-out, but his inner conflicts never spill over into Mimi's life." She was more positive about the relationship between Rodriguez's Angel and Danny Blanco's Collins, which she found believable, adding that Blanco played his role with "a quiet, deeply felt delivery that captures audience empathy."

Later Tours

After a hit Broadway musical has been seen in all the nation's major markets and the "Class A" tours have wound down, if there is deemed to be an appetite for more, sometimes producers will authorize a non-Equity tour. The union and many actors deplore this practice, as it deprives Equity performers of work and the nonunion casts are paid lower salaries and sometimes have to perform in less than ideal circumstances. Still, young performers jump at such opportunities, which frequently provide their first full-time jobs and give them a chance to play huge theaters all over the country in a replica of a popular Broadway production. Most of these tours are booked mainly in smaller cities or towns where the Equity tours haven't been seen; often they play short gigs of only a night or two in each place.

In the case of *Rent*, the Broadway production was still going strong when the Angel and Benny companies completed their tours, so it seemed inevitable that there would be a production company that would want to do a non-Equity version. The new production, again directed by Michael Greif, was produced by On Tour, LLC, and went out in 2001. When the company played Florida in early 2002, Charles Passy of the *Palm Beach Post* found the show exhilarating but mentioned the extreme youth of the cast, adding: "In this case, that makes for plenty of misguided and overly earnest performances. Mimi, Krystal L Washington, comes off especially amateurish, handling her big dance number, Out Tonight, as if she was still learning where to place her feet. Justin Rodriguez's Angel also lacks a drag-queen flair the role demands. Fortunately, Mark (Dominic Bogart) and Roger (Kevin Spencer) are closer to the intended mark, with their big closing duo, What You Own, registering with the right conviction. Ultimately, however, even when the performances are off, it's that sense of community that compensates." (Washington certainly got the choreography down. The next season, she was chosen to take over Mimi in the Broadway company—and got her Equity card.) A string of other short-lived non-Equity tours followed; though Greif directed only the first one, they were generally based on his staging.

If the nonunion casts had their ups and downs, America got to see a Class A tour of *Rent* again in 2009, the year after the show closed on Broadway. Late in the New York run, Adam Pascal and Anthony Rapp had returned to their original roles as Roger and Mark for a brief engagement; the audience response was ecstatic, and both actors were subsequently asked to head up an all-new national company. Greif staged the show with a cast made up mostly of veterans of the Broadway company and the various tours, along with a new Mimi: the youthful Lexi Lawson, who several years later would join the Broadway cast of *Hamilton*.

When the tour hit the Paramount Theatre in Seattle, Washington, Misha Berson of the *Seattle Times* found it a welcome contrast to the "lackluster and/or semi-professional road productions" of the show she had seen most recently. She added: "The unelected leaders of the clan include Rapp's intent chronicler of the scene, Mark, and the grieving, ambivalent Roger. . . . As the latter, Pascal now delivers his big arias in a stronger, ringing voice with a more metallic edge. His wary Roger succumbs very reluctantly to the charms of fetching Lexi Lawson's vulnerable addict and 'exotic' dancer, Mimi. . . . We're now a decade into a new millennium. But for one last hurrah, Pascal and Rapp are still fervently singing about the end of the last one, like they really mean it." In addition to numerous American cities, the tour was booked in Korea and Japan.

That company might have been deemed to have provided a fittingly grand finale to the long history of *Rent* on tour throughout America. But five years later, the show's twentieth anniversary provided the impetus for another non-Equity company, under the auspices of Work Light Productions and executive producer Stephen Gabriel, which played mostly one- and two-night stands all over the country beginning in the fall of 2016. That December, they played an engagement in Tokyo, Japan.

The production was staged on a simplified facsimile of Paul Clay's original set by director Evan Ensign, who had extensive experience with the show, having been associate director for the Broadway company and earlier tours as well as having directed a Montreal company and a tour of the Far East. Original choreographer Marlies Yearby and musical director Tim Weil were

The Twentieth Anniversary Tour cast in the Finale.   *Carol Rosegg/courtesy of Work Light Productions*

back on board working with him. Casting director Joy Dewing rounded up a group of fresh-faced young performers, most of them recent grads of BFA programs.

Though Ensign was hired for his knowledge of the musical's history, he told Michael Gioia of Playbill.com that the new tour would not be an exact duplicate of Greif's production. He said the lighting design was going to be all new "because we're going to be using moving lights that didn't exist back then." He added: "It's not only about finding that the piece is relevant to politics today and racial issues that are going on today, but we have a cast that comes at it from a whole different point of view than we did 18 or 20 years ago. . . . There's aspects of this play that they don't even know, and we have to talk a lot about, but they find things in their own lives that relate to it, and we are having lots of those discussions. It's beautiful." Yearby experimented with some new choreography based on the bodies of the cast and the way they moved. Original costume designer Angela Wendt also came back to take a fresh look. Having completely redesigned the show for the 2011 Off-Broadway revival, this time around she returned mostly to the original 1996 look, but she improvised some new pieces, especially on the ensemble members.

When the production played Dallas, Jessica Fritsche of Theaterjones.com said: "The tour is directed by Evan Ensign, who has been involved with *Rent* since almost the very beginning, and is extremely faithful to the show's legacy, showing off the heart of the original production thanks to the youthful vigor of the non-equity cast. They're professionals, no doubt, but not yet perfectly polished. And that's a good thing—it makes it easier to imagine them as the young bohemians of New York City on the cusp of the new Millennium, and they bring enough energy to shake the foundations of the Winspear Opera House."

"Another Time—Another Place"

Rent Crosses the Pond

Broadway and the West End have always traded shows enthusiastically, and when a musical becomes a megahit on one side of "the pond," it is almost sure to receive a production on the other. Still, the two cities have different tastes and very different theatrical cultures. *Rent* made it to London in 1998, two years after the New York opening, but even before it arrived the British press began predicting it might have a hard time repeating its American success with English audiences. The week before the show opened, David Gritten of the *Telegraph* expressed some of the reasons: "Firstly, this is a hugely competitive season for new musicals in the West End. Hal Prince's revival of *Show Boat* (admittedly a very different, much more traditional show) . . . has already performed prodigiously at the box office. And few would bet on *Rent* outstripping *Saturday Night Fever*, the new stage version of the mega-hit film. . . . Lastly, it is unclear if the marginalised community of poverty-stricken artists in *Rent* will strike a chord outside the US. Americans love to see minorities struggling to overcome obstacles, achieving their dreams and redeeming themselves; we British, in particular, find all that self-regarding and sentimental."

The West End Premiere

Still, a lot of excitement and hype attended the London opening. Michael Greif recreated his Broadway staging in the 1,400-seat Shaftesbury Theatre. Built in 1911, the venue had housed the London productions of several popular Broadway musicals over the years, including *Gentlemen Prefer Blondes*, *How to Succeed in Business Without Really Trying*, *They're Playing Our Song*, and *Follies.* Jonathan Larson would probably have been pleased that it had also been the West End home of *Hair*, which enjoyed a tremendously successful run of 1,998 performances there; it could have run even longer, but part of the ceiling caved in in 1973, and the theater closed for a year for repairs, reopening with a revival of *West Side Story.*

British Equity is not always flexible about allowing American actors to appear in the West End, but in the case of *Rent* they allowed Adam Pascal, Anthony Rapp, Jesse L. Martin, and Wilson Jermaine Heredia to come over to recreate the roles they had originated. They were joined by Krysten Cummings as Mimi; she had first played the role in the Canadian tour, dubbed the "Collins Company," the previous December. Most of the other cast members were British.

When the production opened on May 12, 1998, Gritten's concerns about how it might be received proved justified. Whether or not the stereotype of the British critic as a caustic intellectual snob is accurate, quite a few of them seemed to be doing their best to live up to it in their reviews of *Rent.* Nearly all of them compared it to *Hair,* and some who questioned the reasons for its popularity in the States tastelessly referred to the timing of Larson's death as a "good career move."

One of the nastiest was Susannah Clapp of the *Observer,* who called the musical "a triumph of mawkishness over modernity," adding: "This is saccharine, ghoulish stuff, made worse by its masquerade of gritty realism. *La Bohème* is hardly a model of ironic incisiveness, but *Rent* is far mushier."

John Peter of the *Sunday Times* used similar adjectives: "The thing that most depresses me about Rent is what will most endear it to its fans: it is the way it wears its warm, mushy heart on its sleeve. Yes, you can take the show out of New York, but you cannot take New York out of the show; and even those who love that great city will recognize that mixture of compulsive exuberance, in-your-face, from-your-heart sincerity and well-meaning but oppressive political correctness that sometimes makes you recoil in despair." (Peter's critique of the show's sociopolitical content was undercut by his impression that the character Angel was a prostitute, a misperception he mentioned no fewer than three times in his review.)

Peter was not the only critic who used his review to express personal attitudes about New York City—or America in general. Robert Butler of the *Independent on Sunday* wrote: "The vision these Nineties bohemians share is tunnel vision. Here they are, a performance artist, a video film-maker, a songwriter, a dancer—artists, that is, who might take an interest in the world beyond the Lower East Side loft in which they're squatting. They live in the wealthiest country in the world during an era of unrivalled prosperity. Do they feel lucky? You must be kidding. 'Anywhere, after New York,' sings one of them in all earnestness, 'would be a pleasure cruise.' Lucky that *Rent* wasn't opening in Jakarta. It would take a lot of nerve to deliver that line."

The original London cast of *Rent*. Shaftesbury Theatre, 1998.   *Robbie Jack/Corbis, Getty Images*

Alex Sierz of the *Tribune* had more respect for Larson's take on life in Manhattan. "*Rent* is not just a tale of love and death and rock 'n' roll, it's also a vivid picture of a city. Yup, the real star of the evening is New York City—once the Big Apple, now the new bohemia, with its vicious extremes of rich and poor, happiness and exploitation, loyalty and betrayal. And, despite the sharp personal conflicts and social satire, it also struts an amazing aura of supreme confidence and shining optimism. Idealistic, raunchy, sincere and incurably sentimental, *Rent* is an exciting, funky—and occasionally moving—evening."

Regardless of the critics' responses to the material, Greif's direction and the performers were almost unanimously praised. According to David Benedict of the *Independent*: "The passionate commitment of the cast is never in doubt. When the London production was first announced there were mutterings about the unsuitability of English actors for such raw emotionalism. As it turns out the four New Yorkers reprising their roles find themselves mostly in excellent company." And according to Robert Gore-Langton of the *Express*: "Star of the show is unquestionably Krysten Cummings's Mimi, a lithe new Tina Turner."

One of the show's British champions, Jane Edwardes of *Time Out London*, found the slightly confusing story, always the aspect of the show most vulnerable to criticism, to be a plus: "The first thing that strikes one about 'Rent,' the most exciting musical opening for a very long time, is that it is about now; about trying to hold together with talent and not much money on the streets of New York today. The second thing is that Jonathan Larson's book contains an extraordinarily complicated plot. So instead of being passively swallowed up by the Lloyd Webber emotional vacuum cleaner, one has to stay alert and remain imaginatively involved. . . . Go and celebrate 'La Vie Bohème' in the style of these dynamic New Yorkers."

And finally, the London critic perhaps most attuned to the show's glories was Nicholas de Jongh of the *Evening Standard*, who wrote: "The West End musical stage recovered a long-lost youthfulness last night when Rent made a triumphal transatlantic cross-over from Broadway. . . . The fraught love-affair flaring between Roger and Mimi . . . is the musical's tremendous, emotional making. . . . Rent celebrates a romantic view of outsiders finding community in their troubles. But there's no real happy ending. Mimi's sudden death-bed recovery is only meant as a short-term remission—the final song's an instruction to enjoy each day as if it's the last. This finale and the musical itself will haunt me beautifully."

If the British critical establishment was slow to come around, the show earned a devoted following among young Londoners, many of whom identified with it strongly. The English actors who joined the four originals in the cast were thrilled to be doing something so new and relevant, and fans told the cast the show was just what London had been needing. The production ran just under a year and a half, closing on October 30, 1999, without having fully recouped its investment.

Rent has made a few brief returns to the West End. In 2001, an all-British touring production directed by Paul Kerryson took up temporary residence at the Prince of Wales Theatre; the new staging, which had originated at the Leicester Haymarket Theatre, and cast were generally well received.

Rent Remixed

One of the oddest twists in *Rent*'s journey was another West End production, which opened in October of 2007 at the Duke of York's Theatre. A drastic rethinking of the show by the director William Baker and the music supervisor Steve Anderson, described in the press materials as "the celebrated creative team behind Kylie" (meaning the Australian pop star Kylie Minogue),

Oliver Thornton as Mark, Denise Van Outen as Maureen, and Jay Webb as Angel in *Rent Remixed*. *Tristram Kenton/Lebrecht Music & Arts*

the production was dubbed *Rent Remixed*, and was generally excoriated both by critics and fans of the original show.

Somehow the team was allowed to restructure the script. They began the evening with "Seasons of Love," as the movie had done two years earlier, and took an early intermission—in order to capitalize on the image of their highest-profile cast member, Denise Van Outen, who played Maureen. "Tango: Maureen" was repositioned to directly anticipate Maureen's dramatic first appearance—after which the act curtain came down on her entrance applause. This meant that "Over the Moon" and "La Vie Bohème," along with most of the traditional second act, were performed after the intermission.

The voicemail messages were prerecorded and performed as spoken text rather than sung recitative. The score was played by a four-person band and a computer, which ran virtual orchestra software. Van Outen's "Over the Moon" was expanded to include a dance break.

While some of the songs sounded much as they had in the original, others were entirely reconceived, with radical new arrangements. "What You Own," for example, became a slow-paced emo ballad primarily for Mark, with Roger's entrance held off until late in the number. "Out Tonight" was staged as old fashioned burlesque and given a jazz arrangement; Mimi had backup singers who came out of the Life Support meeting that had been going on in the previous scene. In "Without You," unbelievable as it may sound, her backup team waved large feathered fans like the chorines in *Chicago*.

Colored strobe lights and S&M fetish wear evoked a nightclub milieu. Little attempt was made to suggest the bohemian East Village setting, as the performers were dressed like fashion models on a stylish white set. According to reviewer Michael Billington in the *Guardian*: "The characters in Baker's updated version now inhabit a white-walled, perspex-screened, skeletal-doored world that shrieks Manhattan chic: if this is raffish Bohemian poverty, I wouldn't mind some of it." Peter Brown of Londontheatre.co.uk added: "Mark Bailey's white brick set and modernist metal walkway and staircases seem more appropriate to the sanitised world of loft-living stockbrokers, than struggling artists eking out a miserable existence squatting in accommodation without electricity or heat. It could easily be a TV set for a pop show. An enormous ticker across the stage lists those (mostly famous) people who have died from AIDS over the years, but the pristine environment doesn't reflect the degrading suffering that victims endured in the 1980s and early 90s, nor the despair felt by those who contracted the disease."

Van Outen had something of a reputation in the musical theater world, having played Roxie Hart in the long-running revival of Kander and Ebb's *Chicago*, as a replacement in both the West End and Broadway companies. She had also been a moderator on NBC's *Grease: You're the One That I Want!*—the reality show used to cast the two leads for the Broadway revival of *Grease*. As Maureen, she was decked out in fishnets, a black bustier, and a leather jacket, like something out of an early Madonna video. Oliver Thornton, who played Mark, had a big voice, having played major roles in *The Phantom of the Opera* and *Les Misérables*; he sang the opening verse of "La Vie Bohème" as an over-the-top impersonation of an operatic tenor. His buff body was seen shirtless in certain scenes—and in some of the production's promotional graphics. Luke Evans, another heartthrob, received the best reviews for his well-sung Roger; he has gone on to a film career with roles in *The Hobbit* and Disney's live-action remake of *Beauty and the Beast*.

Compared to the original production, this one's cast was somewhat deficient in diversity. Jay Webb as Angel eschewed traditional drag for a more up-to-date, muscle-revealing take on gender-bending fashion. Siobhan Donaghy, formerly of the pop group Sugababes, played Mimi; neither she nor Webb was Hispanic, and Francesca Jackson as Joanne was as white and blonde as Van Outen. Angel, Mark, and Mimi were identified as British expats living in New York and performed with their own British accents; the other principal cast members assumed American ones. Many of the specific references to East Village and Alphabet City locations were deleted, while gratuitous instances of the F-word were liberally sprinkled into the script.

Karen Fricker of *Variety*, who felt that credibility was strained by casting performers mostly too old for the roles, commented on some of the individual performances: "Oliver Thornton is likeable as Mark, and Luke Evans has the big voice necessary for Roger's songs, but both are simply too pumped-up gorgeous to make sense as impoverished East Village squatters. Leon Lopez as a soulful Collins and Francesca Jackson as Maureen's feisty

Layton Williams, center, as Angel, with Ross Hunter as Roger and Billy Cullum as Mark, in the 2016 production at the St. James Theatre, London. *John Snelling/Getty Images*

lover Joanne are strongest among the leads in voice and characterization. . . . Siobhan Donaghy . . . alone looks age-appropriate as Mimi, but she's otherwise unsuited to the role, her awkward stage movement failing to make sense of the character's seductive felinity." Charles Spencer of the *Telegraph* felt that "while the singing is strong, most of the acting is abysmal." He concluded that the production offered "cruel and unusual punishment to anyone burdened with a brain."

Twentieth Anniversary UK Tour/London Revival

On December 8, 2016, an all-new production of *Rent*—produced by Robert Mackintosh and Idili Theatricals Limited for RENT 20th Anniversary Productions Ltd.—began preview performances in London. This West End engagement came in the middle of a six-month tour that had begun in October. It was presented in the St. James Theatre, one of London's newest venues, built on the site of the former Westminster Theatre, which was torn down in 2002 after being badly damaged by a fire. The new building opened in 2012 and was purchased by Andrew Lloyd Webber's Really Useful Group in 2016; the limited eight-week run of *Rent* was to be one of the last attractions to play the venue before its name was changed, as of early 2017, to The Other Palace, which under artistic director Paul Taylor Mills will focus on the development of new musicals. The main auditorium seats only 312, making it an unusually intimate space for a major professional production of *Rent*.

Neither a remount nor a "remix," this twentieth-anniversary version, directed by Bruce Guthrie, was a newly staged and designed but thoughtful and respectful interpretation of the musical. There was a greater emphasis on dance than in previous productions, with choreography by Lee Proud. Though London critics had historically been less receptive to the material than the American press, this version was received with considerable enthusiasm.

Fiona Mountford of the *Evening Standard* admitted to not being a huge fan of the material, but she was impressed with the young cast: "The two absolute standouts are the women who dominate, frustrate and illuminate Mark and Roger's lives: angry performance artist Maureen (Lucie Jones) and elusive exotic dancer Mimi (Philippa Stefani). If we hooked these two actresses up to the National Grid, they could power the country with their singing, dancing and all-round attitude until well into the New Year."

Writing for the *Stage*, Mark Shenton said: "Some of the rough-edged rawness of its original Broadway staging (by Michael Greif) has been smoothed out in Bruce Guthrie's more glossy, less gritty production, with its industrial, graffiti-ed, multi-platformed set by Anna Fleischle. But the stunningly well-cast company lend it serious vocal heft, making Larson's rich melodies soar and wound, as we follow two tenderly charted ill-fated romances."

Dominic Maxwell of the *London Times* gave the production an enthusiastic four out of five stars, writing: "There have been some so-so revivals of Jonathan Larson's game-changing requiem for New York's bohemia over the past two decades but, oh boy, this electrifying 20th-anniversary production is not one of them. Lithe but grungy, sexy but sad, it's a gorgeous celebration of this rock musical . . . The director, Bruce Guthrie, had apparently never seen *Rent* on stage. That may be part of how he manages to present it with all the urgency and joy of a show that's never been seen before."

In addition to the leading ladies mentioned above, the cast included Billy Cullum as Mark, Ross Hunter as Roger, Javar La'Trail Parker as Benny, Shanay Holmes as Joanne, Ryan O'Gorman as Collins, and Layton Williams (a terrific dancer who as a child had played the title role in *Billy Elliot* in the West End) as Angel.

The St. James Theatre has a second, smaller performance space, called the Studio. Appropriately enough, Anthony Rapp was performing his cabaret show, which included reminiscences and songs from *Rent*, in that venue the same week the show opened on the main stage. His music director, Daniel A. Weiss, had played keyboard and guitar for the original *Rent* on Broadway.

"Adventure, Tedium, No Family, Boring Locations"

Rent and Its Journey to Film

As the biggest phenomenon to hit Broadway in years, *Rent* seemed an obvious candidate for the movies. And studios did begin approaching the Larson family about rights before the show had even moved to Broadway. But the musical's journey to the screen was more complicated and trouble-plagued than most of its fans would have expected. This was partly because movie musicals, and in particular film versions of Broadway shows, had gone out of style years earlier.

During the so-called "golden age" of the Broadway musical, it was almost a given that any hit show, from the forties through the sixties, would be made into a movie. It may be a surprise today to remember that no fewer than four of the ten films that won the Academy Award for Best Picture during the sixties were adapted from Broadway musicals: *West Side Story* (1961), *My Fair Lady* (1964), *The Sound of Music* (1965), and *Oliver!* (1968). Things started to slow down a bit after that, when the lavish Hollywood adaptations of Jerry Herman's *Hello, Dolly!* and *Mame* didn't do as well as they should have done, though both *Fiddler on the Roof* (1971) and *Cabaret* (1972) found tremendous success, and films of the rock musicals *Jesus Christ Superstar* and *Godspell*, both released in 1973, had their adherents. That decade ended with a trio of major entries—the films of *The Wiz* (a critical and financial flop) and *Hair* (a box office disappointment despite rave reviews) and of course the smash hit adaptation of *Grease* (which became the highest-grossing movie musical in history!)—but this spurt of activity would prove to be almost a last hurrah for a genre that went into near hibernation for the next couple of decades. The disappointing performances of the adaptations of *Annie* and *A Chorus Line*, both of which had been huge Broadway hits and should have been blockbusters on film, made the eighties mostly a washout, and the nineties suffered an almost total drought. The two properties that were the frequent subjects of speculation and rumor were *Dreamgirls*, a hoped-for Whitney Houston vehicle, and *Evita*, in which Meryl Streep and Barbra Streisand were alternately rumored to star. When the movie of the latter was finally released in 1996—starring neither Streisand nor Streep but the pop star Madonna—it represented the decade's only contribution to the genre, and the future looked bleak. If continual rumors of the death of the Broadway musical proved unfounded, the movie adaptation looked like an extinct species. But *Rent* had done much to reinvigorate Broadway. Could it single-handedly revive the movie musical as well?

It had been a long time since a musical had become such a mainstream cultural phenomenon, and *Rent*'s of-the-moment subject matter and contemporary rock score suggested that a film would stand an excellent chance of breaking the musical-theater barrier and finding an unusually wide audience. Most of the major studios were expressing interest, but neither the show's Broadway producers nor the Larson family, who controlled the rights to the property in the aftermath of Jonathan's passing, were immediately convinced the show should be a movie at all. Kevin McCollum has spoken about how the appeal of *Rent* was grounded in its identity as a live event, one that established an especially active and intimate rapport between performers and audience. In keeping with the themes that Larson was writing about, the musical celebrated live human contact in the face of an increasingly virtual world. Its uniquely theatrical energy might be difficult to recreate onscreen.

According to Julie Larson, speaking to Morgan Allen for a Playbill.com interview, there was a major "discussion among our family whether we would allow the whole idea of a movie to be made and whether *Rent* can translate to a film. We weren't sure whether it would or not. We realized that a lot more people would be able to hear Jonathan's music. We also realized what would have kept us from going ahead and making a movie would have been fear. So much of what *Rent* is about is to not choose fear and that was for me a very motivating factor in deciding to take a chance and see if it could be translated."

Julie herself had a substantial background in film, having worked in the industry for eighteen years. She produced commercials and also worked for Propaganda Films, one of the biggest producers of music videos, which launched major film directors like David Fincher and Michael Bay. Her husband at the time, Chuck McCollum, was in the business as well, as an actor and casting director. After her brother's death, Julie put her own career on hold in order to take on the responsibilities for overseeing and caretaking the business of *Rent*—which quickly became and has remained a full-time job. Despite their knowledge of the industry, navigating the sale of the film rights was one of the daunting challenges the family faced in those early days. They had barely had time to grieve for Jonathan's loss when most of the major Hollywood film companies began coming to them with offers and requests for meetings. "It was very heady and scary," Julie said. "It was all happening so quickly and simultaneously."

Choosing a Studio

Early contenders for the rights included Warner Brothers (initially on behalf of director Joel Schumacher) as well as Universal, Fox's Searchlight Division, Fine Line, and Danny DeVito's Jersey Films. With offers on the table from various studios, the family decided on Miramax, the production company founded in 1979 by brothers Harvey and Bob Weinstein. Though it had been acquired by Disney in 1993, the Weinstein brothers continued to run it with an unusual degree of autonomy.

With Miramax intending to provide major financing, Harvey Weinstein asked Jane Rosenthal and Robert De Niro (yes, that Robert De Niro) of Tribeca Films to produce the film, and Rosenthal would remain one of the project's staunchest advocates when the going got rough in subsequent years. One of the major considerations the studio had to face was a five-year wait period. The stage version by that point was situated to run for years, and the Broadway producers didn't want any film to compete with it for audiences until at least 2001.

Writers and Directors

One of Rosenthal's first steps was to hire a screenwriter. She chose Stephen Chbosky, a young writer and filmmaker best known for *The Perks of Being a Wallflower*, his 1999 coming-of-age novel about a sensitive, repressed teenager gradually coming out of his shell during his freshman year of high school. From the Pittsburgh area, Chbosky has claimed F. Scott Fitzgerald, J. D. Salinger, and Tennessee Williams as major influences on his aesthetic; he was mentored by the Hollywood screenwriter Stewart Stern (*Rebel Without a Cause*), and earned a degree from the University of Southern California. His first feature, *The Four Corners of Nowhere* (1995), was an indie he wrote, directed, and acted in; it was screened at the Sundance Film Festival. He also collaborated with the writer/director Jon Sherman on a screenplay adaptation of Michael Chabon's bestseller *The Mysteries of Pittsburgh* (a novel that shares some characteristics with his own work), but that project fell apart; the film version that was released several years later was adapted by a different team. *The Perks of Being a Wallflower* was published by MTV Books, and, though not marketed as a YA title, it became a cult favorite among teenagers and eventually a *New York Times* bestseller. Like *Rent*, the book has often been challenged and even banned because of its frank depictions of drug use and sexuality among young people. The film version, which Chbosky himself adapted, directed, and produced, was not made until 2012. His other post-*Rent* credits include co-creating, producing, and writing for the CBS TV series *Jericho* and penning the screenplay for the live-action remake of the Disney musical *Beauty and the Beast* (2017).

The next major decision of course was choosing the right director. There were numerous contenders, even including, at one point, the legendary Martin Scorsese, one of De Niro's close friends and frequent collaborators. De Niro wooed him for the project, but Scorsese was not happy with the screenplay. Eventually it was announced that the film would be directed by Spike Lee—who, coincidentally, is actually mentioned in the show, in the lyrics to "Light My Candle." (See Chapter 16.) Lee was enthusiastic about the project; he spent the summer of 2001 working with Chbosky on the screenplay and even began casting. But Harvey Weinstein wasn't satisfied with the script and responded by reducing the film's budget from $28 million to just $20 million. Angered by this, Spike Lee quit the film, and it started to look as if the whole project was going to fall apart.

Rosenthal, however, was still very committed to bringing *Rent* to the screen; she scheduled a meeting with Weinstein to try to find a way to move forward. That meeting never took place. Though Weinstein's and Rosenthal's offices were in the same building in downtown New York, the building was located just a block and a half from the World Trade Center—and the meeting had been scheduled for September 11, 2001. Were it not for the terrorist attacks that occurred that day, the subsequent history of the film might have turned out very differently.

As it was, though, Weinstein seemed to be losing confidence in the property. No longer wanting Miramax to shoulder the entire risk, he asked Rosenthal and De Niro to try to find another studio to contribute substantially to the financing, and this proved surprisingly difficult. Rosenthal approached Warner Brothers, HBO Films, Universal, and others. Five years into its Broadway run, *Rent* was still selling well, but it was no longer the latest pop culture sensation as it had been when Miramax first bought the rights. Certain elements of the storyline—including drug addiction, cross-dressing, AIDS, and gay relationships—scared away producers and studio heads who worried that it wouldn't appeal to a mass audience. And then in a surprise move Weinstein himself pitched the property to NBC for a TV adaptation. From a business standpoint, that might have made some sense; the previous few years had seen large-budget made-for-TV remakes of several classic

Broadway musicals, including *Gypsy*, *Bye Bye Birdie*, *South Pacific*, and *Annie*, and there seemed to be a market for this type of production, with more in the pipeline.

The Larson family, however, was not pleased with the idea, and contractually they had the power to stop it. According to Claudia Eller of the *Chicago Tribune*: "In signing over the rights, they had secured veto power over who would be producer and director and a guarantee that no TV project could go forward without their permission." Quite rightly, they maintained that *Rent* deserved a big screen treatment.

Someone who happened to agree with them was the director Chris Columbus, a longtime fan of the musical who had made a bid to direct the film years earlier but had been passed over in favor of Lee. When he heard about the proposed TV deal, he was "stunned" that anyone was even considering foregoing a feature film version of the show. He had his agent set up a meeting with Jane Rosenthal and talked to the Larson family as well. Julie Larson later said that after spending no more than ten minutes with him she felt confident that he was the choice; as she later told Eller, "He just got it."

Columbus had his own production company, 1492 Pictures, with partners Michael Barnathan and Mark Radcliffe. They put together a deal with Tribeca Productions, but financing remained a problem. Miramax was splitting off from Disney, and the Weinstein brothers were no longer in a position to bankroll the project. Columbus had a production deal with Warner Brothers; with Harvey Weinstein's permission he took the project to them, and in early May of 2004 it was announced that Warner would be producing the film. But that deal fell through when the studio set the budget at just $20 million—coincidentally the same figure that had caused Spike Lee to resign from the project years earlier.

Like Lee, Columbus didn't feel that amount was adequate for a film of such importance and magnitude; *Rent* had become his passion project and he was determined to get it made right. The solution finally arrived in the person of Joe Roth of Revolution Studios. Roth and Columbus had a positive history dating back to Roth's days heading 20th Century Fox, which had produced *Home Alone* and *Mrs. Doubtfire*, very successful films directed by Columbus. Roth read the screenplay for *Rent* and was enthusiastic—and it helped that his daughter was a Renthead. Revolution agreed to finance the film; the deal was announced in *Variety* on September 30, 2004.

By this time, Hollywood's faith in the future of the movie musical had quite unexpectedly been restored by the success of the film version of *Chicago*. A project that had languished in development for decades finally came to fruition under director/choreographer Rob Marshall; the 2002 film became an enormous hit and won the Academy Award for Best Picture. (It also provided a huge boost to the box office of the Broadway revival of that musical, which had been running since 1996 and is still going strong as of this writing—suggesting that the five-year hold originally put on the movie version of *Rent* might not have been necessary.)

Weinstein sold the rights to *Rent* for $4 million. Because Columbus had already spent time developing the piece at Warner and the screenplay was ready to go, Revolution was able to fast-track the film, which went into production the following spring and would be released that November, distributed by Sony. The producers of the Broadway *Rent*—Jeffrey Seller, Kevin McCollum, and Allan S. Gordon—were also onboard as executive producers, with Julie Larson as co-producer.

Chris Columbus, Director

Columbus was born in Pennsylvania in 1958 but raised primarily in Champion, Ohio. His parents had both worked in factories, and Columbus got a taste of that life himself when he had to take a summer job in one during his college years at New York University's Tisch School of the Arts—a result of having forgotten to renew his scholarship. He later claimed that the experience had been a major motivating factor in his career, as he had seen what the rest of his life might be like if he didn't find success in his chosen field.

Columbus's career in the film industry began with work as a screenwriter; he was employed by Steven Spielberg's company in the mid-eighties and worked on the scripts for such popular films as *Gremlins* and *The Goonies*. He also worked as a writer and creative consultant on the animated television series *Galaxy High School*. His first feature film as director was *Adventures in Babysitting* (1987), which coincidentally featured a teenage Anthony Rapp. This was followed by *Heartbreak Hotel* and *Only the Lonely*, both of which he wrote and directed. He also directed the very popular film *Home Alone* and its sequel *Home Alone 2: Lost in New York*, as well as the Robin Williams vehicle *Mrs. Doubtfire*, among others. In the years immediately before he was chosen to helm *Rent*, Columbus was at the very top of the entertainment industry as the director of the first two films in the hugely successful Harry Potter series, *Harry Potter and the Sorcerer's Stone* and *Harry Potter and the Chamber of Secrets*, and he also served as producer of the third movie in the series, *Harry Potter and the Prisoner of Azkaban*, which was directed by Alfonso Cuarón.

Columbus is married to Monica Devereux, a former dancer, and they have four children. The family lived in London for a time when the Harry Potter movies were in production. They now live in northern California, deliberately keeping a healthy distance from the high-pressure world of Hollywood, where Columbus remains very busy. He cofounded ZAG Animation Studios and started his own production company, 1492 Pictures, in 1995. (The company is named for the year in which another Chris Columbus sailed for the New World.)

In the years following *Rent*, Columbus has directed *I Love You, Beth Cooper* (2009), *Percy Jackson and the Olympians: The Lightning Thief* (2010), and *Pixels* (2015). But if his output as a director has appeared to slow down slightly, he has continued to produce films with other directors at an impressive rate. These include the *Night at the Museum* movies, *Fantastic Four: Rise of the Silver Surfer*, *It Had to Be You*, and *Tallulah*, as well as *Percy Jackson: Sea of Monsters*. Perhaps inspired by his work on the Harry Potter and Percy Jackson films, Columbus has also tried his hand at writing children's books, coauthoring the *House of Secrets* series with Ned Vizzini.

Throughout his career, Columbus has been celebrated as the creator of popular films with teenage or preteen protagonists, and he has been referred to as "the undisputed king of family films." These attributes, as well as his identification with big-budget, mainstream commercial fare, might have seemed to make him an unlikely choice to helm the movie of *Rent*. Fans of the show might well have expected the Larson family to choose a director with a grittier indie-film background and sensibility, or someone with experience in the world of rock music and videos. But Columbus had long been a devoted admirer of the musical, and with the Harry Potter movies he had proven to be adept at adapting stories from other media with tremendous faithfulness, affection, and respect for the original material.

Columbus saw *Rent* on Broadway, with the original cast, in 1996. He has said it produced a kind of emotion he had never before experienced in a theater, and he was so excited by it that he bought another ticket and saw it again less than a week later. He bought the original cast album and played it all the time for years; it became "the soundtrack to his life." He saw touring companies of the show in Boston, San Francisco, and Las Vegas. As he told Steve Head in an interview for the website IGN.com, he felt an unusually strong connection to the material because he had "lived in Manhattan for 17 years," adding: "I've lived in a loft. I knew all of these people when I was struggling at NYU. I knew these musicians and actors and artists. That was the world I knew."

The Screenplay

By the time Columbus took on the project, Stephen Chbosky had written a complete screenplay and revised it in collaboration with Spike Lee. That script was very different from the one that was eventually filmed. Chbosky and Lee had been concerned that a twenty-first century audience would not accept the artificiality of characters singing, particularly in the context of a realistic, modern story. Long gone were the glory days of the MGM musical, when actors gleefully burst into song at the drop of a hat, and the paucity of new musicals over the preceding twenty years had contributed to the notion that the genre was outmoded. So in the early drafts of his screenplay, Chbosky restructured the story, contriving situations in which characters might realistically be singing, or stylistic conceits that would otherwise justify the transitions into songs. These included rewriting some of the songs and recitative sections as spoken dialogue, repositioning some numbers as fantasy or dream sequences, and setting others up as actual musical performances. (Similar strategies were adapted, with varying degrees of success, in other films of stage musicals that came out around the same time, such as *Chicago*, *Nine*, and *Dreamgirls*.) Examples included the title song, which was reconceived as a performance by Roger's band at CBGB's; "Take Me or Leave Me," in which Maureen "improvised" a vocal to music a band was playing in a bar and Joanne, at first embarrassed by her behavior, eventually joined in; and "Tango: Maureen," presented as a dream sequence. "One Song Glory" was to be sung in voiceover with a montage of scenes from Roger and April's past. Though a couple of these ideas, in modified form, found their way into the finished movie, Columbus (with limited involvement by Chbosky) eventually rewrote most of the screenplay. His version is much more faithful to Larson's original script: though a lot of the recitative is replaced by spoken dialogue, most of the songs arise directly out of the scenes as they do in the stage version, and the movie is unabashedly a musical.

Before the movie began filming (and almost exactly a year before it was released), Paul Wontorek published a piece called "I Should Tell You: A Rent Rant" on Broadway.com. Having read an early interview with Columbus about his plans, Wontorek, a big fan of the musical, had some concerns—especially regarding the director's statement that he would be cutting some of the musical's songs to make room for new dialogue scenes. He wrote: "I can only assume that Columbus will leave the big 'hits' like 'Seasons of Love,' 'One Song Glory,' 'Light My Candle,' 'Out Tonight' and 'Take Me or Leave Me' intact and it's probably safe to say that fans of the 'Tune Up' and 'Voice Mail' segments of the score will have to wave them goodbye. But what of the less known yet emotionally driven songs like 'Will I?' 'Halloween' and 'Goodbye Love'? Will Columbus have the good sense to know what to leave in?" Impressively, with the exception of "Will I?"—which is included in the film—Wontorek's suspicions about which songs Columbus would include and which ones he would cut proved to be exactly correct.

Casting the Film

Though Columbus eventually made the decision to cast most of the principal actors from the original Broadway cast, that choice was in no way a foregone conclusion when he began work on the project. He and the producers considered doing a major search and going with all unknown actors, which would have been in keeping with the show's themes. They also came close to going the exact opposite way and casting pop stars, with the names Justin Timberlake, Christina Aguilera, and Usher rising to the top of the list. In the Steve Head interview, Columbus revealed: "I went so far as meeting Justin, who is a *terrific* guy, by the way . . . But then I started to meet the original cast, and I realized the thing I responded to was the *connection* that they had, partially because of Jonathan Larson's death. . . . There's a chemistry there that, as a director, I had never seen before. And I wanted to catch that."

Of the original eight principals, six were cast in the film. Anthony Rapp (Mark), Adam Pascal (Roger), Idina Menzel (Maureen), Taye Diggs (Benny),

Rent costars Jesse L. Martin and Idina Menzel

Jesse. L. Martin (Collins) and Wilson Jermain Heredia (Angel) were all hired to recreate their original roles. But Fredi Walker, who had played Joanne onstage, and Columbus agreed she was too mature by that point to play the role on film. The original Mimi, Daphne Rubin-Vega, was thirty-five by the time the movie went into production, but the decision on whether she could still be convincing as the nineteen-year-old Mimi was obviated by an extenuating circumstance: she was pregnant at the time.

There was of course substantial competition for the role of Joanne. The contenders included *American Idol* alumna Jennifer Hudson, who lost the part but would shortly thereafter be cast in the plum role of Effie in the big screen version of another hit Broadway musical:

In celebration of the film's release, the November 2005 edition of *Life* magazine offered several alternate cover designs featuring different stars. This one shows Jesse L. Martin and Idina Menzel.

Time & Life Pictures/Getty Images

Dreamgirls. That film, for which Hudson won an Academy Award, was released in 2006, one year after *Rent*.

Tracie Thoms (Joanne)

Tracie Thoms had been a devoted fan of the show since her college days, when she had seen the original cast perform it on Broadway. She remembers it vividly, saying: "It was unlike anything anyone had ever seen. It changed the face of musical theatre. I couldn't believe there was a musical with people like the people I knew onstage; I had a visceral reaction to it. I thought,'I have to be a part of this because this is really important.'"

She auditioned for the Broadway company and the tours nine times over the course of several years; she usually got a callback but never booked the job, and was told several times she was still too young to play Joanne. But she wouldn't give up because the role meant so much to her, claiming: "Finally there's a show for me. An intellectual black woman who's viscerally connected to her community. She's from a well-to-do black family; that's something you very seldom see, so I appreciated that at the time." Even after being accepted into the extremely competitive acting program at Juilliard, she attended one last callback in Washington, D.C., and says, "If I had gotten cast in *Rent* I wouldn't have gone to Juilliard. But life has a way of working out, because that probably would have been a mistake."

She first auditioned for the film while she was still in school, and Spike Lee was attached as director; Lee had her sing Mimi's "Without You" as well as Joanne's part of "Take Me or Leave Me." By the time Chris Columbus had taken over the project, Thoms had graduated from the conservatory and made her Broadway debut in *Drowning Crow*. She went in for an audition at Telsey's studio and sang "Take Me or Leave Me" on tape; a DVD was sent to Columbus, and a month later her agent told her she was a frontrunner for Joanne. She was expecting to be asked to do a formal screen test or to read for the director in person, but Columbus simply watched the footage that had been submitted on all the finalists for the role. When he came to hers, he knew he had found his Joanne.

Thoms recalls that she was leaving for a commercial shoot in the East Village when her agent called her to tell her she had the role: "My agent at Gersh had been a Renthead so this was a big deal for her as well!" Her determination and dedication to the show and the part had finally paid off, and in the biggest possible way. She never had to do a screen test or read for Columbus, but after signing her he flew her out to San Francisco for a couple of days just to meet in person, so they could start to get to know each other.

It was only then that she found out that she would be working with most of the original cast, which she says added "an extra level of crazy. I saw all of them do it. They were the reason I loved it, and now I was going to be acting with them, which was insane." She had never considered herself to be that much of a singer—though anyone who has heard her in the movie or on the soundtrack would surely disagree with that assessment! As soon as she booked the film, she started working with a voice coach in New York.

Autographed photo of Tracie Thoms as Joanne.

Three years after making the film, Thoms finally got her chance to play Joanne on stage as well, when she was asked to join the cast for the final six weeks of the Broadway run; she later reprised the role again at the Hollywood Bowl. She has enjoyed a busy television career, with regular or recurring roles on the series *As If*, *Wonderfalls*, *Cold Case*, *Harry's Law*, and the webseries *Bandwagon* and *Send Me* (for which she received an Emmy nomination). Her film credits include *The Devil Wears Prada*, *I Will Follow*, *Safe House*, *Equity*, *Looper*, *Raze*, *The Drowning*, and the 2014 remake of the musical *Annie*. Thoms has remained close friends with her *Rent* costar Rosario Dawson; the two worked together again in the *Death Proof* segment of Quentin Tarantino and Robert Rodriguez's "double feature" film *Grindhouse* in 2007. Though very successful on both the large and small screens, she has stated publicly: "I think theater will always be my first love. I've been doing it since I was nine, and there's nothing quite like being on stage, having the immediate intake of energy and exchange of ideas" (quoted on her IMDB page). Regional theater credits include *A Raisin in the Sun* at Baltimore Center Stage and *Joe Turner's Come and Gone* at Missouri Repertory Theater. She returned to Broadway in Lydia R. Diamond's play *Stick Fly* and as Dr. Charlotte—one of the "lesbians next door"—in the 2016 revival of the musical *Falsettos*.

(The year after the film of *Rent* was released, the original cast reunited for a concert performance onstage at the Nederlander to celebrate the show's tenth anniversary on Broadway. The original Joanne, Fredi Walker-Browne, played the role one more time that night. In a note she contributed to the program book, she wrote: "For the record, I am very, very pleased with the work Tracie did. She totally 'got' Joanne and I feel she captured her wonderfully for both of us. To use the vernacular—girlfriend worked that mess and I'm lovin' her for it!")

Rosario Dawson (Mimi)

The role of Mimi is especially difficult to cast, requiring not only serious rock and roll chops and exciting dance ability but a combination of youthful vulnerability, street cred, and unleashed sexiness. Determined to get the role, Rosario Dawson choreographed her own complex dance routine for "Out Tonight" but, as she later admitted, was so nervous during her screen test that she froze up and was unable to perform it as she had planned. She left feeling that she had blown it—but Columbus followed her out of the room and offered her the role on the spot.

Born in New York City in 1979, Dawson had resisted seeing *Rent* because she had heard a lot about it and, as a Latina who had grown up dirt poor on the Lower East Side, she suspected it was co-opting her own life experiences.

"Light My Candle": Adam Pascal and Rosario Dawson as Roger and Mimi in the film.
Revolution Studios/Columbia Pictures

(When she finally saw the show on Broadway in preparation for playing the role, she found she loved it.) She never knew her father; her mother, who was only sixteen when Rosario was born, was a singer and writer named Isabel Celeste. At seventeen, Isabel married Greg Dawson, a construction worker, who loved Rosario and raised her as his own, though the marriage ended in divorce. Rosario has a younger brother; for much of her childhood, the family lived as squatters in an abandoned tenement where her parents installed the wiring and plumbing by themselves. She got an early start as a performer with a brief appearance on *Sesame Street*, and then was famously discovered on her front porch at age fifteen by a photographer and a screenwriter who tapped her for a role in the controversial indie film *Kids* (1995). She studied acting at the Lee Strasberg Institute, and by age twenty her career had picked up pace, with some fifteen film roles between 2000 and 2003; the titles include *King of the Jungle*, *Josie and the Pussycats*, *Sidewalks of New York*, *Ash Wednesday*, *Men in Black II*, and *Shattered Glass*.

Though she was becoming known as a serious actress in gritty, realistic roles, Dawson had always had an interest in music and singing; she recorded voiceovers and made appearances in rock videos, collaborating with artists including Prince and the Chemical Brothers. Her performance as Mimi earned her the Satellite Award for Best Supporting Actress in a Motion Picture. In the summer of 2005, just months before the film was released, she made her New York stage debut at the Delacorte Theatre in Central Park, playing Julia in the Public Theater's revival of the 1972 rock musical version of Shakespeare's *Two Gentlemen of Verona*.

Dawson's personal life has included romantic relationships with the actor Jason Lewis and the director Danny Boyle, with whom she worked on the film *Trance*, and in 2014 she adopted a twelve-year-old girl. In the years since *Rent*, she has continued to act regularly in serious films while also pursuing her interests in science fiction and comic books; she appeared in *Percy Jackson and the Olympians: The Lightning Thief* and played Claire Temple in the TV series version of the comic book *Daredevil*, crossing over in the same role to appearances in four other related Marvel Television series for Netflix. She has also done voice roles for numerous animated film projects and video games. Dawson started her own production company, which is known as Trybe, and has been active in philanthropic and political causes, supporting the Lower East Side Girls Club, Amnesty International, Doctors Without Borders, the Nature Conservancy, PFLAG, Save the Children, and other worthy organizations.

Supporting Roles

While the stage version of *Rent* used a small ensemble of young actor/singers to double and triple all the cameos and minor parts, the film of course cast these characters realistically, with age-appropriate performers in each of the individual roles. Some highly prestigious artists agreed to take on very small parts, probably because of their affection for the musical. They include Randy Graff (who has many musical theater credits, including the role of Fantine in the original Broadway cast of *Les Misérables*) as Mark's mother, and the distinguished playwright/solo performer Anna Deavere Smith (*Fires in the Mirror; Twilight: Los Angeles, 1992*) as Joanne's mother. Sarah Silverman, the famously outspoken, hilarious, and sometimes controversial actress/writer/comedian, was cast as TV producer Alexi Darling.

A couple of alums of the stage version appeared in small roles, including Shaun Earl, who played Angel on tour and Paul on Broadway, as a waiter in the Life Café scene, and Aisha de Haas, who didn't get to reprise the "Seasons of Love" solo, which she had sung as a replacement on Broadway, but did memorably recreate her cameo as the "Woman with Bags."

Other important supporting performances included actor/playwright Daniel London (*Patch Adams*) as Life Support group leader Paul; the handsome musical theater actor Wayne Wilcox (*The Light in the Piazza* in Chicago;

TV's *Gilmore Girls*) as Gordon; and singer/actor Aaron Lohr, who has been a professional performer since childhood with credits including the original movie *Newsies*, as Steve. After filming *Rent*, Lohr worked with Idina Menzel again in the Off-Broadway production of Michael John LaChiusa's musical *See What I Wanna See*; it was running at the Public Theater in the fall of 2005 when the movie was released. Over ten years later, in September of 2016, Lohr and Menzel announced that they were engaged to be married.

Rehearsing and Recording

When casting was complete, Jonathan Larson's family and some of his closest friends hosted a Peasant's Feast for the actors. As Jonathan had done for the original cast, they wanted to make them feel like part of the family. They shared memories of Jonathan so the people who hadn't known him could start to feel a connection to who he was, what his life had been like, and why he had written *Rent*. Victoria Leacock had a lot of personal items from Jonathan's apartment, and she presented each of the cast members with a keepsake to remember him by.

Though it's unusual for the cast and director of a movie to spend much time rehearsing before going in front of the cameras, sometimes musicals are the exception. Rehearsals for the film *Rent* stretched over a period of several months at San Francisco's Treasure Island. The actors found Columbus a joy to work with. According to Pascal: "It was a true labor of love for him. He had no other motivating factor for doing it. He valued having us there and valued our opinions and our input."

As is standard for a film musical, the cast recorded the songs in a studio before beginning to film their scenes; the tracks were laid down at George Lucas's Skywalker Ranch. Inspired by the Green Day album *American Idiot* (which incidentally was later adapted as a Broadway musical), Columbus hired one of its producers, Rob Cavallo, to handle the recording, which he said he wanted to sound more like a first-class rock record and less like a Broadway show than the original cast album had—especially in the title song and Mimi's "Out Tonight." Original music director Tim Weil played piano on the soundtrack, with an eight-member band that included several well-known session musicians. Though most of the songs were later performed on set to the prerecorded tracks, Idina Menzel's rendition of "Over the Moon" was sung live on the soundstage during filming. Menzel had requested that specifically so she could stay flexible with the comic timing and interact with the crowd; she knew the number depended on spontaneity and wouldn't work as well if she had to conform to the rhythms of a prerecorded version.

Cavallo produced the resulting soundtrack album, which some people consider to be the definitive recording of the score and perhaps the one Larson would have preferred. It has state-of-the-art music-industry production values, unlike the original cast album, which like most such recordings was put together quite hastily and on a limited budget. (Others, of course, will always prefer the Broadway version for its excitement and sense of immediacy.) The soundtrack album runs to ninety-five minutes on two CDs, each with fourteen tracks. Though it can't be considered a complete record of Larson's score (the phone messages, "We're Okay," and the various iterations of "Christmas Bells" were not included in the film), it does include "Halloween" and "Goodbye, Love," since those two numbers were recorded and filmed before being cut from the movie itself. It also features a bonus track of the cast singing "Love Heals," an inspirational song that Larson had written for an AIDS benefit. Released on the Warner Brothers label, the album was originally issued with eight different slipcovers; you could choose the one with the picture of your favorite character. As with the Broadway recording, a single-disc highlights version was also released, this one including seventeen tracks for sixty-five minutes of music. In addition, Warner Brothers commissioned dance remixes of some of the songs, which were distributed for use in clubs, online, and on CD. There were multiple versions of "Seasons of Love" and "Take Me or Leave Me," done by different DJs, and at least one version each of "Out Tonight" and "Light My Candle."

The Shoot

Having hired so many of the original cast members, some of whom had minimal film acting experience, Columbus might have worried that their acting styles, honed onstage, would be too broad for the camera. To their credit (and to his as a director), this ultimately proved not to be the case: under his guidance, they all gave well-modulated, relaxed performances. On one of the early days of filming, however, when the director and actors were still feeling each other out, Taye Diggs took the opportunity to test Columbus by playing a practical joke. As the director told Barbara Hoffman of the *New York Post* shortly before the film was released: "We did the funeral scene and it was time to do his close-up. I yell 'Action,' and suddenly Taye breaks into this hideous, over-the-top performance. He's crying and his lip is trembling and I thought, this is horrible. What can I possibly say to him that would even help? Then I looked over and saw Jesse, Adam and everyone laughing hysterically. Taye was playing a joke on me. That's the essence of Taye. He always wanted to f___ with you."

Though Columbus wanted to film as many scenes as possible on location in the East Village and Alphabet City, the gentrification of those neighborhoods (which, having already started in the nineties, is itself a major theme of *Rent*) had made them almost unrecognizable. There were a few carefully selected streets they were able to use, but the production ended up building Roger and Mark's block on a backlot at Warner Brothers, and some of the street scenes were actually filmed in Oakland, California. The original Life Café was deemed too small to accommodate the filming of "La Vie Bohème," so it was recreated in a warehouse in Alameda, California. Also, following a spate of rock videos that had been filmed in Manhattan, disturbing the sleep of citizens, an ordinance had been passed banning the playing of music on location shoots after ten o'clock at night; this inconvenient rule sent many of the film's musical numbers hunting for alternate locations. One that didn't have to was Roger's great solo "One Song Glory": the producers applied for an exception and managed to get the cutoff extended to midnight on one particular Friday; the song was really filmed on a Manhattan rooftop.

14

"But He's Got Great Footage"

The Movie

The film of *Rent* begins with the iconic song that opens the second act of the stage show: "Seasons of Love." Director Chris Columbus has said that he wanted to start with that to establish immediately that the film is a musical and get the audience—not as comfortable or conversant with the genre as previous generations were—immediately accommodated to the idea of hearing the actors sing. (Also, the film doesn't have an intermission; after getting into the story, it would have been awkward to go back into such an admittedly presentational, theatrical mode.) Michael Greif had told the original cast that during that number they should allow their own personalities and feelings about the sentiments being expressed to come through, rather than strictly playing their characters, and in the film one is even more immediately aware of the performers as actors. We know we are seeing most of the original leading cast members of this famous musical, standing again on a stage, singing a song that has meant a great deal to them for many years; fans of the show already feel an emotional connection—though whether the opening works as well for *Rent* newbies is open to question.

The idea that we are watching actors more than characters is reinforced by setting the number on the stage of a Broadway theater, with highly theatrical lighting that comes up slowly on the performers at the beginning and fades out dramatically at the end; a couple of shots of the house show the seats to be empty, inviting us to imagine that we are the only audience members—or to remember the many audiences who have sat in those seats and been moved by the show in the past. Like they were in the play, the actors are lined up simply and evenly across the stage, but since the film doesn't use an "ensemble," we see only the eight principals rather than the full cast of fifteen. On Broadway, it was two of the ensemble members who sang the demanding, gospel-flavored solo parts: here, the job falls to Tracie Thoms as Joanne and Jesse L. Martin as Collins, and both prove more than equal to the task.

Roger (Adam Pascal) and Mark (Anthony Rapp) throw their burning eviction notice over the fire escape railing in the dynamic opening scene of the film.

Following the fadeout, we hear a brief voiceover by Mark; he identifies the date as Christmas Eve, 1989. Simultaneously, we see some rough film footage, scenes of New York City at Christmastime: both the glittering lights of uptown (including Radio City Music Hall, home of the spectacular annual Christmas Show) and bleak views of the downtown homeless. (Some of these clips were actually made by film students at NYU Tisch, Columbus's alma mater.) An angry driver pulls away from a homeless man trying to clean his windshield, almost running him over in the process, and the shot then opens to reveal Mark, filming the scene on his 16 mm camera. His outrage over the way the man was treated launches him into the opening bars of "Rent," which he sings while riding his bicycle home through the streets of the city.

None of the opening narration from the stage script is included, but most of the information is established visually over the course of the number. When Roger sings his verse, we see him in the loft with his guitar; the power blows after the first line and he struggles with the fuse box (not realizing that Benny had deliberately had it turned off). When Mark arrives home, he finds an eviction notice on the door; he tears it down and shows it to a horrified Roger, so their first "How we gonna pay?" erupts immediately out of this emergency.

The phone call sequence that onstage precedes this number is omitted, but Collins's arrival and Mark's throwing down of the key are enacted in the middle of the song. We then see Collins's mugging quite graphically and frighteningly portrayed (whereas in the play the violence was stylized with the muggers on the opposite side of the stage from their victim.)

It becomes apparent that in this version Benny has bought not just the one building but several, on both sides of the street; all the neighbors with their eviction notices appear in windows and on fire escapes—including Mimi, who emerges from the apartment below Mark and Roger's. In the play, the use of a metal trash barrel for the "illegal wood-burning stove" could be seen as a stylization, but here it is all too literal: as Mark and Roger continue to sing, they burn not only the eviction notice but Mark's screenplay and a band poster Roger pulls down off the wall. A mighty blaze erupts in the big metal garbage can—but rather than using it to keep warm, the guys carry the can out to the fire escape (the metal doesn't seem to have heated up) and dump the contents down into the street.

Joanne and Benny's phone call sequences are cut, but Benny arrives in person in his Range Rover and is surrounded by protesting neighbors as he gets out of the vehicle just in time to sing his line "Draw a line in the sand and then make a stand." The protesting tenants on both sides of the street throw their burning eviction notices down from their fire escapes as the number climaxes in a gorgeous nightmare vision of rebellion. The cavalier handling of flaming papers—which in real life could have burned down the buildings or scorched people on the street below—is not literal so much as imagistic; the whole scene has a heightened, surreal energy that launches the film in a brilliantly dynamic key, expressing the fierceness of Larson's music and lyrics in thrilling visual terms. Though this scene could be viewed as setting the tone for a vividly stylized, dreamlike take on the musical, it actually raises a somewhat false expectation; the ferocious energy and inventive, majestic visual stylization Columbus brought to this number is not matched by anything else in the film—which shortly settles into something more conventional.

The next scene takes place down on the street; Benny parks the Range Rover, and Roger and Mark come downstairs to talk to him (not before Mimi and Roger have exchanged a flirtatious glance on the fire escape). The sequence combines elements of Benny's rent-demanding phone call to the boys (which in the play comes before the opening number) and "You'll See" from much later in the first act; a bit more exposition is added to make sure

Taye Diggs as Benny.

the audience understands Benny's business plan and his relationship with his investor/father-in-law.

Moving forward, much of the first half of the movie follows the stage script quite closely. Most of the changes result from a few key stylistic choices made by the director regarding how to translate the property to film:

First, in keeping with the more naturalistic medium, much of Larson's sung recitative—admittedly a highly theatrical device—is either cut or transformed into spoken dialogue, sometimes but not always using the original words.

Second, the time frame of the movie was moved back to 1989–90. No year is specified in the libretto, but the assumption when the show opened in 1996 was that it was more or less contemporary. By 2005 it was starting to feel like a period piece, and Columbus's decision to set it even earlier made it more so. It also led to a couple of careless anachronisms. No one cut Angel's reference (in "Today 4 U") to *Thelma and Louise* even though that film didn't come out until 1991. Also, the line in "Over the Moon" about "being tied to the hood of a yellow rental truck, packed in with fertilizer and fuel oil" is an allusion to the bombing of the Alfred P. Murrah Federal Building in Oklahoma City, an atrocity that occurred in 1995.

Third, the various iterations of "Christmas Bells" are all omitted; there is no singing chorus of homeless people in the film at all, nor any singing drug addicts. (The reasoning behind this seems clear. When the original show was being developed, there was much concern and deliberation over how to portray the chorus of street people in a way that wouldn't come off as condescending or offensive. They pulled it off, but on film, with the expectation of greater realism and in the absence of a live audience, those moments could have appeared ridiculous indeed. The convincingly cast, non-singing homeless help keep the film grounded in reality and assure that their plight is taken seriously.)

Fourth, the time frame of the first act has been reconfigured so that, instead of taking place entirely in one night, it now covers three days: Christmas Eve, Christmas Day, and the day after that. This change necessitated slight revisions to a couple of the lyrics in "Today 4 U" and "Out Tonight." It also allows some scenes to take place in daylight, including the trip to the Life Support meeting and the walk along the edge of Tompkins Square Park in "I'll Cover You." It may also make things a little more plausible: in the stage version, the number of events crammed into one night can feel excessive, and it's questionable whether Maureen's show—which isn't exactly *The Nutcracker*—could have attracted much of an audience at midnight on Christmas Eve. (In the film it happens two nights later.) If there's a downside to the change, though, it's that it makes the film seem more episodic and lazily paced by comparison. Onstage, the numbers follow one another with the relentless energy of a rock concert, and though this kind of momentum would actually be easier to achieve on film, Columbus opts for the opposite. He slows things down not just by inserting more spoken dialogue but by beginning some scenes with extended establishing shots and ending them with visual codas, often unaccompanied by music, that fade out to black—almost as if preparing for a commercial break. This contributes to a gentle, contemplative tone that is in marked contrast to the propulsive energy of the stage musical.

Much of Mark's narration is also cut, though visual storytelling is generally effective at picking up the slack. Mark doesn't tell us about April's death, but we do learn a lot about her during "One Song Glory." Shots of Roger singing, on the roof of the building, are interspersed with flashback sequences that show April: first watching him perform with his band in a rock club, then hanging out with him in the bar as they fall in love, and later buying heroin from a dealer on the street and shooting up. The last flashback moment shows the two of them reading the positive results of her HIV test.

Columbus originally considered including a shot of Roger and Mark finding her bloody body in the bathroom; the scene was even filmed, but the idea was abandoned due to the impossibility of fitting such a grisly moment into the musical texture of the song. The result is that in the film April's death is never defined as a suicide; for all we learn, she might have simply died of AIDS.

One criticism frequently lobbed at the film concerns the vast spaciousness of Roger and Mark's apartment, which to some people doesn't suggest the financial straits in which they are meant to be struggling. But the choice can certainly be defended: downtown lofts, especially in rundown converted warehouse spaces like this building seems to be, are often both cheaper and much larger than conventional apartments. We also know that, although Roger and Mark are the only people living there now, the same apartment once housed not only the two of them but Benny, Collins, Maureen, and probably April as well. The large living room we see could have been partitioned at that time to make several bedrooms—as in fact was done to Jonathan Larson's famously ramshackle apartment on Greenwich Street. The choice of a large loft was necessitated particularly by Angel's big number, "Today 4 U." His exuberant dance would not have been possible in a cramped, standard-sized living room, and the big apartment here gives him the opportunity to rock out much like he did on Broadway; the famous jump up onto the table is included, and since the vocal was prerecorded he is able to do even more athletic dance moves than he did onstage.

Mark is seen walking through the tent city to Maureen's performance space, which is marked by a graffiti sign over the door identifying it simply as "The Space." An indoor venue in this version, it turns out to be a decaying, cavernous room, probably an abandoned train station, with a stage already set up for her show. Mark and Joanne's meeting goes much as we remember it—with an odd change of gender for the no-show engineer: Joanne's line "she's three hours late" has inexplicably become "he's three hours late"—hard to justify since this particular character would certainly have made a point of hiring a female if at all possible!

Like "Today 4 U," "Tango: Maureen" is a highly theatrical number. In this case Columbus handles the challenge by making it a fantasy sequence. Joanne and Mark begin to dance in the large room, and halfway through the song she gets him in a dip and then drops him on the floor; he cracks his head and the rest of the number becomes his dream sequence. All of a sudden the space is filled with elegant tangoing couples dressed in formal black—and Maureen herself, in a sexy red dress and dancing with a male partner. She breaks away from him to dance with both Mark and Joanne, and then she abandons both to leave arm in arm with another man *and* another woman! If it seems like a production number out of a classic Hollywood musical that takes us dangerously far out of the world of the film, it is worth acknowledging that the song itself is the closest thing in Larson's score to a traditional, old-fashioned musical comedy number.

"Out Tonight" is also opened up. In the stage version, the first half of the number was understood to be taking place in Mimi's apartment as she dressed for her hoped-for night out with Roger, but her daring, seductive moves on the catwalk were meant to evoke the way she probably dances at the Cat Scratch Club, giving the audience a chance to see a different side of the character: her aggressively sexy persona as a stripper. In the movie, the number actually begins in the club, which is depicted as a surprisingly large, glitzy establishment with a boisterous clientele of well-dressed businessmen. Mirroring the stage blocking, Mimi, very scantily clad, descends an onstage stairway and takes the stage, where she joins four other girls to dance and writhe seductively for the crowd. Though she's singing the whole time, there's no visible microphone and the feeling is that it's not to be taken literally; rather than a song she's actually singing for the patrons, we intuit that we're hearing her inner thoughts—and she's already thinking about Roger. As the song continues, we see her in street clothes, leaving the club and walking home through the neighborhood, which is quiet enough at this late hour that she is able to sashay right down the middle of the street. She briefly stops off in her own apartment, then goes out on the fire escape and dances on the railing much as she did in the stage version. (Rosario Dawson was protected from falling by a tether, the evidence of which was removed digitally in post-production.) Then she climbs the stairs and makes her dramatic entrance into Roger's apartment through the window. He looks mesmerized as he watches her finish the number, which ends with her famous climb onto his table (though without scattering the props) and the big kiss.

As many Mimis and Rogers have found over the years, "Another Day" is one of the hardest scenes in the show to play convincingly; the harshness of Roger's anger can seem to be out of all keeping with the situation. But Adam Pascal understands the character, and lets us see the longing and pain underneath; though he lashes out at Mimi with his own lines, he's achingly open and vulnerable when she sings to him. Tellingly, he and Columbus make the "why do you need smack?" moment a crucial one: the intensity of Roger's response there, and the urgency with which he hustles Mimi out of the apartment, make it clear he's remembering April and the wreckage caused by her addiction—something he simply can't cope with facing again.

Once he's kicked her out, Mimi goes downstairs and leaves the building; Roger comes out on the fire escape and she sings up to him in a sort of reverse Romeo and Juliet setup. Onstage, the end of the number is intertwined with the support group's singing of "no day but today," whereas here Collins,

Angel, and Mark happen to come around the corner—on their way home from the meeting, just in time to provide the vocal backup—and join Mimi in beseeching Roger to come out of his shell. After the dynamic staging of "Out Tonight" and the emotional honesty of the scene in the apartment, this coda looks relatively contrived, but it does preserve the musical integrity of the original number. It ends with Angel embracing the disappointed Mimi, helping to establish the sense of a close friendship between these two characters. (That's something that wasn't really explored in the play, but Dawson told Columbus it was important to her that they build in a relationship between the two, partly to ensure that Mimi's participation in the funeral service scene later in the film would carry the right emotional weight. The director agreed, and thus there are several effective moments in the film where the two are seen connecting nonverbally.)

"Santa Fe" and "I'll Cover You" are both expertly handled, with organic and musically sensitive support from choreographer Keith Young and cinematographer Stephen Goldblatt. "Santa Fe" takes place on a subway, with a playful feeling of improvisation and camaraderie among Collins, Angel, Mark, and Roger; by the end of the song some of the other passengers are dancing with them. They get off the train on the Lower East Side and "I'll Cover You" takes place in afternoon light on the street beside Tompkins Square Park. Since the St. Mark's Place number is not included in the film, Angel buys a new coat for Collins from a street vendor during this song. The camera work and choreography, responsive to every musical transition, capture the energy and flow of the song, and the effortless warmth and joy of Martin's and Heredia's performances, rich with nuance and tender humor, could only have come from their long experience playing the relationship together onstage.

"Over the Moon" finds Maureen performing her piece for a large audience, including most of the homeless people who live on the lot; it has the feeling of an event. Other than adding some large video monitors—which performance artists of the period often did use—Columbus wisely resists any temptation to dress up the number with technical gimmickry, focusing instead on capturing every nuance of Idina Menzel's comic tour de force.

A significant change from the stage version follows. Though Jonathan Larson had originally fought for showing the riot, Michael Greif had talked him out of it, saying it would have been impossible to make the violence genuinely believable onstage. On film of course it is possible, and the riot is shown erupting immediately out of the audience's mooing; the impression is of the police overreacting and escalating the conflict by using unnecessary force—and we see Mark capturing it with his camera.

The Life Café scene and "La Vie Bohème" are bursting with vitality and humor, preserving the wit and inventiveness of Anthony Rapp's indelible performance along with a bracing camaraderie and unforced spirit of celebration among the group. Combined with a lovely, intimate rendition of "I Should Tell You" by Pascal and Dawson—filmed in moonlight under falling snow with a romanticism that recalls *La bohème*—the film reaches the end of "Act One" in triumph; at this point it's hard to imagine any hardcore fan of the musical not feeling that all of his or her hopes for what a movie version could provide were being met and even exceeded.

Moving forward into what onstage was Act Two, however, things start to go awry almost immediately. Following a brief reprise of "Seasons of Love," heard over scenes from Mark's film-in-progress, the movie seems to forget that it's a musical, as we go almost a full ten minutes without a song. Some of the lines from "Happy New Year" find their way into the new spoken dialogue, but the plot has been revised. Rather than showing up on New Year's Eve to break into the building, which in the stage version has been padlocked for a week, the whole gang returns home from their revels on New Year's morning to find the door padlocked for the first time. Almost immediately, Angel

The film cast performs "La Vie Bohème." Top row from left: Idina Menzel, Tracie Thoms, Anthony Rapp, Adam Pascal, Rosario Dawson, Wilson Jermaine Heredia, and Jesse L. Martin.

breaks the lock with a trash can, and they get into the building only to find that all of Mark's, Roger's, and Mimi's belongings have been removed from their apartments—presumably on Benny's orders. A new sequence dealing with Mark's job interview at *Buzzline* is added, with lawyer Joanne acting as his agent in a scene set in Alexi Darling's office. On a busy street afterward, an argument between Joanne and Maureen takes a surprise turn into a "commitment" proposal. This plot development, not paralleled in the play, does add emotional texture to the relationship between the two women, but it's hard to believe that even Maureen would be insensitive enough to have that conversation with Mark standing right there. They return to the apartment, where the furniture has been returned and Benny is trying to make amends; sensing a PR stunt, Mark refuses his peace offering, instead making it clear he intends to pay the full rent with the money he's now making.

Still no song; there follows another new scene set at Joanne's parents' posh country club. Here we finally meet Mr. and Mrs. Jefferson, who are portrayed very differently from how they were onstage. In the play, they are afraid Joanne's lesbian relationship will jeopardize her mother's political career, and they tell her to break up with Maureen, whereas in the movie they are enthusiastically supportive, and are seen hosting an engagement party for the couple, with all their friends in attendance. (Tracie Thoms has said she appreciated that change, as it challenges the negative stereotype of black people as homophobic.) Maureen feels out of her element and can't resist flirting with one of the waitresses, leading to an outburst from Joanne that ignites "Take Me or Leave Me." Though marvelously performed by Menzel and Thoms, the number feels painfully artificial in the realistic confines of the country club setting, with the rest of the embarrassed gang following the two of them from room to room, watching helplessly.

Columbus has been criticized for softening the edges of the material, and indeed the film is bathed in a romantic golden glow that, while often beautiful, can obscure the harshness of the characters' lives. "Without You," however, is one place where realism actually comes to the fore more powerfully than it could have onstage. Mimi's drug addiction and the emotional toll it takes on her relationship with Roger becomes painfully tangible, with Dawson appearing dangerously strung out and emaciated. And Angel's final illness, which was highly stylized in the stage number "Contact," is here depicted with a poignant realism.

The funeral scene, faithful to the original, is moving, though the church feels oddly underpopulated: wouldn't someone like Angel have had more friends? The ensemble and recitative section of "Goodbye, Love"—up to "I can't believe this is goodbye"—is staged on a hillside in a cemetery, surrounded by autumn foliage. And then we come to the most controversial decision Columbus made, moaned and groaned about by *Rent* fans to this day: the deletion of the bulk of that number, including the crucial confrontation between Mark and Roger as well as Mimi's aching aria of farewell; Mark's solo "Halloween" is also omitted. The decision to cut those songs was not made until late in the process; they were in fact filmed, and fans finally got to see them when they were included on the bonus disc in the DVD release of the movie. Columbus has offered several reasons for the decision: Mark and Roger's scenes together up to that point in the film had been mostly realistic spoken dialogue, so he thought it seemed wrong for them suddenly to be singing to each other. In watching the early cuts of the film, he found the rhythm and pace of the movie was improved by the deletion; he feared that, if the songs were left in, the audience would suffer from emotional overload at that point and have nothing left for the all-important final scene of Mimi's near death. (Considering that a major recurring theme in the musical is the admonition not to be afraid of strong emotions, that line of reasoning seems ironic.) It might make sense if Columbus had failed to find effective solutions to translating the two songs to film, but the DVD reveals them to be quite beautiful.

The ending of "What You Own" epitomizes the difference between Columbus's approach to the material and Michael Greif's. Onstage, Roger's and Mark's lines overlap and intertwine, but the two men don't make contact; each is singing in his separate world, and there's a tough bleakness to the end of the number. In the film, Roger returns from Santa Fe and finds Mark on the rooftop; they sing the "you're not alone" sequence directly to each other and end in an embrace. There's a definite emotional payoff to seeing that reconciliation and expression of love between two friends (though it would be more powerful if we had actually gotten to hear their big argument . . .), to the point where some directors of regional productions have borrowed the hug and incorporated it. But Greif had a feet-on-the-ground sensibility that tugged against any tendency toward sentimentality, keeping the story rooted in reality and ambivalence. Throughout, he provided a healthy ballast to Larson's wide-eyed, unabashed romanticism, whereas Columbus plays directly into it.

Throughout the film, the director's clear love for, and determination to be faithful to, the musical is, paradoxically, both his greatest strength and his Achilles' heel. He often finds ways to include clever references to the original visual imagery: for example, the huge Christmas tree/totem pole sculpture that dominated the stage left portion of Paul Clay's original set design finds its way into the set for Maureen's performance piece in the movie, and even the huge paper lantern that suggested the moon onstage turns up onscreen, in a much smaller version, in Mark and Roger's loft. Mimi's use of both the staircase at the Cat Scratch Club and the fire escape of her building to evoke the choreography of "Out Tonight" is effective. But some of the other attempts to recreate imagery from the stage version get very awkward. Since the stage set was non-representational, with big metal tables and folding chairs serving as building blocks for whatever scenic elements were needed, it made sense when Maureen and Joanne jumped up onto the tables during "Take Me or Leave Me"; they were actresses on a stage singing a rock song. But having Maureen climb onto a banquet-room table—and a pool table—in the filmed number seems forced. Even more obvious: by the time we got to Mimi's "death scene" onstage, it was understood that the omnipresent tables had been standing in for beds; in the movie it seems ridiculous that the sick girl's friends lay her out on a hard metal table instead of putting her on a bed or a couch.

Nevertheless, Columbus handsomely pulls off that crucial scene, which could have tripped up a less sensitive director. Mimi's revival, always a controversial and tricky moment, could very easily have descended into camp on film—as could the final "curtain call" reappearance of Angel. But Columbus handles both moments with grace and sensitivity, as do the actors. The love between these characters—and among the actors playing them—is palpable, and so we share their joy in Mimi's second chance. It feels earned, and when Anthony Rapp sings "There is no future . . . ," we get that Mark knows this isn't a fairy-tale happy ending. Mimi probably doesn't have a lot of time left, but she has at least another day, and the final shot of Angel, his Mona Lisa smile captured fleetingly in Mark's film, reminds us all to be grateful for that.

Rating

It was important to Columbus that young people be able to see the film, so he was concerned when the initial cut, on being reviewed by the MPAA, was given an R rating. They gave him a list of about five language points he would need to change, as well as thirty visuals, in order to get the rating changed to PG-13. The studio heads supported him, saying they wouldn't force him to make any changes; they believed in his work and in the property and felt it could be successful at the box office even with the R rating. But Columbus wanted kids in the thirteen to seventeen age range to be able to see it without adult supervision, so he made most of the requested language edits. (Mark surprisingly got to keep his "F-bomb," traditionally grounds for an automatic R rating, in "Tango: Maureen.") However, he submitted the film for reconsideration without changing any of the visual footage, and surprisingly the MPAA, considered a very conservative organization, came around and approved the PG-13 rating anyway. They said they felt the film was strong and believed it was something that young people needed to see.

Reception and Reviews

Morale on the set was good. The actors loved working with Columbus and were thrilled that the show that meant so much to them was getting such grand and faithful treatment. In the days leading up to the release date (November 23, 2005), expectations ran high, so a lot of people were surprised when many of the reviews were lukewarm and the film stumbled at the box office. It did remain in the top ten for three weeks, but quickly dropped off after that; budgeted at $40 million, it ended up taking in just $31.6 million in ticket sales.

Fans of the show will always be grateful that the movie exists. It's an invaluable record of the original cast's tremendous performances, and Dawson and Thoms were also brilliant casting choices. The score is beautifully performed, and Columbus's love and respect for the material are palpable. But among people who were experiencing *Rent* for the first time, the film didn't earn as many converts as it could have.

The popular critic Roger Ebert gave the movie a "marginal thumbs up" on his TV show, *Ebert and Roeper at the Movies*, but only two and a half stars when he rethought it later for a review on his website. He focused on the inherent difficulty of translating such an immediate theatrical experience to film: "The stage production surrounded the audience with the characters and the production. It lacked the song 'We Are Family,' but that was the subtext. On film, 'Rent' is the sound of one hand clapping. . . . If you came to know and love the material in its original form, this is a way to see the characters and actors again, and you will bring those memories with you to the movie, as sort of a commentary track. Those who haven't seen 'Rent' on the stage will sense they're missing something, and they are."

David Rooney of *Variety* wrote: "Director Chris Columbus has pasted the grungy 'La Boheme' update onto film with slavish respect for the original material but a shortage of stylistic imagination and raw emotions. [The] result is like watching a dancer with no rhythm; it approximates the moves but rarely gets an infectious groove on . . . The muscular treatment by ace music producer Rob Cavallo . . . supplies driving power to the songs that's rarely matched in the narrative, while Columbus' cluttered idea of how to film a musical seems to reference 'Fame' in its repeated dancing on tables and seemingly endless running through trash-strewn streets holding hands."

Jim Lane of the *Sacramento News and Review* was more positive, and said he found it difficult to imagine that any fans of the show would be

Cover design for the CD release of the soundtrack album.

disappointed in the film. Though he hadn't always been a fan of Columbus's work in the past, he said: "He's in his element here, and he delivers the goods . . . Under Columbus' direction, Stephen Goldblatt's swooping camera and editor Richard Pearson's razor-sharp cuts are the visual equivalent of Larson's soaring chords and driving beat. And Columbus has an emotional directness that can be shameless when the material is artificial or trite, as it was in *Bicentennial Man* and *Stepmom*. But here the material is real, and Columbus goes at it head-on, moving from dialogue to song and back again without awkwardness or apology." He applauded the casting of the originals and Tracie Thoms and added: "Dawson is remarkable. Her feral sexuality makes her a natural for Mimi."

The usually influential *New York Times* seems like it should have done more for the box office than it did, for A. O. Scott was very positive. He admitted to not having gone into the film as a particular fan of the stage version but added: "Two hours later, I was pleased (and somewhat surprised) to find myself an us, for once, instead of a them." He went on to say: "[Columbus] has managed a feat similar to the one he pulled off with the first two 'Harry Potter' movies; he has taken a source that is fiercely and jealously loved by its core fans and refrained from messing it up. It is not just that he shows dexterity and imagination in transferring the spectacle onto the actual streets of the East Village in Manhattan. The real key to his success is his utter lack of condescension."

15

"Seasons of Love"

The Long Broadway Run and the Closing Performance

A s *Rent* settled into its run as the hottest show in town, celebrities were often in attendance. After performances, many of them greeted the cast in an alley beside the theater. Visitors during the early days included actors Jim Carrey, Tom Cruise, Liza Minnelli, Demi Moore, and Robert De Niro (who would later be involved in producing the film version), as well as Hollywood producers and directors including Sherry Lansing, William Friedkin, and the legendary Steven Spielberg. Jonathan Larson would have been thrilled to see some of the artists who had inspired him to start writing music, like Roger Daltrey and Billy Joel, showing up to see his musical. During the first year of the run, then president Bill Clinton and first lady Hillary Rodham Clinton brought their daughter Chelsea to the show as a present on her seventeenth birthday. They posed for photos with the cast afterward.

"Never Playing the Fame Game"

During the run of *Rent*, the producers of some of the other shows on Broadway, notably the long-running revivals of *Cabaret* and *Chicago*, contrived to boost ticket sales periodically through a practice that became known as "stunt casting": bringing in celebrities—often drawn from the worlds of TV, film, or recording rather than the theater—to play limited engagements in major roles. With its story of struggling young people trying to make art outside the mainstream, *Rent* is not a show that readily lends itself to this type of treatment. The appeal of the original cast came partly from their status as new discoveries, or genuine downtown bohemians; though most of them went on to big careers, none was a celebrity when the show first opened. Nonetheless, as the run continued, it was perhaps inevitable that some of the replacement actors would be recognizable names with a bit of built-in box office appeal. The spirit of the show was never violated by bringing in a superstar, but over the years there would occasionally be a new cast member with enough of a following to ignite some new excitement on the street—and in the press. Some of them had become fans of *Rent* and had their agents approach the production to express interest; others were sought out by the producers. All of them had to audition for, or at least meet with, Michael Greif for final approval.

Some of these higher-profile cast additions came from the world of pop music. Two of the actors who played Mark had been members of popular boy bands: Joey Fatone of *NSYNC and Drew Lachey of 98 Degrees. Girl groups were represented by Melanie Brown, a.k.a. Scary Spice of the Spice Girls, the top-selling female group in recording history; she joined the cast as Mimi in 2004.

A couple of the replacements had followings from their days on *American Idol*. Tamyra Gray, one of the run's last Mimis, had been a top-ten finalist in the reality show's first season and finished in fourth place; by the time she came into *Rent* she had substantial TV and film acting credits and had made her Broadway debut in *Bombay Dreams*. Another *American Idol* alum, Frenchie Davis, came into the show twice and put in four years with the Broadway company overall; she was the only person who got substantial publicity for joining the cast in one of the ensemble tracks (the "Seasons" soloist) rather

Three Marks: Anthony Rapp (right), the original Mark Cohen, is shown here at a 2004 event with two of his replacements in the Broadway company: Matt Caplan (left) and Joey Fatone.

Paul Hawthorne/Getty Images

than a principal role (she also understudied and occasionally went on as Joanne).

By the time Jai Rodriguez came into the Broadway company as Angel in 2004, he had a huge following as the "Culture Vulture" on the reality show *Queer Eye for the Straight Guy*—but his fans may have been unaware that he had first done *Rent* six years earlier on tour and as a Broadway understudy. Another Angel, Wilson Cruz, had opened the Benny Tour before taking over the role on Broadway in 1998; he was known to TV fans for his role as Rickie Vasquez on the landmark teen drama *My So-Called Life*.

Among the show's discerning fans, several of these semi-celebrities were not considered to be among the better exponents of their roles; others did very well. Either way, it was primarily love for the show and the characters themselves, rather than any fame factor, that sustained the box office over twelve years.

Broadway replacement cast members Andy Señor (Angel) and Mark Leroy Jackson (Collins) perform "I'll Cover You."   *Joan Marcus*

Maintaining the Show

Anthony Tommasini of the *New York Times* felt a protective, almost proprietary interest in *Rent*, having seen the final dress rehearsal of the show downtown and then having interviewed Larson only hours before his death. When he went back to see it in the summer of 2002, he published an article in the *Times* called "Some Advice for 'Rent' From a Friend" in which he expressed dismay over the then current state of the Broadway production, which he found to be suffering from "long-run-itis." He wrote: "The performance was not stale, but the opposite: pumped up with a rockish energy that seemed forced and generic, and blaringly loud. . . . The young performers, it appeared, had been encouraged to play the show for raw power. Does no one involved still trust in the subtlety of Larson's characterizations, the textured layers of his music and the impish and poignant lyrics? Right now, you would think that the producers of 'Rent' had lost their trust in the work and decided that the only way to get a reaction from audiences was to bludgeon them." He went on to advise Michael Greif to return to the theater, have the sound levels turned down, and call a rehearsal with the cast to read through the script and reconnect to the lyrics.

Though Tommasini may not have known it, Greif actually stayed more involved with the show throughout its life on Broadway than many directors of long-running hits. He approved all the major cast replacements and came in to work with them; if not at their put-in rehearsals, he would at least be sure to come by to see the show and give them notes after a performance. He also, with choreographer Marlies Yearby, staged a special concert version of the show to celebrate a very special milestone.

The Tenth Anniversary

In the spring of 2006, *Rent* reached the ten-year anniversary of its opening on Broadway. The official anniversary date was Saturday, April 29, but the occasion was celebrated on the previous Monday (which would normally have been the show's dark night) with a special concert performance by the original cast, reunited onstage at the Nederlander Theatre. This proved a moving and unforgettable experience for anyone lucky enough to be there.

The evening was a benefit; its proceeds went to support three organizations: New York Theatre Workshop, the nonprofit, Off-Broadway theater company that had originally produced the show; the Jonathan Larson Performing Arts Foundation, which gives grants to talented young musical theater writers; and Friends In Deed, the support organization for AIDS patients and their families and friends that had inspired the Life Support group depicted in the musical.

The audience was filled with celebrities, and the evening began with a brief round of speeches introduced by producer Allan S. Gordon. Benefit cochairs James M. Nederlander and Jonathan Tisch both addressed the crowd; Tish revealed that the event had raised over two million dollars. New York City's mayor at the time, Michael R. Bloomberg, spoke next, saying, "*Rent* is clearly more than just a Broadway musical; it is a Broadway miracle," and Senator Charles E. Schumer saluted the show as well.

Though done on the set where the show was still being performed eight times a week, this performance was billed as a concert, restaged for the occasion by Greif and Yearby. Most of the dancing was eliminated and the blocking simplified. The actors sat in folding chairs on both sides of the main playing area when not involved in a number; they could clearly be seen enjoying each other's performances, which added immeasurably to the festive ambience.

The script was slightly adapted and reshaped. There was no intermission, and "Seasons of Love" was performed not in its usual position but at the top of the show (as in the movie, which had been released five months earlier).

Then Mark (Anthony Rapp) introduced the story by taking the audience back to "Christmas Eve, last year" with a musical excerpt from "Halloween" (usually performed in the middle of Act Two) rather than the familiar opening monologue. Thereafter the focus was on the musical numbers, with much of Mark's narration deleted and the spoken dialogue reduced to a minimum.

The lighting was simplified and most of the action took place downstage center, though Daphne Rubin-Vega did begin "Out Tonight" on the high catwalk and performed most of the choreography for that number. The Life Support meeting took place downstage rather than on the high platform over the band. The actors mostly wore their own clothes, though Rapp sported the famous black-and-white Mark scarf, which by then was iconic. Wilson Jermaine Heredia did most of the show in jeans and a tank top but donned full Angel drag, complete with makeup and wig, just for "Today 4 U," in which he also demonstrated—twice—that ten years later he could still do the astonishing jump onto the table in platform shoes.

Panoramic view of Paul Clay's set design. Shown onstage at the Nederlander Theatre is the final Broadway cast, 2008. *Photo courtesy of Paul Clay*

Fourteen of the fifteen original cast members appeared. The one exception was Gilles Chiasson; he was in California where his wife had given birth to a baby that very morning! Rapp announced this to the audience in a brief tribute to Chiasson directly preceding "Will I," in which his solo part was sung by Heredia; Rodney Hicks picked up the waiter lines in the Life Café scene.

The close-knit cast was clearly delighted to be together again, and there was a warm and playful sense of camaraderie throughout. Many of them hadn't done the show in eight or nine years, and they had had only two days to rehearse the concert; a couple of them held scripts in some scenes, and there were two or three times when people went up on lines, eliciting good-natured laughs from their castmates and the fans out front. Adam Pascal referred to a single sheet of printed text to get through some fast-paced lyrics in "Happy New Year"; having rattled them off perfectly, he crumpled the paper up into a ball and triumphantly tossed it out into the house, to the delight of the audience. Jesse L. Martin was in exuberant form throughout, improvising some dance spins during "Santa Fe"; when Heredia twirled him into the dance break in "I'll Cover You," Martin laughed and said, "Oh shit, I forgot how fast you were!"

Probably alluding to the evening's high-priced tickets and success as a fundraiser, Gwen Stewart as the bag lady changed her line to Mark from "Hey artist, gotta dollar?" to "Gotta thousand dollars?"—eliciting a big laugh. And at the top of "La Vie Bohème," when Mark sang "you bet your ass" and Idina Menzel pulled down her pants to moon Benny, Taye Diggs playfully spanked her behind—getting an even bigger laugh from the audience, most of whom knew the two actors had gotten married in real life.

Despite the occasional high jinks, the cast's commitment to Larson's message and their love for the material shone through, and they delivered the big moments with searing intensity. Pascal brought new detail and insight to "One Song Glory"; Menzel and Fredi Walker-Browne raised the roof in "Take Me or Leave Me"; Martin was supremely powerful in the "I'll Cover You" reprise; and Rubin-Vega was heartbreaking in "Without You."

Covering the event for the *New York Times*, Anthony Tommasini said: "Though this performance was not intended for review, I can say that the cast did itself proud. Understandably, as actors fumbled for lines now and then, the event became as much an affectionate reunion as a straight-ahead performance. But moment after moment brought you back to the early days of 'Rent' when the show's honesty and power were so stunning."

At the conclusion, they were joined onstage by members of other companies of the show for a rousing reprise of "Seasons of Love." The festive post-show party was at Cipriani.

Joining the Cast

As with any long-running Broadway show, the casts for *Rent* were ever changing. As actors completed their contracts, or left for other projects, new performers were brought in. Often, an actor who had proven him or herself in a role in one of the touring companies would be promoted to the Broadway cast; other times, performers with established reputations would be invited to audition, or submissions would be sought from agents, and periodically Equity required the producers to hold a replacement call, for which union actors (and very optimistic nonunion ones) would line up early in the morning in the hopes of being seen.

Actress Tonya Dixon, who joined the Broadway company as Joanne in 2006, recently spoke about the experience of coming into the show as a replacement. She had seen the original cast do the show in 1996 and was a fan; she remembers waiting in line for hours for the $20 rush tickets several times before the lottery process was initiated. "It was a show I had always wanted to do," she remembers. "I probably saw it a good three or four times before I was ever cast in it." And then, once she was scheduled for an audition, she went back and bought standing room to see it again to refresh her memory.

Dixon was one of the more experienced musical theater performers to join the show; she had numerous regional theater productions as well as four national tours, and a stint in *Ragtime* on Broadway, on her résumé by the time she went in for *Rent.* In fact, at the time she was playing the major role of Fantine in a national tour of *Les Misérables* and had to come in to New York from the road a couple of times on days off for her auditions and callbacks. She was given Joanne's section of "Take Me or Leave Me" to learn, along with a song of her own choice. She was seen two or three times before being offered the role.

Her contract signed, she had at least three weeks to prepare. As she was replacing an actress who was leaving for another job, she was the only new cast member coming in at that particular time, and her first few rehearsals were alone with the stage manager, John Vivian, and the resident director, Evan Ensign. "John Vivian was great," she says. "He had been doing the show right from the beginning so he knew the show backward and forward and knew how to put someone in." Vivian taught her the blocking and choreography, the ins and outs of dealing with props and costume changes. "Evan, being the resident director, was more scene-related. He knew all that stuff too, but he dealt more with your emotions and intentions."

After learning the basics of the role, she also got to rehearse several times with the understudies—who on a Broadway musical will usually rehearse two afternoons a week in order to be ready to go on at any time. As a replacement, she had only one rehearsal with the full cast, which was on a Friday afternoon for four or five hours. This was the one time Michael Greif came in to work with her (though he would later occasionally give notes after a performance). This all-important rehearsal, called a "put-in," was focused completely on her needs as the one new cast member. They ran through all of her scenes and numbers onstage, in costume, but without the band; it's expensive to call the band in for extra rehearsal time, so a put-in is generally done with piano. They skipped scenes and songs she wasn't in so she would have time to go back and repeat her numbers if she needed to; Vivian reminded her that the rehearsal was all about her and continually checked in with her to make sure she had everything she needed. The next time she ran though the show—and the first time she ever sang it with the band—was her opening night performance!

Dixon did the show for more than a year and loved it, though she had some mishaps. One night she damaged her knee quite badly when she did Joanne's jump off the table to the floor during "Take Me or Leave Me": she was out of the show for six weeks on workman's comp. She had been sharing an upstairs dressing room with Jaime Lee Kirchner, who was playing Mimi at the time, but when she came back they gave her a different room closer to the stage so she wouldn't have to climb as many stairs as her knee continued to mend. (The backstage area at the Nederlander is relatively small and there are no star dressing rooms; everyone has at least one roommate.)

She was still in the show in 2007 when original leading men Adam Pascal and Anthony Rapp came back for a return engagement, ten years after they had first departed the Broadway company and almost two years after the release of the film, in which they had also starred. This made for a particularly exciting time for the cast—not to mention the fans. Even though she had been doing the show for a while at that point, Dixon said: "I was nervous about performing in front of Anthony and Adam, and wanting to be good enough. But—and I shouldn't have been surprised—they were such accepting people. They were all about communication. They were very open to supporting you onstage. I never felt like I had to be someone else." She enjoyed rehearsing "Tango: Maureen" with Rapp, who was the third Mark she had done it with. He was careful not to make her do anything that would risk reinjuring her knee, and they found ways to make the number their own. As she put it: "It was always encouraged to explore through our characters and see what happened. And let the moments happen onstage as our characters."

Like many of the performers who have done the show over the years, Tonya Dixon considers it a special memory, saying: "I did feel very honored to be part of it for the short time that I was. Because it was such a show, that changed so much. It opened doors to issues that people had never talked about. The characters were so real and talked about issues that people were afraid to talk about. And we all needed to experience and grow from that and grow from love."

Closing

Though there were times when it felt like the Broadway production of *Rent* might run forever, by 2008 the box office was finally slowing down to the point where the producers decided it was time to think about closing. On January 15, Jeffrey Seller made an official announcement that the show would close on June 1, inviting fans to come see it one more time; the response was so strong that it had to be extended to September 7.

Kathy Kirkpatrick, owner of the real-life Life Café, made a point for years of not trying to capitalize on publicity reflected back on the restaurant by the show. She did put up a *Rent* poster autographed by the cast and hosted a premiere party for the film version in 2005, and occasionally she would host dinners there for casts of out-of-town productions of the show who came to New York to experience the location first hand. Late in the show's run, however, Kirkpatrick realized fans had been stealing the restaurant's menus as souvenirs, and she began to market her own line of *Rent* memorabilia at the café. And when the Broadway production was in its final days in 2008, the café hosted a memorable event: people were invited to submit video entries in a contest that chose fifty devoted fans of the show to come to the café for a party on the Friday night before the closing performance. Al and Julie Larson also attended, as well as some members of the show's marketing team and a few former cast members. The guests were served beer and dinner as the score was played over the restaurant's sound system; at around midnight they pushed the tables together, much like the characters in the show, to make a stage on which they performed their own personal variation on la vie bohème.

Because the show had been both a social and a cultural phenomenon, and had achieved such a long run, various writers attempted to quantify its significance as the closing date approached. Its contribution to the national discourse on AIDS was a major focus. Writing in *POZ*, a magazine for people with HIV, Bob Ickes said: "But the show was remarkably prescient, too. At a time when AIDS was primarily portrayed as a gay white man's disease, *Rent* dared to focus on gay men of color and a heterosexual Latino woman, now two of the demographics most affected by HIV. . . . *Rent*'s cast was also youthful, a reminder that many new infections occurred then—and continue to do so now—in those younger than 30." (Justin Johnston, who played Angel in the closing cast, said he had seen the show change people's lives. So many fans had told him that Angel represented their friends and loved ones who had been lost to AIDS that he came to feel an added responsibility to honor them in his performance.)

One of the most controversial elements in the script has always been Mimi's surprise recovery in the last scene, so different from the other Mimi's tragic death scene at the end of *La bohème*. Charles Isherwood of the *Times* reflected meaningfully on this when he revisited the show the week before it closed: "One of the weaknesses that bothered me a dozen years ago—the ending that finds the doomed Mimi springing back to life after appearing to expire—strikes me today as a flaw that Larson may have recognized but could not bring himself to correct. The integrity of art must have seemed a less urgent priority than the dissemination of hope. The awkward affixing of a happy ending to a fundamentally tragic story was a form of prayer, a plea that life might imitate art. I probably rolled my eyes at this absurd resurrection in 1996; this time I fought back tears."

Rent: Filmed Live on Broadway

To the permanent delight of *Rent* fans, the closing performance of the Broadway run was filmed for posterity by Sony Pictures. The company had released the movie version of the show three years earlier and still held the screen rights; partly because the movie had made less of a splash than anticipated, they decided to provide an alternative version that would preserve the original Broadway staging. It was included in a projected series of filmed special events that was collectively being called "The Hot Tickets." The performance was filmed in high-definition digital video and was screened in over 500 movie theaters in the United States and Canada between September 24 and 28, 2008. It is now available on a DVD, which also includes interviews and backstage footage.

One might think that the closing performance of a twelve-and-a-half-year run, especially of a show with such a devoted audience following, would not be the right one to preserve for posterity; the emotional nature of the event might well be expected to overwhelm the play itself, distracting attention from the telling of the story. But if there are moments when the fraught party atmosphere does threaten to take over, it never does, and that's a tribute to the commitment and artistry of all involved. The cast is able to harness the energy of the moment—which of course includes the awareness that they are being filmed—and let it heighten the stakes: this was their chance to do the ultimate performance of *Rent*, both literally and figuratively, and they were determined not to let the show down. As Renée Elise Goldsberry, who played

An autographed photo of Renée Elise Goldsberry, the last actress to play Mimi in the Broadway company.

Mimi, said in one of the backstage interviews, *Rent* is about "a good-bye being so imminent that you have to embrace the moment that you're in." She added: "I mean that's what almost every line in the show is about: exactly what you're doing when you say good-bye to something that you love. And what we're feeling in that moment is something that, if we're smart, we will use." The "no day but today" theme became a tangible reality with the realization that there would literally never be another chance: the numbers and scenes take on a now-or-never ferocity as the cast seizes each moment with the urgency of a loving farewell. Both Tracie Thoms and Rodney Hicks said in interviews that the cast felt an extra pressure and responsibility to ensure that Jonathan Larson's message got through and his story was told right. The show that night took on a heightened focus and emotional urgency, and television director Michael John Warren's minutely detailed camera work captures it with sustained excitement and intensity.

Some seats were sacrificed to make room for cameras, and there were cameras in both aisles as well. Though the film is billed as the closing performance, and much of it was indeed filmed live that night, it also includes footage from a couple of other performances earlier in the week. There are also a few moments that were shot onstage during the day on August 20, without an audience in the house; these are primarily scenes that couldn't be captured adequately without putting cameras onstage in the playing area. On the final night, there were even more cameras behind the scenes and in the dressing rooms, capturing the emotions that were running high backstage—and providing material for the DVD's bonus features.

The creative team and casting directors put extra care into choosing the closing cast. The last-minute extension from June to September meant that several roles opened up in the final weeks; cast members who had thought they were closing the show had already committed to other projects and had to be replaced in June or July.

Casting *Rent* is always a highly subjective and complex undertaking; especially with memories of the originals looming, no one cast is going to satisfy every fan. But as the DVD proves, the closing company was a highly accomplished group of professionals: a canny combination of veterans of various companies and talented newcomers, on average more mature than most of the previous casts but putting that added experience to good use. Also, compared to most of the earlier groups, this is a cast made up primarily of dyed-in-the-wool musical theater performers.

Gwen Stewart anchors the show in authenticity: recreating her original ensemble role, she is majestic in the iconic "Seasons of Love" solo, still nailing her high notes with breathtaking purity and power. Rodney Hicks, who had also been in the original ensemble and understudied Benny at the time, graduates to that role, to which he brings a rich, characterful sound and a clear and sympathetic take on the man's conflicted motivations. Tracie Thoms, who had first played Joanne in the film, finally got her chance to do it on Broadway for the last six weeks of the run. Costumed and coiffed very differently than she had been in the movie, she brings just the right combination of elegance, smarts, and warmth to her scenes; in "We're Okay," which she hadn't gotten to do in the film, she masterfully juggles the three phone calls and keeps the storytelling crystal clear, every nuance vividly in place. She also strikes sparks with Eden Espinosa's Maureen. Espinosa brings an

Cover of the DVD release of *Rent: Filmed Live on Broadway*, 2008.

admirable simplicity and directness to the role, never going for a cheap laugh; her huge belt voice has a depth and richness that put her in a class by herself.

Michael McElroy had played Tom Collins on and off for a decade—experience that pays off in a wonderfully sensitive and tender portrayal; if his voice is not as boomingly large as some of his predecessors', it is warm and expressive, with tremendous musicality. Justin Johnston, also a longtime veteran of the production, complements him well as a mature and eminently stylish Angel, with a core of toughness and wisdom.

The newcomer in the group was the very young Adam Kantor, cast as Mark while still a student in the theater program at Northwestern University. Kantor's impressive voice and confident presence would soon win him acclaim in the revival of *The Last Five Years*, and here he seems undaunted holding the stage with the veterans. But his Mark lacks a certain warmth and vulnerability, relying too heavily on a self-satisfied, sarcastic smirk.

Will Chase, a *Rent* veteran, came back to reprise his charismatic, powerfully-sung Roger; few actors have as effectively revealed the ache and yearning underneath the angry outbursts of "Another Day." His Mimi is the willowy, golden-voiced Renée Elise Goldsberry (a future Tony winner for *Hamilton*). No better actress or singer ever played the role, and she proves to be a singular dancer as well, endowing Mimi's moves in "Out Tonight" with a feline sexiness. In fact, she brings so much class and genuine leading-lady charisma to the role that it feels ungrateful to question whether those are precisely the right qualities for the character.

Michael Greif worked with the cast and the video director, and it was important to him that the work be preserved with integrity. He recently said: "I was very involved; Michael Warren was very collaborative. We talked a lot about what the cameras should get. I do believe it's an excellent film and I'm very happy with it. I'm very glad there's a great rendition of the production available that will continue to give people a chance to see the work."

On closing night, thirteen members of the original cast (including three of the understudies) joined the company onstage for an extended reprise of "Seasons of Love" in the curtain call; over fifty performers who had been in the show on Broadway or on tour were also in the audience, as guests of the producers, so it felt like a family reunion. Numerous other celebrities and theater-industry notables were also in the house, including producers James M. and James L. Nederlander; songwriters Stephen Flaherty, Tom Kitt, and Amanda Green; playwrights Quiara Alegría Hudes, Jeff Whitty, and Doug Wright; directors Christopher Ashley, Walter Bobbie, Scott Elliott, and David Saint; and actors Blake Lively and Penn Badgley (both then starring on TV's *Gossip Girl*) and Priscilla Lopez (of the original *A Chorus Line*).

Al and Nan Larson, along with their daughter Julie Larson, were of course in attendance and said they were overwhelmed by the performance and the outpouring of love for the show. As producer Kevin McCollum told Harry Haun of Playbill.com: "I had a surreal time tonight because it was bittersweet. I was overwhelmed by the amazing talent of the cast and how many lives this show has touched—and the loss of Jonathan. No matter how successful this show became, Jeffrey and I knew early on it would always be clouded by the loss of Jonathan. Our job as producers is to breathe life into his words. People say, 'How do you cast such great people?' And I say, 'We cast great people because Jonathan wrote a show about building a community where love wins.'"

That triumph was reflected onstage, backstage, and in the audience on that historic closing night. As Goldsberry put it, "*Rent* is one of the most beautiful celebrations of life that exists."

16

"Ginsberg, Dylan, Cunningham, and Cage"

Rent Cultural Literacy

The book and lyrics of *Rent* are full of names of people, places, films, songs, and so on that would mostly have been quite familiar to theater audiences in 1996 but in some cases are more obscure today. Whether you're doing a production of the show or just going to see one, this chapter is your handy-dandy, alphabetical guide to the cultural references in the script.

ACT UP

The AIDS Coalition to Unleash Power ("ACT UP") is an advocacy and political action group devoted to raising awareness of and fighting AIDS as well as improving conditions for people living with AIDS (PWAs). Its creation was spearheaded by the writer Larry Kramer, whose autobiographical play *The Normal Heart* is one of the seminal works of AIDS literature. In 1982, Kramer had been one of the founders of the Gay Men's Health Crisis (GMHC), an early AIDS advocacy and support group, but had become disenchanted and estranged from that organization for its lack of political effectiveness. In March of 1987 he gave a speech at the Lesbian and Gay Community Services Center in Greenwich Village where he posited the need for a more aggressive and politically activist group; ACT UP was formed a couple of days later at an initial gathering of about 300 people. It was founded as a response to the inaction of the federal and state governments, which under the Reagan administration had been shamefully slow in acknowledging and addressing the magnitude of the crisis, and to demand more research, better access to experimental drugs, affordable medical services, safe sex education in the schools, and more. The group soon expanded, forming chapters in cities around the nation. Its tactics involved numerous large demonstrations and acts of civil disobedience at high-profile locations like the General Post Office, the Hearst Building, the New York Stock Exchange, network television studios, and St. Patrick's Cathedral. Without a formal organizing plan or an official leader, ACT UP had a loose, intentionally anarchist structure made up of various affiliated committees that were encouraged to act quickly and independently. Viewing the government as an adversary, the organization was so determined not to have anything to do with the system that it never applied for nonprofit status as a charitable organization, which would have allowed it to solicit and collect tax-exempt donations. Sub-groups included Gran Fury, an art collective that generated and distributed artworks in various media in response to the AIDS crisis, and DIVA-TV ("Damned Interfering Video Activist Television), focused on video and film documentation of AIDS and AIDS activism. Numerous members were arrested during the group's large demonstrations, which could be controversial for their radical and sometimes sacrilegious tactics, but ACT UP has been powerfully successful in educating the public, achieving change, and drawing attention and resources to fighting an epidemic that, largely due to homophobia, had been neglected or ignored for far too long. On a smaller scale, ACT UP is still active today in several cities; it has spawned other effective AIDS service organizations, including Housing Works and Health GAP. In *Rent*, the group is mentioned by name at the end of the first "La Vie Bohème" (right before Roger and Mimi begin "I Should Tell You"), and its ethos is celebrated in "La Vie Bohème B" with the group's shout of "Anarchy" and Collins and Maureen's "Revolution, justice, screaming for solutions, forcing changes, risk and danger, making noise and making pleas."

Alphabet City

A neighborhood on the edge of the Lower East Side of Manhattan, so called because, once you travel east of First Avenue, the avenues are named for letters rather than numbers. This is where most of *Rent* takes place: Mark specifies that he and Roger live at 11th Street and Avenue B, and the Life Café was close by. Though the area still has an arty vibe, the gentrification that was already beginning in the nineties has transformed the neighborhood to the point where the starving-artist types depicted in the show generally can't afford to live there anymore. They would more likely be found today in certain sections of Brooklyn or Queens.

Angelou, Maya (1928–2014)

American author, poet, and civil rights activist. Born Marguerite Annie Johnson in St. Louis, Missouri, Angelou traveled widely and worked as a magazine editor in Egypt; she campaigned alongside both Martin Luther King Jr. and Malcolm X during the civil rights movement and fought against apartheid in South Africa. Celebrated for her wisdom, honesty, and spirit, she emerged as one of the most beloved and respected voices in African-American culture. Her abuse and rape by her mother's boyfriend at the age of eight and the subsequent emotional trauma and recovery are recounted in the first of her seven published memoirs, *I Know Why the Caged Bird Sings* (1969), now a classic. Early years of struggle found her working briefly as a streetcar conductor and a fry cook, but she quickly revealed talents in a dizzying multitude of creative areas: she studied modern dance and performed as a dance team with the young Alvin Ailey, sang and danced to calypso music in San Francisco nightclubs, and toured Europe in the cast of *Porgy and Bess.* Though she considered herself a "reluctant" actress, she was nominated for a Tony Award for her role in *Look Away*, a play that had lasted only one performance on Broadway in 1973, and she appeared in the groundbreaking TV miniseries *Roots.* Angelou recorded albums and wrote and directed plays, and was widely celebrated for her spectacular cooking. She was a screenwriter (*Georgia, Georgia* in 1972) and feature film director (*Down in the Delta* in 1996) and wrote music for films and for recording artists like Roberta Flack and Ashford & Simpson. Angelou's many awards and honors include a National Medal of Arts, a Presidential Medal of Freedom, a nomination for the Pulitzer Prize for Poetry, and over fifty honorary degrees; in her later years she became a mentor to Oprah Winfrey. In 1993, she famously recited her own poem, "On the Pulse of the Morning," at the inauguration ceremony of President Bill Clinton. Though a prolific and popular poet, she is most acclaimed for her seven volumes of memoirs, sometimes described as "autobiographical fiction," which concluded in 2013 with the publication of *Mom & Me & Mom.* According to her *New York Times* obituary: "Throughout her writing, Ms. Angelou explored the concepts of personal identity and resilience through the multifaceted lens of race, sex, family, community and the collective past." This, along with the fact that despite the acclaim and respect she has achieved her books have very often been challenged or banned by schools and parent's groups, makes her a natural heroine to the diverse community of outsiders depicted in *Rent.*

Antonioni, Michelangelo (1912–2007)

Italian film director and screenwriter; one of three highly influential foreign filmmakers whose names are mentioned in a single line of "La Vie Bohème," the other two being Bertolucci and Kurosawa (see below). Antonioni grew up in northern Italy, where as a child he developed strong interests in art and music; he was a violin prodigy and loved to draw. He attended the University of Bologna and graduated with an economics degree, then spent some time as a journalist. He went to film school for only three months before being drafted during World War II, but he rejected Mussolini's fascist government and narrowly escaped execution for joining the Italian resistance. In the early forties, Antonioni began his film career working as a writer and assistant director on several features, soon graduating to directing his own short films. His first full-length feature as a director was *Cronaca di un amore* in 1950, and he established his unique experimental style in 1955 with *Le Amiche*. In the early sixties, he released three films about alienation and discontent in the modern world; because they are stylistically and thematically linked, *L'Avventurra*, *La Notte*, and *L'Eclisse* are thought of as a trilogy and are often considered his masterpieces. For MGM Studios and producer Carlo Ponti, he later worked in England and America on a series of English-language films. The popular *Blowup*, set in London, starred a young Vanessa Redgrave. Antonioni followed it with *Zabriskie Point* (1970), which was less well received; dealing with the American counterculture and featuring music by the Grateful Dead, Pink Floyd, and the Rolling Stones, this one would probably be of special interest to the rebellious young artists of *Rent*. Antonioni's work has always been controversial. In her book *A History of Film*, Virginia Wright Wexman called him a "postreligious Marxist and existentialist intellectual"; he deplored the way most human beings were clinging to rigid and outmoded ideas of "morality" that he found meaningless in the modern world. In 1972, Antonioni went to China where he made a documentary; it was censored by the communist government and not shown publicly there until over thirty years later. His output slowed down after 1985, when his mobility and speech were impaired by a stroke, but he found ways to continue making films, including *Beyond the Clouds* (1995), on which he collaborated with the German director Wim Wenders. In all, Antonioni made sixteen feature films over a forty-five year period; unlike most directors, he also continued to produce shorts throughout his career. He won numerous awards from the Cannes Film Festival, the Venice Film Festival, the Berlin International Film Festival, the Italian National Syndicate of Film Journalists, and the National Society of Film Critics. For *Blowup*, he was nominated for Oscars for both Best Director and Best Screenplay; in 1995, he received an

Honorary Academy Award for his body of work and his stature as one of world cinema's "master visual stylists."

Baldwin, Alec (b. 1958)

American actor, the eldest and best-known of the four acting Baldwin brothers. Not one of *Rent*'s bohemian icons, Baldwin is mentioned in the second act of the show by the character Alexi Darling, who attempts to impress Mark by saying she ran into Baldwin in the Hamptons. The actor studied at NYU's Tisch School of the Arts, where his classmates, coincidentally, included Chris Columbus, who much later would direct the movie of *Rent*. Baldwin has sustained an extremely active and multifaceted career for thirty years, moving freely and frequently between the worlds of film, television, and the New York stage. Though his high-profile and multiple-award-winning role as Jack Donaghy on the TV comedy series *30 Rock* postdated his mention in *Rent*, by 1996 he was already a popular star, having begun on TV in daytime drama and shortly afterward taken on the breakout role of Joshua on the CBS primetime soap *Knots Landing*. His film career took off immediately, with roles in no fewer than five major films all released in the year 1988. Notable film appearances have included *Beetlejuice*, *Working Girl*, *Married to the Mob*, *The Hunt for Red October*, and *The Marrying Man*, on which he met his first wife, actress Kim Basinger. Broadway credits include Caryl Churchill's *Serious Money* and revivals of two Joe Orton plays, *Loot* and *Entertaining Mr. Sloane*. He also played the iconic role of Stanley Kowalski in a Broadway revival of *A Streetcar Named Desire* opposite Jessica Lange, after which he and Lange recreated their roles in a 1995 TV remake. Baldwin's famous temper and volatile personal life have landed him in the news on several occasions, and he coauthored a book, entitled *A Promise to Ourselves: A Journey Through Fatherhood and Divorce*, about his long battle with Basinger over her attempts to deny him contact with their daughter, Ireland. Now married to Hilaria Thomas, he remains a very busy and popular actor. He has hosted *Saturday Night Live* more times than any other performer and received enormous attention for his recurring impersonations of Donald Trump on that show during and after the 2016 election season.

Bertolucci, Bernardo (b. 1940)

Italian film director and writer. The son of an art historian/critic/poet, Bertolucci was inspired by his father to begin writing at an early age, and he published a book while still in his teens; his original goal was a career as a poet. His father had been instrumental in helping the legendary Italian

Bernardo Bertolucci and Michelangelo Antonioni, two of the film directors who get shout-outs in "La Vie Bohème," together at a restaurant in Italy, 1975.

Mondadori Portfolio/Everett Collection

director Pier Paolo Pasolini get his first book published as well, which led to an opportunity for Bernardo to work for the older director as an assistant. Pasolini also wrote the screenplay for the first film Bertolucci, then only twenty-two years old, directed: *La commare secca* (1962). He made his reputation two years later with the highly respected *Before the Revolution*. Bertolucci began his career at the tail end of a period of intense interest in Italian cinema that had produced such luminaries as Pasolini, Luchino Visconti, and Federico Fellini; when funding sources in his home country began to dry up, he began to collaborate with foreign producers, including some in the United States. Known for eliciting especially realistic performances from actors, Bertolucci inadvertently caused a scandal with the controversial *Last Tango in Paris*, released in 1972. The highly graphic film was one of the only serious art films ever to receive an X rating, and the nineteen-year-old actress Maria Schneider later accused Bertolucci of emotional rape for the way he manipulated her on the set. Costar Marlon Brando also denounced Bertolucci, who was prosecuted on obscenity charges in Italy, where the film was censored and taken out of circulation. Internationally, critics were sharply divided on the film: some labeled it pornography masquerading as art, but the influential critic Pauline Kael of *The New Yorker* claimed it had "altered the face of an art form," going on to say that it was "the most powerfully erotic movie ever made, and it may turn out to be the most liberating movie ever made."

Bertolucci's next few films were *1900*, *La Luna*, and *Tragedy of a Ridiculous Man*. His career reached a high point in 1987 with the release of *The Last Emperor*, a historical epic set and filmed in China that won nine Academy Awards, including Best Picture and Best Director. Subsequent films have included *Little Buddha*, *Stealing Beauty*, *The Dreamers*, and, most recently, *Me and You* (2012). His honors have included a Directors Guild of America Award, a Golden Lion Award from the Venice Film Festival, and an Honorary Palme D'Or from the Cannes Film Festival. An atheist and avowed Marxist, Bertolucci has often built his films around controversial political themes. His activism, frankness, and willingness to take risks and tackle taboo subjects in his work would naturally make him a favorite of the left-leaning, artistic free spirits of *Rent*.

Bond, James and Pussy Galore

The characters that inspire the costumes Collins and Angel wear to the New Year's Eve party at the beginning of Act Two are from *Goldfinger*, one of Ian Fleming's perennially popular series of James Bond spy stories. The series probably doesn't need much of an introduction, as it has been estimated that a quarter of the world's population has seen at least one James Bond movie. *Goldfinger* was the seventh book in the series, published in 1959, but the third to be made into a film, and the 1964 movie version is generally considered one of the best of the franchise—which is still going strong today at twenty-four films and counting, the longest-running series in film history. *Goldfinger* established the tone and style for the rest of the series, a mix of high-octane action—and violence—with tongue-in-cheek humor, characterized by beautiful women, eccentric villains, sexy cars, and an array of technologically sophisticated gadgets and gizmos. Bond, a British secret agent played in the film by Sean Connery, is entrusted with thwarting the plans of the evil title character, who, in the book, plans to steal the gold from Fort Knox. Since that plot was later deemed too implausible even for a James Bond movie, in the film he schemes instead to contaminate the gold by detonating a nuclear device inside the building. The producers almost had to change the name of Pussy Galore, the book's "Bond girl," for fear that the intended double entendre wouldn't make it past the censors; they allowed it in the film but it was left off most of the promotional materials. In the book, Pussy Galore is a lesbian and a cat burglar/acrobat; in the film she becomes a small-aircraft pilot working for the villain before being seduced by Bond, and is played by Honor Blackman. The part was tailored to show off the martial arts skills the actress had previously displayed on the TV series *The Avengers*. The line "Bond . . . James Bond," which Bond habitually uses to introduce himself and which Collins repeats in the musical, is one of the most famous and oft-quoted lines in cinematic history. The line requesting a martini ("shaken, not stirred") refers to Bond's drink of choice, and "Miss Moneypenny" (the name Collins playfully calls Mimi when he requests the martini) is another character from the Bond books and films: a secretary to Bond's boss who has an unrequited romantic interest in him.

Bruce, Lenny (1925–1966)

American stand-up comedian who was highly controversial during his brief lifetime but is now considered a pioneer in the field and an icon of the crusade for free speech. Born Leonard Alfred Schneider in Mineola, New York, he lived with a succession of different relatives after the divorce of his parents. He eventually moved back in with his mother, Sally Marr, who supported herself and her son by working as a maid and waitress as well as a dancer, comedienne, and impersonator of famous stars; her comedic style had a strong influence on Lenny's development as a performer. He worked on a farm as a teenager and entered the Navy during World War II, seeing combat in Italy and Northern Africa before being dishonorably discharged;

he had performed in drag for a shipboard comedy show and convinced Navy officials he was a homosexual. Later, claiming he had broken no Navy regulations, he successfully sued to have his status changed to an Honorable Discharge. In reality he was heterosexual: he married a burlesque performer named Honey Harlow and struggled to make enough money so she could quit working as a stripper; his later lovers included jazz singer Annie Ross and film star Faye Dunaway. When he first moved to New York City in the late forties, Bruce struggled to establish himself as a comedian in nightclubs, developing a unique voice and an approach to humor that was influenced by the comics Mort Sahl, Dick Gregory, and especially his mentor Joe Ancis. He was strongly inspired by jazz music and incorporated its emphasis on honesty, spontaneity, and free association into his stream-of-consciousness monologues. During the fifties he wrote screenplays for low-budget films and recorded several albums of comedic material. His routines came to feature political and cultural commentary as he boldly and frankly tackled taboo themes like sexuality, religion, and race relations. But although he had his influential champions, including the comedian and TV host Steve Allen and *Playboy* publisher Hugh Hefner, he was frequently censored and even arrested on obscenity charges. Other legal problems centered on his drug use, which by the sixties was undermining his health as well. During a major obscenity trial in New York City in 1964, Bruce was supported by an impressive group of influential writers, performers, and icons of the counterculture—including Bob Dylan and Allen Ginsberg, both of whom are also mentioned in *Rent*. Nevertheless, he was found guilty. The verdict was appealed, but before the appeal was resolved Bruce died of a drug overdose, aged forty. Though by the time of his death he had been banned from most of the major comedy clubs in the nation, his reputation and work were subsequently reevaluated and he is now considered one of the greatest and most influential of all comedians. His autobiography, first published in serialized form in *Playboy* magazine, was released as a book entitled *How to Talk Dirty and Influence People* in 1967. Julian Barry's play *Lenny*, about his life, was produced on Broadway in 1971 and adapted as a film, directed by Bob Fosse, in 1974. In 2003, Bruce received an official pardon for the 1964 obscenity charges, granted by Governor George Pataki: the first posthumous pardon in New York State history.

Cage, John (1912–1992)

Iconoclastic American composer considered a major figure in the history of the avant-garde. Born in Los Angeles to an old American family, he initially wanted to be a writer. He dropped out of college to travel in Europe, where he was introduced to the work of modern composers like Hindemith and

Stravinsky and began composing while also studying architecture, poetry, and painting, anticipating his lifelong interest in collaboration among the disciplines. After returning to America he studied for two years with the great composer Arnold Schoenberg, who subsequently stated that though Cage was not really a composer, he was "an inventor of genius." He struggled financially for a long time, often taking work as a teacher, composer, or accompanist at various colleges; at Cornish College of the Arts in Seattle, he met the choreographer Merce Cunningham (see below), who was to become his most significant collaborator as well as his significant other for the rest of his life. Their highly unconventional work together became legendary (the reference in *Rent* is to "Cunningham and Cage"), not least for how it redefined the rules of collaboration and challenged received notions of the traditional relationship between dance and music. While working with Cunningham and others at the short-lived avant-garde institution Black Mountain College, Cage staged a multimedia performance event that came to be considered the first "happening": That term, coined by his student Allan Kaprow, would help define performance art in the sixties. Cage had an insatiable and wide-ranging intellectual curiosity about the world; influences on his developing aesthetic ranged from Henry David Thoreau and James Joyce to Indian music, Zen Buddhism, and the *I Ching*, which he used as a tool for composing music according to the principle of chance. He stated that he was more interested in the natural activity of sound than in listening to a composer "talk" to him by imposing his will on the music. One of his most controversial experiments was a piece entitled *4'33"*, for which the musicians were instructed simply to be present but not to play for the four minute, thirty-three second duration of the event; the intention was to focus the audience's attention not on silence but on the natural ambient sounds in the space. Later works included an unexpected return to more conventional music with *Cheap Imitation*, inspired by the work of Erik Satie, as well as continued experiments in other art forms such as poetry, printmaking, and watercolor painting; beginning in 1987 he wrote several operas. Though controversial in his time and still argued about today, Cage's work has profoundly influenced subsequent generations of performers as diverse as Thom Yorke (of Radiohead), Frank Zappa, Steve Reich, and Philip Glass. His wide-ranging interests and shattering of artistic boundaries would naturally have appealed to a visionary like Jonathan Larson.

Carmina Burana

A 1936 musical composition by the German composer Carl Orff (1895–1982). The piece calls for substantial forces, including a large symphony orchestra, two adult choirs, and a boys' choir. The soprano, tenor, and baritone vocal soloists are all required to sing at times in almost unnaturally high registers. The text—in a combination of Latin, Middle High German, and Old French—is taken from a collection of medieval poems of the same name which celebrates the fleeting beauty of life and the return of the spring as well as commenting on the unpredictability of fortune and the pleasures (and dangers) of such sinful activities as gluttony, drinking, and sex. Though the work was extremely popular in Germany during World War II, and Orff's own relationship to the Nazi party has long been a subject of debate, these associations have barely tainted its reputation; *Carmina Burana* has become a permanent part of the classical music repertoire and one of the few pieces generally credited with being able to sell out the hall when included in a symphony orchestra's season. Though Orff called it a "scenic cantata" and intended that it be performed with elaborate visual elements as well as movement and dance, it has only occasionally been produced that way and is more often presented in concert format. Orff combined medieval and early baroque musical techniques within a modern idiom that anticipated minimalism; the work's deceptively simple, driving rhythms and haunting melodies give it both an archaic and a contemporary vitality. In particular, the thunderous, propulsive opening movement, "O Fortuna," has become a pop culture touchstone, overly familiar from its recycling in countless movies, TV shows, and commercials.

Cat (Scratch) Club, The

The lyrics to "Light My Candle" identify the club where Mimi dances (and gets tied up) for a living as "the Cat Scratch Club." Unlike most of the place names in *Rent*, that name is fictitious. But the idea for the club came from a couple of different venues that Jonathan Larson did visit in the eighties and early nineties. One of them, located at 76 East 13th Street, was actually called the Cat Club; posters with a logo of a leather collar and leash advertised exotic dancers "starting at 1 AM." It was also a rock club where bands like L.A. Guns, Poison, and Soundgarden performed early in their careers, which makes it especially plausible that a musician like Roger would have spent time there. Beginning in 1985, the club was managed by the famous nightlife personality Don Hill; in 1993, he moved on and opened the now legendary rock club Don Hill's, located on Greenwich Street not far from Larson's building. Another antecedent for the Cat Scratch Club would have been Area, a legendary venue at 157 Hudson Street that existed only from 1983 to 1987. Larson occasionally attended with friends; the celebrity-studded clientele included Sting, Malcolm Forbes, Madonna, John F. Kennedy Jr.,

Bianca Jagger, Grace Jones, and Boy George, as well as downtown visual artists including Jean-Michel Basquiat, Keith Haring, and Andy Warhol, who wrote about the club in his diaries. Attractions included a swimming pool and a unisex bathroom; the entire décor was redone every six weeks or so in accordance with a new "theme," with elaborate art installations. Bohemians and hipsters and bigger-than-life downtown personalities lined up behind the velvet ropes outside, desperate for a chance to be admitted and let their freak flags fly. The crowds were such that management had to be selective about who got in, but co-owner Eric Goode has said wealth was not the criterion, and arriving in a limo was considered a bad sign. (Readers who are interested in learning more about what these downtown clubs were like are advised not to turn to the movie of *Rent*, where the "Cat Scratch Club" is made to look like a gleaming, glitzy, upscale gentlemen's strip club. That kind of establishment did not exist on the Lower East Side in those days, and the type of affluent businessmen seen in the audience would generally not have ventured down to that neighborhood voluntarily.)

CBGB

An iconic music club that operated from 1973 to 2006 in the East Village. The club was opened and owned by Hilly Kristal, a musician who had formerly managed the Village Vanguard, a well-known jazz club in Greenwich Village. The space, located at 315 Bowery, had previously housed a biker bar; the name came from the initials for "Country, Bluegrass, and Blues," which were originally the kinds of music Kristal planned to present, but the program soon changed and the venue became known as a showplace for punk and New Wave music. For a time there was also a café/record store next door that was converted into a second performance space, CB's 313 Gallery, where acoustic, experimental, folk, and jazz bands were presented. During the era of *Rent* in the mid-nineties, the club also operated a bar/pizza place in an adjacent space on the other side. CBGB became renowned as the launching pad for the careers of major bands and artists like the Ramones, Television, Patti Smith, the Talking Heads, and Blondie. Other acts that played there included Elvis Costello, the Voidoids, and the Police. Following a protracted rent dispute with the landlord, the club was closed in October of 2006; Patti Smith played the final dates. Kristal announced tentative plans to open a new CBGB in Las Vegas, but they never came to fruition, and he died of cancer the following year. The storied venue is the subject of two films: *Burning Down the House*, directed by Mandy Stein, is a 2009 documentary about the club's history, and Randall Miller's *CBGB*, released in 2013, is a fictionalized account starring Alan Rickman as Kristal. In 2008, fashion designer John Varvatos opened a store in the club's former space; in 2013, the building was named to the National Register of Historic Places. The mention in *Rent* comes in the opening scene, when Mark says the apartment he shares with musician Roger has posters on the wall advertising Roger's gigs at CBGB and the Pyramid Club.

"Chestnuts Roasting on an Open Fire"

The familiar tune that Tom Collins starts to sing on Mark and Roger's answering machine is the first line, and officially the subtitle, of "The Christmas Song," a 1945 composition with music by the jazz singer Mel Tormé and lyrics by Tormé and Robert Wells. Initially recorded in several versions by Nat King Cole, and then also by Tormé himself, the song quickly became a standard and is one of the most frequently performed, and most beloved, of all Christmas songs. It has been recorded by countless singers, including pop, jazz, Broadway, rock, and country artists; *Rent* star Idina Menzel included it on her 2014 album *Holiday Wishes*. The song is one of several Christmas standards sampled by Larson in the Christmas Eve musical sequences of *Rent*; these also include Irving Berlin's "White Christmas" (here used as an allusion to heroin or cocaine) and Johnny Marks's "Rudolph the Red-Nosed Reindeer." Although the musical quotes are very brief, their use in the musical is by permission, the arrangements for which are still listed among the credits in programs for productions of the show. The other Christmas classics Larson quotes or twists, including "O Little Town of Bethlehem" and "O Holy Night," are traditional carols in the public domain, so permission was not required.

Clit Club

This was the name of a very popular lesbian dance night at a large club called Mother on 14th Street—certainly an event to which Maureen would have taken Joanne. It was known for featuring techno music and an elaborately eclectic décor combining ancient Greek-style sculpture, comic book art, vinyl couches, and Victorian furniture. After Mother closed, the party was relocated to a different club called Flamingo on Second Avenue south of 14th Street.

Cunningham, Merce (1919–2009)

Pioneering American choreographer and a leading figure in the history of modern dance. From Washington State, Cunningham studied at Cornish College of the Arts before being discovered by Martha Graham, who invited him to New York to join her company. He danced with her for six years, and in 1953, while teaching at Black Mountain College, he founded the Merce Cunningham Dance Company. His work with the ensemble over the next fifty years was distinguished by a highly individual approach to process, which included using the *I Ching* (the Chinese Book of Changes) to determine the order and structure of a piece through the principle of chance. Cunningham was also a proponent of "non-representational" dance, believing that movement could be abstract and not tied to expressing traditional ideas of story or emotion. With the composer John Cage (see above), who also became his life partner, he developed a unique approach to collaboration, famously asserting that a dance and its score could develop independently. His other innovations included extensive incorporation of computer and film technology in his live dance pieces. In addition to composers ranging from Cage and David Tudor to rock bands like Radiohead and Sonic Youth, Cunningham built dances with collaborators from the worlds of architecture, visual art, and design; these included such luminaries as Roy Lichtenstein, Bruce Nauman, Liz Phillips, Robert Rauschenberg, and Andy Warhol. These collaborations reached beyond the dance world to have a profound impact on the American avant-garde in general. Cunningham's countless awards and honors included the Kennedy Center Honors, a MacArthur Fellowship, and the National Medal of Arts, in addition to numerous honorary degrees. Though his company gave its last performance in 2011, many of Cunningham's works are still licensed and performed by other major dance companies today. There's a personal *Rent* connection: Jonathan Larson dated Brenda Daniels, a dancer/choreographer who taught at Cunningham's studio.

"Do You Know the Way to San Jose?"

A popular 1968 song written by composer Burt Bacharach and lyricist Hal David for the singer Dionne Warwick. It tells the story of a singer who wants to return home to San Jose, California, after a failed attempt to hit it big in Los Angeles, though the tune itself is more upbeat than that description would suggest. It was released on Warwick's album *Dionne Warwick in Valley of the Dolls* and also as a single, selling over a million copies and becoming the singer's biggest hit; she won a Grammy Award for Best Female Pop Vocal Performance for the record. The song has been covered by numerous other singers and groups over the years. In *Rent*, it is sampled very briefly toward the end of the song "Santa Fe," with the name of that city replacing "San Jose." Bacharach and David are credited in programs for productions of the show, along with the music publisher, because a musical quote of even just one line requires permission. One of the most popular songwriting duos of their era,

Tom Collins, played by Jonathan Christopher (center), expounds on the glory of "Santa Fe" (with a quote from Burt Bacharach!) as Angel (Thomas Green) and Mark (Michael Quadrino) look on in this scene from Uncompromising Artistry's production at the Edinburgh Fringe, 2015.   *Rob Palin*

Bacharach and David are also remembered by musical theater fans as the songwriters of *Promises, Promises*, a Broadway hit with a book by Neil Simon that opened in 1968, the same year they wrote the song in question.

Dorothy, Toto, and Auntie Em

These three characters probably need no introduction, as they come from a story that is as close as any to being a universally recognized American myth: *The Wonderful Wizard of Oz*, a children's novel by L. Frank Baum published in 1900. In 1939 it was adapted as an MGM movie musical, with the title shortened to *The Wizard of Oz*. One of the most famous and beloved films of all time, it starred a teenage Judy Garland, who as Dorothy introduced the classic Harold Arlen song "Over the Rainbow." In the book, Dorothy and her little dog, Toto, having been transported by a cyclone to the magical Land of Oz, spend most of their time trying to find a way home to Kansas and their beloved Aunt Em, so Mark and Mimi are giving the story an ironic twist in "La Vie Bohème" when they say the girl and her dog went "over the rainbow to blow off Auntie Em"—one example of the rebellious downtown kids' lashing out against the older generation and all it stands for. (See also "Wicked Witch of the West, The" below.)

Dylan, Bob (b. 1941)

Singer, songwriter, and visual artist who is one of the seminal figures in the history of American music. Born Robert Allen Zimmerman to a Jewish family in Minnesota, he played in rock bands in high school, covering songs by musicians like Elvis Presley and Little Richard. Following one year at the University of Michigan, he went to New York to visit his ailing idol, the legendary folk singer and songwriter Woody Guthrie; he shortly became involved with the Greenwich Village folk music scene and signed with Columbia Records. He claimed he found folk music deeper and more serious than rock, and, like many other folk artists of the day, he became aligned with the civil rights movement. Early songs like "Blowin' in the Wind" and "The Times They Are A-Changin'" established Dylan as an important singer/songwriter with a political and an artistic voice; he played keyboard, guitar, and harmonica. His rough, nasal voice and highly idiosyncratic singing style proved an acquired taste; though some fans have always claimed that "No one sings Dylan like Dylan," others found his songs more immediately congenial when covered by other artists—who included Jimi Hendrix, Joan Baez (with whom he became seriously involved both creatively and romantically), the Association, Manfred Mann, and Peter, Paul and Mary, among many others. When he returned to rock music in the mid-sixties and began to include electronic instruments on his recordings and tours, some of his hardcore folk-music fans felt betrayed and went so far as to heckle his concerts. Undaunted, Dylan continued to explore new musical horizons. He went to Nashville and took part in the country music scene, recording duets with Johnny Cash, and in the late seventies became a born-again Christian and recorded a couple of gospel-themed albums—though his religious beliefs, like his musical style, would continue to evolve. While many of his contemporaries self-destructed at early ages, Dylan persevered, overcoming a motorcycle accident and a drug habit, and has remained phenomenally productive over the course of a fifty-plus-year career. His countless hit songs have included "Mr. Tambourine Man" (a hit for the Byrds) and the groundbreaking "Like a Rolling Stone," twice named number one on lists of the "500 Greatest Songs of All Time" compiled by *Rolling Stone* magazine. He has provided songs and scoring for films and has also appeared as an actor in a couple of them, including director Sam Peckinpah's *Pat Garrett and Billy the Kid* and Richard Marquand's *Hearts of Fire*. In 1988 he was inducted into the Rock and Roll Hall of Fame, and in 1991 he received a Grammy Award for Lifetime Achievement. In the late eighties, he cofounded a new band, the Traveling Wilburys, with other music legends George Harrison, Jeff Lynne, Roy Orbison, and Tom Petty, which rejuvenated his career once again. That year he began what has become known as the Never Ending Tour, which has averaged a hundred dates a year and continues as of this writing, and in 2009, at the age of sixty-seven, he had a No. 1 album, *Together Through Life*. He won an Academy Award for a song he wrote for the movie *Wonder Boys* and has received a Presidential Medal of Freedom and a special citation from the Pulitzer Prize jury; in 2016 he was even awarded the Nobel Prize in Literature. When presenting him with a Kennedy Center Honor in 1997, President Bill Clinton said: "He probably had more impact on people of my generation than any other creative artist. His voice and lyrics haven't always been easy on the ear, but throughout his career Bob Dylan has never aimed to please. He's disturbed the peace and discomforted the powerful."

8BC

This reference in "La Vie Bohème" is easy to miss; after they name the Sex Pistols, it can sound like the ensemble is simply shouting out the first three letters of the alphabet. But they're actually saying "8BC," the name of an East Village nightclub/gallery/performance space, called that because of its location on 8th Street between Avenues B and C. The venue was celebrated for presenting the work of numerous innovative musicians and performance artists, but it was in operation for only two years, opening on Halloween 1983 and closing on October 22, 1985. It was housed in an old farmhouse— bought by Cornelius Conboy in 1980—in an area of Alphabet City that at the time was so desolate, with so many ruined and abandoned buildings, that it was known as "Little Dresden," after the beautiful German city that was devastated by bombing during World War II. Conboy had worked on Theatre Row in midtown and wanted to create a venue more hospitable to experimental work. With partner Dennis Gattra, he opened a performance space that could accommodate 200 patrons, with a large stage and an open, casual atmosphere—more nightclub than theater. They presented a wide variety of acts ranging from punk bands to Japanese Butoh to theater and performance artists like Charles Busch, Steve Buscemi, Ethyl Eichelberger, Karen Finley, and Holly Hughes; the band They Might Be Giants performed there frequently. The space also functioned as an art gallery with permanent murals as well as rotating exhibits of work by downtown artists. Having closed eleven years before *Rent* opened, it was a place the older members of the gang of bohemians would definitely have frequented and remembered fondly. The club was a casualty of a multitude of licensing and zoning issues with the city. Several other venues in the area, including the Peppermint Lounge, the Limbo Lounge, and Darinka, had recently suffered similar fates, signaling the end of an era. On 8BC's closing night, Conboy told the *New York Times*:

"We accurately reflected the disordered energies that were being flung with wild abandon on the Lower East Side in the last two years. Look at it as a performance project. We only lost $20,000."

Evita

This name is used in the libretto of *Rent* only as the name of Benny's wife's dog, an Akita. But to any musical theater aficionado (and Jonathan Larson qualified as such) it would immediately bring to mind the 1978 musical by Tim Rice and Andrew Lloyd Webber about the life of the controversial and ambitious Argentine first lady, Eva Perón, played in London by Elaine Paige and on Broadway by Patti LuPone. The show was an early example of the pop opera, imported from England and characterized by bombast and spectacle, that had dominated Broadway in the decade preceding *Rent* and that Larson was reacting against in his efforts to transform the musical theater. The film version, starring Madonna, was released in 1996, the same year *Rent* opened on Broadway. Rice and Lloyd Webber provided the title character with difficult, high-lying vocal passages, sung in the belt register, that were meant to mimic the historical Eva's hectoring style of public speaking, and became known as "the harangue"; Larson could have been winking at this when he appropriated the moniker for a dog that barks so incessantly that a neighbor is driven to hire Angel to engineer her death. Or perhaps he just chose the name because it rhymes with "Akita" . . . Make of it what you will.

Food Emporium

A chain of grocery stores that was at the height of its success in the 1990s, with locations in New York City, Westchester County, Connecticut, and New Jersey; today there are still about eleven outlets, mainly in Manhattan. The upscale stores have a reputation for charging relatively high prices, making them an obvious target for the Robin Hood scheme (robbing from the rich to give to the poor) devised by Tom Collins: in the last scene of the musical, he explains that he rewired an ATM machine at a Food Emporium so that it would provide money to any needy individual who puts in the code A-N-G-E-L.

Gingrich, Newt (b. 1943) and Candace (b. 1966)

A high-profile American politician, writer, and political consultant, Newt Gingrich served in the United States Congress from 1979 to 1999, representing the 6th District of Georgia. At the time of *Rent*'s debut, he had been much in the news for coauthoring the "Contract with America," a plan that was instrumental in the 1994 political campaigns that led to the Republican Party regaining control of the House of Representatives, which they had not held for the previous forty years. In 1995 he became Speaker of the House, under President Bill Clinton, and was a loud and influential voice for conservative causes. An ethics scandal tarnished his reputation, leading to a 1996 election season that was disastrous for Republicans; following much dissension within his party, he resigned as Speaker and eventually from Congress. Still, he has remained in the public eye, publishing many books and competing for the Republican presidential nomination in 2012; in 2016, he was on Donald Trump's short list of potential running mates, though he lost that position to Mike Pence. His political positions and values would certainly not have made him a favorite of Jonathan Larson's, and his last name does not even appear in the libretto, where the reference is simply to "Newt's lesbian sister."

Candace Gingrich, twenty-three years younger than Newt, is actually his half-sister and a liberal democrat who emerged as a highly visible and active figure in the fight for LGBT rights. She was the National Coming Out Project Spokesperson for the Human Rights Campaign in 1995, and in 1996 she published a book: *Accidental Activist: A Personal and Political Memoir*. Known as an avid rugby player, she is still active today on behalf of LGBTQ causes. In 2009, she married Rebecca Jones, a playwright; three years later, her brother Newt, otherwise far to the right politically, encouraged his fellow Republicans to rethink their position on same-sex marriage. In *Rent*, Maureen brings her up in a phone conversation to point out that one of America's most conservative politicians has an openly gay person in his family—and thus hopefully to convince Joanne's parents that her own relationship with their daughter won't hurt Joanne's mother's chances of being confirmed as a federal judge.

Ginsberg, Allen (1926–1997)

American poet and social activist. From New Jersey, he grew up in a Jewish family. His father, Louis Ginsberg, was a high school teacher and a poet, and his mother, Naomi Livergant Ginsberg, was a card-carrying Communist who suffered from a psychological illness and was in and out of institutions; both parents had substantial influence on Ginsberg's creative work. Some of his early poetry was written in rhyme and formal meters, but soon William Carlos Williams, becoming a mentor to the younger man, encouraged him to find his own contemporary American voice, and his work became much freer in structure. It was also free, and significantly ahead of its time, in its use of language and willingness to take on then taboo topics such as drug use, promiscuity, and especially homosexuality. His major 1956 work *Howl*, still probably his most famous poem, put Ginsberg at the center of a well-publicized obscenity trial; the admirably forward-thinking judge ruled that the work could not be considered pornography due to its literary and social significance, and his decision set an important precedent for later cases. Ginsberg graduated from Columbia University. He formed friendships with a number of young writers who were sharing each other's work and discussing art and politics in the bars and coffee shops of Greenwich Village, including Jack Kerouac, William S. Burroughs, Gregory Corso, and others. They formed the nucleus of a group that came to be called the Beat Generation. In their energetic pursuit of new forms and originality, their open embrace of drug use and the free expression of sexuality, their rejection of materialism, and their nonconformity and rebellion against the oppressive conservatism of mainstream fifties American culture, this community of artists had much in common with—and significant influence on—the close-knit family of early nineties downtown creative types Jonathan Larson would later celebrate in *Rent*. Jack Kerouac's novel *On the Road* is one of the most famous pieces of literature to be produced by the Beats; Ginsberg figures in it as a character Kerouac called "Carlo Marx," due to the poet's sympathy with certain aspects of communism. Ginsberg, who never joined the Communist Party, was reportedly not thrilled with the portrayal. Following his initial years in New York, he moved for a time to San Francisco, where he served as something of a bridge between the Beats and a similar group of West Coast writers known as the San Francisco Renaissance; his early works were published by the City Lights Bookshop in that city. He began a relationship with Peter Orlovsky, another poet, which lasted for the rest of Ginsberg's life. They traveled to Morocco and then spent time in Paris with some of the other Beats in a lodging house that became known as the Beat Hotel, where several of the writers did some of their best work and where Ginsberg started his epic poem *Kaddish for Naomi Ginsberg (1894–1956)*. An interest in the teachings of Buddha (also invoked in "La Vie Bohème") and, later, in Hare Krishnaism, informed some of Ginsberg's works, which often involved music and chanting, and he was instrumental in spreading Hare Krishnaism in the United States. He befriended the Venerable Chögyam Trungpa, an exiled Tibetan Buddhist who was in the process of founding the Naropa Institute (now Naropa University) in Boulder, Colorado. With the poet Anne Waldman, Ginsberg established the Institute's Jack Kerouac School of Disembodied Poetics. Though, as he said in his works, he saw many of the best minds of his generation destroyed by drugs and the pressures of their struggles against the status quo, Ginsberg himself endured and served as a link between the

Allen Ginsberg and Bob Dylan, both of whom are named in the lyrics to "La Vie Bohème," on the set of the film *Renaldo and Clara* (1978). *Photofest*

1950s legacy of the Beats and the hippie counterculture of the 1960s, of which he became an important part. He participated in many of the great protest events of the sixties and was a tireless activist, speaking out against the Vietnam War and advocating for free speech, racial equality, gay rights, the legalization of marijuana, and other causes. For the last decade of his life, Ginsberg taught poetry at Brooklyn College, where he was a Distinguished Professor of English.

Hagen, Uta (1919–2004)

A legendary Broadway actress and acting teacher, Hagen was born in Germany and grew up in Wisconsin; she enjoyed early stage successes as Ophelia in *Hamlet*, opposite Eva Le Gallienne, and as Nina in *The Seagull* with Alfred Lunt and Lynn Fontanne. Her most famous roles included Desdemona in *Othello*—opposite Paul Robeson and the Iago of her then husband, José Ferrer—and Blanche DuBois in *A Streetcar Named Desire*, which she played on tour and on Broadway as a replacement for Jessica Tandy. Her two Tony Awards were for *The Country Girl* (1951) and for her most iconic role: Martha in the original cast of Edward Albee's *Who's Afraid of Virginia Woolf?* (1963; it played the Billy Rose Theatre, later renamed the Nederlander, where decades later her name would be shouted out nightly in *Rent*.) She also received a special Tony for Lifetime Achievement in 1999 and a National Medal of Arts in 2002. Hagen began teaching at HB Studios, an acting school in New York City's West Village, in 1948, and she married the school's founder, Herbert Berghof, in 1957. She became one of the nation's most revered acting teachers, and her books *Respect for Acting* and *A Challenge for the Actor* are widely used as college texts. Her approach is based in sense memory, drawing on the actor's own emotional history in the work, and the honest pursuit of actions and objectives—all vital touchstones of actor training to this day. Hagen was blacklisted during the Red Scare of the fifties, which inhibited the establishment of a film acting career, but she did appear in several movies later on, beginning with *The Other* in 1972. In her late years she returned to the New York stage in Off-Broadway productions of *Mrs. Warren's Profession*, *Mrs. Klein*, and *Collected Stories*. Her shout out in the *Rent* song "La Vie Bohème" refers to her simply as "Uta"—as, for many decades, did her students.

Havel, Václav (1936–2011)

Czech writer/statesman who is considered one of the great intellectuals of the twentieth century. A lifelong opponent of communism and a crusader for democracy and personal freedom, he attained success as a playwright years before being elected to lead his country, becoming one of the very few contemporary figures to have achieved greatness in both the artistic and political spheres. His early plays included *The Garden Party*, *The Memorandum*, and *Increased Difficulty of Concentration*; they generally critiqued communism and were written in a style influenced by Theatre of the Absurd. While Czechoslovakia was under communist rule, Havel was considered a dissident and was imprisoned several times, including a four-year sentence from 1979 to 1983. He founded a political party called Civic Forum that was instrumental in the Velvet Revolution that overthrew the communist party in 1989; following this, he was elected president. Havel held that post for two and a half years until the nation of Czechoslovakia was dissolved by its parliament and Slovakia became an independent country. He then became president of the new Czech Republic, an office he held until 2003. A lifelong believer in democracy, Havel also warned against the excesses of capitalism and was a proponent of anti-consumerism, human rights, and environmentalism. Though he remained a somewhat controversial figure in his own country, he was more revered and celebrated abroad, where he received countless international honors and accolades, including the Gandhi

Peace Prize, Amnesty International's Ambassador of Conscience Award, the St. George Victory Order, and the US Presidential Medal of Freedom. After the end of his presidency, Havel remained active in political and environmental causes and also returned to his playwriting career, producing a major work entitled *Leaving* that was partially inspired by *King Lear* and *The Cherry Orchard*; the play was produced internationally and adapted as a film, which Havel directed, in 2011. A fictionalized version of Havel's role in the Velvet Revolution is included in *Rock 'n' Roll*, a 2006 play by the great Czech-born British playwright Tom Stoppard. (Havel had dedicated his own 1984 autobiographical play *Largo Desolato* to Stoppard, who translated it into English.) Havel's memoir of his time as president, *To the Castle and Back*, was published in 2007. Though the reference in "La Vie Bohème" in *Rent* celebrates both his writing and the strength of his political convictions, his first name was mispronounced when the song was performed in the original production. (The correct pronunciation is "Vatslav," as opposed to "Vaklav.") In 2012, New York's Human Rights Foundation, with the support of Havel's widow Dagmar Havlová, established in his honor the Václav Havel Prize for Creative Dissent, intended to "celebrate those who engage in creative dissent, exhibiting courage and creativity to challenge injustice and live in truth."

Heidegger, Martin (1889–1976)

German philosopher who is considered one of the most influential figures in the history of continental philosophy, and whose work and legacy are still subject to controversy forty years after his death. He earned his degrees at the University of Freiburg and published his first and most important book, *Being and Time*, in 1927. From 1933 to 1934 he served a troubled term as rector of the University, and during that time he joined the Nazi Party; though there is some indication that he later regretted it, his relationship to Nazism and anti-Semitism remains controversial. Heidegger's work had a strong influence on Jean-Paul Sartre and the development of existentialism, but he distanced himself from the existentialists and did not wish to be so labeled. His works are notoriously difficult to read, and scholars today argue about whether they are thus deeply complex or simply nonsensical and useless. His writings include theories about "being-in-the-world," the dangers of technology, and conformity versus authenticity, all of which might have some appeal to the characters in *Rent*, though his politics would not. In the famous 1981 film *My Dinner with Andre*, actor/playwright Wallace Shawn sums up Heidegger's theory that "experiencing one's being to the fullest is like experiencing the decay of that being towards one's death, as a part of your experience"— perhaps not so far from Mimi's credo, "I live this moment as my last." Still, Heidegger is not one of the figures celebrated in "La Vie Bohème." His name shows up in the song "Santa Fe," when Tom Collins, a sometime professor of philosophy, dreams about opening a restaurant, where the talk would be about wine rather than Heidegger. Whether he specifically rejects Heidegger's theories, or is just tired of talking about philosophy in general, remains anybody's guess.

Herman, Pee-wee

Popular character created by the comedian/writer/actor Paul Reubens (b. 1952). As a young actor, Reubens appeared in stage productions and had roles in films including *The Blues Brothers* and *Cheech & Chong's Next Movie*. He first created Pee-wee while working with the famed Los Angeles improv group the Groundlings; two of his colleagues from that company, Phil Hartman and John Paragon, helped him develop a stage show based on the character, a childlike eccentric in an undersized gray suit and bowtie. *The Pee-wee Herman Show* played at the Roxy Theatre in L.A. for five months; the run included matinees for children and midnight performances of a different version for adults, and this unique double appeal followed Reubens and his character through subsequent incarnations. After the stage show was featured on HBO, Reubens began giving interviews and appearing on talk shows in character as Pee-wee, and for a time even made efforts to conceal his real name and identity from the public. The first feature film about the character, *Pee-wee's Big Adventure* (1985), was directed by Tim Burton; despite mixed reviews, the low-budget movie became a cult hit and grossed over forty million dollars. It was followed by a sequel and the Saturday morning CBS series *Pee-wee's Playhouse*, which ran from 1986 to 1990. The show was in reruns by the time of Reubens's much-publicized arrest for indecent exposure in a Florida adult movie theater in 1991; though CBS yanked the show, many of Reubens's fans and colleagues were supportive and felt too much was made of the incident. Temporarily leaving the character of Pee-wee behind, Reubens gradually began to take on new roles, with appearances in films (*Buffy the Vampire Slayer, Batman Returns*) and as a voiceover artist for cartoons. In 2009, he finally revived the character of Pee-wee Herman for a new Los Angeles stage production, *The Pee-wee Herman Show*, which eventually played Broadway. In a 1987 *Rolling Stone* interview with writer T. Gertler, Reubens said: "I'm just trying to illustrate that it's okay to be different—not that it's good, not that it's bad, but that it's all right. I'm trying to tell kids to have a good time and to encourage them to be creative and to question things." This outlook neatly summarizes the character's appeal to the creative free spirits of *Rent*.

Hughes, Langston (1902–1967)

American poet, writer, social activist, and a leading figure of the Harlem Renaissance. Hughes was born in Missouri and raised in Kansas, usually living with his grandmother; his mother had to travel in search of work after his father abandoned the family and moved to Mexico. He was of racially mixed ancestry on both sides, but his grandmother and the stories she told were instrumental in instilling in him a great sense of pride in his identity as an African American man. He began writing very early, and one of his most famous poems, "The Negro Speaks of Rivers," was published in the NAACP's magazine *The Crisis* when he was only nineteen. He attended Columbia University for a time, and, though he wanted to pursue a career as a writer, he majored in engineering because his father insisted on that as a condition of helping him pay for his education. Dismayed by racism, he dropped out of Columbia (he later earned a degree from Lincoln University) but was drawn to nearby Harlem, where he lived for most of the rest of his life. In addition to poetry, he wrote short stories and, beginning with *Not Without Laughter* in 1930, novels. Most of his work realistically portrayed the lives of working-class African Americans. He was a pioneer in the genre of jazz poetry, which utilized the rhythms of folk and jazz music; his work generally dealt with racial consciousness and cultural nationalism, encouraging other blacks to embrace their heritage and celebrate their unique culture at a time when some were more concerned with assimilation. He also wrote opera librettos and plays, including *Mule Bone* (coauthored with Zora Neale Hurston in 1931), *Troubled Island*, *Tambourines to Glory*, and *Black Nativity*; he cofounded theater companies in New York, Chicago, and Los Angeles. His published works also include two autobiographical volumes, *The Big Sea* and *I Wonder as I Wander*, and nonfiction books on black culture and history for both adults and children. Politically, like many artists and liberal thinkers of his time, he sympathized with communism but never joined the Communist Party and, after being questioned by Senator Joe McCarthy's witch-hunting committee in the fifties, distanced himself from the movement. In his later years, he was famously generous and supportive of the younger generation of African American writers; those he mentored included Alice Walker and Loften Mitchell. A towering figure in black history, Hughes is often considered a gay icon as well, though some Hughes scholars question whether he was actually homosexual; if so, he was closeted, but he cited the gay poet Walt Whitman as a major influence and reportedly produced a series of love poems to a black man that remained unpublished. His awards and honors started early with a Witter Bynner Undergraduate Poetry Prize, and included a Guggenheim Fellowship, the Anisfield-Wolf Book Award, a Springarn Medal from the NAACP, and several honorary doctorates. Jonathan Larson's bohemians would have revered Hughes for his liberal activism, his uniquely musical poetic voice, his lifelong commitment to cultural pride and diversity, and his role in founding and leading a community of socially conscious artists.

It's a Wonderful Life

A 1946 film, produced and directed by Frank Capra, that has become a Christmas classic. Based on a short story called "The Greatest Gift" by Philip Van Doren Stern, the film tells the tale of George Bailey (played by Jimmy Stewart), a family man in the small town of Bedford Falls, New York, who throughout his life has repeatedly sacrificed his own hopes and dreams in favor of making responsible choices and looking out for others. On Christmas Eve, George's family business faces financial disaster and he himself is on the brink of suicide until a guardian angel named Clarence (Henry Travers) intervenes. Clarence shows George sad scenes of what life for his family and the town would have been like without him, which restores George's faith in life and humanity; the film ends with a joyous Christmas celebration. *It's a Wonderful Life*, which also stars Donna Reed, Lionel Barrymore, and Thomas Mitchell, lost money for RKO Pictures on its initial run; its reviews were mixed, with some critics deriding it as sentimental. But it did receive several Oscar nominations, including Best Picture, and it gradually attained the stature of a classic. By the mid-eighties, after years of annual TV broadcasts during the Christmas season, it had become a perennial holiday tradition almost on a par with *A Christmas Carol* or *The Nutcracker*; it appears on many lists of the best movies ever made, and both Capra and Stewart claimed it as their favorite among all the films they had worked on. The reference in *Rent* comes in the "You'll See" number, also set on Christmas Eve; Mark invokes the movie to chastise Benny, telling him he can't go home and watch the film on TV after wiping out a tent city of homeless people to make room for his personal real estate development project. The point is well taken, since one of George Bailey's good deeds in the film is building Bailey Park, an affordable housing complex for the town's lower- and middle-income families.

Koppel, Ted (b. 1940)

Television journalist best known as the original anchor of the late-night ABC news series *Nightline*, which he hosted from 1980 to 2005. The son of

German Jews who fled Germany to escape the Nazis, Koppel earned degrees at Syracuse and Stanford Universities and began his broadcasting career at ABC, where, at twenty-three, he was the youngest news correspondent ever hired by the network. He started on the radio before moving on to ABC-TV news, for which he covered the Vietnam War and Richard Nixon's campaign for president. He also covered the US State Department, where he began a lifelong friendship with former Secretary of State Henry Kissinger. Though Koppel had a reputation for challenging authority and rarely hesitating to put politicians and elected officials on the spot by asking hard questions, he and *Nightline* were occasionally accused by left-leaning media critics of being mouthpieces for the government establishment and not giving enough airtime to opposing views. However, the show was sometimes criticized by conservatives, too, as when Koppel read on the air a list of the names of soldiers killed in the Iraq War, which some interpreted as an antiwar statement or an attempt to undermine the war effort. After retiring from *Nightline*, Koppel has stayed active on the national journalism scene, including stints with the *New York Times*, the Discovery Channel, National Public Radio, *BBC World News America*, the *NBC Nightly News*, and *CBS News Sunday Morning*. In *Rent*, Koppel is mentioned in the St. Mark's Place scene: Mark stops a police officer from roughing up a homeless person by filming the incident and saying, "Smile for Ted Koppel, Officer Martin!"

Kurosawa, Akira (1910–1998)

Japanese film director and screenwriter. The most famous director in the history of Japanese cinema, he is also considered a giant in the history of the art form internationally. Though he had originally intended to pursue a career as a painter, he entered the Japanese film industry at age twenty-five, soon after the advent of talking pictures; he worked extensively as an assistant director and screenwriter before directing his own first feature, *Sanshiro Sugata*, in 1943. His career flourished during the years of the American Occupation of Japan following World War II. Kurosawa's work often championed humanism and the rights of the individual; critical of the prewar Japanese government, he fought to encourage the development of a more democratic society. He first found international success with the now-classic *Rashomon* (1951), based on a short story that examined the same crime through the conflicting accounts of several different characters. Though not particularly acclaimed in Japan, the film won the prestigious Golden Lion prize at the Venice Film Festival and subsequently became a hit in America, beginning a vogue for Japanese cinema in the West. *The Seven Samurai* (1954), a historical epic set in sixteenth-century Japan, became one of Kurosawa's most influential films; it was adapted by American director John Sturges, who reset it in the American West as *The Magnificent Seven*, a star-studded Hollywood epic, in 1960. *Battle Beyond the Stars*, a 1980 American film directed by Jimmy T. Murakami, resets the same story in a science fiction milieu, and a remake of *The Magnificent Seven* is in the works as of this writing. Though Kurosawa was fascinated by Japanese history and made a number of samurai pictures, he was often inspired by European literature as well, and some of his films are adaptations of works by such authors as Dostoyevsky and Gorky. Two of his greatest films are based on Shakespeare: *Throne of Blood* (1957) is a Noh-inspired take on the story of *Macbeth*, while the epic *Ran* (1985) borrows plot elements from *King Lear*. Kurosawa's countless awards and honors include the Cannes Film Festival's Palme D'Or for *Kagemusha* (1980), a Golden Jubilee Award from the Directors Guild of America (1986), and an Oscar for Lifetime Achievement, presented at the 1989 Academy Awards. The director's work inspired not only a whole generation of younger Japanese directors but some of the biggest names in European and American cinema history as well, including George Lucas and Steven Spielberg, both of whom were so devoted to the master's work that, when the Japanese film industry was in a slump, they helped him secure foreign financing for some of his later works. Other great directors who cited Kurosawa as a major influence included Ingmar Bergman, Federico Fellini, and the Italian Bernardo Bertolucci (see above), whose name is linked with the Japanese director's in the lyrics to "La Vie Bohème" in *Rent*.

Lee, Spike (b. 1957)

Toward the end of his first scene with Mimi, Roger wonders aloud whether what they have been interpreting as romantic moonlight might really be artificial lighting, since he has heard that "Spike Lee's shooting down the street." Not unlikely, as the famed and sometimes controversial filmmaker has been based in New York since moving to Brooklyn from Atlanta with his family as a small child; his production company, called 40 Acres and a Mule Filmworks, is located in that borough today. The company is named for the deal that was offered (and later revoked) to freed black men as an attempted reparation for slavery following the Civil War; this reflects Lee's lifelong concerns with social and economic injustice and African American history, all of which he has explored from many angles throughout his prolific career. Born Shelton Jackson Lee, he was nicknamed Spike by his mother in childhood, and it stuck. He made his first student film while studying at Morehouse College and then entered the graduate program in Film & Television at NYU; he earned his MFA there and later joined the faculty of the school, which is located in the East Village, just blocks from the locations where *Rent* takes place. He has also taught at Harvard. While still a student at NYU, Lee made a sixty-minute film called *Joe's Bed-Stuy Barbershop: We Cut Heads*, which was shown in the New Directors/New Films Festival at Lincoln Center; it also won a student Academy Award. He founded 40 Acres and a Mule in 1983 and has turned out thirty-five films in the past thirty-three years. A cinematic polymath, he is not only a director but a producer, screenwriter, and actor—often fulfilling two, three, or even all four of these roles on a single film. His first feature, the comedy *She's Gotta Have It* (1986), was filmed on a budget of $175,000 and made over $7 million at the box office. As early as 1989, the young filmmaker earned an Academy Award nomination for Best Original Screenplay for his acclaimed film *Do the Right Thing*, about racial tensions in a Brooklyn neighborhood. Often appearing on lists of the greatest films of all time, the film was honored by selection for the National Film Registry at the Library of Congress. Since then, Lee's output has included comedies, dramas, thrillers, documentaries, and more experimental projects. He has worked with many of today's finest actors, including Denzel Washington, who earned an Oscar nomination playing the title role in Lee's film *Malcolm X* and also collaborated with him on *Mo' Better Blues*, *He Got Game*, and *Inside Man*. One of Lee's most ambitious films is the controversial historical epic *Miracle at St. Anna* (2008), which tells the often overlooked story of black American soldiers in World War II. Lee is quoted in his IMDb bio as saying of young filmmakers: "I hope they're doing it because they love it, not because they want to be rich or famous. Not that those things can't happen, but the main reason, the focus is, 'This is what I want to do for the rest of my life and I love it.'" That philosophy would certainly have spoken to Jonathan Larson, not to mention *Rent*'s aspiring filmmaker Mark Cohen, who demonstrates a social conscience simpatico with Lee's. In addition to being mentioned in the show, Lee very nearly directed the film version of *Rent* (see Chapter 13). A self-professed fan of Hollywood musicals, he later directed the 2009 movie of the stage musical *Passing Strange*.

The Life Café

The restaurant where the musical's characters celebrate following Maureen's performance was a real place. Mark announces the exact location in the show's libretto ("the corner of 10th Street and Avenue B"); the official address was 162 Avenue B. The café was opened in 1981 by David and Kathy Kirkpatrick. David was an artist, and Kathy, who later went by the name Kathy Life, was famous for her vegetarian chili, which initially was priced at fifty cents a bowl in order to be affordable by the struggling artists who frequented the restaurant. The couple originally included an antique store adjacent to their coffee shop space, until they realized denizens of the low-rent neighborhood were not interested in purchasing antiques. The building was decrepit, and David and Kathy received a credit on rent in exchange for improving the space. At one point they used wheat paste to reinforce the insecure front wall with a new façade made up of pages from their collection of old issues of *Life* magazine; this led to the idea for the new café's name. The place was eclectically furnished with pieces from David's antique collection and discarded furniture found on nearby streets. In addition to providing inexpensive food, the restaurant became a haven for East Village artists and performers, hosting poetry readings, comedy shows, and musical events. There were performance art and theater evenings as well, and the work of local visual artists was displayed on the walls. By the end of the eighties, David had left the business to open a yoga center; Kathy stayed and ran the café herself, expanding the service from the initial coffee shop offerings to a full menu focused on vegetarian and vegan entrees. Though Jonathan Larson ate there on occasion, the myth that he wrote much of *Rent* in the café has been debunked by personal friends. But according to the restaurant's website,

Anthony Rapp as Mark (center) leads the cast in their celebration of the icons of Bohemia: "La Vie Bohème." Original cast, 1996.   *Joan Marcus*

Lifecafe.com: "He observed the neighborhood people who regularly met at Life Café. They came because, after all, there was never enough room in Lower East Side apartments or enough heat, or hot water. And sometimes there was no water at all." Once *Rent* became a hit, business at the restaurant prospered, as Rentheads made a point of visiting the location so they could experience their favorite show's milieu firsthand and say that they too had eaten at the Life Café. The sign over the door read "Enjoy Life Every Day," which could be construed as a paraphrase of the show's theme. But changes to the economy of the neighborhood eventually made it hard for the institution to stay afloat. As *Rent* publicist Richard Kornberg told the *Daily News*: "The East Village of 'Rent' is a very different place than the East Village of today. 'Rent' helped gentrify that neighborhood, but unfortunately places like Life which were once institutions could no longer fit in the market." The café closed in September of 2011, in preparation for structural repairs that were sorely needed, and never reopened; the space was listed as available by the end of February 2012. On the café's website, Kathy Life specifically attributed the closing to the fact that she "could no longer carry the huge business losses caused by the two warring landlords who fought over structural repairs to their property." In 2001, she had opened a second, similar venue, Life Café 983, in Bushwick, Brooklyn, but sadly it too closed before the end of 2012 when the landlord chose not to renew the lease. It was immediately reopened under different ownership with the name simplified to just 983 (the address is 983 Flushing Avenue), and the new management has made a point of preserving a sense of the original ambience and spirit, with an affordable menu featuring American, Mexican, and Italian dishes. Kathy Life was proud of the way her restaurant was immortalized in *Rent*. On the closing of the two establishments, she summed up what she and her husband had intended and achieved: "Life Café has always been about the relationship between the staff and patrons. A café is more than a place to eat and drink. It's where special relationships are fostered and melded through conversation, laughter and camaraderie. That's what a good café is. It's far more than food and drink. It's about human connection."

"Musetta's Waltz"

A soprano aria from the Puccini opera *La bohème*, the story of which was the original inspiration for *Rent*. The aria is sometimes called by its Italian title, "Quando m'en vo' soletta" ("When I walk alone"), which is the first line of its text. It's the most familiar tune from the opera and has been heard or quoted in countless films and even TV commercials over the years. Portions of the melody are played on guitar three times in the course of the musical;

in addition, the lyrics inspired the opening verse of "Take Me or Leave Me." (See also Chapter 2.)

Neruda, Pablo (1904–1973)

Chilean poet and politician. His real name was Ricardo Eliécer Neftalí Reyes Basoalto, and he chose his pen name to honor the Czech poet Jan Neruda. Though the name change was attributed to the fact that his father disapproved of his pursuing a writing career, Neruda achieved very early success, beginning to write poetry at age ten and publishing by thirteen. His early output also included essays and articles. His most renowned work, *Veinte poemas de amor y una canción desesperada* (*Twenty Love Poems and a Song of Despair*), a collection of erotic love poetry, was published when he was only twenty years old and has since sold millions of copies. At the time his writing was not lucrative, and he began to support himself by serving in a variety of diplomatic posts in remote locales like Burma, India, Ceylon, and Singapore. While stationed in Barcelona, Spain, he became friends with a variety of literary luminaries, including the playwright Federico Garcia Lorca, who was executed by followers of the dictator Francisco Franco. These events turned Neruda into a committed Communist, and his subsequent works, including the 1938 volume *Spain in My Heart*, took on an overtly political character. He was especially proud of his role in a mission to relocate 2,000 Spanish emigrants from French refugee camps to Chile in 1938. Neruda's increasingly fervent allegiance to Joseph Stalin gradually drove a wedge between him and some of his leftist contemporaries. He later regretted his loyalty to the Russian dictator and denounced the "personality cults" that corrupted the regimes of Communist leaders like Stalin and China's Mao Tse-tung, but he remained committed to the basic tenets of Communism. He served as a senator in Chile but was forced to go underground when that country's leadership turned against the Communist Party; in exile, he spent time in Argentina and traveled widely. He later returned to favor in Chile under the Socialist administration of Salvador Allende and was even appointed Chilean Ambassador to France, but he remained a controversial figure on the world stage: revered as a leading left-wing thinker and writer, he was simultaneously reviled as a Communist, which remained a dirty world in the West throughout the Cold War era. He was awarded the Nobel Prize in Literature in 1971—a controversial decision given his politics—and became one of the world's most widely read poets, his works translated into countless languages. He died in 1973, reportedly of cancer, but rumors persisted that he had been poisoned on order of General Augusto Pinochet, the new Chilean dictator who had overthrown Allende; forty years later, Neruda's remains were exhumed in an inconclusive effort to prove or disprove the theory. Jonathan Larson was far from the only writer to show an interest in Neruda, whose poetry has been set to music by many composers and songwriters over the years. An episode during Neruda's exile in Italy, when he inspired a love of poetry in a postman whom he befriended, became the subject of a novel by Antonio Skármeta. The book was adapted as a film entitled *Il Postino* and later as an opera of the same name by Daniel Catan.

Pyramid Club, The

An East Village nightclub founded in 1979 and located at 101 Avenue A in a building dating from 1876. This is one of two clubs (the other being CBGB, see above) where Mark says Roger had performed his music, and the Pyramid Club is especially representative of the subculture represented by the characters in *Rent*. According to Wikipedia: "In the late 70s and early 80s, when mega-clubs like Studio 54 and The Limelight, dominated New York nightlife, the struggling artists, actors, musicians, and drag queens who lived in the East Village created their own, more intimately-scaled scene . . . The club became a hangout for 'a new breed of politicized drag performers' like Lypsinka, Lady Bunny, and RuPaul, whose first New York City show was at the Pyramid Club in 1982." This would suggest that Angel might be more likely to have performed there than Roger, but the club also featured rock bands like Nirvana and the Red Hot Chili Peppers. The events were initially presented and promoted by a trio made up of Bobby Bradley, Alan Mace, and Victor Sapienza, who had all worked together previously at a more mainstream nightclub called Interferon. Madonna did an AIDS benefit at the Pyramid Club (her first of many). Plays were also presented there, including a popular stage serial called *Chang in a Void Moon*, written and directed by filmmaker John Jesurun, and later a Monday midnight series by a company called Blacklips Performance Cult. Drag actor Ethyl Eichelberger, who had been a mainstay of Charles Ludlam's Ridiculous Theatrical Company, also appeared there regularly. By the end of the eighties, when the club had received national media attention and had begun to attract a more mainstream crowd, the experimental, theatrical, and gay-oriented offerings were mostly replaced by rock bands, and the club lost some of its alternative vibe. By the late nineties, though, dance nights with an eighties theme were being offered, appealing to both gay and straight patrons. Unlike CBGB, the Pyramid Club is still in operation as of this writing. Along with numerous other buildings in its East Village neighborhood, it was declared a Historic Landmark in 2012.

Saks Fifth Avenue

A luxury department store founded by Andrew Saks in 1898. Though it's now a chain with stores around the country, the flagship store, opened in 1924, is still located on Fifth Avenue and 50th Street in midtown Manhattan. Renowned for its lavish holiday window displays and situated near the famous Rockefeller Center Christmas tree, the store, which features expensive international luxury brands, epitomizes upscale New York City holiday culture. In *Rent*, the five homeless people sing that "Christmas bells are ringing," but only "on TV—at Saks," emphasizing the difference from their own bleak experience of the season.

Sex Pistols, The

British band, active from 1975 to 1978, that was instrumental in launching the punk movement and had enormous influence on other punk and alternative rock bands over the next couple of decades. The band evolved from an earlier group called the Strand; Malcolm McLaren—a visual artist/performer who ran a clothing shop called Too Fast to Live, Too Young to Die (which became a meeting place for the burgeoning punk crowd)—came on board to manage guitarist Steve Jones, bassist Glenn Matlock, and drummer Paul Cook. Shortly after John Lydon (a.k.a. Johnny Rotten) was chosen as lead vocalist, the group was officially dubbed the Sex Pistols; following disputes between Rotten and Matlock, the latter left the group and was replaced by John Beverley (a.k.a. Sid Vicious), who was hired for his look and attitude but reportedly couldn't play the bass at all. (He subsequently taught himself by listening to Ramones recordings.) Fueled by anger over an antiquated British social system that was causing massive unemployment at the time, the Sex Pistols spoke to a generation of similarly disenfranchised young people by spitting in the face of the establishment. The conservative British public was outraged by the single "God Save the Queen," whose lyrics claimed Queen Elizabeth II was "no human being," to the point where factory workers refused to participate in manufacturing the actual records. Other scandals included a TV interview where a drunken Rotten and Jones spouted profanities to show host Bill Grundy, and numerous incidents of violence at their concerts, involving scuffles with other bands, destruction of sound equipment, and injury to audience members. The group's one studio album, *Never Mind the Bollocks, Here's the Sex Pistols*, was released in 1977 by Virgin Records. Following a truncated and trouble-plagued US tour in early 1978, Rotten left the band and it split up, though the other three members worked on recording numbers for *The Great Rock 'n' Roll Swindle*, a mockumentary film about the band spearheaded by McLaren and director Julien Temple. Vicious went on to a brief solo career as a singer but was quickly derailed by the violently codependent relationship he developed with his American girlfriend/manager, Nancy Spungen. A former groupie and sometime prostitute, Spungen was a diagnosed schizophrenic, and both she and Vicious became addicted to heroin. Vicious was widely believed to have stabbed Spungen to death in the Hotel Chelsea in New York in 1978, though he was never tried for the crime due to his own death from a heroin overdose four months later; some theorize that one of Spungen's drug dealers was actually responsible. The other members of the band went their separate ways, but in 1996 the original four (including Matlock, who had preceded Vicious as bass player) reunited for a revival tour—which they called the "Filthy Lucre Tour"—and they continued to perform together on and off into the new millennium. Debate on their legacy has often focused on whether the musicians themselves had any artistic vision or valid point of view or if the band was actually created and manipulated by McLaren to satisfy his own commercial agenda, as suggested by his film.

Sondheim, Stephen (b. 1930)

American composer/lyricist, widely considered to be the greatest musical theatre writer of the second half of the twentieth century. Sondheim was mentored by the great Oscar Hammerstein II and studied composition seriously with Milton Babbitt; before establishing himself as a composer, he provided lyrics for two of the most iconic American musicals: *West Side Story* (1957; music by Leonard Bernstein) and *Gypsy* (1959; music by Jule Styne). He followed these up with the first Broadway show for which he wrote both music and lyrics—*A Funny Thing Happened on the Way to the Forum*, a hit in 1962. After that, he returned just once to writing only lyrics: a collaboration after Hammerstein's death with his late mentor's legendary partner, Richard Rodgers, on *Do I Hear a Waltz?* (1965). Sondheim's second effort as a composer/lyricist, *Anyone Can Whistle*, ran only nine performances on Broadway in 1964, but it has since developed a cult following. He followed this up with three back-to-back collaborations with director Harold Prince in the early seventies, all masterworks of the musical theater canon: *Company, Follies*, and *A Little Night Music*. With the last-named show's librettist, Hugh Wheeler, he later wrote one of his masterpieces, *Sweeney Todd: The Demon Barber of Fleet Street* (1979). His other musicals include *Pacific Overtures, Merrily We Roll Along*, and three later-career collaborations with librettist/director James Lapine: *Sunday in the Park with George, Into the Woods*, and *Passion*. Though his most recent musical had a troubled journey (it had developmental productions at several regional theaters, and several title changes, before landing at the Public Theater in New York as *Road Show* in 2008, and has never been seen on Broadway), Sondheim's work has been introduced to a wide new twenty-first century audience through the successful film versions of *Sweeney Todd* and *Into the Woods*. As Hammerstein had mentored him, Sondheim in turn became an inspiration and source of encouragement and support to the young Jonathan Larson. He stated that he thought Larson was one of very few composers who had a gift for fusing rock music with the needs of musical theater. In addition to dropping Sondheim's name in "La Vie Bohème" in *Rent*, Larson paid tribute to the older writer by gently parodying his style in "Sunday," a song in *tick, tick . . . BOOM!* that pays obvious homage to *Sunday in the Park with George*. Though much imitated and emulated, the wit and complexity of Sondheim's lyrics, combined with the challenging subject matter he has chosen to adapt and the richness of his music, put him in a class by himself; few musical theater writers have approached the genre with anywhere near the subtlety and depth he has brought to it. Meryle Secrest's biography *Stephen Sondheim: A Life* was published by Knopf in 1998.

Sontag, Susan (1933–2004)

American writer/activist who was an influential social and cultural critic during the second half of the twentieth century. Her widely varied interests included human rights, the AIDS crisis, photography, and the influence of media on culture. Sontag studied literature, history, and philosophy at the University of Chicago and Harvard, and she subsequently taught at a variety of American colleges and universities, including Columbia. She began her writing career as a novelist (*The Benefactor, Death Kit*) and returned to fiction writing late in her career with *The Volcano Lover* and *In America*; she also directed plays and films and wrote the play *Alice in Bed* as well as an adaptation of Henrik Ibsen's *The Lady from the Sea*. Her nonfiction and critical writings included *Against Interpretation, On Photography*, and *Illness as Metaphor*. Though she was widely respected as a pioneering feminist and liberal theorist, her audaciously expressed views were sometimes so far to the left that she alienated herself from other feminists and from the liberal community itself. Her famous comment that the white race had historically been a "cancer" on the world occasioned much controversy; she herself eventually retracted it, but only because she had come to the realization that the use of cancer as a metaphor was a disservice to people actually suffering from the disease! Her personal life was also subject to much conjecture and analysis: after a youthful marriage to the writer/sociologist Philip Rieff, she had romantic relationships with numerous luminaries, both male and female, including painter Jasper

Johns, writer Joseph Brodsky, playwright Maria Irene Fornés, and, for the last several years of her life, the prominent photographer Annie Leibovitz. Sontag's openness (unusual at the time) about her unconventional sexuality, along with her bold questioning of the status quo both in art and politics, would make her a natural for the bohemians' list of heroes. More specifically, Larson stated that he was influenced by her book *AIDS and its Metaphors* in formulating his own approach to portraying the disease onstage in *Rent*.

Stein, Gertrude (1874–1946)

American writer and art collector whose Paris salon became a legendary gathering place for some of the brightest artists and writers of her time. Stein was born into an upper-middle-class family in Pennsylvania. She grew up mainly in Oakland, California—a locale that, when she revisited it many years later, inspired one of her most famous lines: "There is no there there." The phrase has found its way into popular contemporary lingo, though commentators have never been able to agree on exactly what she meant by it at the time. Showing an early interest in biology and psychology (as a student of the famous William James), Stein graduated from Radcliffe College and then entered medical school at Johns Hopkins University, but she was unhappy there and never became a doctor. In an age when women tended to be corseted, painted, and coiffed to please men, Stein, a large woman, eschewed makeup, cut her hair mannishly short, was sometimes seen wearing sandals, and favored long, robelike garments; her idiosyncratic appearance and vivid personality inspired painters, including Félix Vallotton and Pablo Picasso, to do portraits of her. In 1903, she moved to Paris with her older brother Leo, an aspiring painter; they set up house together at 27 rue de Fleurus, where they made many important connections in the art world and quickly amassed an extraordinary collection of paintings focused on post-impressionist and modernist artists. Their uncanny ability to identify genius artists early in their careers led not only to prescient art purchases but to the gathering of a group of friends who initially visited their home to see the art and ended up staying to talk about politics, literature, and the social and cultural phenomena of the day. Gertrude was soon hosting weekly Saturday evening salons attended by such luminaries as Picasso, Guillaume Apollinaire, Henri Matisse, F. Scott Fitzgerald, Ernest Hemingway, and Thornton Wilder. She is often credited with coining the term "Lost Generation" to refer to her creative contemporaries; together they were instrumental in defining the modernist movement. While Gertrude talked art and politics with these mostly male artistic and literary lights, her life partner, Alice B. Toklas, often entertained their wives and girlfriends in another room. Gertrude and

Alice became early icons of the lesbian community for their successful long-term relationship; Stein's book *The Autobiography of Alice B. Toklas*, actually a memoir of her own experiences, became a bestseller and sealed her fame as an author. She also produced numerous poems, stories, speeches, novels, plays, and opera libretti, developing an idiosyncratic style characterized by humor, repetition, and a playful, musical use of words and language. Though critics have always been divided on the true importance and quality of her literary achievement, Stein is considered an important figure in cultural and social history. Even there, though, she has been controversial, especially in her much argued-about activities during and after World War II. Though Jewish, she managed to continue to live in France during the Occupation, and many felt this was because she made use of her close relationship with Bernard Faÿ, an important official in the Vichy government—a regime she openly admired even after the war had ended. One view of her fascinating contradictions was summed up vividly by historian Blanche Wiesen Cook, who wrote: "She was not a radical feminist. She was Jewish and anti-Semitic, lesbian and contemptuous of women, ignorant about economics and hostile to socialism." As an open lesbian who flouted society's restrictive rules and nurtured a community of artists bent on redefining art and its place in society, her appeal to the *Rent* crowd is obvious.

Thelma and Louise

A popular American movie, released in 1991, directed by Ridley Scott and written by Callie Khouri, who won an Academy Award for her screenplay. A feminist twist on the classic genre of the road movie or buddy picture, the film follows Thelma (played by Geena Davis) and Louise (Susan Sarandon), two friends feeling oppressed by dreary lives, as they head off on what is intended to be a simple two-day road trip. When a man they meet in a bar tries to rape Thelma, Louise shoots him, and the women's simple vacation becomes a flight from the law across the western United States. One mishap and violent misadventure follows another until the two friends are cornered by the FBI just yards from the Grand Canyon. Rather than turn themselves in, they embrace and hit the gas, driving Louise's 1966 Ford Thunderbird convertible over the canyon wall. That powerful final image, a unique amalgam of despair and exhilaration, helped make *Thelma and Louise* a huge critical and popular success, and the film is now considered a classic, though some commentators continue to debate its sexual politics. The iconic final scene has been much parodied and imitated, and it is to that moment that Angel is alluding in his big number, "Today 4 U," when he compares a dog's suicide to Thelma and Louise's desperate act. The flippant comment may not be one of *Rent*'s more illuminating or clever conceits, but it's reasonably in keeping with Angel's irreverent, spontaneous sense of humor.

Village Voice, The

A weekly newspaper that has been published in New York City for over sixty years. It was originally produced out of a two-bedroom apartment in Greenwich Village, where it was founded in 1955 by four men: Ed Fancher, Norman Mailer, John Wilcock, and Dan Wolf. The paper was initially distributed only in that neighborhood, but by the sixties it was covering more of the city and it was eventually available nationwide. Though the *Voice* originally charged a cover price, it was distributed for free in New York City beginning in 1996 (readers in other cities still paid), and it was the model for a type of tabloid that has come to be called the "alternative weekly," with numerous successful imitators in major cities all over the nation. Considering its reputation as a liberal-leaning publication founded during the heyday of the Beat Generation, and the fact that its first real office was located in Sheridan Square (a center of gay life in the West Village), it may come as a surprise that the paper did not start out as particularly supportive of the gay community; early articles went so far as to use the words "faggot" and "dyke" in reporting on the Stonewall riots. But in later decades the editors made up for this early failing and became high-profile supporters of the gay rights movement, producing an annual Pride issue and, in 1982, becoming only the second organization nationwide to extend domestic partner benefits to employees. The *Voice* published pieces by numerous important and celebrated writers, often early in their careers: to name just a few, these have included James Baldwin, e. e. cummings, Allen Ginsberg, Nat Hentoff, Lorraine Hansberry, Henry Miller, Katherine Anne Porter, and Tom Stoppard. Cartoonists whose work has been featured include Jules Feiffer (also known as a playwright), Lynda Barry, Matt Groening, and M. Wartella. The paper's edgy reputation rested partly on the inclusion of sex advice columns and a well-known section of ads for various "adult services" in the back pages. Since 2005, *The Village Voice* has experienced several controversial changes in ownership and editorial staff, but in 1996 it was enjoying its peak years as a touchstone of the New York underground artistic and cultural scene, particularly the jazz and hard rock music communities, and as such was justly celebrated by the young bohemians of *Rent*. In addition to groundbreaking investigative political reporting, the *Voice* has always been a leader in promoting and reviewing alternative and underground artists in music, film, literature, and drama; its editors founded the annual Obie Awards, which have honored excellence in Off-Broadway theater since 1956; in 1964 the field was widened to include

Off-Off-Broadway as well. Since 2014 the Obies have been jointly administered by the Voice and the American Theatre Wing, which also co-produces the Tony Awards. Given a shout-out in the "La Vie Bohème" number in *Rent*, the *Voice* returned the favor by honoring Jonathan Larson, Michael Greif, and the show's cast with a Special Citation at the Obie Awards in 1996. In August of 2017, the paper's owner, Peter D. Barbey, announced that *The Village Voice* would be ceasing print publication and would soon be available only online, marking the end of an era

Wicked Witch of the West, The

Another character from the children's classic *The Wonderful Wizard of Oz* (see listing for "Dorothy, Toto, and Auntie Em" above). The evil, dog-stealing sorceress is the villainess of the story. When Mark's mother phones him in the second act of *Rent*, she jokingly identifies herself as the Wicked Witch of the West—her implication being that that is how he must perceive her, since he hardly ever returns her calls. There's another *Rent* connection that Larson could not have foreseen: the numerous works inspired by the original Baum book include Gregory Maguire's novel *Wicked*, which retells the story from the Witch's point of view. That book was the basis for the hugely successful Broadway musical of the same name by Stephen Schwartz and Winnie Holzman, which opened in 2003 and is still running as of this writing. The character of the Witch is named Elphaba, after the initials of the original book's author, L. Frank Baum. In *Wicked* on Broadway, the role was created by Idina Menzel, *Rent*'s original Maureen, who won a Tony Award for her performance. Other prominent *Rent* alumni who have appeared in *Wicked* include Taye Diggs, Toby Parker, Norbert Leo Butz, and Kendra Kassebaum. The powerful singing actress Eden Espinosa was one of Menzel's successors in both musicals; she closed the Broadway run of *Rent* as Maureen, and her performance is preserved on the DVD *Rent: Filmed Live on Broadway*.

17

"Don't Look Back or You May Drown"

The Return of *Rent* to Off-Broadway

T hough successful new musicals had been moving from Off-Broadway to Broadway as far back as *Hair* and *A Chorus Line*, and much more frequently since the huge success of *Rent*, the reverse of that trajectory—meaning a show closing after a long Broadway run and then reopening Off-Broadway—was almost unheard of until quite recently. But in 2009, the year after *Rent* closed at the Nederlander, the musical *Avenue Q* (another show produced by Jeffrey Seller and Kevin McCollum) also ended a long Broadway run and, within a month, reopened in a much smaller, Off-Broadway theater in the New World Stages complex on 50th Street; the transfer proved very successful, and the show continues to run there as of this writing. In 2010, the hit Broadway comedy *The 39 Steps* closed in January and reopened in March, also at New World Stages (where there are five theaters), where it continued to draw audiences. So in 2011, it seemed like *Rent*, with its army of devoted fans and a new generation of theatergoers who had not yet discovered it, would be a reasonable candidate for similar treatment.

Because it had been almost three years since the show had closed on Broadway, a direct transfer of that production wouldn't have been possible. And when original producers Seller, McCollum, and Allan S. Gordon approached director Michael Greif about putting together an Off-Broadway company of the musical (also to play New World Stages, in a 499-seat house), he surprised them by saying he would like to start afresh and create an all-new production, with new staging and completely reconceptualized design elements. The producers agreed.

The New Look

Greif has said that, since the move from NYTW to the Nederlander had been undertaken so quickly in 1996, there had been very little time to rethink the staging for the new space—or the new audience. Other than some necessary adjusting of blocking for the different sight lines, the Off-Broadway production was moved basically intact. So the new 2011 incarnation was offering the director the chance to, as he put it, address some things he thought he probably should have addressed fifteen years earlier, as well as approach the piece with a fresh eye and the experience of another decade and a half as a director.

Larry Keigwin provided new choreography, and Will Van Dyke was the musical director. Original costume designer Angela Wendt returned, but with the understanding that she would be redesigning the show, and Mark Wendland and Kevin Adams were hired as the new set and lighting designers, respectively. Brian Ronan designed the sound.

Like the original set, Wendland's new one included scaffolding and levels, but there was more extensive structure, and a few pieces of realistic furniture to evoke specific locations. The set suggested a streetscape, with a cleverly designed collection of "puzzle pieces" that could be rotated to evoke different locations. There were moving stairs, and the actors were able to use the metal scaffolds like a jungle gym, often climbing or pulling themselves up onto higher levels, allowing for staging that made dynamic use of vertical space. And where the original production had used film, projected on the walls, to represent Mark's documentary in the last scene, the new one added onstage video monitors that were used more extensively throughout the evening. During "What You Own," they showed documentary footage of late twentieth-century events, including political campaigns, ACT UP demonstrations, and the Tompkins Square Park riot.

Wendt talked to interviewer Yale Breslin of Ny.racked.com about her work on the revival: "I've tried to look at the show with a new perspective as if I've never designed it before. It was definitely a challenge. It was helpful to design it for a small theatre; going back to the roots of *Rent* in a way. This time around, the designs are more detailed; more accessories and pattern and more gritty and distressed." A few familiar pieces from the original design reappeared.

When asked whose look had changed the most, she replied: "I'd have to say Angel. His character is now more boyish and edgy and represents more of a club kid." Rather than the famous Santa Claus drag of the original, the new Angel (MJ Rodriguez) was dressed as a Christmas present, complete with an oversized fabric bow. Along with a short platinum-blonde wig, he wore a close-fitting, tailored jacket with an old-fashioned, romantic cut; it had a detachable piece that could be worn either as tails or as a cape.

Another of Wendt's innovations was the costume that Maureen (played by future Tony-winner Annaleigh Ashford) wore for "Over the Moon." The original Maureens had all worn simple street clothes, but, in keeping with the nursery-rhyme imagery in the number, Ashford was given a perky mini-dress that suggested a milkmaid or a farm girl costume, worn over bright blue leggings. And in "Out Tonight," Mimi (Arianda Fernandez) wore a glittering blue tube top that, with a quick downward tug, she converted to a skirt when she sang "Wanna put on a tight skirt and flirt with a stranger."

"Over the Moon": Annaleigh Ashford as Maureen in the Off-Broadway revival, New World Stages, 2011.   *Joan Marcus*

Some of Greif's new staging was intended to clarify plot points audiences had sometimes been confused about in the original. For example, because Roger, who we know has HIV, never shows any symptoms of illness, people have wondered whether or not he has full-blown AIDS. During the musical-beds staging of "Without You" in the Broadway version, he briefly sat on the "hospital bed" (represented by one of the metal tables with a sheet on it) that had previously been occupied by Angel—but audiences didn't always catch the intended significance. In the new staging, Greif had two of the ensemble actors, playing nurses, lead Roger to the bed, making it very clear that he too was suffering from the disease.

A New Cast

Telsey + Company, the original casting directors, were charged with discovering a fresh ensemble of talented young performers to breathe new life into the now-iconic characters. Open calls were held in New York and Los Angeles. For those who couldn't attend, a new strategy this time around was the *Rent* Online Audition Contest, whereby hopefuls around the country could submit videos of themselves singing one-minute excerpts from the score. (Of course, this also served as a publicity tactic to increase anticipation over the production itself.) The videos were posted on the production's website, and fans could vote for their favorites. The winner was Jessie Hooker, a Pennsylvania resident who sang Joanne's part in "Take Me or Leave Me" and received a whopping 12,945 votes. Her prize was an expense-paid flight to New York for an audition in person with the casting directors.

They sought performers who would bring their own personalities to the characters rather than trying to mimic the original cast. A couple of the actors chosen had prior experience with the show: Marcus Paul James, in the male "Seasons of Love" soloist/Mr. Jefferson track, was the lone returnee from the final Broadway cast, and Arianda Fernandez, cast as Mimi, had done the show on tour.

The new Mark was Adam Chanler-Berat, who had made his Broadway debut under Greif's direction in *Next to Normal*. He bore a distinct resemblance to Jonathan Larson, which seemed appropriate given that Mark, the Jewish boy from Westchester County documenting the lives of his friends, has often been seen as something of an autobiographical sketch. Reinforcing the parallel, Wendt put him in a flannel shirt and wool cap that recalled the way Larson often dressed.

The new Roger was Matt Shingledecker, who had recently been a replacement Tony in Arthur Laurents's Broadway revival of *West Side Story*. The

Matt Shingledecker (Roger) and Arianda Fernandez (Mimi) perform "Light My Candle" in the Off-Broadway revival, New World Stages, 2011.   *Joan Marcus*

producers of *Rent* were initially skeptical that such a clean-cut, classically-trained tenor would be right for the role of the grungy, angst-ridden rocker, but Shingledecker eventually proved convincing. As he told Broadway.com: "I've taken a lot of inspiration from Jeff Buckley. To be true to this piece, you really have to get in touch with some deep places in your soul. It's therapeutic but exhausting."

When Shingledecker departed the cast in early 2012, his replacement came as a surprise to fans. Justin Johnston, who had a long history with the character Angel, both on tour and in the final Broadway cast, returned to the show to take on the very different role of Roger. Johnston played the role for six months and in July was replaced by Anthony Fedorov, who had been a finalist on the fourth season of *American Idol*. Chanler-Berat was succeeded as Mark by the equally talented Josh Grisetti, a lanky, dark-haired actor who also looked a bit like Larson.

A New Era

When asked by Esther Zuckerman of *The Village Voice* what had changed about the show's milieu since 1996, Greif responded: "Actually, the big difference is not really about the East Village, it's about HIV treatments in terms of the psychology of the characters. The real heart of the piece has always been that Jonathan wrote it in honor of some friends he believed were dying, some who had died. The psychologies of the characters are very much a part of that time in New York when an HIV diagnosis really did or could be a death sentence. . . . So the characters' psyches are caught up with learning that their time on the planet might be very limited." Greif spent considerable rehearsal time showing videos and discussing the history of the AIDS crisis with the young cast to ensure that they were grounded in the reality of what those years had been like, and he recommends that directors rehearsing future productions do the same. Helpful films to watch would include *Paris is Burning*, the documentary *How to Survive a Plague*, *Longtime Companion*, and the TV version of *Angels in America*.

The revival opened on August 10 and though it ran for over a year—very respectable for an Off-Broadway show—the transfer didn't stick the way it had for *Avenue Q*. The production cost $1.5 million, and with a cast of fourteen, plus swings and a band of five, its weekly payroll was unusually high for an Off-Broadway-sized house. Box office returns were less than expected, disappointing fans who had hoped the show had found a new permanent New York home. It closed on September 9, 2012, having played 32 previews and 450 performances.

Reviews

Though many critics, as well as fans, were delighted to have *Rent* back onstage in New York, reactions to the new production were mixed. Joe Dziemianowicz of the *New York Daily News* found the score as beautiful as ever but was disappointed that the new cast seemed to lack a breakout star performance, adding: "A couple of actors stand out for dubious reasons. Shingledecker has sturdy pipes but is stuck wearing jeggings-like pants that just look . . . off. Annaleigh Ashford plays performance artist Maureen with such cutesy-poo narcissism she recalls Glinda from 'Wicked.' Did the Good Witch's floating bubble drift off-course and land at 'Rent' by mistake? Greif's revised staging of the anthemic group number 'La Vie Bohème' and the depiction of the doomed Angel's fate don't pack the emotional wallop of the original."

Adam Chanler-Berat as Mark in the Off-Broadway revival, New World Stages, 2011.
Joan Marcus

Scott Brown of Vulture.com also caught the Glinda connection but viewed it in a much more positive light, praising the new Maureen as "a wonder to behold." Brown added: "Ashford, whose comic timing is as tight as her diamond-cut voice, looks like she's vying to be the next Kristin Chenoweth, and there's every indication she'll succeed. She's well-matched with Corbin Reid's smoldering Joanne . . . who matches her flubbery inamorata note for note and step for step. Nicholas Christopher's Collins—a part originated by that ebullient *papi* Jesse Martin—is a quieter, more contemplative sort. . . . His relationship with Rodriguez's more poised, more androgynous, more fashion-plate-y Angel takes on a refreshing new vibe when it's less clear who wears the pants."

According to Steven Suskin of *Variety*: "It's already back, and the news is all to the good. 'Rent' is not so provocative as it was in back 1996, but even so, the tuner is plenty effective in its new Off Broadway guise. . . . The original 1996 cast . . . created their parts so memorably that the new crop can't be expected to compete. Even so, the 2011 group has a distinct advantage over the dozens of cast replacements on Broadway and on tour, benefiting from a full rehearsal period with director Greif and with each other. As a result, they play well together."

Chris Caggiano, reviewing the show on his blog Everythingmusicals.com, commented on the use of video: "The new stage design also includes what have now become obligatory in professional productions in New York and beyond: projections, designed here by Peter Nigrini. . . . Admittedly, some of it works quite well, but somehow digital projections don't seem very '90s. They did, however, provide a really stunning effect during 'What You Own.' Initially, the projections during this song are isolated on a couple of screens, but when the song modulates, the projections suddenly wash the entire set. It was a really nice touch, and added greatly to the power of the song, and the moment."

Ben Brantley devoted much of his review in the *New York Times* to praising the material and recalling how powerfully it had affected him when he first saw the show in 1996. But he was dissatisfied with the revival: "To me this 'Rent' feels neither close enough to nor different enough from the original to warrant revisiting. It is visually busier than its prototype, with jittery new choreography (by Larry Keigwin) and slapdash mood- and place-defining projections (by Peter Nigrini) . . . The cast is passable but seldom more than that . . . Only Annaleigh Ashford as Maureen . . . adds a revitalizing grit to her role. She is more precise and funnier than was Ms. Menzel (whose strengths were of a different stripe) in evoking the particular world of downtown performance that's being satirized here."

"Seasons of Love": Autographed photo of the company of the Off-Broadway revival of *Rent* at New World Stages. Shown here is the 2012 cast including replacements; newcomers included Josh Grisetti, far right, as Mark.

Joan Marcus

Matthew Murray of Talkinbroadway.com wasn't sold on the new cast and felt the production lacked urgency, but he reaffirmed the power of the material itself: "It all works not just because it's all real and all unique, but because Larson was a true theatre artist, the kind of writer who knew—and cared—about what was necessary to properly tell a story: real rhymes; rock-solid characters; sweeping variety; and startlingly specific honesty. . . . *Rent* is at once a lush emotional spectacle in the Golden Age tradition and a pulsating New Idea, one with a core of intelligence and strength that will allow it to thrive in productions at all levels for decades to come."

18

"It'd Be Another Play"

tick, tick . . . BOOM!

The terrible irony of the story of *Rent* was that Jonathan Larson passed away just as he was on the threshold of seeing his work finally achieve the kind of recognition that he had been struggling for and dreaming of for over fifteen years. But though his family and friends took some comfort in the fact that *Rent* was out in the world and people were finally hearing Jonathan's voice, some of them were also very aware that the show was only one part of his vast output of music, and they worried that the other wonderful songs and shows he had worked so hard on might never see the light of day. Victoria Leacock, always one of his most devoted champions, recalls that when she spoke at his memorial service on February 3, 1996, she made an impassioned plea that people had to know about his other work.

As a very close friend, Victoria felt a strong connection with Jonathan even in death, saying: "[By 1999] I honestly believed, whether it's true or not, that Jonathan's spirit was very much in touch with me. Jonathan's spirit was almost harassing me to get his other work out there!" She had been helping with benefits at the Second Stage, one of the theaters where his one-man musical *Boho Days* had been workshopped, and she contacted Robyn Goodman, that theater's cofounder, about maybe doing a show built around songs Larson had written for various unproduced projects. They put together a piece with the title *½ MT House* (pronounced "Half Empty House") and did a reading of it; participants included Pippin Parker, Jason Gould (son of Elliott Gould and Barbra Streisand), Mary Testa, and Amy Spanger; David Armstrong, who had worked with Larson in college, directed. But the reading didn't lead to anything.

In mid-2000, Leacock and Goodman got together for lunch. Goodman, too, had been a champion of Larson's work; she was no longer at the Second Stage but had just opened her own production office and was looking for properties to produce, so Leacock reminded her of the Larson project.

Goodman was interested, but instead of doing a composite piece she suggested going back to *tick, tick . . . BOOM!* (the final title of the musical that had started life as *30/90* and then changed to *Boho Days*; see Chapter 1.) The show dealt in a very personal way with Jonathan's thoughts about turning thirty before having found success in his chosen field; his frustration over his thwarted attempts to get his large-scale musical *Superbia* produced; a turning point in his relationship with his dancer girlfriend; and his reaction on learning that his best friend Michael (based on Matt O'Grady) had HIV.

Enthused about the possibilities, Leacock approached the Larson family to ask for their permission. At first they were reluctant. They had seen Jonathan perform the show himself, and it was about his life; they found it painful to think about anybody else doing it. But, like Victoria, Al Larson had also been thinking about how important it was for Jonathan's neglected works to be heard, and eventually they came around.

Because Larson had worked on the show for so long, there were five different drafts of the script available to work from. In addition to the 1990 workshop at the Second Stage, he had performed it as part of a monologue series at New York Theatre Workshop and twice at the Village Gate. In those versions, Larson had performed all the dialogue and songs, accompanying himself at the piano, with an onstage rock band and sometimes one backup vocalist.

Choosing Collaborators

Goodman and Leacock, now co-producers, considered various directors, including Diane Paulus, before settling on Scott Schwartz, an up-and-coming director and the son of the Broadway and film composer Stephen Schwartz. Working with music supervisor Stephen Oremus, who was tasked with arranging and orchestrating the score, Schwartz came up with the idea of expanding the piece into a musical for three actors. One would play "Jon," the character based on Jonathan, and the other two would play his girlfriend Susan and his best friend Michael. The actors playing Susan and Michael would also take on all the other cameo roles as needed.

They decided to hire a playwright to handle the script adaptation, and the only person Goodman and Leacock considered was David Auburn, a young writer who had very recently emerged from obscurity to become the toast of the town. His play *Proof* had opened at the Manhattan Theatre Club to ecstatic reviews and then transferred to Broadway; like *Rent*, it won a Pulitzer Prize. But success was new to Auburn; Leacock remembers telling him, "You're the perfect person to be doing this project because you understand all those hopes and dreams." For his part, Auburn said, "Victoria was

Jonathan Larson performing the original one-man version of *tick, tick . . . BOOM!* at the Village Gate, 1991.   *Victoria Leacock Hoffman*

a very good guide to what was autobiographical in the material. It was very helpful to have her."

Shaping the Material

Goodman gave Auburn a stack of different drafts of the piece that Larson had written, along with a cassette tape of the songs; he immediately realized that it was a complete score of very high quality. As he told Theatremania. com, as a young writer he related to the story and the way Larson told it: the ambition and frustration and insecurity. He said he was drawn to "the rawness of it," adding: "I liked how kind of brutal he was about his own feelings and how he didn't shirk from portraying himself as being sometimes a little bit arrogant, a little bit irritated. He put all of his warts on display as well as all his incredible gifts, which I thought was a brave thing to do."

Given the well-known circumstances of Larson's death, Auburn was concerned about certain lines in the script that seemed eerily prescient.

There were scenes where Jonathan had written about how hard his heart was pounding, or how he felt like it was going to burst if he didn't get his show on; Auburn actually ended up cutting some of those lines because they were so on-the-nose that he was afraid audiences would think he had written them himself to exploit Larson's death. In the end, he estimated that about 80 percent of the words in the final version of the book are Larson's.

One of Auburn's key contributions was to heighten the dramatic stakes by restructuring the time frame of the story. In Larson's drafts of the one-person version, the show began with his thirtieth birthday party; he depicted himself looking back at the workshop of *Superbia* and all the attendant angst. As Auburn put it: "I felt that you needed to see . . . him anticipating it and looking forward to it and having hopes invested in it and then share his disappointment when it didn't turn into what he wanted and then watch him come out of that." So the time frame was changed to begin before the workshop and take the audience through that experience, arriving at the birthday party only at the end.

"Come to Your Senses"

Since the show was now going to include the workshop of *Superbia* as a major scene and turning point in the plot, Auburn came up with the idea of inserting one song from that show into the score, allowing the audience to see a bit of the earlier musical as a play-within-the-play. The original plan was to use the song "LCD Readout," one of *Superbia*'s key numbers and a song that Stephen Sondheim had said he considered to be one of Larson's best. It made sense because the song was also quoted in "Why," the penultimate song in *tick, tick . . . BOOM!* But Leacock wasn't thrilled about the idea of using that particular song because it was such an integral part of *Superbia* and she was still hopeful that that show, in its entirety, would also one day be resurrected. Trying to figure out a solution, she found herself standing in front of a wall display where cassette tapes of many of Larson's songs were stored, and the tape of "Come to Your Senses" literally jumped out of its compartment at her. Once again, she felt a message from Jonathan. That song was a beauty—but he had cut it from the later drafts of *Superbia*, so there was no reason for it not to have a life separate from the show.

There is now a scene in *tick, tick . . . BOOM!* where Jon welcomes his friends to the workshop and then sits down to watch the presentation, in which the character Karessa—*Superbia*'s leading lady—sings "Come to Your Senses." The discovery of the song not only solved a dramaturgical problem, it provided something the creative team had been lacking: a strong showpiece number for the actress in the cast. It works beautifully in performance, because not only is it genuinely from *Superbia*, it also relates thematically to the problems in Jon and Susan's own relationship, and thus provides a link between Karessa and Susan (played by the same actress) who, by the song's end, seem almost to have become one. The song "Why," sung later in the show, was adapted to include a brief sample of that song rather than "LCD Readout."

"Why" is another song for which we have Victoria Leacock to thank. When Larson was first writing the show, and venting about all the frustrations of pursuing a career as a songwriter, she had told him she thought he needed to add a song to express *why* he was still doing it. He replied with the moving song that is perhaps his simplest and clearest expression of his love for his work.

Casting

Finding an actor to play Jon was a major challenge, and the producers engaged David Caparelliotis, the casting director from the Manhattan Theatre Club, to handle the search. They saw many people but no one seemed quite right; the fact that Goodman and Leacock had known the real Larson set their expectations very high. A couple of the actors who had been in *Rent* were recommended, but Leacock didn't want to do that; she said: "I didn't want the show to be compared to *Rent*; I wanted it to be a unique theatre experience and not a mini-*Rent*. I really feel *tick, tick . . . BOOM!* is its own beautiful show."

Caparelliotis was excited about an actor who had recently relocated to New York from Chicago: Raúl Esparza. Though Esparza had mainly done serious acting roles in straight plays, he was at that time demonstrating his powerful rock tenor as Riff Raff in the Broadway revival of *The Rocky Horror Show*. He came in to audition and sang "Walking in Memphis." According to Leacock: "He had this light shining in him. He was relaxed, and the song had so much hope." They offered him the role immediately—and he turned it down. He didn't want to leave the security of a Broadway show for the uncertainty of an Off-Broadway contract. But Leacock felt so strongly that she called him up and, thankfully, was able to talk him into it. As she recently said, "Basically, he had to make the leap of faith that Jonathan made."

Amy Spanger, who had toured as Maureen in *Rent* and had been in the reading of *½ MT House*, was cast as Susan, and Jerry Dixon as Michael. Choreographer Christopher Gattelli was brought on board to do musical staging. With Dede Harris, Lorie Cowen Levy, and Beth Smith as co-producers, the show was booked into the Jane Street Theatre, a venue on the far west side of the West Village that had a club-like atmosphere; it had also been the original home of *Hedwig and the Angry Inch*.

Reception and Revivals

Despite the phenomenal popularity of *Rent*, then in its sixth season on Broadway, Leacock and Goodman found that raising money and attracting audiences for *tick, tick . . . BOOM!* was somewhat harder than they had expected. But even if the critics couldn't help comparing it to *Rent*, the show was well received.

Charles Isherwood reviewed it for *Variety*: "The show's navel-gazing subject is a sign that, at the time it was written, Larson hadn't quite achieved the perspective of a fully mature artist—the show's central themes are the same ones given more theatrically satisfying life in 'Rent.' But its execution equally illustrates how rich were the gifts just about to reach fruition. As in 'Rent,' the songs are melodic and instantly appealing, blending pop-rock orchestrations with classic musical theatre structures; you can hear the strong influence of Stephen Sondheim . . . but the music also evokes Billy Joel with an angry edge."

Ben Brantley of the *New York Times*, who had always been a passionate devotee of *Rent*, found *tick, tick . . . BOOM!* "sweet, simple and hopeful . . . an

The original cast of the Off-Broadway production of *tick, tick . . . BOOM!* is shown here taking their curtain call on opening night at the Jane Street Theatre, 2001. Left to right: Jerry Dixon (Michael), Raúl Esparza (Jon), and Amy Spanger (Susan).   *Victoria Leacock Hoffman*

amiable public exercise in the sort of soul-searching sure to befall anyone approaching a milestone birthday haunted by specters of unfulfilled ambitions." He added: "Compared with 'Rent,' 'Tick' inevitably feels small and conventional, suggesting that Larson benefited greatly from stretching his imagination beyond his immediate self . . . But perceived as a sort of sketchbook for 'Rent,' in which the same themes are developed with richer idiosyncrasy and breadth, 'Tick' has its gentle fascination. And it allows its sure-voiced young singers and a four-member band to remind us of what an infectiously tuneful composer Larson could be."

tick, tick . . . BOOM! has now been done successfully all over the country and even internationally. When the show was revived in concert form for one weekend in 2014 as part of the New York City Center's Encores! Off-Center series, the role of Jon was played by none other than Lin-Manuel Miranda, who has said his experience seeing *Rent* on Broadway at age seventeen was what inspired him to start writing his own musicals. When Isherwood reviewed this production for the *New York Times*, he said: "In the lovably scrappy, terrifically moving revival of the show . . . the struggling composer, Jon, is portrayed by Lin-Manuel Miranda, whose funny, anguished and heartbreaking performance throbs with a sense of bone-deep identification. Not too many years ago, Mr. Miranda was himself a struggling young musical-theater composer living hand-to-mouth in New York, teaching high school English while scribbling songs on the side. He, of course, would find

George Salazar as Michael, Nick Blaemire as Jon, and Lilli Cooper, who replaced Ciara Renée as Susan, in Keen Company's 2016 revival of *tick, tick . . . BOOM!*
Ben Jay/courtesy of Keen Company

success when his musical 'In the Heights' transferred to Broadway and won the Tony Award for best musical—before he turned the appalling age causing such agony for Jon."

Two years later, the show got a full-scale New York revival produced by Keen Company, a respected Off-Broadway group led by artistic director Jonathan Silverstein. This time again, the role of Jon was played by an actor who is also a writer of musicals: Nick Blaemire, whose own show *Glory Days* had opened on Broadway when he was just out of the University of Michigan. His physical resemblance to Larson was noted, and in his program bio he said he was "honored to be playing one of his heroes." Ciara Renée played Susan, and George Salazar was Michael. Silverstein directed, with musical direction by Joey Chancey and choreography by Christine O'Grady.

Reviewing the revival for the *New York Times*, Alexis Soloski said she would have appreciated more development of the character relationships, but added:

> Those relationships are more fully realized in "Rent," of course, and just as it's impossible to avoid reading "Tick, Tick . . . Boom!" autobiographically, it's also impossible not to read it retrospectively . . . Jonathan's agent summarizes the discouraging reaction to the "Superbia" workshop. "I think everyone was just so intrigued by your talent, and they can't wait to see what happens next," she says. What happened was "Rent," a musical whose blend of rock and romance and realism has proved so influential that a predecessor like "Tick, Tick . . . Boom!" now feels a little passé. That's a paradox Larson should have lived to enjoy.

As a realistic expression of the fears and challenges that go with trying to make a life in the arts, and Larson's most personal statement of why he loved what he did, *tick, tick . . . BOOM!* is, at least for those of us who work in the theater, at least as moving a show as *Rent*, and the score is a gem. Leacock, Goodman, Auburn, Oremus, and Schwartz did a great service by giving it a new life, and they felt Larson guiding them. As Leacock has said: "Jonathan's mighty spirit can be very proactive. As much as we try to do for him, he still does for us."

19

"I Escape and Ape Content"

Spoofs and Imitations

L ike any property that achieves enormous worldwide success and becomes a pop culture phenomenon, *Rent* has come in for its share of teasing, including spoofs, parodies, and knockoffs. Attempting to remember the old saw that "Imitation is the highest form of flattery," we survey three high-profile examples here:

Forbidden Broadway Strikes Back (1996–1997)

Writer/director Gerard Alessandrini has long been known for his witty and affectionate, if sometimes biting, musical revues satirizing the Broadway scene. The first installment opened in 1982, and there have since been more than a dozen revised versions, updated to feature spoofs of the latest hit musicals. *Forbidden Broadway Strikes Back* was the 1996 edition; it opened at the Triad, a cabaret theater on the Upper West Side of Manhattan, and later moved to Ellen's Stardust Diner in the Theater District. It included numbers poking fun at that year's crop of Broadway shows, including *Victor/Victoria*, *Big*, *Beauty and the Beast*, *Sunset Boulevard*, and the revivals of *Show Boat*, *Chicago*, and *A Funny Thing Happened on the Way to the Forum*.

Since *Rent* was by far the biggest phenomenon to hit Broadway that season, there was a five-song medley lampooning that show, which was rechristened "Rant." Targets included the frenetic hype surrounding the musical and the impossibility of obtaining a ticket. Actress Donna English as Daphne Rubin-Vega performed a new version of "Out Tonight"—squirming in the famous form-fitting vinyl pants and squealing the adapted lyric: "Ouch! They're Tight." Bryan Batt played both Roger and Angel; the latter's "Today 4 U" was refashioned as "Too Gay for You—Too Het'ro for Me," and, in a couple of numbers, David Hibbard (replaced by Tom Plotkin when he got a real Broadway gig) impersonated Anthony Rapp as Mark. Rubin-Vega herself

Another Unoriginal Cast Recording

JOHN FREEDSON, HARRIET YELLIN
and JON B. PLATT present

Created, Written and Directed by

**GERARD
ALESSANDRINI**

Starring
BRYAN BATT
DONNA ENGLISH
CHRISTINE PEDI
TOM PLOTKIN
MATTHEW WARD

FORBIDDEN BROADWAY STRIKES BACK!

VOLUME 4

Liner notes cover design for the cassette release of *Forbidden Broadway Strikes Back!*

recently recalled seeing the show and laughing when, at Mimi's death, Batt wailed out "Daaaphneeee!" A cast album was recorded and released by DRG Records. At the 1997 Drama Desk Awards, the show was nominated for Outstanding Revue and Alessandrini won for Outstanding Lyrics. The evening's finale was a rewrite of "Something Wonderful" from *The King and I* (also revived that year); some people took it to mean that, after a worrisome dry spell, there was indeed a wonderful new musical on Broadway.

Team America: World Police (2004)

A movie produced by Scott Rudin in association with writer/director Trey Parker and writers Matt Stone and Pam Brady—a trio best known for their outrageous TV cartoon series *South Park*—*Team America: World Police* is a spoof of big-budget action movies. The twist is that it is all done not with live actors but with supermarionettes, a type of highly expressive puppet originally developed for the British TV series *Thunderbirds. Team America* is meant to satirize both overzealous American international "peacekeeping" forces, which sometimes do more harm than good, and the sanctimonious Hollywood celebrities who criticize them. Early in the film, the fictitious governmental paramilitary group of the title recruits a new member: Broadway actor Gary Johnston (voice by Parker), who is initially seen performing in a show called *Lease: The Musical*. On a towering set of metal scaffolding, we see a cast of puppets (mostly wearing costumes that recognizably represent specific *Rent* characters) singing a song called "Everyone Has AIDS." Wearing the iconic black-and-white "Mark scarf," the boyish, floppy-haired Gary gives an impassioned speech about the tragedy of the epidemic and the need for activism; a Broadway audience (also made up of marionettes) is seen weeping and applauding. Another musical theater reference later in the movie has a character recalling how as a teenager he was sexually abused by the cast of *Cats*.

The film is designed to offend the left, the right, and everyone in between. Most of the puppets representing present-day Hollywood stars are seen meeting violent deaths, and the film narrowly escaped an NC-17 rating; a few cuts and edits eventually got it an R. It also got good reviews, and many find it to be a laugh riot. Parker and Stone had always had a predilection for musical theater, and several years later they created their own contribution to the genre, *The Book of Mormon*, a show that became one of the biggest Broadway hits since . . . well, *Rent*.

Smash (2013)

During its two-season run, musical theater buffs followed the soapy NBC primetime TV series *Smash* with great interest, as it depicted (with songs!) the backstage turmoil and rocky rehearsal processes of two new musicals headed for Broadway. The series was the creation of playwright Theresa Rebeck, and many of the producers, writers, and directors who worked on it came from the New York theater community, giving the show a definite whiff of insider savvy.

Though the first season dealt exclusively with the trials and tribulations of *Bombshell*, a musical bio of Marilyn Monroe, in the second season there appeared an upstart, rival musical: *Hit List*, written by two very green up-and-comers whom leading lady Karen Cartwright (played by Katharine McPhee) discovers working in a Theater District bar. Neither the songwriter, Jimmy Collins (played by Broadway heartthrob Jeremy Jordan), nor the book writer, Kyle Bishop (Andy Mientus), seems particularly like a personality portrait of Jonathan Larson, but right away other characters start predicting that *Hit List* could be the next *Rent*. After a trouble-plagued tryout run at the "Winter Fringe Festival," the show is picked up and developed by a hip Off-Broadway institution called Manhattan Theatre Workshop—and in case the name wasn't enough of a clue that this was an allusion to New York Theatre Workshop, exterior and lobby scenes were actually filmed there. Jesse L. Martin (*Rent*'s original Collins) played the artistic director, called Scott Nichols (after James Nicola?), and actor Daniel Abeles was cast as the company's attractive young lighting designer, called Blake (after Blake Burba, the designer of *Rent*?). The gentle, doe-eyed Kyle is secretly in love with the emotionally volatile Jimmy, a former drug addict with a shady past (Jeremy Jordan would make a great Roger), but becomes romantically involved both with Blake and with *Bombshell*'s much more experienced songwriter, Tom Levitt (Christian Borle), while Jimmy gets entangled in a love triangle with Karen and the womanizing director Derek Wills (Jack Davenport).

Though many of these dramatic complications don't resemble anything in the history of *Rent*, more and more parallels revealed themselves as the season progressed. When the script of *Hit List* doesn't seem to be coming together, Nichols decides to help Kyle by hiring a dramaturg—a term most musical theater fans might never have heard were it not for the well-known controversy surrounding the dramaturg who worked on *Rent*. The edgy *Hit List*, with its rock score, tempestuous love story about a songwriter and two singers, and modern-dance-infused choreography, becomes a cult hit downtown and seems poised to take Broadway by storm. And then, before it officially opens, Kyle is run over by a car late one night and killed. The following evening's presentation of *Hit List* for a grief-stricken audience, which begins as a concert reading but spontaneously transforms into a full-out performance, is an all-too-obvious effort to recreate the now-legendary events of January 25, 1996, on East 4th Street. And in the final episode of the series, Kyle is posthumously presented with the Tony Award for Best Book of a Musical.

The executive producer and showrunner for that season of *Smash* was Joshua Safran, an NYU-educated playwright who had been involved with one of *Rent*'s original cast members during the musical's early days; he thus had inside information on the show and felt a connection to it. He reported conferring with both Martin and Daphne Rubin-Vega (who also had a recurring role on *Smash*, as a press agent) to make sure they were comfortable with the way he and the writers were adapting true events for the storyline, and he said he would have scrapped it if they had felt it was in any way exploitative.

In an interview with Tvline.com, Andy Mientus was asked if he worried whether the show was exploiting Larson's story, as some viewers had suggested. He replied that not only had he been in a production of *Rent* (as Mark with the Pioneer Theatre Company) but that the musical was his inspiration:

the reason why he had chosen to pursue acting and was also trying to be a writer. As he said: "Jonathan Larson and his story is something that I really don't take lightly. He was such a genius. . . . Hopefully Kyle has mirrored Jonathan Larson's enthusiasm and his light and positivity in a way that will make that parallel something that's a tribute and not exploitative. It's about this kid who loves this art form more than anything, and has worked so hard and struggled so much to get the show to where it is, and then can't be there to see it through. Hopefully that's the story that we're telling."

20

"For Someone Who Longs for a Community of His Own"

The Larson Legacy

I n the wake of Jonathan Larson's untimely death and the tremendous success, both artistic and financial, of *Rent*, Larson's family, friends, colleagues, and admirers recognized the importance of finding appropriate ways to honor his memory. Over the years, they have instituted several distinguished programs, using the resources provided by the show both to perpetuate his creative legacy and to support and nurture the next generation of artists.

The Jonathan Larson Collection

Larson's collected papers, songs, and documents are in an archive at the Library of Congress in Washington, D.C. They were donated by his family, at the request of archivist Mark Eden Horowitz, to become part of an extraordinary collection of rough drafts, recordings, and correspondence from the files of some of the greatest songwriters in musical theater history, including Rodgers and Hammerstein, Lerner and Loewe, Leonard Bernstein, George and Ira Gershwin, and others.

The task of organizing and cataloguing such materials requires a specialist, and Horowitz recommended Amy Asch, who had already done work on the Irving Berlin collection for the archive. Most of Larson's materials were found in boxes and battered filing drawers in his Greenwich Street apartment and on the hard drive of his computer; Al Larson and Jonathan Burkhart set up a music office for the purpose of going through all the documents, listening to music on more than 500 cassettes and digital audio tapes, and registering all the songs with the copyright office. They incorporated as Unky's Music, Ltd., after the nickname that Larson's two young nephews had given their uncle; Asch and her assistants Kari O'Donnell and Adriana Rowe took to calling themselves the Unky Girls.

As Asch later wrote in an article for Playbill.com: "We started making a database of every song title—who the lyricist was (in early years Jon didn't write his own); the approximate date; what project it belonged to; what recordings we had of it; and whether there was any notated music. We collected anything Jonathan said about the work he was trying to do and his descriptions of particular songs. . . . We cranked the music loud and sang along with Jonathan's demos. I hoped that I was putting the clues together correctly." They also interviewed some of Larson's friends and collaborators, and teachers from his college days.

Jonathan Larson at the keyboard with his nephews, Matthew and Dylan McCollum.   *Photo courtesy of the Larson family*

Because of the computer technology available at the time he was writing, in the eighties and nineties, Larson saved his work on floppy disks, which he originally stored in shoeboxes; the archive has 189 of them. The disks were analyzed by Doug Reside, a devoted theater fan who was also the digital curator for performing arts at the New York Public Library. They contained around forty separate drafts of the text of *Rent*, and by analyzing them with advanced equipment and vintage software Reside was able to see the order in which changes were made, down to the level of individual keystrokes. To Jennifer Schuessler of the *New York Times*, Reside said: "Larson was 'a little advanced' technologically . . . despite his ambivalence about the Big Brother-ish aspects of technology . . . Most notably, he was an avid early adopter of the digital composition software Performer, which made it easy to orchestrate—and repeatedly reorchestrate—his music himself. If 'Rent' had been composed 10 years earlier, before such software was available, 'it might have been a radically different show.'"

An invaluable resource, the documents and recordings are now fully catalogued and available at the library in Washington, D.C., where they can be studied by researchers.

The Jonathan Larson Grants

When the box office receipts from *Rent* began building to what seemed like astronomical amounts, more than even the producers had anticipated, Larson's family was faced with serious decisions regarding the royalties earned. They of course considered it Jonathan's money, and since he wasn't there to spend it they asked themselves how he would want it to be used.

Because Jonathan had been a generous spirit who had believed in helping others, because *Rent* is about the plight of creative young people struggling financially as they try to come into their own as artists, and because Jonathan had so often expressed the goal of transforming the American musical theater, it seemed right to establish a foundation to support the work of emerging composers and lyricists writing new musicals.

The grants and fellowships Jonathan himself had won, even when the amounts were small, had provided him with important encouragement and validation; his family decided they wanted to pass that kind of support on to other deserving artists who were beginning their careers. The Jonathan Larson Grants became the perfect way to celebrate Larson's legacy. In addition to librettists, composers, and lyricists, some of the early grants were awarded to other nonprofit organizations and theaters that were commissioning or producing new musicals. Today they are all awarded to the writers.

The program was initially administered by the Jonathan Larson Performing Arts Foundation, Inc., under executive director Nancy Kassak Diekmann. Since 2008, the grants, which come with an award of $10,000, have been administered by the American Theatre Wing, also co-producer of the Tony Awards. As described on the Wing's website: "We celebrate the standards of tomorrow by supporting the songwriters of today. New musical classics push the envelope of convention and infuse musical theatre with contemporary, joyful urban vitality. Our financial support, recognition and residency opportunities allow us to invest in the changing landscape of the American musical, one writer at a time."

Though the grants are specifically for writers out in the professional world and not intended as scholarship money, there are no other restrictions on how the funds may be used. The annual deadline for writers and teams wishing to be considered is September 30; guidelines and an application are available at http://americantheatrewing.org/program/jonathan-larson-grants.

Jonathan Sings Larson

The Library of Congress produced a concert on October 23, 2006, in celebration of the acquisition of the Jonathan Larson Collection and the tenth anniversary of *Rent*. Musical director Tim Weil led a band and cast made up mainly of alumni of the show in a program of Larson's music, along with songs written and performed by Cynthia Hopkins, Joe Iconis, and Steven Lutvak—all past recipients of the Jonathan Larson Grants.

Cover design for the 2007 CD *Jonathan Sings Larson*.

In conjunction with the archive and the concert, the Library of Congress also sponsored the production of a deluxe CD/DVD package entitled *Jonathan Sings Larson*, released in 2007 on the PS Classics label as part of its Songwriter Series. The CD consists of recordings of fifteen of Larson's songs, mostly previously unreleased demo recordings—including numbers written for *Rent, tick, tick . . . BOOM!*, *Superbia*, and other projects—performed by Larson himself. Also included is a recording of "Boho Days," a cut song from the show that became *tick, tick… BOOM!*, as performed at the October concert by a trio of *Rent* alums: Jeremy Kushnier, Michael McElroy, and Anthony Rapp. The DVD, produced by Victoria Leacock Hoffman, is a video of Larson performing four numbers from *tick, tick . . . BOOM!* in a November 1991 performance of the original one-man version at the Village Gate. Remembered as an excellent actor and singer, Larson proves on these recordings to have been a vital and engaging interpreter of his own work, singing with warmth and humor in a pleasing, expressive baritone voice. Listening to the composer himself perform "One Song Glory" and "Why" is a uniquely moving experience.

The Jonathan Larson Fund

After Larson's death, his family learned that the aortic aneurysm that killed him was probably the result of Marfan Syndrome, a genetic disorder that effects the body's connective tissue. Signs of the condition vary from person to person, but can include a tall, lanky build, long arms, flat feet, and loose joints. Chest pains and shortness of breath can be warning signs that the heart is being affected. Because the disorder was obscure and little understood even in the medical community, too many cases, like Jonathan's, went undiagnosed, so another way in which the Larson family determined to honor his memory was through working to educate the public about the condition. In 2000, they established the Jonathan Larson Fund to support the Marfan Foundation's awareness campaign; funds were raised through curtain speeches and collections at performances of *Rent*. With the goal of preventing the loss of more lives, the family produced, with filmmaker Jonathan Burkhart, informational videos on the disease: one aimed at medical professionals and one designed to educate the general public. As Al Larson told the *New York Times* in June of 2001: "If we save just one life by getting this information out there, I will feel that my mission has been fulfilled. . . . The key thing is, if somebody else had done this 7 to 10 years ago, Jonathan would be alive." Information and resources can be found on the Marfan Foundation's website, https://www.marfan.org.

21

"Anywhere You Could Possibly Go After New York"

Rent in a Town Near You

Though foreign companies of *Rent* played in numerous countries, and many languages, while the show was still running on Broadway, U.S. stock and regional rights were not released until 2009. At that point, theaters and schools that had wanted to do the show for years finally had the opportunity to license it through Music Theatre International (MTI) and put on their own productions.

Rent has become a particular favorite of high school drama clubs and youth theater groups, and yet these productions have often engendered controversy. Though the music, story, and characters appeal mightily to young people, sometimes their parents and other adult authority figures find the show's frank depiction of sexuality and drug use inappropriate for teens. But Jonathan Larson's message is positive and powerful, and important for kids to hear; numerous young people have written to his family to say *Rent* literally saved their lives. The show's emphasis on embracing diversity and celebrating creativity has been a lifeline to sensitive, artistic kids who feel like misfits in their communities, and especially to LGBTQ teens struggling with coming-out issues, who are thrilled to discover a musical with characters they can identify with.

In an attempt to make the show more accessible to youth groups, MTI, with the approval of the Larson family and the active participation of Al Larson, prepared a special version of the show called *Rent School Edition* that tones down some of the rough language and deletes the sexually explicit number "Contact." The edited script was workshopped in 2006 at Stagedoor Manor, the famed theater camp in the Catskills, and most schools that do the show now use that version. Still, school boards, principals, and religious organizations have frequently sought to censor these productions, often with success; productions in several states have been shut down before they even opened, disappointing students and denying them what can be an empowering growth experience.

In Rowlett, Texas, parents even complained about the scene where Tom Collins talks about rewiring an ATM machine to provide money for the homeless, claiming that it set a bad example for kids by glorifying stealing! The weeks of debate and controversy over whether they should be allowed to do the show became so heated that the drama teacher in that case ended up cancelling it voluntarily out of concern for the pressure all the fighting was putting on the students.

In some cases, though, students and teachers have fought back against attempted censorship and managed to prevail, getting the show on in the face of intolerance and disapproval. A couple of their inspiring stories are included in the alphabetical survey below, along with productions at all levels, from big-budget regional theaters to small community groups.

American Theatre Company, Chicago, IL, 2012

Despite its institutional-sounding name, the American Theatre Company is actually a very small (less than 150 seats), though highly respected, Chicago theater. Its production of *Rent* was a co-production with another Chicago Off-Loop company, About Face Theatre; it received national press attention due to its director, David Cromer, a product of the Windy City's storefront theater scene who returns there periodically though he is now one of the most revered and in-demand directors in the country. His reputation has soared in recent years due to his rapturously received Off-Broadway productions of *Our Town*, in which he also played the leading role of the Stage Manager, and *Tribes*. He has also directed Broadway revivals of *Brighton Beach Memoirs* and *The House of Blue Leaves*, and he received a MacArthur Fellowship in 2010. In a press release, the late PJ Paparelli, then artistic director of the theater, said that he and Bonnie Metzgar, artistic director of About Face Theatre, "wanted to produce *Rent* at our companies because we wanted to bring a stark reality to this musical, a reality that accurately depicts life in the Village in 1990." Though he had initially planned to direct the show himself, he said he was thrilled when Cromer, who had a long history with the theater, asked him to let him take it on instead. Cromer said of the musical: "The forces at work in *Rent* are just so exhilarating. What's richer than exploring that time in your life when you're freezing cold, and terrified, and in love, and completely broke and inspired, and besieged. And hopeful, and hopeless, and somehow strong enough to survive all (or most of) that?" (Quoted on the website Theatreinchicago.com.) At the first read-through, the director told the cast that their production was going to be the first major "re-look" at the show, and said that though there was no reason why they should copy any previous production, they were not "turning *Rent* on its ear." He said: "It's just going to be as deep and as dense and as complicated and as truthful as we can make it. . . . We're not throwing *Rent* out to do some kind of inversion of it, but we're just trying to look at it as if it hadn't been done before." Theater critic Chris Jones of the *Chicago Tribune* wrote: "There are revelations in David Cromer's intensely-textured, hyper-naturalistic 'Rent,' staged, alley-style . . . on a set designed by Collette Pollard to feel entirely like a gritty extension of the songwriter Roger and filmmaker Mark's 1990s loft. . . . He points up the contrast between the upper-middle-class kids whose rebellion is a choice and those with whom they share the frigid streets for whom poverty is a reality unshakable by performance art . . . This feels like a show that stretched everyone with its ambition—a fine thing, in so many ways, given the richness of the vision." But he went on to point out that most of the leads were unable to handle the vocal and musical demands of the score, which he called a "crippling problem"; he singled out Alex Agard (who played Tom Collins) and Lili-Anne Brown (Joanne) as exceptions, the two strongest singers in the cast. Jones blamed some of the problem on ineffective amplification, the high placement of the band, and the lack of a conductor that the actors could see. Hilton Als, reviewing the production for the *New Yorker*, called the production "radical" and said: "[Cromer and his designers] create a kind of emotional milieu where despair and the need to connect physically alternate from number to number, adding up to something bittersweet, and true. . . . Cromer doesn't use the music in ways we're familiar with—to encourage resolution, and happiness—but to emphasize the distance the characters feel in their separate prisons of ill health and distrust." Of the cast, he said: "For the most part, these are not show-business veterans, hardened by some inner mechanism on how to please an audience, but new, young performers who are willing to try almost anything to communicate something of themselves." They included Alan Schmuckler (also known as a composer of musicals) as Mark, Grace Gealey (now known for her TV work under her married name, Grace Byers) as Mimi, Derrick Trumbly as Roger, and Aileen May as Maureen.

Bristol Riverside Theatre, Bucks County, PA, 2012

By the time this 300-seat professional regional theater produced it, *Rent* had become a well-known entity in the Philadelphia area, where various smaller groups had done the show and the national tours had come through a couple of times. Wendy Rosenfield reviewed the production (her fifth) for the *Philadelphia Inquirer*, saying the choice was "unusual for Bristol, which favors All-American classics but has gently leaned toward the topical in recent seasons." She added: "Theirs is a scrappy version, maybe closest to the experience of seeing it in a workshop during those heady days of ACT UP and the Clintons . . . Director Jose Zayas remains mostly, but not entirely, faithful . . . Mark's iconic striped scarf seems to have gone missing. In addition, Benny (Joseph Michael O'Brien), the group's former friend-turned-sellout landlord, is white, rather than African American. These are changes I've never seen, and they will matter only to diehard Rentheads; but if you're one, consider yourself warned."

In his review for *U.S. 1 Newspaper*, Jonathan Elliott singled out a performer with a unique take on her role: "Jamila Sabares-Klemm, as the newly Sapphic performance artist Maureen, is a charmer through and through, a flirt who cares little about the consequences of her actions until the costs become apparent. Sabares-Klemm also illustrates an interesting point of this production: in the role that made a star out of Idina Menzel (prior to 'Wicked' and 'Glee'), she opts to go in a completely different direction, impish and coy where Menzel was erotic and edgy. While both held the right amount of humor and humanity in their roles, finding a new interpretation that works brings a new life to this Maureen." Brit West, who had previously played Joanne at the John W. Engeman Theater (see below) was Mimi this time. The cast also included Mark Willis Borum (Roger), James LaRosa (Mark), Tracie Franklin (Joanne), Julian Alvarez (Angel), and Tyrone Roberson (Collins). Keith Baker, the theater's artistic director, was the production's musical director.

Broadway Palm Dinner Theatre, Fort Myers, FL, 2011

Though dinner theaters were popular throughout the seventies and eighties, providing affordable dinner-and-show packages for middle-class urban and suburban audiences and employment opportunities for hundreds of young musical theater performers, this type of venue began to die out in the nineties. Numerous long-running institutions have gone out of business as their audiences have aged or been lured away by more up-to-date entertainment options. The few dinner playhouses that remain have had to rethink their comfortable programming and marketing strategies in an effort to attract new audiences who might not be drawn to the standard Rodgers and Hammerstein or Neil Simon fare. When the Broadway Palm Dinner Theatre presented *Rent*, the theater's marketing director and general manager, Susan

Johnson, spoke about the challenges in an interview with Nancy Stetson of *Fort Myers Florida Weekly*. She admitted that *Rent* is "as far from what you picture at a dinner theater as you could imagine." But the theater had recently made successful attempts to reach out to younger audiences with productions of *The Full Monty* and *Hairspray*, so they decided they were ready for *Rent* as the next step. Said Johnson: "You hang onto some of the traditional means of marketing a show, but you have to toss a lot of them out of the window and start fresh." The show was publicized in Sarasota and Tampa as well as Fort Myers, with hotel discounts offered, and advertised on late-night and reality TV shows. The theater posted highlights videos on YouTube for the first time, and even placed an ad on Craigslist "calling all Rentheads," to attract those fans who will go to lengths to seek out productions of their favorite musical. Special "Girls' Night Out" packages were promoted, with a specially designed cocktail called a "Rentini," and the theater offered talkbacks after the Friday night performances. The experiment was largely successful. According to Chris Silk of the *Naples Daily News*: "Broadway Palm unleashed rock opera 'Rent' on the unsuspecting population of Fort Myers last week. An artistic stretch from the middle-of-the-road musicals that usually dock at Broadway Palm, 'Rent' proves 'there's no day like today' to try something new. The vibrant, throbbing show pulses with life and resonates with emotion. More concert than show—audiences rarely get this kind of treat . . . Tuesday's crowd seemed divided between 'love it' and 'I don't know about this.'" He added, "The stellar ensemble pounds out the big set pieces with fire and verve."

Directed and choreographed by Andy Ferrara, the production, with most but not all of the same leading actors, had played a previous engagement at the Broadway Palm's sister theater: the Dutch Apple Dinner Theatre in Lancaster, Pennsylvania (seemingly an even less likely environment for this show!). Both Non-Equity theaters are run by the Prather Entertainment Group. The Broadway Palm cast included Brie Cassil as Mimi, Gus Curry as Roger, E. J. Marotta as Mark, Kaitlin Doughty as Maureen, Marisha Wallace as Joanne, William Bailey as Angel, and a resonant-voiced George L. Brown as Tom Collins.

Casa Mañana, Fort Worth, TX, 2012, 2016

Originally a theater-in-the-round, this long-running Texas venue was thoroughly renovated in 2003 and now features a thrust configuration seating over 1,000. Both of the company's productions of *Rent* were directed by Tim Bennett. The first mounting was plagued by electrical and sound glitches on press night; according to Ashlea Palladino of Thecolumnonline.com: "Casa

Mañana's production of *Rent* reflected real life; it was beautiful at times, but also wrought with imperfections. A solid cast kept the ship afloat but not without some difficulty." She added: "As Mimi Marquez, Karmine Alers reprised the role she played on Broadway . . . Ms. Alers was incredibly energetic as the warm-hearted, drug-addicted Mimi and her 'Out Tonight' was the up-tempo highlight of the show. She evoked a wide range of emotions with her performance, especially during 'Goodbye Love.'" Palladino also appreciated Walter Lee Cunningham Jr. as Angel, saying: "[He] shared a stunningly open-hearted, thoughtful, and incredibly generous drag persona. Not only were his boots to die for, his ability to run and dance and jump in them colored me three shades of green." The cast also included Jason Wooten—complete with shoulder-length dark hair—as Roger, Maurice Johnson as Collins, Kia Dawn Fulton as Joanne, and Jennifer Boswell as Maureen. Company regular Christopher J. Deaton, a white actor, played Benny, and Adam Hose appeared as Mark for the third time, having previously played the role in the regional premiere at the Hangar Theatre and later taken over mid-run at the John W. Engeman Theater (see below).

When the theater presented *Rent* again in February of 2016, Bennett repeated as director; the one principal cast member to return from the 2012 production was Johnson as Collins. This time the opening seems to have gone more smoothly. According to Punch Shaw of the *Fort Worth Star-Telegram*: "Music director James Cunningham does a superlative job of leading his crew . . . and even at the opening night performance seen for this review, the mix created by sound designer Kyle McCord was right on the money." Noah Putterman, the company's director of children's theater and education, played Mark; reviewing the production for the website Theaterjones. com, Jessica Fritsche said: "It's clear that he's having a blast during songs like 'Tango: Maureen' and 'What You Own,' and that makes him a lot of fun to watch. Putterman is a good foil for John Arthur Greene's showy, angsty Roger Davis, who seems to need a Xanax in addition to his AZT. Greene has a big Broadway voice and the pedigree to match, but it gets lost in the hair-raking, fist-pumping gestures that make up his character's limited emotional range. He's best when he leaves all the emoting behind and just sings—his rendition of 'Your Eyes' is beautiful and heartfelt." This time Benny (Calvin Scott Roberts) was African American, as is traditional for this role. Kalyn West played Mimi, with Mackenzie Bell as Maureen, Phyre Hawkins as Joanne, and Tyler Hardwicke as Angel. As Shaw summed it up: "Bennett has directed and choreographed several musicals at Casa . . . and his work continues to impress on every level. When you see one of his shows, you feel you are seeing the players involved at their absolute peaks."

Edinburgh Festival Fringe, Edinburgh, Scotland, 2015

This renowned annual event is billed as the world's largest arts festival, presenting artists from all over the world and performances in all genres at an enormous variety of mostly nontraditional venues. In 2015, a trio of young producers (Samantha Chuna, Michael Quadrino, and Erin Mizer)—who had been involved with a previous production of *Rent* as students at Hofstra University and had started a theatre company called Uncompromising Artistry—decided to mount an all-new production of the musical for the Fringe. Anthony Rapp, the original Mark, had worked with them on the show at Hoftstra and came on board as an artistic consultant. This *Rent* was one of 3,314 separate productions presented at the Fringe that year, at a total of 313 venues. The company's performance space, Paradise in Augustine's, was an old church converted into a 110-seat theater; the team at the venue was very supportive and even purchased new sound equipment (all-important for any production of *Rent*, even in a small space) for the show at no cost to the company. Rapp suggested Nicola Murphy, a young Irish director who had been studying and working in New York, to stage the piece, and he worked with her closely on casting and throughout the process. Murphy says Rapp "was a great collaborator as an artistic consultant and we worked really well together," adding, "I think inherently we have the same artistic sensibilities and so it was quite a harmonious relationship!" Murphy described herself as a *Rent* newbie, having never seen a professional production of the show, so she approached it fresh, without the baggage of anyone else's imagery, and found herself profoundly affected by the musical's themes. She says: "Personally I had lost my father just a couple years previous to directing the show, and grief, and how to deal with grief, is such a huge part of the show that it allowed me an opportunity to deal with that in a way I wasn't necessarily expecting. Mimi's line 'the heart may freeze or it can burn, the pain will ease if I can learn . . . ,' that was my in, and it was that line that I always came back to if I ever got stuck. I think it's the key to *Rent*, for me, anyways in the sense that we have two roads we can take in terms of how we want to live our lives—with courage or with fear."

Working with Murphy, designer Steven Royal devised a versatile set for the small space. The principal elements were two large ladders, used in various inventive configurations to suggest doorways, the phone booth, the Christmas tree, and more. Murphy said: "The lighting overall was quite simple; we lit the real altar of the church above and behind the blacks during Angel's funeral, and these work lights were also very effective during 'Contact' as we used a white fabric that became known as the Angel sheet, and so using backlighting on that was really simple and effective. Actually, for the longest time we couldn't figure out how to project Mark's video . . . we didn't want to bring down a screen, and then one day I thought 'why don't we bring back Angel's sheet and project on that.' It felt like the perfect choice!"

The cast included both Equity and nonunion New York actors. Janet Krupin (Maureen) had appeared with Rapp and the original Maureen, Idina Menzel, in the Broadway production of *If/Then*, and Johnny Newcomb (Roger) had made his Broadway debut in *American Idiot*. Michael Quadrino, one of the producers, was highly praised by critics for his performance as Mark. The other principals were Jonathan Christopher as Collins, Lyonel Reneau as Benny, Thomas Green as Angel, Zia as Joanne, and Magdiel Cabral as Mimi. "Everyone is here for the love," Newcomb told Meredith Ganzman of Playbill.com. Like other festival artists, the cast members handed out flyers on the streets of Edinburgh and tweeted about the show to fill seats; they also worked together to strike the set after each performance, clearing the venue for other shows, and bonded as a family. Reviewing them for the magazine *ScotsGay*, Brett Heriot wrote: "This production has perhaps the best cast ever assembled for a Fringe show with every single performer excelling in their roles and when working together create spine tingling moments."

The company announced plans to perform the show again in Aruba—one of the few places in the world where *Rent* had never been seen before—during the 2017–2018 season, produced by new international production company On The Quays in partnership with Cas Di Cultura and Dyvents Entertainment Aruba.

Fifth Avenue Theatre, Seattle, WA, 2012

Seattle is a major theater town, so it may come as a surprise that, though the touring productions had been through multiple times, there was no major professional production of *Rent* with a local cast until four years after the show had closed on Broadway. In the summer of 2012, that was remedied by the Fifth Avenue Theatre, a large downtown venue that presents a season of both locally-produced shows and national tours. The homegrown *Rent* was staged by Bill Berry, whose direction was described by reviewer David Edward Hughes of Talkinbroadway.com as "faithful, spirited and not overly reverential." Aaron C. Finley played Roger, Naomi Morgan was Mimi, and Daniel Berryman was Mark; the cast also included Brandon O'Neill (Collins), Jerick Hoffer (Angel), Logan Benedict (Benny), and Ryah Nixon (Maureen). Hughes singled Nixon out for praise, calling her "dazzling and stunningly original in the role of Maureen." He added: "Nixon is a rocket-powered vocal and emotive wonder, and her 'Over the Moon' not only goes exactly there, but takes the whole audience along for the bracing ride. She has real chemistry with Andi Alhadeff's grounded, no-nonsense Joanne, and their 'Take Me or Leave Me' is a second-act standout." Daniel Cruz provided choreography, and the show featured set design by Martin Christoffel, lighting by Tom Sturge, and costumes by Pete Rush.

5th Floor Theatre Company, Long Island City, NY, 2015

This nonunion production was one of two September mountings of the show staged in New York City in honor of the musical's twentieth anniversary; it shared a set designer, Carl Tallent, with the other one, staged by the Harbor Lights Theater Company, which played concurrently at a much larger venue on Staten Island (see below). 5th Floor doesn't have its own performance space, and their *Rent* was presented in a rented venue: the Secret Theatre—a very intimate space that seats ninety-nine in a three-quarter thrust configuration—in Long Island City, a neighborhood in Queens. The entire five-day run sold out before opening night. Dedicated to supporting emerging artists as they begin their careers, 5th Floor has an all-volunteer staff, including casting director Nikki Grillos, who, in tandem with the production's director, Nick Brennan, put together a very strong group of young performers. Dan Rosenbaum, who played Roger, had done the role in one of the non-Equity tours; Lindsay Lavin (Maureen) had also played her role before, at the Orlando Shakespeare Theatre. Bernard Holcomb (Tom Collins) was making his musical theater debut in the production but was a trained and experienced opera singer: having played the leading tenor role of Rodolfo in *La bohème*, he is possibly the only performer to play major roles in both *Rent* and the opera on which it's based!

Other cast members included Nina Negron as Mimi, Daniel Clayton Smith as Mark, André Revels as Benny, and Mia Johnson as Joanne. Director Brennan staged the show effectively for the small space; Tallent's set included two rolling staircases, which moved Mimi around the stage during "Out Tonight." Rock posters decorated the walls of the house as well as the set, creating an authentic nightclub atmosphere. According to actor Anthony Wright, who played Angel: "You hear a lot about *Rent* bringing people together and it is one hundred percent true. I am still incredibly close with the cast members because the material itself forces the cast to create life-long bonds. In the beginning we only rehearsed two days a week which was extremely difficult in terms of building relationships and chemistry at first. We would make progress and then we wouldn't see each other for three or four days. However, we didn't let that stop us from creating what I feel was one of my favorite theatrical experiences, to date." Wright and Kevin Lagasse, who played Gordon and the "Will I?" soloist, both returned to the stage of the

Secret Theatre a couple of months later, playing Richie and Al, respectively, in the fortieth anniversary New York production of *A Chorus Line*.

Hangar Theatre, Ithaca, NY, 2009

The Hangar was one of the first regional theaters to get the rights to produce *Rent*, and their production of the musical provided the finale to their 2009 summer season. The director/choreographer Devanand Janki (known for the Off-Broadway musical *Zanna, Don't!*) used the space inventively: according to reviewer Kathryn Andryshak of the *Ithaca Times*: "The quaint theater had . . . been transformed into a gritty cityscape, situating some of its staging and props within the audience. A streetlamp, public telephone, fire escape, chain link fence, graffiti, crumpled flyers and rainbow Christmas lights put me closer to the stage than I was actually sitting." Mark Fifer was the musical director. The company of twenty-five was substantially larger than the cast used on Broadway, and though the theater imports most of its leading actors from New York City, they made a point of announcing that the ensemble included several members of the local community. Jared Zirilli and Adam Hose led the cast as Roger and Mark, respectively, with Anisha Nagarajan as Mimi, Eric Jordan Young as Collins, Jonathan Burke as Angel, Maria-Christina Oliveras as Joanne, Catherine Stephani as Maureen, and Nik Walker as Benny.

Harbor Lights Theater Company, Staten Island, NY, 2015

This was one of two productions of the musical presented concurrently in New York in honor of the twentieth anniversary of the show's premiere. It shared a set designer (Carl Tallent) with the other one, which was produced by 5th Floor Theatre Company in Long Island City (see above). Harbor Lights is a much larger operation, an Equity company run by the husband-and-wife team of Jay Montgomery and Tamara Jenkins. They presented the show, like most of their other productions, in the Snug Harbor Music Hall, a beautifully maintained venue with a large proscenium stage and an orchestra pit that is billed as one of the two oldest theaters still in operation in New York City (the other being Carnegie Hall).

Harbor Lights brought in an exemplary sound system that helped the singers project the lyrics into the large house with unusual clarity. Alex Perez, a director/choreographer with several previous productions of *Rent* already under his belt, added substantial dance elements to the show this time around. These included ensemble tangoing during Mark and Joanne's "Tango: Maureen," and choreographed interaction among the actors during

Tom Collins (played by Monté J. Howell) sings the reprise of "I'll Cover You" as the spirit of Angel (Michael J. Mainwaring) looks on from above. Harbor Lights Theater Company, 2015.   *Bitten By A Zebra*

"Seasons of Love"—though the traditional lineup of all fifteen cast members across the stage was seen briefly a couple of times before the end of the number. Most notably, two of the ensemble members, on an upper platform level, danced a *pas de deux* reenacting the story of the end of Roger and April's relationship while Roger was singing about it downstage in "One Song Glory"—an innovation that some audience members interpreted as a nod to the flashbacks seen during that song in the movie of *Rent*. Though some of the added dance routines were distracting and seemed self-consciously arty, others were more organic and contributed to the visual energy of the show. Abetted by the outstanding lighting design of Kia Rogers, Perez's staging was distinguished by uncommonly clear and vivid storytelling. His casting deviated from the standard template, using actors of unexpected physical types in several of the roles. Travis Artz, the possessor of an exciting musical-theater tenor, was a fresh faced Roger with shoulder-length dark hair. Reversing the usual racial casting, Madeline Fansler, a white actress with a powerhouse voice, played Joanne opposite an African American Maureen, Zuri Washington. Emily Jeanne Phillips (Mimi) looked like she was from the Midwest but brought down the house with strong belting and high-energy dance moves in a memorable "Out Tonight."

The Hollywood Bowl, Los Angeles, CA, 2010

The landmark Los Angeles venue presented *Rent* in 2010 as that year's entry in its annual series of fully staged musicals. One of the most highly publicized remounts of the show, this outdoor production was notable as being staged in the biggest venue ever to host a production of the musical (the 17,500-seat bowl is billed as the largest outdoor amphitheater in the United States) as well as a rare instance of *Rent*, which even in its original Broadway production was deliberately cast with unknowns, being presented with something of an "all-star cast."

The show was directed by Neil Patrick Harris, the very popular actor who much earlier in his career had played Mark in the original LA company of *Rent*, with the original costume designer (Angela Wendt) and musical director (Tim Weil) recreating their work for the outdoor stage. The band was augmented with brass that gave some of the numbers a different, almost seventies-style vibe. Vanessa Hudgens (of Disney's *High School Musical*) as Mimi was not asked to perform "Out Tonight" on the standard catwalk and stairs. Instead, Harris had her begin the number seated at a vanity table downstage left; she then walked onto a ramp that took her out into the audience. The cast, which got only a week of rehearsal followed by three performances, also included Aaron Tveit (Broadway's *Next to Normal* and *Catch Me if You Can* and

In rehearsal for the 2010 production at the Hollywood Bowl, director Neil Patrick Harris (left) uses a model of the set to explain blocking to Vanessa Hudgens, who played Mimi, and Aaron Tveit (Roger). *Lawrence K. Ho/Getty Images*

TV's *Gossip Girl*) as Roger, Nicole Scherzinger (lead singer of the Pussycat Dolls and a winner on TV's *Dancing with the Stars*) as Maureen, and popular comedian/television host Wayne Brady as Tom Collins. Mark was played by Skylar Astin, an original cast member of Broadway's *Spring Awakening* who would shortly go on to star in the *Pitch Perfect* movies. Gwen Stewart represented *Rent*'s original cast, recreating her "Seasons of Love" solo, and Tracie Thoms returned to the role of Joanne, which she had played in the movie and in the final Broadway cast.

The show was slightly abridged, the most notable cuts including Joanne's "We're Okay" and most of the "Contact" sequence. Reviewing the show for the *Los Angeles Times*, Charles McNulty reported that Harris lacked the directorial experience that might have enabled him to block the show efficiently and tell the story with optimal clarity on the huge stage, but singled out several of the performers for individual praise, opining that "Tveit's Roger has both the rock-star charisma and lost-boy inwardness to entice Mimi." He went on to say: "The surprise for me was the confident intensity of

Brady's portrayal of Tom Collins, whose romance with Angel (a vibrant Telly Leung) was the most moving element of Harris' production. The staging tended to lock the couple into variety-show frames, but the richness of vocal feeling between them burst the bounds with a passion that flirted with opera, gospel, rock and R&B."

Due to the size of the venue, the cast size was increased from the usual fifteen to twenty-five; the ensemble included Yassmin Alers, who had been

Vanessa Hudgens as Mimi and Aaron Tveit as Roger onstage at the Hollywood Bowl, 2010.   *Mathew Imaging/Getty Images*

an understudy in the original Broadway company, and director Harris's spouse, actor David Burtka. As in the rock concerts frequently presented at the Bowl, close-up views of the action were presented on Jumbotron video screens beside the stage.

Ivoryton Playhouse, Essex, CT, 2016

This venerable Connecticut venue has a history going back to the early thirties, when Katharine Hepburn starred in a season of summer stock produced by Milton Stiefel, a close associate of the legendary David Belasco; it became known as the "first self-supporting summer theatre in the United States," and Stiefel operated it until 1973. Now under the auspices of a nonprofit foundation, the theater has become a year-round operation and is listed on the National Register of Historic Places. It has been run for over twenty years by Jacqueline Hubbard, who serves as both executive director and artistic director. Having loved *Rent* for years, Hubbard had wanted to direct it for some time, but it was a departure from the usual fare at the theater, and she wasn't sure how their audience would respond. As she put it: "*Rent* was always going to be a risk for us as we had painted ourselves as a theatre with a demographic audience of well over sixty-five that preferred mild mannered theatre so I was prepared for the twenty or so audience members who left every intermission.

Patrick Clanton (Collins), Tim Russell (Mark), and Johnny Newcomb (Roger) at the Ivoryton Playhouse, 2016.   *Anne Hudson*

I was prepared for the 'I am offended by the language, subject matter, etc.' What I was not prepared for was this whole new demographic that came out of the woodwork. Where had they been hiding? So many young people that came back two and three times. So many groups of LGBTQ teens from all over Connecticut. I was especially moved by the HIV positive teens that came all the way from Bridgeport Young Adult Services. But more importantly for us, I was not prepared for the older demographic that loved the play; that brought their grandchildren; that wept and remembered friends that they had lost. It was humbling for me and a renewed lesson in not judging by the walkers and hearing aids."

Reviewing the show for Talkinbroadway.com, Zander Otter said: "Director Jacqueline Hubbard, working with choreographer Todd Underwood, keeps the stage teeming with life, helping to fill the show with both humor and heartache. . . . This production, in general, is reminiscent of the original Broadway show and yet finds new and significant moments that feel entirely fresh."

Johnny Newcomb repeated his outstanding Roger, which he had played in the much-publicized production at the Edinburgh Festival Fringe the previous summer (see above), Alyssa V. Gomez was both sexy and sweetly tender as Mimi, and Stephanie Genito was a sophisticated, very funny Maureen. The uniformly strong cast included Tim Russell as Mark, Maritza Bostic as Joanne, Collin L. Howard as Benny, Jonny Cortes as Angel, and Patrick Clanton as Tom Collins. Sandra W. Lee, who performed strongly in the "Mark's Mom" track in the ensemble, was a self-proclaimed disabled combat veteran of the Iraq War; she spoke movingly of having found with this cast the same close-knit sense of community that she had experienced with her squad in the US Army.

Many productions of the show in smaller theaters have encountered serious sound balance issues, as the band tends to drown out the singers; faced with this issue in tech rehearsals, Hubbard and musical director Michael Morris removed the band from their usual position onstage and put them under the stage, where they couldn't be seen but the sound mix could be controlled—with the result being that the cast was able to put across every one of Larson's lyrics clearly. At the end of the show, Hubbard made sure the musicians got to come onstage for a well-deserved curtain call.

John W. Engeman Theater, Northport, NY, 2009

Taking a cue from the show's story, the community-minded Engeman Theater, a professional venue on Long Island, donated a portion of the proceeds from every ticket sold to two area AIDS charities: the Long Island

Association for AIDS Care and Thursday's Child. Director Alan Souza was a regular at the Engeman; he told interviewer Brian Scott Lipton of Theatermania.com: "[I] just had to explain to some of the young kids in the cast about what ACT-UP was like in the 1990s—but it remains so relevant today. There's still this sense of a community coming together during times of strife, like now, and there have been plenty of fascinating things to discover in the script as we've taken it apart and interpreted it. In a lot of ways, we feel like we're putting on this show for the first time."

Actor Mike Backes, who had done three other shows at the theater, was playing his dream role as Roger, having auditioned for the Broadway production about a dozen times. He was praised for his work, as were Stanley Bahorek (Mark), Betsy Morgan (Maureen), and Alan Mingo, Jr. (Collins). Reviewing the show for the *New York Times*, Anita Gates opined: "The athletic, vibrant, strong-voiced young cast . . . stylishly directed by Alan Souza, works hard to evoke the era, and largely succeeds. There are moments when the show's energy flags. Some performances could be more focused . . . And some of Johnny Davenport's costume designs look more J. Crew than Avenue B. But those flaws are easy to overlook when so much about 'Rent' is right." The cast also featured Lakisha Anne Bowen as Mimi, Miles Johnson as Benny, Reymundo Santiago as Angel, and Brit West as Joanne. Scenic design was by Todd Ivins, lighting by Cory Pattak, and sound by Richard Dionne.

La Mirada Theatre for the Performing Arts, La Mirada, CA, 2015

The plays and musicals at this 1,251-seat Southern California venue are produced by McCoy Rigby Entertainment, a company owned by producers Tom McCoy and his wife Cathy Rigby, the Olympic gymnast-turned-musical theater star known especially for her many appearances as Peter Pan. Director Richard Israel took a fresh approach to the production's visuals, moving the band from their usual position onstage into the orchestra pit to make room for an unusual set designed by Stephen Gifford. Reviewer Eric Marchese of the *Orange County Register* wrote: "Gifford's scenic design features the massively tall brownstone walls of the characters' home in New York City's East Village circa 1989. While it first appears monolithic, it ingeniously offers the cast multiple places to enter and exit, including moving from the stage to elevated levels." Steven Stanley, editor of Stagescenela.com, called it a "spectacular, multi-level . . . set that is both literal (we actually feel we are in Roger and Mark's industrial loft) and figurative enough to allow us to believe (thanks to Jonathan Infante's vivid projections) that we are all over New York . . . Much is made of second, third, and even fourth-floor spaces . . . letting multiple vignettes take place simultaneously in clearly distinct areas." Stanley singled out several cast members for praise, including Lawrence Cummings, whose "fabulously fierce Angel is the finest of the ten Angels I've seen (I felt I was seeing the role reinvented) and no Angel could ask for a dreamier Collins than (John) Devereaux, the twosome sharing palpable stage chemistry." In the *San Gabriel Valley Tribune*, Frances Baum Nicholson especially liked Mark Whitten. Nicholson wrote: "[Mark Whitten] makes Mark a mixture of joy and fatalism—just a bit goofy, with an elemental love for the people and the purpose of his part of the city. Devin Archer makes Mark's . . . roommate Roger fragile and damaged, but with a particular kind of resolute purpose. As Mimi, the heroine-addicted [sic] exotic dancer Roger falls for, Cassie Simone makes much of the pathos, the manipulativeness and the openness of a young girl trying to find her space in the world." Cooper Howell played Benny, Emily Goglia was Maureen, and Amber Mercomes, who had sung the "Seasons of Love" solo in the LA regional premiere six years earlier, was Joanne. The cast numbered sixteen, one more than the Broadway company.

Stephen Gifford's towering set, as lit by Steven Young, and Jonathan Infante's evocative projections made for an unusually atmospheric production at California's La Mirada in 2015. Shown here is the final scene, with Devin Archer (Roger) and Cassie Simone (Mimi) at center stage.

Jason Niedle

Musical Theatre West, Long Beach, CA, 2009

Opening fifteen months after the musical's closing performance on Broadway, Musical Theatre West's version was announced as the first professional regional theater production of *Rent* in the Los Angeles area. Playwright Obed Medina, a devoted fan who had seen the show over thirty times previously, reviewed the production for the blog LA Live on Stage. He praised director Nick DeGruccio for incorporating ingenious ideas of his own into a staging that also honored the original, adding, "The set, provided by Plan B Entertainment, is a scaled down version of the original with some inspiring additions that allow the characters to move and interact in a way they've never been able to do."

A certain amount of celebrity cachet was provided by two cast members: Sabrina Sloan (Mimi) had been an *American Idol* finalist, and Jai Rodriguez, well known for his regular appearances on the TV reality show *Queer Eye for the Straight Guy,* reprised the role of Angel, which he had played as a replacement on Broadway. Eric Marchese of the *Orange County Register* praised both: "Sloan's Mimi is both minx and delicate flower. Rodriguez nearly walks off with the show, his girlishly feminine Angel clad in a Santa Claus coat, zebra leggings and steep platform shoes. His dance scenes carry an energy similar to Michael Jackson's." According to Medina: "Jai Rodriguez is absolute heaven to watch as the tender, loving AIDS-ridden cross-dressing Angel. He is the glue that holds this makeshift family together and Rodriguez is just the right actor to portray him with humor and poignancy." He praised most of the cast but had reservations about P. J. Griffith as Roger, whose interpretation he described as a cross between Iggy Pop and Keith Richards. Steven Stanley of Stagescenela.com, however, said: "Griffith's stellar work here comes from the heart and the gut, and his singing, never anything less than powerhouse, comes from the perspective of an *actor* and not just a vocalist. I guarantee you, you won't have seen a better Roger than Griffith." The cast also included Beau Hirshfield as Mark, Callie Carson as Maureen, Mel Robert as Collins, Nicole Tillman as Joanne, and Andrew Johnson as Benny. According to Marchese: "Musical director Michael Paternostro infuses Larson's rock score with equal parts energy and tenderness, while Alisan Porter's choreography creates frequently pleasing visual counterpoint to the show's 22 songs." (Paternostro and Porter both had Broadway acting credits; they had recently performed together as Greg and Bebe in the 2006 Broadway revival of *A Chorus Line.*) James Scarborough, reviewing the production for the culture blog What the Butler Saw, had a unique take on *Rent,* whose first act is set on Christmas Eve, as holiday entertainment: "At first you think it's a curious choice, a Christmas season production that's *hardly* silent, with no shining stars, no rejoicing at the manger, and where heroin takes the place of frankincense and myrrh. By the end, though, the story's hope, faith, and redemption resonate as much as any traditional iteration of the greatest story ever told."

New Line Theatre, St. Louis, MO, 2014

Founded in 1991 by director Scott Miller, New Line Theatre has embraced the moniker "The Bad Boy of Musical Theatre." According to the company's website: "New Line was founded to involve the people of the region in the creation and exploration of provocative, alternative, politically and socially relevant works of musical theatre—daring, muscular, intelligent theatre about politics, race, violence, drugs, sexuality, religion, art, obscenity, the media, and other contemporary issues." Given that description, *Rent* seems like a natural choice for them.

It may seem surprising the company waited so long to tackle it, but, in his Director's Notes, Miller acknowledged that several potential patrons had told him they disliked the show because they saw the characters as whiny and selfish. His response: "These people are not entirely wrong. But they're also missing a lot. . . . Every protagonist in every story has to learn something. In *Rent*, these kids need to learn to see beyond their own selves, their own lives, their immediate wants; to learn that we're all interconnected, we're all responsible for each other, or as Sondheim put it so elegantly, 'Careful, no one is alone.'" Miller saw Angel as the "wise wizard . . . She's there to teach the others (*and us*) a valuable lesson, to see the world in terms of what we can give instead of what we can get." Miller had waited a long time to tackle the show because, as he told *American Theatre* magazine, he had found Michael Greif's original production to be "so exactly right, so perfect, why would I change anything?" He felt liberated, though, when he saw how much Greif had rethought the work for his own Off-Broadway revival; this effectively gave him permission to explore the show in his own way.

The production and its very young non-Equity cast were rapturously received by the press. Judith Newmark of the *St. Louis Post Dispatch* credited Miller and assistant Mike Dowdy with giving all the actors equal opportunity to shine, rather than focusing on a couple of leads: "Though Evan Fornachon as Roger and Jeremy Hyatt as Mark are fine in their roles, this is truly an ensemble piece. The actors run through the aisles, teeter on low walls and dance atop the tilted table that is the centerpiece of the set (lavishly tagged and effectively lit by Rob Lippert)." Feeling that the intimacy of the 210-seat space added to the impact of the show, she added: "In her blue wig and twinkly makeup, Sarah Porter is hilarious as Maureen in 'Over the Moon,' a piece of performance art that blossoms in a small theatre. (That's where performance pieces tend to happen.)" Paul Friswold of the *Riverfront Times* claimed he had never before been a fan of the material but said: "Theirs is a *Rent* that is sharp, incisive and viscerally moving. These characters matter; their struggles to find themselves in the wastelands of their early twenties are a potent reminder of what it's like to feel lost in your own life, and that even small steps toward maturity can feel immense. In Miller and Dowdy's hands, *Rent* is a show that deserves every bit of its formidable reputation as the musical that revivified musicals for the next generation."

Anna Skidis as Mimi was widely acknowledged for her powerful voice. The cast also included Luke Steingruby and Marshall Jennings as Angel and Collins, Cody LaShea as Joanne, and Shawn Bowers as Benny. In addition to playing Maureen, Sarah Porter did the costume designs, along with Marcy Wiegert, and music director Justin Smolik headed the five-man band.

New Repertory Theatre, Watertown, MA, 2011

Billed as the third-largest theater in the Greater Boston area, this company opened their seventh season in residence at the Arsenal Center for the Arts with *Rent*. It was the first professional regional theater production of the show in New England. Much attention focused on Rep regular Aimee Doherty in a tour de force comic performance as Maureen; her many previous roles at the theater had included Susan in a 2007 production of Larson's *tick, tick . . . BOOM!* The cast also included Eve Kagan as Mimi, Robert St. Laurence as Roger, John Ambrosino as Mark, Robin Long as Joanne, Maurice E. Parent as Collins, and Nick Sulfaro as Angel.

Director Benjamin Evett, the Founding Artistic Director of the Actors' Shakespeare Project, wrote in a press release about his approach to Jonathan Larson's work: "He created extraordinary characters that young people can really relate to, then and now. It's their journey, from naïve self-absorption to an appreciation of the real value of life and family, where I want to focus our energy. I want to create a world that is rough, exciting, chaotic, and inspirational for the characters living in it, and hopefully for the audience, too." Reviewing the show for the *Boston Globe*, Don Aucoin said, "Under the sure-handed direction of Benjamin Evett, this 'Rent' navigates that fine line between the heart-on-its-sleeve earnestness essential to the success of this 1996 musical and the melodramatic excess that perpetually threatens to capsize it." He also pointed out that the socioeconomic themes of the piece felt more relevant than ever: "[In 1996] the title song, with its half-angry, half-desperate refrain about housing and money woes—'How we gonna pay?'—registered as the cry of impoverished and marginalized outsiders. In 2011, amid rampant foreclosures and a still-reeling economy, those margins are getting more crowded by the day, and the bohemians' insistent refrain could almost serve as the new national mantra."

New York University, New York, NY, 2016

The Tisch School of the Arts at NYU has the largest undergraduate theater program in the nation. BFA students receive their acting training, and do most of their production work, at a variety of independent acting schools and studios around the city. This leads to a certain amount of separation, but there is also a program called NYU Tisch StageWorks that produces plays and musicals that students from all the different studios can audition for. In February 2016 they staged *Rent* in honor of the musical's twentieth anniversary. The director, Kenneth Noel Mitchell, is head of acting at the New Studio on Broadway, where NYU acting majors focusing on musical theater study and train.

Reviewing the show for Verge Campus, the university's news website, Elizabeth Katz pointed up some of the innovations in this nontraditional production. When audience members entered the tiny Abe Burrows Theater, there was already one actor onstage. According to Katz: "A single ensemble member bundled in a white scarf sat on a step shivering, making the audience immediately aware of the homeless epidemic in the world we were entering. The set featured many levels with bare bone metal staircases and platforms. Yet, rather than doing the typical dark color scheme, this production washed everything—walls, floors, stairs, and props—white; even the entire ensemble of people living on the streets was costumed in white . . . The choice represented the humanity of the characters dealing with impossibly difficult situations, and of people who are unwilling to be defined by their struggles." The wintry white set provided the opportunity for extensive use of projections.

Two of the student actors (Sammy Ferber, who played Mark, and David Merino, who played Angel) were hired shortly afterward to go into the company of the Twentieth Anniversary Tour of the show. The cast also included Trevor Bunce as Roger, Mia Gerachis as Mimi, Marcus Guerrier as Collins, Gabi Garcia as Maureen, and Sierra Leverett as Joanne. In May, the cast performed a medley of songs from the show as part of the school's commencement ceremony, the Tisch Salute, at Radio City Music Hall.

Performing Arts for Children and Teens, Tullahoma, TN, 2015

Under the auspices of the South Jackson Civic Center, this community group, located in a town with a population of less than 20,000, has a mission which, according to their website, is focused on "enriching the lives of children and teens. We strive to make theater accessible to any youth who wants to participate in the performing arts. PACT FOR kids . . . is leading by example—children need to witness quality theater as much as they need to be a part of it. We do projects that involve ALL ages so that kids can be surrounded by quality talent and learn from the example of others."

Though their productions are usually family-oriented, with recent efforts including *Oliver!*, *Pinocchio*, *Peter Pan*, and the Christmas opera *Amahl and the Night Visitors*, in 2015 the group decided to take on *Rent*, a musical beloved of teenagers, though its subject matter, particularly as concerned with sexual relationships and drug use, has often been described as "adult." Civic Center Board Chair Kathryn Hopkins suggested the show to Robert Allen, a freelance director who had just completed a production of *Big River* for the theater. Though he had never been particularly enamored of the musical and had jokingly referred to it as *Rant* with his theater students, he realized it could be a good fit for a group of older teens and young adults that had gotten involved with the organization; its message and themes would provide them with a vehicle to express themselves and say what they wanted to say to the adults in their community. But the choice became a controversial one, with opposition launched by Pastor James Zidan of the town's Christ Community Church. Feeling the show's content was inappropriate, he expressed his views in an e-mail to other clergy that was later picked up and circulated by Pastor Wayne Wester of Highland Baptist Church. The only concession PACT made to the content concerns was to ask MTI for permission to delete the song "Contact," with its graphic dance moves and frank evocation of intercourse, from the production; MTI agreed (the song is at any rate not included in their official "School Edition" of the show) but the rest of the musical was presented intact. The religious objections were focused primarily on whether the show was an appropriate one for performance by and for kids, though the cast included only three actual minors and they all had the support of their parents, who were also involved in the production and signed waivers granting them permission to take part.

Although cast and crew members were taunted by their peers and even family members for taking part, only two dropped out of the show and PACT was undeterred. In the words of director Allen, "theatre is a powerful catalyst for social engagement and change, and the choice to do it comes with great responsibility." He told *The Tullahoma News*: "We have (actors) who are HIV positive, who have eating disorders, who have abusive relationships, who are disconnected from life, who struggle with sexuality issues. These are real people to them. When someone says 'you're so awful, we can't have you portrayed onstage because it's so disgusting,' it's a horrible message. [The show] has given a voice to people who don't have a voice or who have actively sought to be silent."

The theater's leaders brought in a psychologist to lead discussions with the actors (the show was double cast) during rehearsals and help them express their feelings about the controversy; they also scheduled moderated "feedback sessions" for audience members after two performances. As a protest, a prayer vigil was held outside the theater on the show's opening night, but the church groups chose not to disrupt the production. Robert Viagas quoted both Zidan and Allen for an article in Playbill.com. Significantly, Allen mentioned a high school guidance counselor who attended the show and told him the information it contained was crucial for students, remarking, "You are doing the work the schools are failing at." Pastor Zidan said, "I don't believe our community has an interest or appetite for such fare." However, he admitted his protest didn't get as much traction in the community as he had expected, adding, "Ultimately it is up to our parents and local theater leadership; and apparently they are all asleep at the wheel." Surprisingly, director Allen himself quoted scripture in summing up the production's success: "We've realized the Parable of the Sower and the Seed from Matthew 13. Good seed in good soil from a good sower will bring good fruit. All those things combined here and a change is coming."

Pioneer Theatre Company, Salt Lake City, UT, 2011

This professional regional theater production was staged by Karen Azenberg, who at the time was the President of the Society of Stage Directors and Choreographers, a labor union that is the equivalent of Equity for directors. Azenberg had worked with Jonathan Larson, directing a production of his early work *Blocks*. While in rehearsal for *Rent* at PTC, she told Kenneth Jones of Playbill.com: "I realized just how much *Rent* has changed the theatrical landscape at our auditions. In 1996, when *Rent* first opened, casting the show was a real challenge; musical theatre performers were not comfortable with this rock-based musical style. Now, it's practically a requirement and I have reaped the benefits 15 years later with a cast of singers, actors and dancers who have all trained to do this style of musical theatre—and they are extraordinary."

Her cast included several New York performers with Broadway and/ or national tour experience. Andy Mientus, who played Mark, had already toured in *Spring Awakening* and would go on to appear in the Broadway revivals of that show and *Les Misérables*. Halle Morse (Mimi) had been on Broadway in *Mama Mia!*, and Adrienne Muller (Joanne) toured in *The Lion King*. Fabio Monteiro played Roger, with Rachel Moulton as Maureen, Nik

Walker as Collins, Jason Gotay as Angel, and Gregory L. Williams as Benny. The production had a cast of sixteen—one more than the Broadway version—and departed from tradition by casting white singers (Ginger Bess and Daniel T. Simons) as both of the "Seasons of Love" soloists. Reviewer Barbara M. Bannon wrote in the *Salt Lake Tribune*: "Should I praise the free-flowing spontaneity of Karen Azenberg's direction? At the show's start, Mark tells us, 'From here on in, I shoot without a script,' and this production has the feel of being invented as it goes along, a seamless collaboration of director and actors." The production opened in June at the tail end of the theater season, and Bannon called it the best theater production to play Salt Lake City during that year, "and possibly several others."

Ridge High School, Basking Ridge, NJ, 2011

Drama teacher Megan Kern and her students were in the middle of auditions for their annual musical, *Rent School Edition*, on December 17, 2010, when they were informed that the show had been cancelled by the school board superintendent, Valerie Goger. According to Linda Sadlouskos of the *Basking Ridge Patch*, the board had received numerous e-mails objecting to the musical's "themes of drug use, AIDS and homosexuality." One school board member, Michael Byrne, "said he views the 'controversial' and 'avant garde' play as an attempt to force changes on a community such as Basking Ridge. Byrne noted the play stresses drug use and poor conduct by its main characters. 'It shows no self constraint of the people involved,' Byrne said." But the superintendent was impressed when, after the cancellation was announced, a large number of students contacted her. "She said students were especially eloquent in stressing the play's anti-bullying message and stated goal of practicing tolerance," wrote Sadlouskos, adding that student Susanna Vogel had pointed out "that the 'elephant in the living room' is that there are two homosexual couples in 'Rent,' and challenged that as the basis for pulling support for the play." As of January 2, Goger's decision to cancel had been reversed, and auditions were able to resume, a little bit behind schedule.

Rather than emulating the standard skeletal staging and design, this production of *Rent* was something of a spectacle. In Kern's Director's Note in the program, she revealed that the drama club had taken a trip into New York City to see Franco Zeffirelli's famously lavish production of *La bohème* at the Metropolitan Opera; she used the facilities of the school's well-equipped new Performing Arts Center to emulate that production's panoramic cityscape in the set for her production of *Rent*. According to Kern: "Myself, along with an amazing team of collaborators, plus the student 'crew' and the performers have hopefully created a production which promotes the intent of the

"You Okay, Honey?": Angel (played by Drew Michael Gardner) introduces himself to Tom Collins (Alex Wilke) on the Zeffirelli-inspired set (designed by Jason Stewart) at Ridge High School, 2011.   *Photo courtesy of Drew Gardner*

original show while allowing our large 'tent city' ensemble, staging and sets to give off some of the grandness of what we saw at the opera last December."

In keeping with the epic concept, the cast numbered over fifty students, including Nicholas Siccone as Mark, Julius Trombino as Roger, Alex Ursino as Mimi, Alex Wilke as Collins, Peter Hughes as Benny, Emily Cleary as Joanne, Lauren Dennis as Maureen, and Drew Michael Gardner as Angel. But the controversy in the community continued. As Kern recently recalled: "Drew and I both admitted back then, that we were afraid when he came onstage just before 'Today 4 U,' he might get harmed (shot). The homophobia we had experienced up to that point was so bad, they had two armed guards at our show, and we were all on alert, since our theatre seats almost 1000 and we were packed. Fortunately there were no bad incidents during the shows, and Drew performed to standing ovations every night, and even earned himself the 'Best Supporting Actor' Award from Paper Mill Playhouse's 'Rising Stars' program."

Ritz Theatre Company, Oaklyn, NJ, 2015

This renovated vaudeville theater in Haddon Township is known for revivals of classic plays and big musicals as well as extensive youth and family programming. Though it's generally considered a professional non-Equity theater, the production of *Rent*, directed and designed by the company's founding artistic director, Bruce Curless, featured Krysten Cummings—a veteran of the show's Canadian, West End, and Broadway companies—in the role of Mimi. She had been nominated for an Olivier Award when she played the role in the first London production in 1998. In an interview with Ted Otten of the *Times of Trenton*, Cummings said: "I came to the Ritz as a teenager and did musicals like . . . 'A Chorus Line,' but I've been all over the world in shows like 'Rent' and 'Jesus Christ Superstar,' and now I'm back at the place where I found out where I belonged, just like my character in this show does." Similarly, Otten quoted Cory Wade, a reality TV star who portrayed Angel, as saying, "When I was in school and told people that I wanted to be an actor, they all told me I was too feminine and couldn't and wouldn't be cast in practically anything, but since Angel is a transsexual, that makes Angel the perfect role for me." (Though Angel is generally seen as a biological male not undergoing a sex change, Wade's use of the term transsexual can be considered technically correct, as Merriam-Webster defines it as "a person who tries to look, dress, and act like a member of the opposite sex.") The cast also included Joshua Bessinger (who had previously played Angel in another production of the show at the nearby Eagle Theater) as Mark, Eric Lawry as Roger, Michael Hogan as Tom Collins, Larisa Bunch as Joanne, Martha Marie Wasser as Maureen, and Vincent Leggett as Benny.

Reviewing the show for Talkinbroadway.com, Cameron Kelsall wrote: "Cummings burrows under the skin of her character and gives a fully realized performance, which you'd expect from someone who has been playing the character off and on for 20 years. Of course, she's far too old for the role—she gives the line 'I'm nineteen, but I'm old for my age' a whole new meaning—but if you're willing to suspend disbelief, you're in for a treat." Musical Director Brian Bacon led a four-piece band, and Lindsey Krier did the choreography.

Slow Burn Theatre Company, Boca Raton, FL, 2015

This small company, a relative newcomer on the South Florida theater scene, has in six years built a reputation for dynamic productions of challenging musicals. They have a predilection for rock shows, having produced *Chess*, *Bat Boy*, *Next to Normal*, *Avenue Q*, and two productions of *The Rocky Horror Show*; the repertoire has also included several Sondheim titles and other sophisticated contemporary pieces, and they have given second chances to several musicals, like *High Fidelity*, *Bonnie & Clyde*, and the notorious *Carrie*, that flopped on Broadway. Shortly before beginning their current residency at the Broward Center for the Performing Arts, the company staged *Rent* at West Boca High School, moving for the last week of the run to the Aventura Arts and Cultural Center.

The production was directed and choreographed by the company's artistic director, Patrick Fitzwater. In a press release, he said: "We're so excited to breathe fresh new life into this classic musical of love, friendship and community; it's the kind of show Slow Burn Theatre is in existence to produce. I look forward to re-examining this piece with fresh eyes and ears and to present *Rent* to a new generation, as well as remind the 'Renthead Generation' why they fell in love with this show, and help them discover something new."

The cast included Equity actors Mike Westrich as Mark and Amy Miller Brennan as Maureen, along with Abby Perkins (Mimi), Bruno Faria (Roger), Rayner Garranchan (Benny), Darrick Penny (Collins), and Bruno Vida (Angel). Christina Alexander, highly praised for her performance as Joanne, also got to sing the "Seasons of Love" solo. The musical director was Caryl Fantel. Michelle F. Solomon, writing for the website Floridatheateronstage. com, had mixed feelings about the production, calling it "ambitious, daring, electric and 2 hours and 30-something minutes of nonstop rock 'n' roll—a no-holds-barred, take chances, go-out-on-a-limb spectacle," and adding that the fresh vision "allows for some forgiveness for some of the weaker elements—characters that appear shallower than the stories they are telling, and choreography here and there that seems a bit too difficult for the skill level of some of the players." Hap Erstein of the *Palm Beach Post* was more positive: "The Broadway production was staged as a rock concert with a plot, while Fitzwater anchors the show in more defined locales on Sean McClelland's multi-level unit set of scaffolding, industrial debris, a mobile staircase and an ominous, retro clock. The result, along with Pat Ward's exacting sound design, renders the story and songs more clearly, even as the score verges on high-amp rock . . . Fitzwater's production dispels any doubt about the lasting quality of 'Rent,' a vivid, wrenching, ultimately uplifting tale for our times."

The Staples Players, Westport, CT, 2011

Founded in the fifties by teacher Craig Matheson and a group of student actors that included Christopher Lloyd and Mariette Hartley, the Staples Players is the name of the drama program at Staples High School—a public school—and one of the most accomplished and acclaimed such programs in the United States. The program is now run by drama teacher David Roth, who codirected the school's production of *Rent* with his wife, Kerry Long, a professional photographer; both are alumni of the school. Unlike some of the other public high schools that have presented the show, Staples has a progressively minded principal and a school board that enthusiastically supports the theater program and defends Roth's prerogative to choose works with challenging contemporary themes. The Players generally produce a big season that includes a straight play (in a small black box theater), a one-act festival, and student directed works, in addition to three full-scale musicals per year in the school's well-equipped 1,000-seat auditorium. The third annual musical is put on during the summer, when school is not in session, and students from other high schools in neighboring towns are able to audition.

Rent, which received five and a half weeks of rehearsal, was one of these summer productions; it featured a cast of some fifty teenagers who swarmed the stage effectively in the group numbers. Westport itself is mentioned a couple of times in the script of *Rent* as the town Benny's wife ("Alison Grey of the Westport Greys") is from. Larson chose the name because Westport is famous as an affluent and mostly white Connecticut town; by moving there Benny is very obviously selling out his community and his roots in the struggling, ethnically diverse Lower East Side. So doing *Rent* with a cast of privileged kids from that town, however well trained and committed to musical theater, presented unique challenges.

Roth began by giving the students a solid understanding of the milieu and time period of the play, what was happening in New York at the time, and especially what it was like to live there during the early days of the AIDS epidemic; a former Broadway actor who is also an alum of the school came in to talk to the cast about living through those years and coping with the illness and deaths of so many colleagues. The stories he told affected the young actors deeply. Roth and Long worked with them to find ways to connect emotionally with the material, especially those who were playing roles that took them far outside the range of experiences they had had in their own lives so far. Maureen (played by Eva Hendricks) and Joanne (Kathryn Gau) provided the first same-sex kiss that had been seen on the Staples stage; several cast members were struggling to come to terms with their own sexualities, and Roth could see that it was cathartic and important for them to be in a show that dealt so frankly with sexual identity. The cast also included David Ressler as Collins and Charlie Greenwald as Benny. The other principals were double cast, with Clay Singer and Steve Autore alternating performances as Roger, Chris McNiff and Dan Shure as Mark, Michelle Pauker and Audrey Twitchell as Mimi, and Johnny Shea and Tyler Jent as Angel.

Backed by a cast of nearly fifty students, David Ressler as Tom Collins sings the reprise of "I'll Cover You." Staples Players, 2011.   *Kerry Long*

Surflight Theatre, Beach Haven, NJ, 2011

This picturesque summer theater, located on Long Beach Island off the Jersey Shore, had been in operation since 1950. Their production of *Rent* was directed by Jen Bender, the resident director for *The Lion King* on Broadway, and starred Justin Guarini. A recording artist well known since his runner-up finish on the first season of *American Idol*, Guarini has substantial TV and film credits; he had appeared on Broadway in both *Women on the Verge of a Nervous Breakdown* and *American Idiot* by the time he was cast to play Roger at Surflight. Most theaters have eschewed celebrity casting for *Rent*, a show about struggling artists, but in an interview with Tammy La Gorce of the *New York Times*, Surflight's producer Roy Miller said that the theater, which was operating under Chapter 11 bankruptcy protection at the time and trying to increase its audience base, was considering the importance of bringing in bigger-name actors; their season that year also included appearances by Judd Hirsch and Cindy Williams in other plays. According to Miller: "The level of talent we're bringing in is something that's never been done here before, and I hope that will help make us successful."

Charlie Smith designed the set and Jeremy Randall was the music director; costumes by Caitlin Reed closely followed the iconic original Angela Wendt designs for the leads. The cast also included Drew Gasparini (himself a songwriter and musical theater composer/lyricist) as Mark, Katrina Rose Dideriksen (soon afterward a swing in the Off-Broadway revival of *Rent*) as Mimi, Chelsea Lovett as Maureen, Dean-Carlo Grant as Collins, Joshua Cruz as Angel, and Carla Stewart as Joanne.

Syracuse Stage/Syracuse University, Syracuse, NY, 2011

Though there are several MFA acting programs that have affiliations with major regional theaters, giving their students the chance to perform as interns in professional productions, Syracuse University is one of the few schools that offers a similar opportunity to undergraduates. According to Patrick Finlon in an article on the university's website: "'Rent' marks the 11th time since the year 2000 that Syracuse Stage and SU Drama have co-presented a large-scale show, continuing a mutually beneficial relationship that allows Syracuse Stage the resources to produce fully realized productions with large ensembles, while offering a learning opportunity for SU Drama students that is unique among undergraduate theater programs."

Professional actors played the eight principal characters, while the eleven students in the cast played all the ensemble roles and understudied the leads. In an interview with Melinda Johnson for Syracuse.com prior to the opening, director Anthony Salatino emphasized the difficulty—and vital importance—of making sure all of Larson's lyrics were audible over the onstage rock band, a challenge some other productions have failed to meet. He described his work with the actors: "It's difficult because it's relentless. It keeps driving forward. But I've been making many attempts to articulate and to really know what the operative words are when you're singing and how does that directly move the plot forward or expose your character further. It's a constant focus for me to do that because the backbeat of this rock, you can get lost in that backbeat."

Nevertheless, David Feldman, reviewing the production for Instantencore.com, pointed out some sound system glitches on opening night. Not particularly a fan of the material, he liked the production, writing: "What holds this particular production solidly together is the energy and verve of the cast, Salatino's choreography (so carefully crafted it seems spontaneous) and Troy Hourie's well-used, multi-level set. The moment when Angel ascends the stairway in the rear wall to eternity just on the other side is genuinely affecting. Dawn Chiang's lighting is often excitingly obtrusive, and Jessica Ford's costumes are appropriately grubby."

The cast included Jene Hernandez as Mimi, Ken Clark as Roger, Jose Sepulveda as Angel, Jordan Barbour as Collins, and Stanley Bahorek repeating the role of Mark, which he had previously played at the Engeman Theatre.

Theo Ubique Cabaret Theatre, Chicago, IL, 2016

This uniquely intimate production of *Rent*, presented in the show's twentieth anniversary year, became the toast of the (very discerning and demanding) Chicago theater community and press. It was presented in a space called the No Exit Café, which reminded at least one viewer of the Life Café, the real Alphabet City restaurant where the final scene of Act One takes place. Not only that, but the cast bonded with the audience before the show by serving them an (optional) meal of "Alphabet City Salad" and baked chili mac and cheese (suggested by the Life Café's menu).

Director Scott Weinstein, respected for his work with larger Chicago companies, devised an environmental staging on a set designed by Adam Veness that used the space's exposed pipes and brick walls, decorated with graffiti by numerous local street artists. According to Colin Douglas in Chicagotheatrereview.com: "[The show] explodes all over the tiny No Exit Café. Down the center aisle, on an elevated platform and on petite playing areas perched all over the theatre, Scott Weinstein has staged his story so close to theatergoers that we can almost feel the heat of their passion." The

From left: Jaymes Osborne (Benny), Savannah Quinn Hoover (Mimi), Courtney Jones (Maureen), Matt Edmonds (Mark), and Patrick Rooney (Roger) in Theo Ubique Cabaret Theatre's 2016 production of *Rent*.   *Adam Veness*

interpretation was compared to the equally intimate but darker and bleaker version by the American Theatre Company, another small Chicago theatre, that had been much discussed and highly praised four years earlier (see above). Theo Ubique's take, featuring a cast of up-and-coming young musical theater actors, was more focused on musical values.

Kris Vire of *Time Out Chicago*, while acknowledging that some of the lyrics were drowned out (a common problem in productions of the show in intimate spaces that don't use amplification), mentioned that the show featured "at its center, via Jeremy Ramey's resonant music direction, a 'Seasons of Love' rendered in gorgeous and all-natural surround sound." Kelly Kleiman of the website Duelingcritics.net found the show to be "flawlessly cast," adding: "Aubrey McGrath deserves a special acknowledgment: he plays drag-queen Angel, a part written for a Latino actor, with such life-giving energy that any and all prejudices—for or against drag queens; for or against casting against ethnic type—simply melt away." The unanimously praised non-Equity cast also included Matt Edmonds as Mark, Patrick Rooney as Roger, Savannah Quinn Hoover as Mimi, Courtney Jones as Maureen, Nicole Michelle Haskins as Joanne, Charles Benson as Collins, and Jaymes Osborne as Benny.

Hedy Weiss of the *Chicago Sun Times* pinpointed the appropriateness of the low-budget milieu: "There could be no better way to celebrate this show about aspiring artists living on the edge than to see it on the intimate stage of Theo Ubique Cabaret Theatre, where a cast of supremely talented young performers (who double as waiters) probably earn just enough to pay their mobile phone bills and their fare on the L."

The run sold out every performance and was extended—but then the planned extension was announced as cancelled: the rights had been withdrawn due to the announcement of the forthcoming twentieth-anniversary tour. However, original *Rent* producer Kevin McCollum, though not directly involved with the tour, intervened on Theo Ubique's behalf and persuaded the powers that be to let them do their extension: given the themes of the show—which McCollum has always understood instinctively—it seemed inappropriate and indeed ironic to let a small storefront theater's production be shut down by a large corporate one, and happily reason prevailed.

Town Hall Arts Center, Littleton, CO, 2010

Popular Denver-area actor/director Nick Sugar staged the musical for this suburban theater. The Arts Center, founded in 1982, is housed in a beautifully renovated 1920 building which originally was the actual Town Hall of the city of Littleton; the theater is on the second floor and seats 260 in an intimate three-quarter thrust configuration.

Reviewing the production for 303magazine.com, Noah Jordan praised the cast, especially the Maureen and Joanne: "Amanda Earls plays the confident, leather-clad, outspoken, flirtatious Maureen Johnson. She rouses the crowd with 'Over the Moon,' the performance art/protest number her character Maureen delivers. Ashlie-Amber Harris, who plays Maureen's lover Joanne Jefferson, brings power and a new spice to the role, this Joanne isn't the same one you saw years ago on Broadway, she's the 2010 edition. With Earls and Harris playing opposite each other, the two are a force to be reckoned with making 'Take Me or Leave Me' one of the strongest duets in the production." The cast also included Russell Mernagh as Roger, Anna Gibson as Mimi, Mark Lively as Mark, Ryan Belinak as Collins, Danny Harrington as Angel, and Matt LaFontaine as Benny. Donna Debreceni was the musical director.

Towson University, Towson, MD, 2011

Though several academic productions of the show have generated controversy, the dispute surrounding the version presented at Towson, a large Maryland university, was of a different sort. After the first preview performance, the Internet was abuzz with consternation over the way the last scene had been handled by the director, faculty member Diane Smith-Sadak. She had her own take on the apparent death/surprise recovery of Mimi—which has always been one of the more controversial moments in the show. Feeling that Mimi's sudden awakening wasn't ringing true in rehearsal, the director decided to try something more akin to the bleak, tragic denouement of *La bohème*. She took it upon herself to cut the lines about Mimi's recovery, moving from Roger's grief-stricken wailing over her body directly into the finale. According to theater blogger Jeff Linamen of Theatre from the Center Aisle, Smith-Sadak had said she wanted to leave the ending ambiguous and allow the audience to decide whether they believed Mimi lived or died, but "in the end, when Angel joined the cast for curtain call, she had him touch Mimi and she got up and joined the cast. Unless she changed something else in the script, Angel dies halfway through the second act." Such a staging choice could potentially be interpreted either as Angel's spirit greeting Mimi's and sending her back to the world of the living (akin to the original intention, as expressed in the lines that had been cut), or as acknowledging her death, with one "angel" welcoming another into heaven.

The issue was the deleted lines, as Music Theatre International (MTI), which licenses the show, provides a contract that clearly prohibits any cuts or changes to the script or score. Following the first preview performance, someone posted a comment about the production on the message board at Broadwayworld.com and started a heated thread. When the staff at MTI heard about it they issued a "cease and desist" order, informing the university that they had a choice: restore the cut lines or close the production. Smith-Sadak called an emergency rehearsal and the scene was performed as written on the official opening night; the director praised her young cast for their professionalism in handling the situation and learning and incorporating the changes quickly.

However, the controversy didn't end there. Smith-Sadak claimed that she had not seen the contract—though the language is standard for the licensing of any play or musical. She put a note in the production's program explaining that the version of *Rent* she had intended to present had been suppressed: "Like the characters in RENT who faced the ongoing struggle to create art in an increasingly corporate mindset and money-driven and fear-driven attitude, we in tonight's production came in and reworked our ending into what you will see tonight. The 'traditional' ending of RENT. We complied only under duress . . . Copyright law has its place, and playwrights have valid arguments about their work needing protection, but at what point do we take that inflexibility too far?" She reiterated her position in an open letter to *The Towerlight*, the university's online newspaper.

In response to all the controversy, and to clarify the situation for the theater community, MTI president Drew Cohen issued a statement, available on the company's website. It concluded: "This was not about commerce or fear or delegating responsibility to lawyers. This was about one person deciding that she could write a better show than the one that was licensed and opting to present it in violation of the performance license. Respectfully, that is simply not allowed."

The production's cast included Thomas Hedgpeth as Roger, Andrew Worthington as Mark, Nellie Glover as Mimi, Skye Pollard as Joanne, Nurney Mason as Angel, Anthony Conway as Collins, and Nina Kauffman as Maureen. Charlotte Evans was the musical director.

Trumbull High School, Trumbull, CT, 2014

One of several teen productions of *Rent* that have ignited controversy in their communities and were nearly shut down, this one received national media attention due to the efforts of a particularly committed and diplomatic student. Larissa Mark, then a senior at the public high school, was the president of the school's Thespian Society when drama teacher Jessica Spillane selected *Rent School Edition* as the spring musical. In November, before the show had been cast, the high school's principal, Marc Guarino, who was then in his first year at the school, announced that he was cancelling the production due to the "controversial and sensitive" nature of the material, which was deemed inappropriate for high school students. Larissa quickly organized a campaign to have the decision reversed, collecting 1,500 student signatures and circulating a survey via Facebook to find out how parents and other adults in the town of Trumbull felt about the show going on (97 percent of the respondents were in favor of it). She also attended a meeting of the Trumbull Board of Education, where she advocated in favor of the show and its relevance to current social issues.

As Mark eloquently expressed it to theater blogger Chris Luner of Luberontheatre.com: "*Rent* is a play of love and acceptance. We want to present that to our community. Trumbull is a place of love and acceptance despite all of what has happened and *Rent* is a reflection of this school and community. We just want to spread that message." She also expressed to her schoolmates the importance of being respectful of the principal and his point of view at all times; she defined her goals as collecting data for the administration's reconsideration, and led the campaign with civility and dignity.

At first Guarino held to his original decision, though various compromises were suggested, including an unsuccessful attempt to have the production adopted by the Trumbull Youth Association, a community theater group in the town, rather than produced by the high school. But Mark and her friends were persistent; after further discussion the principal was persuaded that the show could have a positive impact, but only if there could be an educational component devised to address the controversial topics in the script and foster constructive discussion. In order to provide time to prepare the requisite educational materials, he suggested postponing the production to late April or May, but due to other school events and exam schedules many students would not have been able to participate if that had happened, and parents protested.

The controversy became a national issue, with emotional online debate and widespread media attention. The professional theater community rallied around the students, as did the family and friends of Jonathan Larson, and the Dramatists Legal Defense Fund (DLDF) enlisted Dramatists Guild president Scott Schwartz (whose many directing credits included the 2001 Off-Broadway production of Larson's *tick, tick . . . BOOM!*) to write a letter to Guarino. Finally, in mid-December, following a contentious school board meeting at which parents and students pushed to have the original dates reinstated, Guarino met with the Thespian troupe and told them he was relenting and would allow the show to proceed: it would open the last week in March as originally intended, with Mark as stage manager and assistant director. As Guarino told Patrick Healy of the *New York Times*: "We've worked diligently to get this all worked out, and the students have been awesome, with a lot of great ideas about ways to have a wider conversation about the issues raised in the show." After the decision was announced, Julie Larson posted on Trumbull for Rent, the show's Facebook page: "Congratulations to all of you. Thank you for your passion, dedication and activism and for your understanding of the broader messages contained in *Rent*. My brother, Jonathan, would be extremely proud of all your efforts and your deep desire to perform his work."

In February, while the production was still in rehearsal, Larissa Mark was honored for her efforts on behalf of the show with the first-ever DLDF Defender Award, presented to her at the Dramatists Guild's annual awards ceremony at the Lambs Club in New York City. Jessica Spillane directed the production, with veteran Broadway actor Jerold Goldstein as musical director; the student cast included Michael Ell, a senior with substantial professional acting experience, as Mark, Zac Gottschall as Roger, Ava Gallo as Mimi, Matt Buckwald as Angel, Michael LePore as Collins, Emily Ruchalski as Maureen, Casey Walsh as Joanne, and Daniel Satter as Benny.

University of Michigan School of Music, Ann Arbor, MI, 2008

With one of the largest and most competitive musical theater training programs in the country, the University of Michigan boasts numerous alumni working on Broadway; graduates include *Rent* producer Jeffrey Seller and original cast member Gilles Chiasson. The university's School of Music presented one of the first licensed college productions of the show in their Lydia Mendelssohn Theatre, opening just six weeks after the closing of the Broadway production.

The cast was made up of students in the BFA Musical Theatre program, and the director was faculty member Mark Madama. In his program note, Madama recalled living in New York City himself during the time the show takes place: "I lived in a building featured on the cover of *New York* magazine captioned as a 'Westside apartment building longtime famous for drugs, prostitution and white slavery.' I, like any youth, found joy and excitement in these times and the horrors of the present were only a part of the city's social landscape. Working on Rent surprised me with memories both good and bad, brought up anger and sadness and sorted out many mysteries of my past."

The musical director was Cynthia Kortman Westphal. As is typical with U of M productions, several of the cast members have already gone on to big things. Ashley Blanchet (Mimi) has performed in the Broadway companies of *Memphis, Beautiful,* and the revival of *Annie.* Cary Tedder (Mark) has been in several Broadway shows, including playing the role of Dick in the 2015 Broadway premiere of *Dames at Sea,* and appeared as both Snowboy and Tony in the first national tour of the revival of *West Side Story;* he is also well known as a New York dance teacher. Kent Overshown (Collins) did the national tours of *The Gershwins' Porgy and Bess* and *Memphis.* Mark Ayesh (Roger) would go on to recreate his role in *Rent* at the Westchester Broadway Theatre (see below), and Corbin Reid would reprise her Joanne in the original cast of the 2011 Off-Broadway revival.

Wagner College, Staten Island, NY, 2013

Wagner College's production of *Rent* was a homecoming of sorts for the show: Some twenty years earlier, Jonathan Larson had submitted a cassette tape of an early draft of the musical to the college's annual Stanley Drama Award competition; he won the award, which came with a check for $1,000. Wagner has long had a reputation as an outstanding undergrad theater program, with an emphasis on musical theater.

The director of this production was the Tony-winning actress Michelle Pawk, an Associate Professor in the Theatre Department; coincidentally, she is also the former wife of original *Rent* producer Kevin McCollum. In an interview with Michael J. Fressola for the website Silive.com, she said: "I think what is really important is that, even though it is now more of a period piece, the ideas that are written about so beautifully in this play are still important. It's about love, life and not wasting a second, because 'you have no day like today.'"

The student cast numbered seventeen (two more than on Broadway) and featured Olivia Puckett as Mimi, Alex Boniello as Mark, Robby Haltiwanger as Roger, Anthony Colasuonno as Angel, Jenny Kelly as Joanne, Dave Resultan as Collins, Justin Stevens as Benny, and Melanie Brook as Maureen. Senior Anthony Freitas designed the set, and Ashley Delane Burger, a recent grad, did the choreography; Brandon Sturiale was the musical director.

Westchester Broadway Theatre, Elmsford, NY, 2010

The 449-seat facility, which opened in 1991 with a production of *A Chorus Line*, has a thrust configuration: the audience is seated at tables on tiered levels on three sides of the large stage. There's something appropriate, if somehow ironic, about *Rent* making an appearance at a dinner theater in affluent, suburban Westchester County, as Jonathan Larson himself grew up in White Plains but left to pursue the life of a struggling composer in the big city.

The implications were not lost on Marisa LaScala, who reviewed the production for *Westchester* magazine: "Sure, it's all about living a gritty, artist's life in New York City, but the musical *Rent* is just as much about the suburbs as it is about the city—at least in subtext . . . It doesn't seem like a loving portrayal of the suburbs—that they're a shameful part of one's past that must be repressed at all costs. But I don't really see it that way. I see it as Larson saying that once you grow up in the suburbs, they'll always be a part of you (no matter how hard you try to deny it)."

Whether or not it was a concession to conservative suburban sensibilities, this version was one of the only professional productions on record to omit the highly sexual "Contact"—the number officially deleted from the "School Edition" of the show. Tom Holehan, reviewing for the Connecticut Post Chronicle, was enthusiastic: "This soulful rock fable . . . is just as dynamic as ever in a polished, first-rate revival currently at the Westchester Broadway Theatre. It may even rival its Broadway predecessor . . . Boldly directed and choreographed by Patricia Wilcox, this 'Rent' sizzles with energy and emotion. The casting is so evenly balanced—there's not a weak link in the crew—that all the stories seem to carry equal weight and importance."

The cast included Mark Ayesh as Roger, Andy Kelso as Mark, Angelo Rios as Tom Collins, Steena Hernandez as Mimi, Justin Senense as Angel, Sara Ruzicka as Maureen, Gabrielle Reid as Joanne, and Justin Keyes as Benny. The musical director was Christopher McGovern.

Yale Dramatic Association, New Haven, CT, 2010

The Dramatic Association, known informally as the Yale Dramat, is the longstanding student-run theater company at the Ivy League university. Though undergrad students produce the plays and make up the casts, they often hire professional New York directors, and sometimes designers, to helm the major productions. The group's *Rent* was directed by Mike Donahue, an up-and-coming young director who had graduated from the Yale School of Drama's MFA Directing Program two years earlier. In his program notes Donahue said: "I am not interested in reproducing a facsimile of the original production. But I am equally uninterested in entirely deconstructing the piece. For me, it's about finding the right balance between the familiar and the new, about honoring it while breathing new life into it. . . . *Rent* is a show about hope. About not dwelling in fear, but seizing the moment, because you never know what's coming next. It's about the power of love and human connection to overcome the greatest fears."

One of his main goals was to give the show a feeling of immediacy and event by breaking down the fourth wall and creating the sense that cast and audience were all in the room together. The set, made up mainly of tall metal lighting towers and large black-painted crates, looked like a stage for a rock concert; the concert atmosphere was taken a step further by having the singers all hold hand microphones. In "Over the Moon," several of the leading characters, including Mark with his camera, took places in the back of the house to watch Maureen's show; Sarah Cohen as Maureen performed it in an oversized, white, man's dress shirt, black boots, and panties. Backed up by three female vocalists who also mimed comedic business behind her, she moved through the theater's center aisle and spoke directly to individual audience members; the cast in the house contributed to egging the spectators on to an enthusiastic and extended communal mooing session at the end of the number.

Based on the available student population, the cast was less ethnically diverse than usual, but the production was notable for including Matthew McCollum among the cast. A Yale undergrad at the time, the young actor, who played Benny, is Jonathan Larson's nephew; he has since gone on to earn his MFA in Acting at Yale, and is now continuing the family legacy by writing his own musicals. Castmate Liz Dervan went to law school after graduating and is now an attorney—just like Joanne, the character she played in the show. The cast also included Devon Martinez as Mimi, Miles Jacoby as Roger, Sam Bolen as Mark, Scott Hillier as Collins, and Sam Tsui as Angel. Martha Burson was the student producer.

Appendix One
Rent Timeline

Chronological List of Major Events in the History of the Show

February 1, 1896   World premiere of Giacomo Puccini's *La bohème* at the Teatro Regio, Turin, Italy

February 4, 1960   Jonathan Larson born in Mt. Vernon, New York

June 17, 1993   First reading of *Rent* at New York Theatre Workshop

October 29, 1994   Opening of studio production (eight performances) at New York Theatre Workshop

December 18, 1995   Peasant's Feast for the newly-hired Off-Broadway cast at Larson's home

December 19, 1995   First rehearsal for the Off-Broadway production

January 25, 1996   Death of Jonathan Larson, aged thirty-five, on the date of what would have been the show's first Off-Broadway preview performance. That evening, the cast sings through the show for Larson's family and friends.

January 26, 1996   First public preview Off-Broadway at New York Theatre Workshop

February 3, 1996   Memorial service for Larson at the Minetta Lane Theatre

February 13, 1996   Off-Broadway opening night

April 1, 1996   Last performance at NYTW

April 9, 1996   Jonathan Larson's *Rent* wins the Pulitzer Prize for Drama

April 16, 1996   First preview on Broadway at the Nederlander Theatre

April 29, 1996   Broadway opening night

June 2, 1996   *Rent* wins four awards at the fiftieth annual Tony Awards

August 26, 1996   Cast performs "Seasons of Love" at the Democratic National Convention

August 27, 1996   Release of the original cast recording on DreamWorks Records

November 18, 1996   The first national company, known as the "Angel Tour," begins performances at the Shubert Theatre in Boston

July 1, 1997   The second touring company, known as the "Benny Tour," begins performances at the La Jolla Playhouse in San Diego

May 12, 1998   West End production opens at the Shaftesbury Theatre, London

October 30, 1999	Closing performance in London
May 23, 2001	Premiere of *tick, tick . . . BOOM!* at the Jane Street Theatre
March 14, 2005	Filming begins on the movie version of *Rent*
June 27, 2005	Final day of filming
September 23, 2005	Release of the soundtrack album
November 23, 2005	Release of the movie of *Rent*, directed by Chris Columbus
April 24, 2006	Tenth anniversary concert performance at the Nederlander, reuniting the original cast
September 7, 2008	Closing performance of the Broadway run
July 14, 2011	First preview of the Off-Broadway revival of *Rent*
August 10, 2011	Off-Broadway revival opens at New World Stages
September 9, 2012	Off-Broadway production closes at New World Stages
October 20, 2016	Off-Broadway revival of *tick, tick . . . BOOM!* opens on Theatre Row

Appendix Two
Cast List
(with All Replacements)
for Original Broadway
Production, 1996-2008

(Many actors alternated in and out of the show several times; they are listed in the order in which they first took over the role.)

Role	Original Actor	Replacements	
Roger	Adam Pascal	Norbert Leo Butz Richard H. Blake Luther Creek Manley Pope Dean Balkwill Sebastian Arcelus	Ryan Link Jeremy Kushnier Cary Shields Tim Howar Declan Bennett Will Chase*
Mark	Anthony Rapp	Jim Poulos Christian Anderson Trey Ellett Matt Caplan Joey Fatone	Drew Lachey Christopher J. Hanke Harley Jay Adam Kantor*
Collins	Jesse L. Martin	Michael McElroy* Rufus Bonds Jr. Alan Mingo Jr. Mark Leroy Jackson	Mark Richard Ford Destan Owens Troy Horne
Benny	Taye Diggs	Jacques C. Smith Stu James	D'Monroe Rodney Hicks*
Joanne	Fredi Walker	Shelley Dickinson Gwen Stewart Alia León Kenna J. Ramsey Danielle Lee Greaves Natalie Venetia Belcon	Myiia Watson-Davis Merle Dandridge Nicole Lewis Tonya Dixon Tracie Thoms*

continued

Role	Original Actor	Replacements	
Angel	Wilson Jermaine Heredia	Wilson Cruz Shaun Earl Jose Llana	Jai Rodriguez Andy Señor Justin Johnston*
Mimi	Daphne Rubin-Vega	Marcy Harriell Krysten Cummings Maya Days Loraine Velez Karmine Alers Krystal L. Washington	Melanie Brown Antonique Smith Jaime Lee Kirchner Tamyra Gray Renée Elise Goldsberry*
Maureen	Idina Menzel	Sherie Rene Scott Kristen Lee Kelly Carla Bianco Jessica Boevers Tamara Podemski Cristina Fadale	Maggie Benjamin Kelly Karbacz Ava Gaudet Nicolette Hart Caren Lyn Manuel Eden Espinoza*
Mark's Mom/Alison/ Others	Kristen Lee Kelly	Jessica Boevers Tamara Podemski Carly Thomas Maggie Benjamin Kendra Kassebaum Haven Burton	Jodi Carmeli Amy Ehrlich Tracey Langran Caren Lyn Manuel Tracy McDowell*
Christmas Caroler/ Mr. Jefferson/ Pastor/Others	Byron Utley	Marcus Paul James* Destan Owens Todd E. Pettiford	
Mrs. Jefferson/ Woman with Bags/ Others	Gwen Stewart*	Shelley Dickinson Aisha de Haas Maia Nkenge Wilson	Catrice Joseph Frenchie Davis Trisha Jeffrey
Gordon/The Man/ Mr. Grey/Others	Timothy Britten Parker	Mark Setlock Chad Richardson Colin Hanlon Peter Matthew Smith	Luther Creek Matt Caplan Jay Wilkison* Kyle Post
Steve/Man with Squeegee/Waiter/ Others	Gilles Chiasson	Will Chase Matthew Murphy Owen Johnston II Robin De Jesús Scott Hunt	Justin Johnston Enrico Rodriguez Andy Señor Telly Leung*
Paul/Cop/Others	Rodney Hicks	Darryl Ordell Leslie Odom Jr. Robert Glean	Nick Sanchez Shaun Earl*
Alexi Darling/ Roger's Mom/ Others	Aiko Nakasone	Tina Ou Kim Varhola Mayumi Ando Sala Iwamatsu	T. V. Carpio Yuka Takara Andrea Goss*

*Denotes final company/closing night cast, September 8, 2008

Appendix Three
Opening Cast Lists for Touring and International Productions, 1996-1998

Role	Angel Tour Boston, 11/96	Benny Tour La Jolla, 7/97	Collins Tour Toronto, 12/97	Original London Cast, 5/98
Roger	Sean Keller	Christian Mena	Luther Creek	Adam Pascal
Mark	Luther Creek	Neil Patrick Harris	Chad Richardson	Anthony Rapp
Collins	C. C. Brown	Mark Leroy Jackson	Danny Blanco	Jesse L. Martin
Benny	James Rich	D'Monroe	Damian Perkins	Bonny Lockhart
Joanne	Sylvia MacCalla	Kenna J. Ramsey	Karen LeBlanc	Jacqui Dubois
Angel	Stephan Alexander	Wilson Cruz	Jai Rodriguez	Wilson Jermaine Heredia
Mimi	Simone	Julia Santana	Krysten Cummings	Krysten Cummings
Maureen	Carrie Hamilton	Leigh Hetherington	Jennifer Aubry	Jessica Terzier
Mark's mom, others	Amy Spanger	Carla Bianco	Tamara Podemski	Angela Bradley
Christmas caroler, others	John Eric Parker	Kevin "Kye" Brackett	David St. Louis	Mykal Rand
Mrs. Jefferson, others	Queen Esther	Sharon Brown	Divine Brown	Rachel McFarlane
Gordon, others	Christian Anderson	Curt Skinner	Dean Balkwill	Josh Cohen
Steve, others	Lambert Moss	Andy Señor	Gavin Hope	Robert J. Solomon
Paul, others	D'Monroe	Brent Davin Vance	Thom Allison	Leon-Maurice Jones
Alexi Darling, others	Julie Danao-Salkin	Sala Iwamatsu	Tricia Young	Claire Coates
Directed by	*Michael Greif*	*Michael Greif*	*Michael Greif*	*Michael Greif*

Appendix Four
Opening Cast Lists for Tours and Revivals, 2001–2016

Role	OnTour, LLC Non-Equity Tour, 2001	Mark Tour, 2009	New World Stages Off-Broadway Revival, 2011	Twentieth Anniversary Non-Equity Tour, 2016
Roger	Kevin Spencer	Adam Pascal	Matt Shingledecker	Kaleb Wells
Mark	Dominic Bogart	Anthony Rapp	Adam Chanler-Berat	Danny Harris Kornfeld
Collins	Bruce Wilson Jr.	Michael McElroy	Nicholas Christopher	Aaron Harrington
Benny	Matthew Morgan	Jacques C. Smith	Ephraim M. Sykes	Christian Thompson
Joanne	Bridget Mohammed	Haneefah Wood	Corbin Reid	Jasmine Easler
Angel	Justin Rodriguez	Justin Johnston	Michael Rodriguez	David Merino
Mimi	Krystal Washington	Lexi Lawson	Arianda Fernandez	Skyler Volpe
Maureen	Sara Schatz	Nicolette Hart	Annaleigh Ashford	Katie LaMark
Mark's mom, others	Clark Mims	Caren Lyn Manuel	Morgan Weed	Natalie Lipin
Christmas caroler, others	Brandon L. Pearson	Toby Blackwell	Marcus Paul James	John Devereaux
Mrs. Jefferson, others	Haneefah Wood	Gwen Stewart	Tamika Sonja Lawrence	Alia Hodge
Gordon, others	Jay Wilkison	Adam Halpin	N/A	Sammy Ferber
Steve, others	Cole McClendon	Telly Leung	Michael Wartella	Jordan Long
Paul, others	Damien DeShaun Smith	Andy Señor	Ben Thompson	Timothy McNeill
Alexi Darling, others	Jackie Maraya	Yuka Takara	Margot Bingham	Futaba Shioda
Directed by	*Michael Greif*	*Michael Greif*	*Michael Greif*	*Evan Ensign*

(Tables compiled with data from *Theatre World*, *The Best Plays*, ibdb.com, Ovrtur.com, and production Playbills.)

Bibliography

Books

Asch, Amy. *Jonathan Larson: A Guide to His Songs, Shows & Scores*. New York: Finster & Lucy Music, Ltd., 2001.

Benstock, Shari. *Women on the Left Bank: Paris 1900–1940*. Austin: University of Texas Press, 1987.

Bloom, Ken. *Show & Tell: The New Book of Broadway Anecdotes*. New York: Oxford University Press, 2016.

Chbosky, Stephen. *The Perks of Being a Wallflower*. New York: Gallery Books, 1999.

Coenen, Margaux. *That Doesn't Remind Us of 'Musetta's Waltz'- An Analysis of the Adaptation from the Opera La Bohème to the Broadway Musical Rent to the Film Musical Rent*. Master's thesis,Vrije University, Brussels, Belgium, 2010.

Gruber, Paul (editor). *The Metropolitan Opera Guide to Recorded Opera*. New York: W. W. Norton & Company, 1993.

Gruber, Paul (editor). *The Metropolitan Opera Guide to Opera on Video*. New York: W. W. Norton & Company, 1997.

Guernsey Jr., Otis L. (editor). *The Best Plays of 1994–1995* through *1999–2000*. New York: Limelight Editions, 1995–2000.

Herrington, Joan (editor). *The Playwright's Muse*. New York: Routledge, 2002.

Hodges, Ben and Scott Denny (editors). *Theatre World Volume 68 (2011–12)*. Milwaukee: Applause Theatre & Cinema Books, 2013.

Hodges, Drew. *On Broadway: From Rent to Revolution*. New York: Rizzoli, 2016.

Jenkins, Jeffrey Eric (editor). *The Best Plays Theater Yearbook 2000–2001* through *2007–2008*. New York: Limelight Editions, 2001–2009.

Kenrick, John. *Musical Theatre: A History*. New York: Bloomsbury Academic, 2010.

Larson, Jonathan. *Rent by Jonathan Larson*. Interviews and text by Evelyn McDonnell with Katherine Silberger. New York: Rob Weisbach Books, 1997.

Larson, Jonathan. *Rent: The Complete Book and Lyrics of the Broadway Musical*. New York: Applause Theatre & Cinema Books, 2008.

Larson, Jonathan. *tick, tick . . . BOOM!: The Complete Book and Lyrics*. New York: Applause Theatre & Cinema Books, 2009.

Lipsky, David. *The Creation of Rent*. Booklet distributed at the Nederlander Theatre, 1996.

Mordden, Ethan. *The Happiest Corpse I've Ever Seen: The Last 25 Years of the Broadway Musical*. New York: Palgrave Macmillan, 2004.

Puccini, Giacomo, with libretto by Giuseppe Giacosa and Luigi Illica. *The Metropolitan Opera Presents Giacomo Puccini's La Bohème: Libretto, Background, and Photos*. Milwaukee: Amadeus Press, 2014.

Rapp, Anthony. *Without You: A Memoir of Love, Loss, and the Musical Rent*. New York: Simon & Schuster, 2006.

Simon, John. *John Simon on Theater: Criticism, 1974–2003*. New York: Applause Theatre & Cinema Books, 2005.

Singer, Barry. *Ever After: The Last Years of Musical Theater and Beyond*. New York: Applause Theatre & Cinema Books, 2004.

Stempel, Larry. *Showtime: A History of the Broadway Musical Theater*. New York: W. W. Norton & Company, 2010.

Viagas, Robert and Louis Botto. *At This Theatre: 110 Years of Broadway Shows, Stories & Stars*. New York: Applause Theatre & Cinema Books, 2010

Viertel, Jack. *The Secret Life of the American Musical: How Broadway Shows Are Built*. New York: Farrar, Straus and Giroux, 2016.

Wexman, Virginia Wright. *A History of Film*. Boston: Pearson, 2006.

Willis, John and Ben Hodges (editors). *Theatre World Volume 52 (1995–1996)* through *Volume 65 (2008–2009)*. New York: Applause Theatre & Cinema Books, 1996-2010.

Articles

Andryshak, Kathryn. "Center Stage: Review of *Rent*." *Ithaca Times*, August 12, 2009.

Anonymous. "No Rest for the Parents of the Parent of 'Rent.'" *New York Times*, June 12, 2001.

Aucoin, Don. "Recession-era 'Rent' is Even More Relevant." *Boston Globe*, September 10, 2011.

Benedict, David. "How the Wild West End Will Be Won." *Independent*, May 5, 1998.

Benedict, David. "'Rent' Review." *Independent*, May 13, 1998.

Berson, Misha. "Theatre Review: 'Rent' Holds Up Well in Tour at Paramount, With Refreshed Staging, Impressive Music." *Seattle Times*, June 17, 2009.

Billington, Michael. "Theatre Review: Rent." *Guardian*, October 16, 2017.

Blumenthal, Ralph. "Calling All Unsung Superstars: 'Rent' Needs Singers." *New York Times*, July 13, 1996.

Boyle, Christina. "NYC Nightclub Legend Don Hill, Owner of Cat Club and Don Hill's, Dead at 66." *New York Daily News*, April 2, 2011.

Brantley, Ben. "Soul-Searching at the Milestone Age of 30." *New York Times*, June 14, 2001.

Brantley, Ben. "That Ragtag Bohemian Army Returns." *New York Times*, August 11, 2011.

Brantley, Ben. "Theatre Review: Enter Singing: Young, Hopeful and Taking on the Big Time." *New York Times*, April 30, 1996.

Brantley, Ben. "Theatre Review: 'J.P. Morgan' and Some Heavy Site-Specificity." *New York Times*, June 16, 1995.

Brantley, Ben. "Theatre Review: Rock Opera a la 'Boheme' and 'Hair.' *New York Times*, February 14, 1996.

Brustein, Robert. "The New Bohemians." *New Republic*, April 22, 1996.

Butler, Robert. "'Rent' Review." *Independent on Sunday*, May 17, 1998.

Clapp, Susannah. "'Rent' Review." *Observer*, May 17, 1998.

Czaplinski, Kate. "Larissa Mark to be Honored as 'Defender' of School Musical." *Trumbull Times*, February 20, 2014.

de Jongh, Nicholas. "'Rent' Review." *Evening Standard*, March 13, 1998.

Dziemianowicz, Joe. "'Rent' Review: Classic Broadway Production Has All the Talent of Original, But Less Emotional Pull." *New York Daily News*, August 12, 2011.

Edwardes, Jane. "'Rent' Review." *Time Out London*, May 20, 1998.

Edwards, Sharon Kay. "'Rent' in Twain: Division in a Small Town." *Huffington Post*, July 6, 2015.

Eller, Claudia. "Long Journey Made 'Rent' Overdue." *Chicago Tribune*, November 29, 2005.

Elliott, Jonathan. "Review: 'Rent.'" *U.S. 1 Newspaper*, May 16, 2012.

Erstein, Hap. "Boca Troupe Puts On Vivid, Uplifting Tale of Our Times." *Palm Beach Post*, April 17, 2015.

Fields-Meyer, Thomas. "The Wrong Call." *People*, February 24, 1997.

Fleming, Michael and Marc Graser. "'Rent' Rolls from WB to Revolution." *Variety*, September 30, 2004.

Fox, Margalit. "Maya Angelou, Lyrical Witness of the Jim Crow South, Dies at 86." *New York Times*, May 28, 2014.

Fricker, Karen. "Review: 'Rent Remixed.'" *Variety*, October 16, 2007.

Friedlander, Mira. "Review: 'Rent.'" *Variety*, January 4, 1998.

Friswold, Paul. "A Rent to Own: New Line Breathes New Life Into the Musical that Defined the '90s." *Riverfront Times*, March 13, 2014.

Gates, Anita. "Evoking Triumph and Tragedy in the '90s." *New York Times*, September 18, 2009.

Gerard, Jeremy. "Review: 'Rent.'" *Variety*, April 30, 1996.

Gertler, T. "The Pee-wee Perplex." *Rolling Stone*, February 12, 1987.

Gore-Langton, Robert. "'Rent' Review." *Express*, May 13, 1998.

Grimes, William. "'Rent' on the Road With a New Life, Beginning in Boston." *New York Times*, November 20, 1996.

Gritten, David. "Rent is Due But Will We Pay Up?" *Telegraph*, May 9, 1998.

Gross, Michael. "The Party Seems to be Over for Lower Manhattan Clubs." *New York Times*, October 26, 1985.

Gussow, Mel. "Jonathan Larson, 35, Composer of Rock Opera and Musicals." *New York Times*, January 26, 1996.

Healy, Patrick. "Connecticut High School Cancels Student Production of 'Rent.'" *New York Times*, December 4, 2013.

Healy, Patrick. "Connecticut School's Production of 'Rent' is Back On." *New York Times*, December 16, 2013.

Heriot, Brett. "SGFringe: 'Rent' Review." *ScotsGay*, August 27, 2015.

Hoffman, Barbara. "Village People—The Original Cast of 'Rent' Retells their NYC Story for the Movies." *New York Post*, November 20, 2005.

Holden, Stephen. "In 'Acoustically Speaking,' a 'Rent' Duo Returns." *New York Times*, October 11, 2016.

Holehan, Tom. "A Dynamic 'Rent' at Westchester Broadway Theatre." *Connecticut Post-Chronicle*, September 7, 2010.

Ickes, Bob. "Rent Decrease." *POZ*, October, 2008.

Isherwood, Charles. "The Aging of Aquarius." *New York Times*, September 16, 2007.

Isherwood, Charles. "A Creator and His Doubts." *New York Times*, June 24, 2014.

Isherwood, Charles. "525,600 Minutes to Preserve." *New York Times*, September 17, 2008.

Isherwood, Charles. "Review: 'Rent.'" *Variety*, July 15, 1997.

Isherwood, Charles. "Review: 'Rent.'" *Variety*, September 30, 1997.

Isherwood, Charles. "Review: 'Tick, Tick . . . BOOM!'" *Variety*, June 13, 2001.

Istel, John. "Jonathan Larson Talks About His Writing Process and Making 'Rent.'" *American Theatre*, July/August, 1996.

Istel, John. "'Rent' Check: Did Jonathan Larson's Vision Get Lost in the Media Uproar?" *American Theatre*, July/August, 1996.

Johnson, Malcolm. "Passions Charge 'Rent' at Boston's Shubert Theatre." *Hartford Courant*, November 20, 1996.

Kael, Pauline. "Last Tango in Paris." *New Yorker*, October 28, 1972.

Kiley, Brendan. "Theater Is an Inconvenient Business: An Interview with Kevin McCollum." *Stranger*, September 23, 2010.

La Gorce, Tammy. "Starting a New Season With Youthful Energy." *New York Times*, May 20, 2011.

Lahr, John. "Hello and Goodbye: Jonathan Larson's 'Rent' Tries to Update the Musical." *New Yorker*, February 19, 1996.

Lane, Jim. "Bohemian Rhapsody: Rent." *Sacramento News and Review*, November 24, 2005.

Lapczynski, Kelly. "'Rent' Opens Friday Amid Controversy." *Tullahoma News*, July 9, 2015.

LaScala, Marisa. "Rent at the Westchester Broadway Theatre." *Westchester*, August 2010.

Lipworth, Elaine. "Chris Columbus: My dad said, 'Don't do a job you hate.'" *Guardian*, April 26, 2013.

Marchese, Eric. "La Mirada delivers a slick 'Rent.'" *Orange County Register*, October 30, 2015.

Marchese, Eric. "'Rent' Worth the Price in Long Beach." *Orange County Register*, December 9, 2009.

Maxwell, Dominic. "Theatre: Rent at the St James Theatre, SW1." *London Times*, December 16, 2016.

McNulty, Charles. "Theatre Review: 'Rent' at the Hollywood Bowl." *Los Angeles Times*, August 8, 2010.

Milzoff, Rebecca. "Rent: The Oral History." *New York*, May 2, 2016.

Miranda, Lin-Manuel. "Pursuing the Muse Against the Clock." *New York Times*, June 19, 2014.

Mountford, Fiona. "Rent, Theatre Review: Female Stars Shine in this Onslaught of Music." *Evening Standard*, December 14, 2016.

Newmark, Judith. "New Line Gives 'Rent' Fresh Proportions." *St. Louis Post-Dispatch*, March 10, 2014.

Nicholson, Frances Baum. "McCoy Rigby's revival of the musical 'Rent' still resonates." *San Gabriel Valley Tribune*, October 27, 2015.

Nicholson, Joe, and Anne E. Kornblut. "State Faults Hospitals for 'Rent' Tragedy." *New York Daily News*, December 13, 1996.

Oliver, Myrna. "Carrie Hamilton, 38; Drug Fight Publicized." *Los Angeles Times*, January 21, 2002.

Otten, Ted. "Theater: 'Rent' at Oaklyn's Ritz Theatre." *Times of Trenton*, October 28, 2015.

Otterman, Sharon. "As 'Rent' Ends 12-Year Run, a Gathering of Fans Overflows With Emotion." *New York Times*, September 6, 2008.

Pacheco, Patrick. "Life, Death and 'Rent.'" *Los Angeles Times*, April 14, 1996.

Pacheco, Patrick. "Many Are Called But Few Will Be Chosen for 'Rent.'" *Los Angeles Times*, July 18, 1996.

Passy, Charles. "A Florida Treat: 'Rent' Exhilarates Despite Obstacles." *Palm Beach Post*, January 20, 2002.

Pastorek, Whitney. "'Rent' Review." *Entertainment Weekly*, August 7, 2010.

Pastorek, Whitney. "'Rent': The Cast Looks Back." *Entertainment Weekly*, April 10, 2008.

Peter, John. "'Rent' Review." *Sunday Times*, May 17, 1998.

Portantiere, Michael. "*Rent* Stabilization." *Playbill*, May, 1996.

Preston, Rohan. "Touring the Past in 'Rent' Revival." *Minneapolis Star Tribune*, March 24, 2009.

Reedy, R. Scott. "A Role for Anthony Rapp." *MetroWest Daily News*, June 29, 2016.

Rich, Frank. "Journal: East Village Story." *New York Times*, March 2, 1996.

Riedel, Michael. "Every Day a 'Rent' Party: Hardcore Fans of the Hit Musical Form a Squatters Camp at the Box Office." *New York Daily News*, March 3, 1997.

Robertson, Campbell. "Bohemia Takes Its Final Bows." *New York Times*, July 13, 2008.

Rooney, David. "Review: 'Rent.'" *Variety*, November 19, 2005.

Rosenfield, Wendy. "A Scrappy 'Rent' at Bristol Riverside Theatre." *Philadelphia Inquirer*, May 11, 2012.

Sadlouskos, Linda. "A School Version of 'Rent' Will Be Staged at Ridge High School." *Basking Ridge Patch*, January 2, 2011.

Saltz, Jerry. "Tower of Rabble: An Elegy for the City's Folk-Art Monumentalism." *New York*, May 25, 2008.

Schuessler, Jennifer. "Tale of the Floppy Disks: How Jonathan Larson Created 'Rent.'" *New York Times*, February 1, 2012.

Scott, A. O. "New Tenants in Tinseltown." *New York Times*, November 23, 2005.

Shaw, Punch. "Theater Review: 'Rent' at Casa Mañana." *Fort Worth Star-Telegram*, February 28, 2016.

Shenton, Mark. "Rent the Musical Review at St James Theatre, London—'Larson's rich melodies soar.'" *Stage*, December 13, 2016.

Sidman, Amanda P. "Space That Housed the Life Cafe, the Setting for 'Rent,' Is Itself Up for Rent, Ending an Era." *New York Daily News*, February 26, 2012.

Sierz, Alex. "'Rent' Review." *Tribune*, May 29, 1998.

Silk, Chris. "Review: Broadway Palm Signs a New Lease on Cool, Rocks Out with Fantastic 'Rent.'" *Naples Daily News*, April 13, 2011.

Sokolove, Michael. "The C.E.O. of 'Hamilton' Inc." *New York Times Magazine*, April 5, 2016.

Soloski, Alexis. "'Tick, Tick. . .Boom!' is Jonathan Larson's Run Up to 'Rent.'" *New York Times*, October 20, 2016.

Spencer, Charles. "Rent Rimixed: Unfair Punishment as Grunge Comes Clean." *Telegraph*, October 16, 2007.

Stein, Joshua David. "It Was the Hottest Club in Town. (And That Was Just the Bathroom). Memories of Area." *New York*, November 3, 2013.

Stetson, Nancy. "Rent comes to the Broadway Palm Dinner Theatre." *Fort Myers Florida Weekly*, April 6, 2011.

Suskin, Steven. "Review: 'Rent.'" *Variety*, August 11, 2011.

Taylor, Markland. "Review: 'Rent.'" *Variety*, November 30, 1996.

Tommasini, Anthony. "Another Season of Love: The Original Cast Reassembles for a 'Rent' Anniversary." *New York Times*, April 26, 2006.

Tommasini, Anthony. "A Composer's Death Echoes in His Musical." *New York Times*, February 11, 1996.

Tommasini, Anthony. "Like Opera Inspiring It, 'Rent' Is Set to Endure." *New York Times*, September 5, 2008.

Tommasini, Anthony. "The Seven-Year Odyssey That Led to 'Rent.'" *New York Times*, March 17, 1996.

Tommasini, Anthony. "Some Advice for 'Rent' From a Friend." *New York Times*, July 28, 2002.

Van Gelder, Lawrence. "On the Eve of a New Life, an Untimely Death." *New York Times*, December 13, 1996.

Vire, Kris. "A 'Rent' Resized Pays Off for Theo Ubique." *Time Out Chicago*, March 20, 2016.

Weinert-Kendt, Rob. "Those Magic Changes." *American Theatre*, July/August, 2014.

Weiss, Hedy. "A Winningly Authentic 'Rent' at Home in Theo Ubique's Storefront." *Chicago Sun Times*, March 16, 2016.

Zuckerman, Esther. "Michael Greif, Director, and Angela Wendt, Costume Designer, Revisit *Rent*." *The Village Voice*, July 29, 2011.

Websites

http://ctarts.blogspot.com

http://dramaturgyforrent.blogspot.com/

http://ny.racked.com

http://theatrecenteraisle.blogspot.com

http://thecolumnonline.com

http://vergecampus.com

www.angelfire.com/mn/angeltour

www.angelfire.com/in2/everythingisrent

www.billyaronson.com

www.broadway.com

www.broadwayworld.com

www.chicagotheatrereview.com

www.duelingcritics.net

www.everythingmusicals.com

www.facebook.com

www.floridatheateronstage.com

www.ibdb.com

www.ign.com

www.imdb.com

www.lansingcitypulse.com

www.lifecafe.com

www.lunerontheatre.com

www.merriam-webster.com

www.mtishows.com/rent

www.northwestmilitary.com

www.playbill.com

www.silive.com

www.stagescenela.com

www.talkinbroadway.com

www.theaterjones.com

www.thsmusicals.com

www.vulture.com

www.wikipedia.com

Index

Page numbers in italics refer to illustrations.

*NSYNC, 228
½ MT House, 292, 296
1492 Pictures, 200, 202
1776, 2
1900, 248
1984, 7
20/20, 118
20th Century Fox, 200
24, 117
30 Rock, 246
30/90, 8–9, 293
39 Steps, The, 282
4'3", 251
40 Acres and a Mule Filmworks, 269–70
5th Floor Theatre Company, 318–19
8BC, 258–59
98 Degrees, 228
983, 272

ABBA, xx
Abeles, Daniel, 303
About Face Theatre, 311–12
Abyssinia, 116
Academy Awards, 102, 109, 196, 201, 205, 245–46, 248, 258, 267, 269, 270
Accidental Activist: A Personal and Political Memoir, 260
ACT UP, 242–43, 283, 313, 326
Acting Company, The, 106
Actors Equity Association, 16, 183–84
Actors Theatre of Louisville, 106
Actors' Shakespeare Project, 330
Adams, Kevin, 283
Adams, Lee, xviii
Adelphi University, 3, 5

Adirondack Theatre Festival, 101
Adventures in Babysitting, 113, 201
after the quake, 110
After the Rain, 105
Against Interpretation, 277
Agard, Alex, 312
Agnes of God, 63
Aguilera, Christina, 204
Ahmanson Theatre, 180
Aida, 109, 111
AIDS and HIV, xi, xx, xxi, xxii, 13–14, 18, 33, 34, 35, 37, 43, 45, 50, 53, 67, 72, 75, 77, 78, 79, 80, 91–92, 122, 125, 126, 127, 137, 142, 148, 199, 211, 217–18, 235–36, 242–43, 274, 277, 285, 287, 293, 302, 325–26, 328, 332, 334, 339
AIDS and its Metaphors, 278
Ailey, Alvin, 244
Ain't Misbehavin', 116
Albanese, Licia, 39
Albee, Edward, 263
Albis, Theron, 105
Alers, Karmine, 315, 354
Alers, Yassmin, 12, 82, 323–24
Alessandrini, Gerard, 300–1
Alexander, Christina, 337
Alexander, Stephan, 178, 355
Alfano, Franco, 22
Alfred P. Murrah Federal Building, 217
Alhadeff, Andi, 318
Alice in Bed, 277
All Shook Up, 117
Allan S. Gordon Foundation, 62
Alleluia! The Devil's Carnival, 112
Allen, Robert, 332–33
Allen, Steve, 250

Allende, Salvador, 273
Allison, Thom, 355
Ally McBeal, 102, 106
Alvarez, Julian, 313
Amahl and the Night Visitors, 332
"Amazing Grace," 86
Ambrosino, John, 330
American Academy of Arts and
    Letters, 50
American Dance Festival, 66
American Festival of Theatre and
    Dance, 66
American Idiot, 210, 317, 340
American Idol, 204, 228, 286, 328, 340
American Music Theatre Festival, 66
American Passenger, 105
American Primitive, 112
American Theatre Company, 311–12,
    342
American Theatre Wing, 281, 307
Amnesty International, 209
Ancis, Joe, 250
Anderson, Christian, *177*, 179, 353, 355
Anderson, Judith, 143
Anderson, Laurie, 56, 73
Anderson, Steve, 190
Ando, Mayumi, 354
Andrews, Julie, 153–54
Angel Tour, xii, *175*, 175–79, *177*, 355
Angelou, Maya, 244
Angels in America, 64, 287
Anna in the Tropics, 115
Annie, 196, 200, 207, 347
"Another Day," 55, 89, 127, 141, 219,
    240
Antonioni, Michelangelo, 245, *247*
Anyone Can Whistle, 276
Anything Goes, xxi
Apollinaire, Guillaume, 278
Apollo of Bellac, The, 105
Apollo Theatre, 104
Arcelus, Sebastian, 353
Archer, Devin, 327, *327*
Arden, Elizabeth, 64
Area, 252–53
Arena Stage, 47, 63, 106, 161
Aristophanes, 166
Arlen, Harold, 256

Armstrong, David Glenn, 3, 7, 292
Aronson, Anna, 45
Aronson, Billy, 13, 20, 42–46, *43*, 55, 58
Aronson, Jake, 45
Arsenal Center for the Arts, 330
Art Room, The, 46
Artz, Travis, *31*, *133*, 321
As If, 207
ASCAP, 5–6, 7, 8
Asch, Amy, 305–6
Ash Wednesday, 208
Ashford & Simpson, 244
Ashford, Annaleigh, 283–84, *284*,
    287–89, 357
Ashley, Christopher, 240
Ask the Dust, 109
Askins, Robert, 61
Association of Press Agents and
    Managers, 176
Association, The, 257
Astin, Skylar, 322
Aubry, Jennifer, 355
Auburn, David, 293–95, 299
Audition, 166
Australian Opera, 41
Author's Voice, The, xiii
Autobiography of Alice B. Toklas, The, 279
Autore, Steve, 339
Avengers, The, 249
Aventura Arts and Cultural Center,
    337
Avenue Q, xiv, 60, 61, 282, 287, 337
Avenue X, 116
Awakenings, 117
Away We Go!, 12, 54
Ayesh, Mark, 347, 349
Azenberg, Karen, 333–34

Babbitt, Milton, 276
Bacharach, Burt, 255–56
Backes, Mike, 326
Backyardigans, The, 112
Bacon, Brian, 337
Bacon, Kevin, 115
Badgley, Penn, 240
Baez, Joan, 257
Baggage Claim, 102
Baher, Peggy, 166

Bahorek, Stanley, 326, 341
Bailey, Mark, 192
Bailey, William, 314
Baker, Keith, 313
Baker, William, 190–91, 192
Baldwin, Alec, 246
Baldwin, Ireland, 246
Baldwin, James, 280
Balkwill, Dean, 353, 355
Baltimore Center Stage, 63, 207
Bandwagon, 207
Banshee, 104
Barbour, Jordan, 341
Barker, Cheryl, 41
Barn Theatre, 4
Barnathan, Michael, 200
Barnhouse, Mark, xii
Barry, Julian, 250
Barry, Lynda, 280
Barrymore Awards, 105
Barrymore, Lionel, 267
Bart, Roger, 44
Basinger, Kim, 246
Basquiat, Jean-Michel, 253
Bat Boy, 337
Batman, 134
Batman Returns, 265
Batt, Bryan, 300–1
Battle Beyond the Stars, 269
Baum, L. Frank, 256, 281
Bay Street Theatre, 60
Bay, Michael, 197
BBC World News America, 268
Beals, Greg, 6
Beals, Jennifer, 6
Beat Hotel, 261
Beatles, The, 1
Beautiful, 347
Beautiful Mind, A, 114
Beauty and the Beast, 192, 199, 300
Beetlejuice, 246
Before the Revolution, 248
Being and Time, 264
Belasco Theatre, 102
Belasco, David, 22, 324
Belber, Stephen, 105
Belcon, Natalie Venetia, xiv, 353
Belinak, Ryan, 343

Bell, Mackenzie, 315
Benacková, Gabriela, *31*
Bender, Jen, 340
Benedict, Logan, 317
Benefactor, The, 277
Bengal Tiger at the Baghdad Zoo, 61
Benjamin, Maggie, 354
Bennett, Declan, 353
Bennett, Michael, xix, xx
Bennett, Tim, 314–15
Benny Tour, 179–83, *181*, 229, 355
Benson, Charles, 342
Berghof, Herbert, 263
Bergman, Ingmar, 269
Berkeley Repertory Theatre, 114
Berlin International Film Festival, 245
Berlin, Irving, 254, 305
Bernstein, Leonard, 40, 276, 305
Berry, Bill, 317
Berryman, Daniel, 317
Bertolucci, Bernardo, 245, 246–48, *247*, 269
Bess, Ginger, 334
Bessie Award, 66
Bessinger, Joshua, 336–37
Best Man Holiday, The, 102
Best Man, The, 102
Between Us, 102
Beyoncé, 175
Beyond the Clouds, 245
Bianco, Carla, 354, 355
Bicentennial Man, 226
Big C, The, 118
Big Deal, 44, 117
Big River, 44, 62, 105, 116, 332
Big Sea, The, 266
Big: The Musical, 154, 300
Billie Holiday Theatre, 104
Billy Elliot, 195
Billy Rose Theatre, 143
Bingham, Margot, 357
Bitter End, The, 86
Black Donnellys, The, 101
Black Mountain College, 251, 255
Black Nativity, 266
Blackbird, 114
Blacklips Performance Cult, 274
Blackman, Honor, 249

Blackwell, Toby, 357
Blaemire, Nick, *298*, 299
Blake, Paul, 60
Blake, Richard H., 353
Blanchet, Ashley, 347
Blanco, Danny, 183, 355
Blankenship, Beth, 48
Blinding Light, 112
Blindside, 104
Blitz, Rusty, 7
Blockbuster Award, 115
Blocks, 12–13, 333
Blondie, 253
Bloomberg, Michael R., 230
Bloomingdale's, 159, *167*
"Blowin' in the Wind," 257
Blown Sideways Through Life, 170
Blowup, 245
Blues Brothers, The, 265
Bobbie, Walter, 240
Boddie-Henderson, Deirdre, 54
Boevers, Jessica, 354
Bogart, Dominic, 184, 357
Bogosian, Eric, 9
Bohanek, James, 48
Boho Days, 8–9, 45, 292, 293
"Boho Days" (song), 309
Boitano, Brian, 147
Bolen, Sam, 350
Bombay Dreams, 228
Bonds Jr., Rufus, 353
Boniello, Alex, 348
Bonnie & Clyde, 337
Book of Mormon, The, 302
Booking Office, The, 57, 60–61
Borle, Christian, 303
Boros, Eddie, 162
Borum, Mark Willis, 313
Bostic, Maritza, 325
Boswell, Jennifer, 315
Boublil, Alain, xx
Bowen, Lakisha Anne, 326
Bowers, Shawn, 330
Bowie, David, 147
Boyle, Danny, 209
Brackett, Kevin "Kye," 355
Bradley, Angela, 355
Bradley, Bobby, 274

Brady Brunch, The, 151
Brady, Pam, 301
Brady, Wayne, 322–23
Brando, Marlon, 248
Brennan, Amy Miller, 337
Brennan, Nick, 318
Brescia, Kenny, 65
Briggs, Pat, 54, 80
Bright Lights, Big City, 63, 106
Bright Room Called Day, A, 50
Brighton Beach Memoirs, 311
Brighton Fringe, 114
Bring in 'da Noise/Bring in 'da Funk, 154
Bring in the Morning-A Wake-Up Call, 104
Brinkley, Christie, 147
Bristol Riverside Theatre, 312–13
Broadway Arts Theatre for Young
    Audiences, 12
Broadway Bound, 101
Broadway Palm Dinner Theatre,
    313–14
BroadwayCon, 114
Broderick, Matthew, 109, 154
Brodsky, Joseph, 278
Brook, Melanie, 348
Brooklyn College, 262
Brooks, Mel, 7
Broward Center for the Performing
    Arts, 337
Brown, C.C., *177*, 355
Brown, Divine, 355
Brown, George L., 314
Brown, Lili-Anne, 312
Brown, Melanie, 228, 354
Brown, Sharon, 180, 355
Browne, Jackson, 143
Bruce, Lenny, 249–50
Brustein, Robert, 3
Brynner, Yul, 113
Buckley, Jeff, 286
Buckwald, Matt, 346
Buddha, 261
Buddy Holly Story, The, 117
Buell Theatre, xii
Buffy the Vampire Slayer, 265
Bunce, Trevor, 331
Bunch, Larissa, 337

Burba, Blake, 54–55, 153, 163–64, 170, 303
Burdick, Jacques, 3
Burger, Ashley Delane, 348
Burke, Jonathan, 319
Burkell, Scott, 4
Burkhart, Jonathan, 6–7, 8, 10, *10*, 12, 14–15, 16–17, 93, 145–46, 305–6, 309
Burnett, Carol, 176, 179
Burning Down the House, 253
Burroughs, William S., 261
Burson, Martha, 350
Burtka, David, 324
Burton, Haven, 354
Burton, Tim, 265
Buscemi, Steve, 258
Busch, Charles, 258
Butler, Karen, 12
Butz, Norbert Leo, 102, 281, 353
Bye Bye Birdie, xviii, 200
Byers, Grace (Gealey), 312
Byrds, The, 257
Byrne, Michael, 334

Caballé, Montserrat, 40
Caban, Angel, 48–49
Cabaret, xvii, 111, 112, 196, 227
Cabral, Magdiel, *76, 134*, 317
Cabrini Medical Center, 16–17, 19
Cage, John, 250–51, 255
Cage, Nicholas, 56
Camelot, 60, 104
Camp, 111
Canal Jeans, 168
Candide, 40
Cannes Film Festival, 245, 248, 269
Caparelliotis, David, 296
Caplan, Matt, *228*, 353, 354
Capra, Frank, 267
Cargo Car, 6
Carlos, Laurie, 66
Carmeli, Jodi, 354
Carmina Burana, 251–52
Carmody, Brian, 17, 18
Carnegie Hall, 319
Carnegie Mellon University, 175
Carousel, 102

Carpio, T.V., 354
Carreras, José, 41
Carrey, Jim, 227
Carrie, 337
Carroll, Diahann, 154
Carson, Callie, 328
Carter, Nell, 116
Cas Di Cultura, 317
Casa Mañana, 314–15
Cash, Johnny, 257
Cassil, Brie, 314
Cat Club, 252–53
Catan, Daniel, 274
Catch Me if You Can, 321
Cats, 5, 163, 302
Cavallo, Rob, 210–11, 225
Cavaluzzo, Jon, 44, 49, 80
CB's 313 Gallery, 253
CBGB, 77, 145, 203, 253–54, 274
CBGB (film), 253
CBS News Sunday Morning, 268
Celeste, Isabel, 208
Central Park, 209
Chabon, Michael, 198
Challenge for the Actor, A, 263
Chancey, Joey, 299
Chang in a Void Moon, 274
Chanler-Berat, Adam, 285, *288*, 357
Charleston, Janet, 14
Charlie Brown Christmas, A, 11
Charlie Rose Show, xii
Charmed, 117
Chase, Will, xiv, 240, 353, 354
Chautauqua Theatre Company, 161
Chbosky, Stephen, 198–99, 202–3
Che gelida manina, 37
Cheap Imitation, 251
Cheech & Chong's Next Movie, 265
Cheek, John, *31*
Chekhov, Anton, 53
Chelsea Piers, 147
Chemical Brothers, 208
Chenoweth, Kristin, 113, 289
Cher, 56
Cherry Lane Theatre, 170
Cherry Orchard, The, 264
Chess, xix–xx, 109, 112, 337

"Chestnuts Roasting on an Open Fire," 254
Chiang, Dawn, 341
Chiasson, Gilles, 54, 81, 85, 100–101, 232, 347, 354
Chicago, 102, 112, 150, 192, 200–201, 203, 227, 300
Childhood's End, 166
Chivian, Cybele, 112
Chocolate Me!, 102
Chorus Line, A, xvii, 155, 196, 240, 282, 319, 328, 336, 348
Choudhury, Bikram, 110
"Christmas Bells," 38, 55, *90*, 129–30, 163, 211, 217
Christmas Carol, A, 65, 106, 113, 267
"Christmas Song, The," 254
Christoffel, Martin, 318
Christopher, Jonathan, *256*, 317
Christopher, Nicholas, 289, 357
Chrysalis, 101
Chuna, Samantha, 316
Churchill, Caryl, 48
Cilento, Wayne, 110
Cipriani, 232
Circle Line, 176
City Center, xxiii
City Center Encores!, 109, 298
City Lights Bookshop, 261
City of Angels, 65
Civil War, 269
Civil War, The, 101
Clanton, Patrick, *324*, 325
Clark, Ken, 341
Clay, Paul, 159–66, 176, 185, 223
Cleary, Emily, 336
Cleveland Playhouse, 106
Clinton, Bill, 227, 244, 258, 260, 313
Clinton, Chelsea, 227
Clinton, Hillary Rodham, 227, 313
Clit Club, 254
Clooney, George, 147
Clunie, James, 6
Coates, Claire, 355
Cobain, Kurt, 77
Cohen, Drew, 345
Cohen, Josh, 355
Cohen, Sarah, 349

Colasuonno, Anthony, 348
Cold Case, 112, 207
Cole, Nat King, 254
Coleman, Chris, 105
Collected Stories, 263
Collins Tour, 183, 355
Columbia University, 261, 266, 277
Columbus, Chris, 200–5, 207, 210, 211–12, 213–26, 246
Come From Away, 105
Come to the Edge, 14
"Come to Your Senses," 295–96
Company, 276
Conboy, Cornelius, 258–59
Congdon, Constance, 63
Connery, Sean, 249
"Contact," 55, 68, 137–38, 174, 222, 310, 316, 322, 348
Conway, Anthony, 345
Cook, Paul, 275
Cool J, LL, 166
Cooper, Alice, 87
Cooper, Lilli, *298*
Coraggio, Linus, 163
Cornish College of the Arts, 251, 254
Coronet Theatre, 170
Corso, Gregory, 261
Cort Theatre, 63
Cortes, Jonny, 325
Costanzo, Tommy, 115
Costello, Elvis, 253
Country Girl, The, 262
Coward, Noël, 61, 143
Crash, 101
Creek, Luther, 178, 179, 183, 353, 354, 355
Crimp, Martin, 166
Crisis, The, 266
Criss, Darren, 102
Croft, Dwayne, *27*, *31*
Cromer, David, 310–11
Cronaca di un amore, 245
Cruise, Tom, 227
Cruz, Daniel, 318
Cruz, Joshua, 340
Cruz, Nilo, 115
Cruz, Wilson, 180, 229, 354, 355
Cuarón, Alfonso, 201

Cullum, Billy, *193*, 195
cummings, e.e., 280
Cummings, Krysten, 183, 188, 189, 336–37, 354, 355
Cummings, Lawrence, 327
Cunningham Jr., Walter Lee, 315
Cunningham, James, 315
Cunningham, Merce, 170, 251, 254–55
Curless, Bruce, 336
Curry, Gus, 314
Cybele's Free To Eat, 112

D'Monroe, 180, 353, 355
D'onde lieta usci, 38
Daffy's, 168
Dallas Theater Center, 60, 65
Daltrey, Roger, 227
Dames at Sea, 347
Damn Yankees, 61
Danao-Salkin, Julie, 355
Dance Party USA, 104
Dancing with the Stars, 322
Dandridge, Merle, 353
Daniels, Barbara, 40
Daniels, Brenda, 255
Daphne's Dive, 115
Daredevil, 209
Darinka, 258
Dartmouth College, 51
Davenport, Jack, 303
Davenport, Johnny, 326
David Searching, 113
David, Hal, 255–56
Davis Jr., Sammy, 104
Davis, Frenchie, 228, 354
Davis, Geena, 279
Davis, Sheila Kay, 54
Dawson, Greg, 208
Dawson, Rosario, 77, 207–9, *208*, 219, 220, 221, *221*, 222, 225, 226
Days, Maya, 354
Dazed and Confused, 53, 113
de Billy, Bertrand, 40
de Haas, Aisha, 209, 354
de Haas, Darius, 82
De Jesús, Robin, 104, 354
De Niro, Robert, 198, 199, 227
Dear Evan Hansen, xxiii, 64

Death and the King's Horseman, 117
Death Kit, 277
Death of a Salesman, 62
Death Proof, 207
Deaton, Christopher J., 315
Debreceni, Donna, 343
DeBuono, Barbara, 19
"Defying Gravity," 108
DeGruccio, Nick, 328
Del Campo, Eduardo, *27*
Delacorte Theatre, 209
Dennis, Lauren, 336
Denver Center for the Performing Arts, xii
Derricks, Cleavant, 117
Dervan, Liz, 350
Descent, 104
Destiny of Me, The, 113
Deutsch, Kurt, 112
Devereaux, John, 327, 357
Devereux, Monica, 201–2
Devil Wears Prada, The, 207
DeVito, Danny, 147, 198
Dewing, Joy, 186
Diamond, Liz, 63
Diamond, Lydia R., 207
Diary of Anne Frank, The, 105
Dickinson, Shelley, 54, 70, 82, 85, 353, 354
Dideriksen, Katrina Rose, 340
Diekmann, Nancy Kassak, 307
Different Drummer, 60
Diggs, Marcia, 101
Diggs, Taye, 69, 86, 89, 101–2, 109, 204, 211, *216*, 232, 281, 353
Diggs, Walker, 109
Dio, Ronnie James, 111
Dionne Warwick in Valley of the Dolls, 255
Dionne, Richard, 326
Directors Guild of America, 269
Dirty Blonde, 48
Disaster!, 44, 113
Disney, 108, 109, 111, 117, 143, 198, 200
Dixon, Jerry, 296, *297*
Dixon, Tonya, 233–34, 353
DLDF Defender Award, 346
Do I Hear a Waltz?, 276
Do the Right Thing, 270

"Do You Know the Way to San Jose?"
128, 255–56
Doctors Without Borders, 209
Doherty, Aimee, 330
Domingo, Plácido, 40
Domsey's 168
Don Hill's, 170, 252
Don't Tell Mama, 4
Donaghy, Siobhan, 193, 194
Donahue, Mike, 349
Donizetti, Gaetano, xxi
Doogie Howser, M.D., 180
"Door/Wall," 97
Dornhelm, Robert, 40
Dostoyevsky, Fyodor, 269
Doughty, Kaitlin, 314
Douglass, Frederick, 117
Dowdy, Mike, 329–30
Down in the Delta, 244
Down to Earth, 117
"Downtown," 4
Downtown Art Company, 160
Drama Desk Awards, 67, 103, 153, 166,
301
Drama League, xiii, 153
Dramatists Guild, 8, 346
Dream, 110
Dreamers, The, 248
Dreamgirls, xix, 116, 180, 197, 203, 205
Driver, David, 82
Drooker, Eric, 163
Drowning Crow, 205
Drowning, The, 207
Dubois, Jacqui, 355
Dude, xix
Duke of York's Theatre, 190
Dunaway, Faye, 250
Dutch Apple Dinner Theatre, 314
Dylan, Bob, xii, 250, 257–58, *262*
Dyvents Entertainment Aruba, 317

Eagle Theater, 336
Earl, Shaun, *177*, 209, 354
Earls, Amanda, 343
Easler, Jasmine, *182*, 357
Ebb, Fred, 104, 112
Ebersole, Christine, 64
Ebert, Roger, 225

Ebert and Roeper at the Movies, 225
Echo's Hammer, 106
Edelstein, Barry, 166
Edgar, 21
Edinburgh Festival Fringe, *76*, 114,
134, 256, 316–17, 325
Edmonds, Matt, 342, *342*
Edoff, Larry, 112
Edwards, Blake, 154
Egan, Ann, 6, 11
Ehrlich, Amy, 354
Eichelberger, Ethyl, 258, 274
El Barrio USA, 115
Elizabeth II, Queen, 275
Ell, Michael, 346
Ellen's Stardust Diner, 300
Ellett, Trey, xiv, *178*, 179, 353
Elliott, Scott, 240
Emmy Awards, 207
En Garde Arts, 13, 66
Enchanted, 109
English, Donna, 300
Ensemble Studio Theatre, 46, 61, 106
Ensign, Evan, 185–86, 233, 357
Entertaining Mr. Sloane, 246
Equilibrium, 102
Equity, 207
Esbjornson, David, 63
Esparza, Raúl, 296, *297*
Esper, William, 114
Espinosa, Eden, 238–40, 281, 354
Estefan, Gloria, 53
Esther, Queen, 355
Ettinger, Wendy, 51
Evans, Charlotte, 345
Evans, Luke, 192, 193
Evans, Maurice, 143
Evett, Benjamin, 330
Evita, 59, 113, 197, 259
Eyen, Tom, xix

Fadale, Cristina, 354
Fair Game, 117
Falling Star, 112
Falsettos, 207
Fame, 225
"Fame" (song), 4
Fancher, Ed, 280

Fansler, Madeline, *31*, 321
Fantastic Four: Rise of the Silver Surfer, 202
Fantel, Caryl, 337
Faria, Bruno, 337
Fatone, Joey, 228, *228*, 353
Faust, 63
Faÿ, Bernard, 279
Federal Hall National Memorial, 13
Fedorov, Anthony, 286
Feiffer, Jules, 60, 280
Feingold, Michael, 147
Feinstein's/54 Below, 114
Fellini, Federico, 248, 269
"Female to Female," 56
Fenley, Molissa, 166
Ferber, Sammy, 331, 357
Fermat's Last Tango, 101
Fernandez, Arianda, 284, 285, *286*, 357
Ferrara, Andy, 314
Ferrer, José, 262
Fichandler, Zelda, 47
Fiddler on the Roof, 2, 196
Fifer, Mark, 319
Fifth Avenue Theatre, 317–18
"Finale A," 140–41
"Finale B," 141
Fincher, David, 197
Fine Line, 198
Finley, Aaron C., 317
Finley, Karen, 43, 258
Finster and Lucy, 6
First Day of School, 46
Fischer, Kurt, 96
Fisher Theatre, 59
Fitzgerald, F. Scott, 198, 278
Fitzwater, Patrick, 337, 338
Flack, Roberta, 244
Flaherty, Stephen, 240
Flamingo, 254
Flash, The, 107
Flashdance, 6
Flawless, 104, 115
Fleischle, Anna, 194
Fleming, Ian, 248
Fly, 60
Follies, 187, 276

Fontanne, Lynn, 262
Food Emporium, 79, 259
Forbes, Malcolm, 252
Forbidden Broadway Strikes Back, 300–301
Ford, Mark Richard, 353
Ford's Theatre, 65
Forever 21, 168
Forever Plaid, 101
Forman, Milos, 117
Fornachon, Evan, 329
Fornés, Maria Irene, 278
Fosse, Bob, 44, 250
Foster, Hunter, 173
Four Corners of Nowhere, 198
Fox's Searchlight Division, 198
Franco, Francisco, 273
Frankel, Scott, 64
Franklin, Tracie, 313
Freedom, 117
Freitas, Anthony, 348
Freni, Mirella, 39
Friedkin, William, 227
Friends In Deed, 91–92, 230
Frozen, 108
Full Monty, The, 61, 314
Fulton, Kia Dawn, 315
Funny Shorts, 46
Funny Thing Happened on the Way to the Forum, A, 276, 300
FUQs: Frequently Unanswered Questions, 115

Gabriel, Stephen, 185
Galas, Diamanda, 73
Galati, Frank, 110
Galaxy High School, 201
Gallo, Ava, 346
Garber, Victor, 147
Garcia, Gabi, 331
Garden Party, The, 263
Gardner, Drew Michael, *335*, 336
Garland, Judy, 256
Garranchan, Rayner, 337
Gasparini, Drew, *78*, 340
Gaston, Jeremy, *78*
Gattelli, Christopher, 296
Gattra, Dennis, 258

Gau, Kathryn, 339
Gaudet, Ava, 354
Gay Men's Health Crisis, 242
Gaye, Marvin, 85, 107
Geffen, David, 147, 150
Gemignani, Elvira, 22
Genito, Stephanie, *73*, 325
Gentlemen Prefer Blondes, 187
George, Boy, 253
Georgia, Georgia, 244
Gerachis, Mia, 331
Gerber, Tony, 164
Gersh Agency, 205
Gershwin, George, 305
Gershwin, Ira, 305
Gertz, Ali, 13–14
Ghostwriter, 117
Giacosa, Giuseppe, 21
Gibson, Anna, 343
Gifford, Stephen, 326
Gilmore Girls, 210
Gingrich, Candace, 259–60
Gingrich, Newt, 12, 129, 259–60
Ginsberg, Allen, 250, 260–62, *262*, 280
Ginsberg, Louis, 260
Ginsberg, Naomi Livergant, 260–61
Giordani, Marcello, *27*
Girl from the Naked Eye, The, 104
Girl of the Golden West, The, 22
Glass, Philip, 251
Glean, Robert, 354
Glee, 109, 313
Glimmerglass Opera, 170
Glory Days, 299
Glover, Nellie, 345
Go, 102
"God Save the Queen," 275
Godspell, xix, 3, 196
Goger, Valerie, 334
Goglia, Emily, *136*, 327
Gogol, Nikolai, 106
Goldblatt, Stephen, 220, 226
Golden, Bob, 12, 49
Golden Boy, 104
Goldfinger, 248–49
Goldman, Seth, 7
Goldsberry, Renée Elise, 236–37, *237*,
    240, 241, 354

Goldstein, Jerold, 346
Gomez, Alyssa V., *75*, 325
"Goodbye, Love," 38, 55, 56, 77,
    138–39, 203, 211, 222–23, 315
Goode, Eric, 253
Goodman Theatre, 64
Goodman, Robyn, 20, 292–94, 296,
    297, 299
Goods: Live Hard, Sell Hard, The, 117
Goodspeed at Chester, 65
Goodspeed Opera House, 109
Goonies, The, 201
Goranson, Alicia, 166
Gordon, Allan S., 58, 62, 83, 97, 99,
    171, 201, 230, 282
Gordon, Haskett & Co., 62
Gorky, Maxim, 269
Goss, Andrea, 354
Gossip Girl, 240, 322
Gotay, Jason, 334
Gottschall, Zac, 346
Gould, Elliott, 292
Gould, Jason, 292
Government Inspector, The, 106
Gozzi, Carlo, 22
Grabowski, Christopher, 48
Graff, Randy, 65, 209
Graham, Katharine, 46
Graham, Martha, 254–55
Graham, Stephen, 46
Grammer, Kelsey, 106
Grammy Awards, 40, 255, 257
Grant, Dean-Carlo, 340
Grateful Dead, The, 245
Gray, Spalding, 9
Gray, Tamyra, 228, 354
Grease, xix, 173, 192, 196
Grease: You're the One That I Want!, 192
"Great Balls of Fire," 86
Great Pretenders, The, 166
Great Rock 'n' Roll Swindle, The, 275–76
"Greatest Gift, The," 267
Greaves, Danielle Lee, 353
Green Day, 210
Green, Amanda, 240
Green, Thomas, *134*, *256*, 317
Greenberg, Richard, xiii
Greene, John Arthur, 315

Greenwald, Charlie, 339
Gregory, Dick, 250
Greif, Michael, xii, 18, 50–51, 53, 54,
    57, 62–64, *64*, 73–74, 83–90,
    92–94, 96–97, 106, 111, 114,
    116, 119, 124, 147, 153, 154,
    161, 162, 164, 166, 168, 171–72,
    174, 178, 179–80, 184, 187, 189,
    194, 213, 220, 223, 228, 229–30,
    234, 240, 281, 282–83, 285, 287,
    289, 355, 357
Gremlins, 201
Grey Gardens, 63
Grey's Anatomy, 102
Griffith, P.J., 328
Grillos, Nikki, 318
Grimm, 105
Grindhouse, 2071
Grisetti, Josh, 286, *290*
Groban, Josh, 109, 112
Groening, Matt, 280
Groundhog, 101
Groundlings, The, 265
Grundy, Bill, 275
Guare, John, 113
Guarini, Justin, *78*, 340
Guarino, Mark, 345–46
Guerrier, Marcus, 331
Guiding Light, 102
Guip, Amy, 151
Guns N' Roses, 151
Gustafson, Nancy, *31*
Guthrie Theatre, 64, 65, 104
Guthrie, Bruce, 194–95
Guthrie, Woody, 257
Guys and Dolls, xvii
Gypsy, 2, 200, 276

H&M, 168
Haag, Christina, 14
Hackady, Hal, 12
Hadley, Jerry, 40
Hagen, Nina, 166
Hagen, Uta, 262–63
Hair, xviii–xix, xx, 2, 43, 109, 117, 187,
    188, 196, 282
Hairspray, 62, 314
Hall, Michael C., 102

Hall, Sky, 173
"Halloween," 56, 89, 138, 203, 211, 223,
    231
Halpin, Adam, 357
Haltiwanger, Robby, 348
Hamburger, Annie, 13
Hamburger Harry's, 5
Hamilton, Carrie, 176, 179, 355
Hamilton, Joe, 179
Hamilton, xxiii, 60, 153, 155, 240
Hamlet, 262
Hammerstein II, Oscar, 149, 154, 276,
    277, 305, 313
Hampden, Walter, 143
Hampson, Thomas, 40
Hand to God, 61
Hangar Theatre, 315, 319
Hanke, Christopher J., 353
Hanlon, Colin, 354
Hansberry, Lorraine, 280
"Happy New Year," xxi, 38, *134*,
    134–35, 162, 221, 232
"Happy New Year B," 69
Harbor Lights Theater Company, *31*,
    133, 318, 319–21, *320*
Hardwicke, Tyler, 315
Haring, Keith, 253
Harlem Stages, 66
Harlow, Honey, 250
Harnick, Jay, 147
Harriell, Marcy, xiv, 354
Harrington, Aaron, 357
Harrington, Danny, 343
Harris, Ashley-Amber, 343
Harris, Dede, 296
Harris, Neil Patrick, 102, 180, *181*, 321,
    322, 322–24, 355
Harrison, George, 257
Harry Potter and the Chamber of Secrets,
    201–2, 226
Harry Potter and the Prisoner of Azkaban,
    201
Harry Potter and the Sorcerer's Stone,
    201–2, 226
Harry's Law, 207
Hart, Nicolette, 354, 357
Hartford Stage, 117
Hartley, Mariette, 338

Hartman, Phil, 265
Harvard Law School, 62, 70
Harvard University, 270, 277
Haskins, Nicole Michelle, 342
Hatcher, Jeffrey, 63
Havel, Václav, 263–64
Havlová, Dagmar, 264
Hawkins, Phyre, 315
HB Studios, 263
HBO Films, 199
He Got Game, 270
"He Looks Beyond My Faults," 116
Health GAP, 243
Heartbreak Hotel, 201
Hearts of Fire, 257
Hedgpeth, Thomas, 345
Hedwig and the Angry Inch, 102, 105, 114, 297
Hefner, Hugh, 250
Heidegger, Martin, 264–65
Heidi Chronicles, The, 105
Helen Hayes Award, 66
Hellman, Lillian, 48
Hello, Dolly!, 196
Hemingway, Ernest, 278
Hendricks, Eva, 339
Hendrix, Jimi, 257
Hentoff, Nat, 280
Hepburn, Katharine, 324
HERE, 161
Heredia, Wilson Jermaine, 67, 68, *85*, 86, 89, *103*, 103–4, 153, 155, 188, 204, 220, *221*, 231, 232, 354, 355
Herman, Jerry, 5, 196
Hernandez, Jene, 341
Hernandez, Steena, 349
Herron, Matt, 166
Hetherington, Leigh, 355
Hibbard, David, 300
Hicks, Rodney, 12, 81, *90*, 104–5, 116, 174, 232, 237–38, 353, 354
High Fidelity, 61, 337
High School Musical, 321
Hilfiger, Tommy, 159
Hill, Don, 252
Hill, Erin, 54
Hill, Lauryn, 104

Hill, Linda, 170
Hillier, Scott, 380
Hindemith, Paul, 250
Hirsch, Judd, 340
Hirshfield, Beau, 328
Hobbit, The, 192
Hobson, David, 41
Hochschule der Kunste, 166
Hodge, Alia, 357
Hodges, Drew, 150–51
Hoffer, Jerick, 317
Hoffman, Philip Seymour, 115
Hofstra University, 316
Hogan, Michael, 337
Holcomb, Bernard, 318
Holiday Wishes, 254
Holiday, Billie, 65
Hollywood Bowl, 117, 207, 321–24, *323*
Holmes, Shanay, 195
Holzman, Winnie, 281
Home Alone 2: Lost in New York, 201
Home Alone, 200, 201
"Honestly Sincere," xviii
Hong, Hei-Kyung, *27*
Hooker, Jessie, 285
Hoover, Savannah Quinn, 342, *342*
Hope & Faith, 105
Hope, Gavin, 355
Hopkins, Cynthia, 308
Hopkins, Kathryn, 332
Horne, Troy, 353
Horowitz, Mark Eden, 305
Hose, Adam, 315, 319
Hotel 41, 164
Hotel Chelsea, 276
Hotel Shocard, 164
Hourie, Troy, 341
House of Blue Leaves, The, 311
House of Secrets, 202
Housing Works, 243
Houston, Whitney, 197
How Stella Got Her Groove Back, 102
How to Succeed in Business Without Really Trying, 109, 110, 187
How to Survive a Plague, 287
How to Talk Dirty and Influence People, 250
Howar, Tim, 353

Howard, Collin L., 75, 325
Howell, Cooper, 327
Howell, Monté J., 320
Howl, 261
Hoylen, Tony, 49, 54, 57
Hubbard, Jacqueline, 324–25
Huckleberry Finn, 62
Hudes, Quiara Alegría, 115, 240
Hudgens, Vanessa, 321, 322, 323
Hudson, Jennifer, 204–5
Hughes, Holly, 258
Hughes, Langston, 266–67
Hughes, Peter, 336
Hunt, Scott, 354
Hunt for Red October, The, 246
Hunter, Ross, 193, 195
Hurston, Zora Neale, 266,
Hustling, 115
Hyatt, Jeremy, 329

I Ching, 251, 255
I Know Why the Caged Bird Sings, 244
I Love You, Beth Cooper, 202
I Make Me a Promise, 12–13
I pagliacci, 22
"I Should Tell You," 38, 44, 45, 46, 55,
    56, 89, 132, 148, 221, 243
I Was Looking at the Ceiling and Then I
    Saw the Sky, 104
I Will Follow, 207
I Wonder as I Wander, 266
Iconis, Joe, 308
ID, 166
Idili Theatricals Limited, 194
If/Then, 63, 109. 114, 152, 317
Il Postino, 274
"I'll Cover You," 55, 80, 94, 128, 138,
    217, 220, 229, 232, 320, 339
Illica, Luigi, 21
Illness as Metaphor, 277
In America, 277
In the Heights, xxiii, 60, 61, 299
Increased Difficulty of Concentration, 263
Infante, Jonathan, 326
Inherit the Wind, 143
Innocents, The, 110
Inside Man, 270
Intar, 103

Intelligent Homosexual's Guide to
    Capitalism and Socialism with a
    Key to the Scriptures, The, 64
Interlochen Arts Camp, 113
Interpreter, The, 117
InTheater, xi
Into the Woods, 5, 276, 277
Iphigenia and Other Daughters, 161
Iraq War, 268
Irving Berlin's White Christmas, 61
Israel, Richard, 326
Isreal, Mark, 173
It Had to Be You, 202
It's a Wonderful Life, 267
Ivins, Todd, 326
Ivoryton Playhouse, 73, 75, 324, 324–25
Iwamatsu, Sala, 354, 355

J. Crew, 326
J. Glitz, 4
J.P. Morgan Saves the Nation, 13, 83
Jack Goes Boating, 115
Jack Kerouac School of Disembodied
    Poetics, 261
Jackson, Francesca, 193–94
Jackson, Mark Leroy, 229, 353, 355
Jackson, Michael, 68, 328
Jacob's Pillow, 66
Jacoby, Miles, 350
Jacques Brel is Alive and Well and Living in
    Paris, 104
Jagger, Bianca, 253
James, Henry, 110
James, Marcus Paul, 285, 354, 357
James, Stu, 353
James, William, 278
Jane Street Theatre, 296–97, 297
Janki, Devanand, 319
Jay, Harley, 353
Jeffrey, Trisha, 354
Jenkins, Tamara, 319
Jennings, Marshall, 330
Jent, Tyler, 124, 339
Jericho, 199
Jersey Films, 198
Jesurun, John, 274
Jesus Christ Superstar, xix, xx, 2, 86, 104,
    196, 336

Jett, Joan, 106
Joe A. Callaway Award, 66
Joe Turner's Come and Gone, 207
Joe's Bed-Stuy Barbershop: We Cut Heads, 270
Joel, Billy, 1, 147, 227, 297
Joey Breaker, 110
John W. Engeman Theater, 313, 315, 325–26
John, Elton, 1, 109, 111
Johnny Was, 104
Johns Hopkins University, 278
Johns, Jasper, 277–78
Johnson, Andrew, 328
Johnson, G.R., xiii
Johnson, Maurice, 315
Johnson, Mia, 318
Johnson, Miles, 326
Johnson, Susan, 313–14
Johnston II, Owen, 354
Johnston, Justin, 235, 240, 286, 354, 357
Jonathan Larson Foundation, xxiii, 65, 230, 307–8
Jonathan Larson Fund, 309
Jonathan Larson Lab, 48
Jonathan Sings Larson, *308*, 308–9
Jones, Bambi, 49
Jones, Courtney, 342, *342*
Jones, Grace, 253
Jones, Jeffrey M., 13, 63
Jones, Leon-Maurice, 355
Jones, Lucie, 194
Jones, Rebecca, 260
Jones, Steve, 275
Jones, Walton, 63
Jordan, Jeremy, 302–3
Joseph and the Amazing Technicolor Dreamcoat, 60
Joseph, Catrice, 354
Joseph, Rajiv, 61
Joshua Tree, The, 87
Josie and the Pussycats, 208
Joyce, James, 251
Juilliard School, 166, 175, 205
Jumpers, 65
Jungle Book, The, 7

Kaddish for Naomi Ginsberg (1894–1956), 261
Kafka on the Shore, 110
Kagan, Eve, 330
Kagemusha, 269
Kamitsuna, Mako, 166
Kander, John, 104, 112
Kansas Lied Center for the Performing Arts, 66
Kantor, Adam, 240, 353
Kaprow, Allan, 251
Karbacz, Kelly, 354
Kassebaum, Kendra, 281, 354
Katya, 166
Kauffman, Nina, 345
Keen Company, *298*, 299
Keigwin, Larry, 283, 289
Keller, Sean, 178, 179, 355
Kelly, "Cowboy" Ray, 163
Kelly, Jenny, 348
Kelly, Kristen Lee, 81, *90*, 105–6, 110, 354
Kelso, Andy, 349
Kennedy Jr., John F., 14, 252
Kennedy, Patricia, 105
Kennedys of Massachusetts, The, 105
Kern, Jerome, 63
Kern, Megan, 334–36
Kerouac, Jack, 261
Kerryson, Paul, 190
Kevin Hill, 102
Keyes, Justin, 349
Khouri, Callie, 279
Kids, 208
Kimball, Chad, 112
King and I, The, 50, 113, 301
King Jr., Martin Luther, 105, 244
King Lear, 264, 269
King of the Jungle, 208
Kirchner, Jaime Lee, xiv, 234, 354
Kirkpatrick, David, 270–71
Kirkpatrick, Kathy, 235, 270–71
Kissing Jessica Stein, 109
Kissinger, Henry, 268
Kitchen, The, 170
Kitt, Tom, xxiii, 63, 114, 240
Knots Landing, 246
Knowlton, Sarah, 54, 56

Knox, Bethany, 174–75
Koppel, Ted, 267–68
Korie, Michael, 64
Kornberg, Richard, 271
Kornfeld, Danny Harris, 357
Kraine Theatre, 105
Kramer, Larry, 242
Krieger, Henry, xix
Krier, Lindsey, 337
Kristal, Hilly, 253
Krupin, Janet, 317
Kuper, Peter, 163
Kurosawa, Akira, 245, 268–69
Kushner, Tony, 48, 63, 64, 170
Kushnier, Jeremy, 309, 353

L.A. Guns, 252
L.A. Stage Alliance Ovation Award, 117
L'Avventura, 245
L'Eclisse, 245
La bohème, xi, xxii, 1, 18, 20–41, *27, 31,
        35*, 42–43, 45, 48, 53, 61, 68, 69,
        77, 101, 114, 119, 121, 149, 154,
        188, 221, 225, 236, 272, 318,
        334, 344
La Bohème (restaurant), 19
La Cage aux Folles, 104
La Chiusa, Michael John, 210
La commare secca, 248
La fanciulla del West, 22
La gioconda, 20
La Jolla Playhouse, 62, 63, 115, 179–80
La Luna, 248
La Mirada Theatre for the Performing
        Arts, *136*, 326–27, *327*
La Notte, 245
"La Vie Bohème," xxi, 55, 71, 72, 79,
        82, 94, 131–32, 154, 157, 162,
        170, 174, 190, 191, 192, 212,
        221, *221*, 232, 243, 245, 256,
        258, 261, 263, 264, 265, 269,
        271, 277, 281, 287
"La Vie Bohème B," 132, 243
LAByrinth Theater Company, 114
Lachey, Drew, 228, 353
Lady Bunny, 274
Lady Day at Emerson's Bar and Grill, 65
Lady from the Sea, The, 277

LaFontaine, Matt, 343
Lagasse, Kevin, 318–19
LaMaMa Experimental Theatre Club,
        161
LaMark, Katie, *182*, 357
Lambs Club, 346
Lane, Nathan, 154
Lane Bryant, 118
Lange, Jessica, 246
Langham, Michael, 106
Langley, Charles, 173
Langran, Tracey, 354
Lansing, Sherry, 227
Lapine, James, 8, 276
Largo Desolato, 264
LaRosa, James, 313
Larry and Me, 112
Larson, Al, 1, *15*, 93, 96, 146, 171–72,
        176, 235, 241, 293, 305–6, 309,
        310
Larson, Jonathan,
        As actor/performer, 3–5, 309
        As collaborator, 42–46, 48–49, 54,
                58, 83–84, 88–91, 100, 220,
                333
        Childhood, 1–2, 348
        Creative goals and influences,
                xviii, xxii, 5, 9, 227, 277
        Critical responses to work of, 147–
                49, 179, 180, 183, 188–90,
                195, 287–91, 338
        Education, 2–3
        Family, 1–2, 305, 349–50
        Friendships, 3, 6–7, 9–12, 14–15,
                91–92, 110, 145–46, 176
        Honors and awards, 146, 153–55,
                281, 347
        Illness and death, 16–19, 92, 171,
                188, 204, 229, 241, 292,
                305, 309
        In casting process, 53, 84–86, 111
        Lesser known songs, 211, 292, 295
        Romantic relationships, 14, 255
        More: xi, *4, 6, 10, 15*, 72, 77, 118,
                152–53, 162, *294, 306*
Larson, Julie, 1, 7, 16, 154, *155*, 176,
        197–98, 200, 201, 235, 241, 346

Larson, Nan, 1, *15*, 93, *155*, 171–72, 176, 241
LaShea, Cody, 330
Last Emperor, The, 248
Last Five Years, The, 240
Last Ship, The, 61
Last Tango in Paris, 248
Lathan, John, 54
Laurents, Arthur, 61, 285
Lavin, Lindsay, 318
Law and Order, 106, 110, 117, 118
Law and Order: Criminal Intent, 105
Law and Order: Special Victims Unit, 104, 105, 114, 117
Lawrence, Gertrude, 143
Lawrence, Tamika Sonja, 357
Lawry, Eric, 337
Lawson, Lexi, 184–85, 357
"LCD Readout," 295–96
Le Amiche, 245
Le Gallienne, Eva, 262
Le villi, 21
Leacock Hoffman, Victoria, 3, 6, *6*, 7, 8, 9, *43*, 50, 67, 146, 171, 210, 292–97, 299, 309
Leave It to Beaver, 1
Leaving, 264
LeBlanc, Karen, 355
Lee, Sandra W., 325
Lee, Sherri Parker, 101
Lee, Spike, 117, 199, 200, 202–3, 205, 269–70
Lee Strasberg Institute, 208
Leggett, Vincent, 337
Lehrer, Josh, 60
Leibovitz, Annie, 278
Leicester Haymarket Theatre, 190
Lena Horne: The Lady and Her Music, 143
Lenat, Jesse Sinclair, 54
Lenny, 250
Leo, Jamie, 163
León, Alia, 353
Leoncavallo, Ruggero, 21
LePore, Michael, 346
Lerner and Loewe, 305
Les Misérables, xx, 5, 65, 101, 115, 192, 209, 233, 333

Lesbian and Gay Community Services Center, 242
"Let It Go," 108, 109
Leung, Telly, 323, 354, 357
Leupp, Clinton, 49
Levenson, Steven, 64
Leverage, 105
Leverett, Sierra, 331
Levine, David, 49
Levine, James, 41
Levy, Lorie Cowen, 296
Lewis, Jason, 209
Lewis, Nicole, 353
Library of Congress, 270, 305–7, 308–9
Libro de Buen Amor, 3
Lichtenstein, Roy, 255
Life, *204*, 271
Life Café, 38, 78, 82, 123, 131, 162, 209, 212, 221, 232, 235, 243, 270–72, 341
Life Café 983, 271
"Life Support," 126–27
Light in the Piazza, The, 209
"Light My Candle," xxi, 55, 57, 89, 123, 126, 148, 199, 203, *208*, 211, 252, *286*
Light Years, 46
"Like a Rolling Stone," 257
Lilith Fair, 109
Lima, Luis, *31*
Limbo Lounge, 258
Limelight, 166, 274
Limon, José, 65
Lincoln Center, 42, 66, 103, 104, 117, 270
Lincoln Center Theatre, 102
Lincoln University, 266
Link, Ryan, 353
Lion King, The, 117, 333, 340
Lipin, Natalie, 357
Lippa, Andrew, 60, 102, 109
Lippert, Rob, 329
Lipsky, Jeff, 166
Little Buddha, 248
Little Foxes, The, 143
Little Night Music, A, 101, 276
Little Prince and the Aviator, The, 113
Little Richard, 257

Little Shop of Horrors, 113, 117
Lively, Blake, 240
Lively, Mark, 343
Llana, Jose, 354
Lloyd Webber, Andrew, xix, 154, 190, 194, 259
Lloyd, Christopher, 338
Lockhart, Bonny, 355
Lohr, Aaron, 109, 210
London, Daniel, 209
Long Island Association for AIDS Care, 325–26
Long Wharf Theatre, 104
Long, Jordan, 357
Long, Kerry, 338
Long, Robin, 330
Longtime Companion, 287
Look Away, 244
Looper, 207
Loot, 246
Lopez, Leon, 193–94
Lopez, Priscilla, 240
Lorca, Federico Garcia, 273
"Losing My Religion," 53
Lotto, 104
"Love Heals," 211
Love, Janis, 105
Love, Ludlow, 166
Lovett, Chelsea, 340
Lower East Side Girls Club, 209
Lucas, George, 210, 269
Ludlam, Charles, 274
Luhrmann, Baz, 41, 61, 101
Luisotti, Nicola, 41
Lunt, Alfred, 262
LuPone, Patti, 64, 115, 259
LuPone, Robert, 84
Lutvak, Steven, 308
Lyceum Theatre, 106
Lydia Mendelssohn Theatre, 347
Lydon, John, 275
Lynne, Jeff, 257
Lypsinka, 274
Lysistrata, 166

Mabou Mines, 160
Macbeth, 117, 269
MacCalla, Sylvia, 179, 355

MacDermot, Galt, xviii–xix
Mace, Alan, 274
Machado, Eduardo, 161
Machinal, 50, 63
Mack, Steve, 65
MacKay, Andy, 105
Mackintosh, Robert, 194
Madama, Mark, 347
Madama Butterfly, xx, 22
Madonna, 173, 192, 197, 252, 259, 274
Magee, Rusty, 49
Magnificent Seven, The, 269
Maguire, Gregory, 281
Mailer, Norman, 280
Mainwaring, Michael, J. *320*
Majestic Theatre, 154
Malcolm X, 117, 270
Malfitano, Catherine, *35*
Mama Mia!, 333
Mame, 196
Mamet, David, 61, 105
Man in the Ceiling, The, 60
Manfred Mann, 257
Manfredi, Doria, 22
Manhattan Theatre Club, 101, 102, 106, 109, 293, 296
Manic Panic, 163
Mann, Emily, 115
Manon, 21
Manon Lescaut, 21
Mantovani, Nicolette, 39
Manuel, Caren Lyn, 354, 357
Maraya, Jackie, 357
Mardin, Arif, 151
Marfan Foundation, 309
Marfan Syndrome, 19, 309
Margulies, Donald, 61, 161
Marisol, 166
Mark, Larissa, 345–46
Mark Taper Forum, 63
Mark Tour, 114, 117, 357
Marks, Johnny, 254
Marotta, E.J., 314
Marquand, Richard, 257
Marr, Sally, 249
Married to the Mob, 246
Marrying Man, The, 246
Marshal, Susan, 161

Marshall, Heidi, 173
Marshall, Rob, 102, 200
Martin, Jesse L., 5, 80, 85, *85*, 106–7, *107*, 110, 188, 204, *204*, 211, 213, 220, *221*, 232, 289, 303, 353, 355
Martinez, Devon, 350
Mascagni, Pietro, 21
Mason, Nurney, 345
Massachusetts Institute of Technology, 79, 124–25
Massenet, Jules, 21
Matheson, Craig, 338
Matisse, Henri, 278
Matlock, Glenn, 275, 276
May, Aileen, 312
Mayer, Michael, 113
Mazzie, Marin, 4
McAnuff, Des, xx, 62
MCC Theater, 61, 84
McCarthy, Joe, 266
McCarthy, Michael, 156
McClelland, Sean, 338
McClendon, Cole, 357
McCollum, Chuck, 197
McCollum, Dylan, 16, *306*
McCollum, Kevin, xii, xxi, 20, 41, 57, 58, 60–62, *64*, 83, 97, 99, 142, 146, 150, 151, 159, 171, 197, 201, 241, 282, 343, 347
McCollum, Matthew, *15*, 16, *306*, 349–50
McCord, Kyle, 315
McCoy, Tom, 326
McCoy Rigby Entertainment, 326
McDonald, Audra, 65
McDonald's, 59
McDonnell, Evelyn, 152
McDowell, Tracy, 354
McElroy, Michael, 240, 309, 353, 357
McFarlane, Rachel, 355
McGinn/Cazale Theatre, 13
McGovern, Christopher, 349
McGovern, George, 1
McGrath, Aubrey, 342
McInerney, Jay, 63
McKeown, Erin, 115
McKinstry, Scott, xiii

McLaren, Malcolm, 275, 276
McLaughlin, Ellen, 161
McNeill, Timothy, 357
McNiff, Chris, *124*, 339
McPhee, Katharine, 302
Me and You, 248
Meara, Anne, 147
Medium, 104
Memorandum, The, 263
Memphis, 112, 347
Men in Black II, 208
Mena, Christian, 180, 355
Menzel, Idina, 54, 63, 74, 86–87, 89, 91, *98*, 102, 105, 107–9, *108*, 111, 112, 114, 153, 204, *204*, 210, 220, *221*, 222, 232, 254, 281, 289, 313, 317, 354
Merce Cunningham Dance Company, 255
Merce Cunningham Studio, 170
Mercer, Johnny, 110
Merchant of Venice, The, 106
Mercomes, Amber, *136*, 327
Mercury, Freddie, 111
Merino, David, *68*, 331, 357
Mernagh, Russell, 343
Merrily We Roll Along, 276
Metropolitan Opera, 1, 20, 22, *27*, *31*, 40–41, 42, 334
Metzgar, Bonnie, 311
MGM Studios, 203, 245, 256
Michigan State University, 5
Midsummer Night's Dream, A, 117
Mientus, Andy, 302, 303–4, 333
Milan Conservatory, 20
Miller, Henry, 280
Miller, Randall, 253
Miller, Roy, 340
Miller, Scott, 329–30
Miller, Tim, 43
Mills, Paul Taylor, 194
Mims, Clark, 357
Minetta Lane Theatre, 19, 142
Mingo Jr., Alan, 326, 353
Minnelli, Liza, 227
Minogue, Kylie, 190
Miracle at St. Anna, 270
Miramax, 198, 199, 200

Miranda, Lin-Manuel, xxiii, 60, 298–99
Miss Saigon, xx, 22, 163
Miss You Like Hell, 115
Missouri Repertory Theater, 207
Mitchell, John Cameron, 102
Mitchell, Kenneth Noel, 331
Mitchell, Loften, 266
Mitchell, Thomas, 267
Mixed Me!, 102
Mizer, Erin, 316
Mizrahi, Isaac, 147
Mizusaki, Naomi, 151
Mo' Better Blues, 270
Mode, 118
Model Apartment, The, 161
Moesha, 117
Mohammed, Bridget, 357
Mom & Me & Mom, 244
Mondo Kim's, 163
Monteiro, Fabio, 333
Montgomery, Jay, 319
Moonchildren, 3
Moondance Diner, 5, 12, 16, 83, 106
Moonstruck, 56
Moore, Demi, 227
Morehouse College, 269
Moresco Productions, 101
Morgan, Betsy, 326
Morgan, Matthew, 357
Morgan, Naomi, 317
Morissette, Alanis, 173
Morris, Michael, 325
Morse, Halle, 333
Moss, Lambert, 355
Most Fabulous Story Ever Told, The, 118
Mother, 254
Mother Courage, 106
Motown the Musical, 62
Moulton, Rachel, 333
Mountaintop, The, 105
Movin' Spirits Dance Theater, 65–66
Mowgli, 7
Mozart, Wolfgang Amadeus, xxi
MPAA, 224–25
"Mr. Tambourine Man," 257
Mrs. Doubtfire, 200, 201
Mrs. Klein, 263

Mrs. Warren's Profession, 263
Mule Bone, 266
Mullally, Megan, 109
Muller, Adrienne, 333
Municipal Opera Company of St. Louis, 60
Murakami, Haruki, 110
Murakami, Jimmy T., 269
Murder in the First, 102
Murger, Henri, 21, 33, 37
Murphy, Matthew, 354
Murphy, Nicola, 316–17
"Musetta's Waltz," 28, 38, 56, 121, 141, 272–73
Music and Art Academy, 118
Music Box Theatre, 64
Music Man, The, xvii
Music Theatre International (MTI), 310, 332, 344–45
Musical Theatre West, 328–29
Musical Theatre Works, 172–73
Mussolini, Benito, 245
Mute, 111
My Dinner with Andre, 264
My Fair Lady, 196
My Favorite Things," xxi
My Gay Roommate, 104
My So-Called Life, 180, 229
Myers, Troy, 110
Mysteries of Pittsburgh, The, 198

NAACP, 266, 267
NAACP Image Awards, 102
Nada, 161
Nagarajan, Anisha, 319
Nailed, 104
Nakasone, Aiko, 82, 106, 109–10, 354
Naked Angels, 110
Naropa University, 261
National Actors Theatre, 106
National Black Arts Festival, 66
National Endowment for the Arts, 43, 161
National Theatre, 143
Nature Conservancy, 209
Nauman, Bruce, 255
NBC Nightly News, 268
Nederlander, David Tobias, 143

Nederlander, James L., 240
Nederlander, James M., 230, 240
Nederlander Organization, 143, 164–65
Nederlander Theatre, xii, xiii, 64, 143–44, *144*, 145–46, 155, 163, 164–66, *165*, 174, 176, 178, *178*, 207, 230, *231*, 282
"Negro Speaks of Rivers, The," 266
Negron, Nina, 318
Nelson, Lora, 160
Nelson, Richard, xx, 114
Neruda, Jan, 273
Neruda, Pablo, 273–74
Nessun dorma, 22
Netrebko, Anna, 40
Never Gonna Dance, 63
Never Mind the Bollocks, Here's the Sex Pistols, 275
New Americans, The, 103
New Group, The, 61
New Line Theatre, 329–30
New Repertory Theatre, 330–31
New World Stages, 61, 166, 282, *290*
New York City Opera, 20
New York Drama Critics Circle, 153
New York Institute of Technology, 111
New York International Fringe Festival, 104
New York Musical Theatre Festival, 61
New York Public Library, 306
New York Shakespeare Festival, 63, 64, 65, 106, 166
New York Stage and Film, 166
New York State Department of Health, 16–17, 19
New York Theatre Workshop, 16, 17–18, 19, 46–55, 57–58, 59, 62–63, 83–84, 92–99, 101, 105, 107, 142, 145, 147, 149, 150, 161–62, 166, 170, 176, 180, 230, 282, 293, 303
New York University (NYU), 79, 84, 106, 108, 117, 118, 125, 201, 202, 214, 246, 269–70, 303, 331
Newcomb, Johnny, *76*, 317, *324*, 325
Newman, Randy, 63
Newsies, 210

Newsome, Joel, 49
Next to Normal, xxiii, 63, 114, 285, 321, 337
Nichols, Mike, 91
Nicola, James C., xxi, xxii, 17, 18, 46–49, *47*, 50–51, 53, 58, 59, 83, 92–93, 96–97, 145, 161, 303
Night and the City, 117
Night at the Museum, 202
Nightline, 128, 267–68
Nigrini, Peter, 289
Nine, 203
Nirvana, 54, 274
Nixon, Richard, 268
Nixon, Ryah, 317–18
No Day But Today: The Story of Rent, 7, 94–95
"No Es Asi," 103
No Exit Café, 341
Nobel Prize, 258, 273
Nocturne, 114
Noonan, Tom, 161
North Shore Music Theatre, 117
Northwestern University, 62, 240
Not Without Laughter, 266
Nunn, Trevor, xx
Nutcracker, The, 217, 267
NYPD Blue, 105, 117, 162

"O Fortuna," 252
"O Holy Night," 254
"O Little Town of Bethlehem," 254
O Mimì, tu più non torni, 39
O soave fanciulla, 38
O'Brien, Joseph Michael, 313
O'Connor, Nancy, 49
O'Connor, Sinead, 53
O'Donnell, Kari, 306
O'Gorman, Ryan, 195
O'Grady, Christine, 299
O'Grady, Matthew, 2, 7, 11–12, 13, 14, 15, 91, *155*, 293
O'Horgan, Tom, 117
O'Neal, Cynthia, 91
O'Neill, Brandon, 317
Oberlin, Karen, 49
Obie Awards, 111, 153, 280–81
Odom Jr., Leslie, 354

Oedipus Rex, 56
Oklahoma!, xvii, 50, 105
Oleanna, 61, 105
Oliver! 113, 196, 332
Oliveras, Maria-Christina, 319
Olivier Awards, 103, 336
On a Mission from God, 104
"On Broadway," 5
On Photography, 277
"On the Pulse of the Morning," 244
On The Quays, 317
On the Road, 261
"On the Street," 127–28
On Tour, LLC, 184, 357
Once, 48
"One Last Kiss," xviii
One Life to Live, 104
"One Song Glory," xii, xxi, 56, 97–99,
    123, 203, 212, 217, 309, 321
Only the Lonely, 201
"Open Road," 56
Opera House, The, 6
Opera Theatre of St. Louis, 170
Orbison, Roy, 257
Ordell, Darryl, 354
Oremus, Stephen, 293, 299
Orff, Carl, 251–52
Orlando Shakespeare Theatre, 318
Orlovsky, Peter, 261
Orton, Joe, 246
Orwell, George, 7
Osborne, Aaron, 65
Osborne, Jaymes, 342, *342*
Othello, 105, 117, 262
Other Palace, The, 194
Other Woman, The, 114
Other, The, 263
Ou, Tina, 354
Ouellette, Corry, 173
Our Country's Good, 143
Our Town, 311
"Out Tonight," xii, xiv, xxi, 55, 76, 77,
    127, 149, 161, 168, 169, 184,
    192, 203, 207, 210, 211, 217,
    219, 220, 224, 231, 240, 284,
    300, 315, 318, 321, 322
Outer Critics Circle Awards, 101, 113,
    153

"Over the Moon," 56, 73, 74, 130, 168,
    191, 192, 210, 216, 220, 283,
    284, 317, 329, 343, 349
"Over the Rainbow," 256
Owens, Destan, 353, 354
Oxley, Jennifer, 46

Pacific Overtures, 276
Pacini School of Music, 20
Pacino, Al, 106
Paige, Elaine, 259
Pajama Party, 114
Palatchi, Stefano, *27*
Palminteri, Chaz, 147
Panache, 4
Paparelli, PJ, 311
Paper Mill Playhouse, 336
Paper, 166
Papp, Joseph, xviii, 47
Paradise in Augustine's, 316
Paragon, John, 265
Paramount Theatre, 184
Parent, Maurice E., 330
Paris is Burning, 287
Parker, Javar La'Trail, 195
Parker, John Eric, 355
Parker, Pippin, 110, 292
Parker, Sarah Jessica, 110, 154
Parker, Timothy Britten (Toby), 81, *90*,
    110, 281, 354
Parker, Trey, 301–2
Pascal, Adam, xi, xiv, 44, 77–78, 87, 88,
    89, 94–95, *95*, 99, 109, 111–13,
    114, 148, *151*, 152, 153, 178,
    179, 184–85, 188, 204, *208*, 210,
    211, *214*, 219, 221, *221*, 232,
    234, 353, 355, 357
Pascal, Lennon, 112
Pascal, Montgomery, 112
Pasek, Benj, xxiii, 64
Pashalinski, Lola, 147
Pasolini, Pier Paolo, 248
Passanante, Jean, 46
Passing Strange, 270
Passion, 276
Pat Garrett and Billy the Kid, 257
Pataki, George, 250
Patch Adams, 209

Paternostro, Michael, 328
Patricia Field, 53, 168
Pattak, Cory, 326
Pauker, Michelle, 339
Paul, Justin, xxiii, 64
Paulus, Diane, 293
Pavarotti, Luciano, 22, 39
Pawk, Michelle, 348
Peacock, Chiara, 49
Pearlman, Rhea, 147
Pearson, Brandon L., 357
Pearson, Richard, 226
Peckinpah, Sam, 257
Pee-wee Herman Show, The, 265
Pee-wee's Big Adventure, 265
Pee-wee's Playhouse, 265
Peg + Cat, 46
Pence, Mike, 260
Pennies from Heaven, 3
Penny, Darrick, 337
Penumbra Theater, 66
Peppermint Lounge, 258
*Percy Jackson and the Olympians: The
    Lightning Thief*, 202, 209
Percy Jackson: Sea of Monsters, 202
Perez, Alex, 319–21
Performance Space 122, 66, 161
Performing Arts for Children and
    Teens, 331–33
Pericles, 63
Perkins, Abby, 337
Perkins, Damian, 355
Perks of Being a Wallflower, The, 198–99
Perón, Eva, 259
Perry Street Theatre, 47
Perry, Lynnette, 61
Perry, Steve, 111
Peter and the Starcatcher, 48
Peter and Vandy, 106
Peter Pan, 332
Peter, Paul and Mary, 257
Peterson, Lisa, 63
Pettiford, Todd E., 354
Pettiford, Valarie, 44
Petty, Tom, 257
Pfeiffer, Michelle, 147
PFLAG, 209
Phantom of the Opera, The, xix, 5, 192

Philadelphia Theatre Company, 105
Phillips, Emily Jeanne, *31, 133*, 321
Phillips, Liz, 255
Picasso, Pablo, 278
Pielmeier, John, 63
Pink Floyd, 245
Pinocchio, 332
Pinochet, Augusto, 273
Pioneer Theatre Company, 303,
    333–34
Pippin, xix, 101
Pitch Perfect, 322
Pixels, 202
Plan B Entertainment, 328
Play with Repeats, 166
Playboy, 250
Playwrights Horizons, 8, 13, 42, 63, 110
Plotkin, Tom, 300
Plotnick, Jack, 113
Podemski, Tamara, 354, 355
Poison, 252
Police, The, 253
Pollard, Collette, 312
Pollard, Skye, 345
Ponchielli, Amilcare, 20
Ponti, Carlo, 245
Pop, Iggy, 328
Pope, Manley, *178*, 179, 353
Popol Vuh, 103
Porgy and Bess, 244, 347
Port Authority, 144
Porter, Alisan, 328
Porter, Katherine Anne, 280
Porter, Sarah, 329–30
Portland Center Stage, 105
Post Theatre Company, 118
Post, Kyle, 354
Potter, Jeff, 65
Potts, Michael, 54
Poulos, Jim, 353
Power, Jim, 163
Prather Entertainment Group, 314
Precious Sons, 113
Presley, Elvis, xviii, 257
Prévost, Abbé, 21
Priest, Maxy, 166
Primary Stages, 161
Prince of Wales Theatre, 190

Prince, 68, 208
Prince, Hal, 187
Private Lives, 61
Private Practice, 102
Producers, The, 44, 155
Producing Office, The, 61
Promise to Ourselves: A Journey Through Fatherhood and Divorce, A, 246
Promises, Promises, 256
Proof, 293
Propaganda Films, 197
Proud, Lee, 194
Psych: The Musical, 114
Public Theater, xviii, 47, 60, 63, 64, 172, 209, 210, 277
Puccini, Antonio, 22
Puccini, Giacomo, xi, xix, xx, xxii, 20–23, 33–39, 51, 148, 149, 154
Puckett, Olivia, 348
Pulitzer Prize, 60, 63, 115, 146, 150, 153, 154, 244, 258, 293
Puncture, 106
Punk Is Dead, 112
Purlie, 143
Pussycat Dolls, The, 322
Putterman, Noah, 315
Pyramid Club, 166, 254, 274

Quadrino, Michael, *256*, 316–17
Quando m'en vo' soletta, see "Musetta's Waltz"
Queer Eye for the Straight Guy, 183, 229, 328
Quills, 170
Quiz Show, 110

Radcliffe, Mark, 200
Radcliffe College, 278
Radio City Music Hall, 214, 331
Radiohead, 251, 255
Rado, James, xviii
Ragni, Gerome, xviii
Ragtime, 61, 233
Raised in Captivity, 113
Raisin in the Sun, A, 207
Raitt, Bonnie, 86
Ramey, Jeremy, 342
Ramones, The, 253, 275

Ramsey, Kenna J., 353, 355
Ran, 269
Rand, Mykal, 355
Randall, Jeremy, 340
Randall, Tony, 106
Ranks, Shabba, 166
Rannells, Andrew, 102
Rapp, Adam, 113, 114
Rapp, Anthony, xi, xiv, 12, 51–53, 55, 63, 71, 85, *85*, 88, 89, 94–95, *95*, 109, 112, 113–14, 147, 154, 179, 184–85, 188, 195, 201, 204, *214*, 221, *221*, 224, *228*, 231, 234, *271*, 300, 309, 316, 317, 353, 355, 357
Rapp, Mary, 113
Rashomon, 268
Rauschenberg, Robert, 255
Raze, 207
Reagan, Ronald, 242
"Real Estate," 56
Real Live Brady Bunch, The, 62
Really Useful Group, 194
Réaux, Angelina, 40
Rebeck, Theresa, 302
Rebel Without a Cause, 198
"Red Hill Mining Town," 87
Red Hot Chili Peppers, The, 274
Redemption Songs, 115
Redgrave, Bobby, 156
Redgrave, Vanessa, 245
Reed, Caitlin, 340
Reed, Donna, 267
Reggae, 117
Reich, Steve, 251
Reid, Corbin, 289, 347, 357
Reid, Gabrielle, 349
R.E.M., 53
Reneau, Lyonel, *134*, 317
Renée, Ciara, 299
RENT 20th Anniversary Productions Ltd., 194
Rent Remixed, 190–94
Rent School Edition, 310, 334, 345
Rent: Filmed Live on Broadway, 236–41, *239*, 281
"Rent" (song), 44, 46, 72, 121–22, 203, 210, 214–15, 330–31

Rentheads, 155–58, 271, 337
Reprise Theatre Company, 101
Reside, Doug, 306
Respect for Acting, 263
Ressler, David, 339, *339*
Restaurant, 106
Resultan, Dave, 348
Reubens, Paul, 265–66
Revels, André, 318
Revolution Studios, 200, 201
Rice, Tim, xix, xx, 111, 259
Rich, James, 355
Richard Rodgers Awards for Musical Theatre, 50
Richards, Keith, 328
Richardson, Chad, 183, 354, 355
Rickman, Alan, 253
Ricordi, Giulio, 21
Ridge High School, 334–36, *335*
Ridiculous Theatrical Company, 274
Rieff, Philip, 277
Rigby, Cathy, 326
"Right Brain," 56
Ringwald, Molly, 176
Rios, Angelo, 349
Ripley, Alice, 106
Risa Bramon & Billy Hopkins Casting, 84
Rise of Little Voice, The, 61
Ritz Theatre Company, 336–37
Rivera, José, 63, 166
Rivers, Joan, 65
Rivington School, 162–63
RKO Pictures, 267
Road Show, 277
Road Trip, 114
Roberson, Tyrone, 313
Robert, Mel, 328
Roberts, Calvin Scott, 315
Robeson, Paul, 1, 262
Rock 'n' Roll, 264
Rockefeller Center, 275,
Rocky Horror Show, The, xix, 105–6, 110, 115, 296, 337
Rodgers, Aggie Guerard, 169
Rodgers, Richard, 8, 50, 149, 154, 276, 305, 313
Rodriguez, Enrico, 354

Rodriguez, Jai, 183, 229, 328, 354, 355
Rodriguez, Justin, 184, 357
Rodriguez, MJ (Michael), 283, 289, 357
Rodriguez, Robert, 207
Rogers, Gordon, 13–14
Rogers, Kia, 321
Roht, Ken, 106
Rolling Stone, 257
Rolling Stones, The, 245
Romani, 23,
Romberger, James, 163
Romeo and Juliet, 8, 64, 219
Ronan, Brian, 283
Rooney, Patrick, 342, *342*
Roots, 244
Rose, Billy, 143
Rose, Charlie, xii
Rosenbaum, Dan, 318
Rosenstein, Eddie, 6, 12, 16, 17, 95
Rosenthal, Jane, 198, 199, 200
Rosewood, 102
Ross, Annie, 250
Ross, Jeff, 147
Rosselini, Isabella, 147
Roth, David, 338–39
Roth, Joe, 200
Rowan, Richard, xi
Rowe, Adriana, 306
"Roxanne," 53
Roxy Theatre, 265
Royal Alexander Theatre, 183
Royal, Steven, 316
Rubinstein, Helena, 64
Rubin-Vega, Daphne, 18, *52*, 53, 55, 57, 75, 76, 85, 89, 99, 106, 110, 114–15, 148, *151*, 152, 153, 168, 179, 204, 231, 300–301, 303, 354
Ruchalski, Emily, 346
Rudetsky, Seth, 113
Rudin, Scott, 301
"Rudolph the Red-Nosed Reindeer," 254
Runaways, 103, 110
RuPaul, 274
Rush, Pete, 318
Russell, Tim, *324*, 325

Rusty's Storefront Blitz, 7
Ruzicka, Sara, 349

Sabares-Klemm, Jamila, 313
Sacrimmoralinority, 3
Safe House, 207
Safran, Joshua, 303
Sahl, Mort, 250
Saint, David, 240
Saks, Andrew, 275
Saks Fifth Avenue, 159, 275
Salatino, Anthony, 341
Salazar, George, *298*, 299
Salinger, J.D., 198
Sally Marr. . . and her escorts, 65
Salvation Army, 168
Sammy Cahn in Person-Words and Music,
    62
San Francisco Playhouse, 104
San Jose State University, 65
Sanchez, Nick, 354
Sanford, Tim, 42
Sanshiro Sugata, 268
"Santa Fe," 44, 46, 55, 79, *84*, 128, 140,
    174, 220, 232, 255, 265
Santana, David, 116
Santana, Julia, *35*, 180, 355
Santiago, Reymundo, 326
Sapienza, Victor, 274
Sarandon, Susan, 279
Sartre, Jean-Paul, 264
Satellite Award, 209
Satie, Erik, 251
Satter, Daniel, 346
Saturday Night Fever, 187
Saturday Night Live, 3, 246
Save the Children, 209
*Saved!-An Immoral Musical on the Moral
    Majority*, 7
Scarlet Pimpernel, The, 101
Scènes de la vie de bohème, 21, 22–23
Schatz, Sara, 357
Scherzinger, Nicole, 322
Schmuckler, Alan, 312
Schneider, Maria, 248
Schoenberg, Arnold, 251
Schönberg, Claude-Michel, xx
School of Rock, 112

School of the Arts (Rochester), 101
School Ties, 113
Schreier, Dan Moses, 13
Schumacher, Joel, 198
Schuman, Howard, 105
Schumer, Charles E., 230
Schwartz, Scott, 293, 299, 346
Schwartz, Stephen, xix, 108, 281, 293
Scorsese, Martin, 199
Scott, Ridley, 279
Scott, Sherie Rene, 109, 112, 354
Scotto, Renata, 41
Scottsboro Boys, The, 104–5
Screaming Mimi's, 168
Seagull, The, 53, 262
Season of Youth, 106
"Seasons of Love," xi, xxi, 54, 55, 81,
    94, 116, 132–34, 138, 151, 154,
    180, 191, 203, 209, 211, 213,
    221, 230, 232, 238, 240, 285,
    290, 321, 322, 327, 334, 337,
    342
"Seasons of Love B," 137
Sebastian's Caribbean Carnival, 102
Seckinger, Anna, 49
Second Stage, 9, 49, 63, 64, 114, 292
Secrest, Meryle, 277
Secret Theatre, 318
See What I Wanna See, 109, 210
Seeger, Pete, 1
Sellars, Peter, 104
Seller, Jeffrey, 9, 41, 49, 57, 58, 59–61,
    64, 83, 97, 99, 142, 146, 150,
    154, 158, 171, 175, 183, 201,
    235, 241, 282, 347
Send Me, 207
Senense, Justin, 349
Señor, Andy, *229*, 354, 355, 357
Sepulveda, Jose, 341
Serious Money, 246
Sesame Street, 12, 86, 208
Setlock, Mark, 54, 82, 85, 354
Seven Samurai, The, 268–69
Sex Pistols, The, 258, 275–76
Sexual Healing, 107
Shaftesbury Theatre, 187–88, *189*
Shakespeare, William, xix, 3, 47, 63,
    106, 113, 117, 166, 209, 269

Shattered Glass, 208
Shaw, Pam, 13–14
Shawn, Wallace, 264
She Loves Me, 60
She's Gotta Have It, 270
Shea, Johnny, 339
Shear, Claudia, 170
Sherman, Jon, 198
Shields, Cary, 353
Shingledecker, Matt, 285–86, *286*, 287, 357
Shioda, Futaba, 357
Sh-K Boom Records, 112, 115
Show Boat, 187, 300
Showtime at the Apollo, 116
Shrek the Musical, 65
Shubert Theatre (Boston), 176
Shubert, Franz, 9
Shuberts, 143
Shure, Dan, 339
Shyamalan, M. Night, 112
Sì, mi chiamano Mimì, 37
Siccone, Nicholas, 336
Sidewalks of New York, 208
Signature Theatre, 64, 115
Silberger, Katherine, 152
Silverman, Sarah, 209
Silverstein, Jonathan, 299
Simon & Kumin Casting, 84
Simon, Neil, 256, 313
Simone, 82, 178, 179, 355
Simone, Cassie, 327, *327*
Simone, Nina, 179
Simons, Daniel T., 334
Simpson, Jim, 147
Singer, Clay, 339
Six Degrees of Separation, 113
Skármeta, Antonio, 274
Skidis, Anna, 330
Skinner, Curt, 355
Skinner, Steve, 11, 13, 44, 65, 151
Skywalker Ranch, 210
Slavs!, 170
Sleight of Hand, 63
Sloan, Sabrina, 328
Sloane, Robin, 150, 151
Slow Burn Theatre Company, 337–38
Slow Down, 101

Smash, 106–7, 115, 302–4
Smith, Anna Deavere, 61, 209
Smith, Antonique, 354
Smith, Beth, 296
Smith, Charlie, 340
Smith, Damien DeShaun, 357
Smith, Daniel Clayton, 318
Smith, Jacques C., 353, 357
Smith, Patti, 253
Smith, Peter Matthew, 354
Smith-Sadak, Diane, 344–45
Smolik, Justin, 330
Snug Harbor Music Hall, 319
Society of Stage Directors and Choreographers, 333
Soho Rep, 161
Solitary Confinement, 143
Solomon, Robert J., 355
Solti, Georg, 40
Some Americans Abroad, 114
Something Rotten!, 62, 113
"Something to Talk About," 86
"Something Wonderful," 301
Sondheim, Stephen, xii, xxi, 5, 8, 50, 276–77, 295, 297, 329
Sonic Youth, 255
Sontag, Susan, 277–78
Sony Pictures, 201, 236
Sophisticated Ladies, 44
Sophistry, 113
Sound of Music, The, xxi, 50, 196
Soundgarden, 252
Sousa, John Philip, 13
South Jackson Civic Center, 331
South Pacific, xvii, 65, 200
South Park, 301
Souvenir, 115
Souza, Alan, 326
Soyinka, Wole, 117
Spain in My Heart, 273
Spamalot, 62
Spanger, Amy, 179, 292, 296, *297*, 355
Spencer, Kevin, 184, 357
Spice Girls, 228
Spice, Scary, 228
Spielberg, Steven, 201, 227, 269
Spillane, Jessica, 345, 346
Spin City, 104

"Splatter," 55
Spot Design, 150
SpotCo, 150–51
Spring Awakening, 322, 333
Springsteen, Bruce, 54, 77, 85
Spungen, Nancy, 276
St. James Theatre (London), *193*, 194, 195
St. Laurence, Robert, 330
St. Louis, David, 355
St. Vincent's Hospital, 17, 19
Stagedoor Manor, 111, 310
Stained, 66
Stalin, Joseph, 273
Stanford University, 268
Stanley Drama Award, 347
Staples Players, *124*, 338–39, *339*
Starlight Express, 110
Starmites, 116
State Fair, 154
Stealing Beauty, 248
Steely Dan, 43
Stefani, Philippa, 194
Stein, Gertrude, 23, 278–79
Stein, Leo, 278
Stein, Mandy, 253
Steinem, Gloria, 147
Steingruby, Luke, 330
Stephani, Catherine, 319
Stephen Sondheim: A Life, 277
Stepmom, 226
Steppenwolf Theatre, 110
Stern, Philip Van Doren, 267
Stern, Stewart, 198
Stevens, Fisher, 102
Stevens, Justin, 348
Stewart, Carla, 340
Stewart, Gwen, 81, *90*, 116–17, 232, 238, 322, 353, 354, 357
Stewart, Jason, 335
Stewart, Jimmy, 267
Stick Fly, 207
Stiefel, Milton, 324
Still I Can't Be Still, 109
Stiller, Jerry, 147
Stilwell, Richard, 41
Sting, 61, 252
Stipe, Michael, 53

Stone, Matt, 301–2
Stones in His Pockets, 61
Stoppard, Tom, 65, 264, 280
Strand, The, 275
Stratas, Teresa, 41
Stravinsky, Igor, 251
Streep, Meryl, 197
Streetcar Named Desire, A, 115, 246, 262
Streisand, Barbra, 197, 292
Strouse, Charles, xviii
Student Affairs, 105
Studio 54, 274
Studio Arena Theatre, 117
Sturge, Tom, 318
Sturges, John, 269
Sturiale, Brandon, 348
Styne, Jule, 276
Suds, 116
Sugababes, 193
Sugar Mountain, 105
Sugar, Nick, 343
Sulfaro, Nick, 330
Summer of 42, 109
Sundance Film Festival, 198
Sunday in the Park with George, 8, 276, 277
"Sunday," 277
Sunset Boulevard, 154, 300
Superbia, 8, 9, 50, 110, 293, 295, 309
Supremes, The, xix
Surflight Theatre, *78*, 340
Swados, Elizabeth, 103, 110
Swayze, Patrick, 147
Sweeney Todd, xvii, 2, 276, 277
Sweet Valley High, 179
Sykes, Ephraim M., 355
Syracuse Stage, 340–41
Syracuse University, 101, 268, 340–41

Takara, Yuka, 354, 357
"Take Me or Leave Me," 38, 56, 71, 91, *98*, *136*, 136–37, 179, *182*, 203, 205, 211, 221, 224, 233, 234, 273, 285, 318, 343
Tales from the Tunnel, 104
Talking Heads, 253
Tallent, Carl, 318, 319
Tallulah, 202
Tambourines to Glory, 266

Tandy, Jessica, 262
"Tango: Maureen," 38, 57, 126, 191,
    203, 218–19, 224, 234, 315, 319
Tarantino, Quentin, 207
Tate, Robert, 49
Tattered Cover Book Store, xii
Team America: World Police, 301–2
Tedder, Cary, 347
Television, 253
Telsey, Bernard, 84–87, 172–73
Telsey + Company Casting, 84, 173–75,
    205, 285
Tempest, The, 64
Temple, Julien, 276
Temptation, 112
Tennessee Rep, 166
Terzier, Jessica, 355
Testa, Mary, 292
TheaterWeek, xi
Theatre at Boston Court, 106
Theatre Communications Group,
    160–61
Theatre World Awards, 111, 115, 153
Thelma and Louise, 216, 279–80
Theo Ubique Cabaret Theatre,
    341–43, *342*
They Might Be Giants, 258
They're Playing Our Song, 187
thirtysomething, 44
Thomas, Carly, 354
Thomas, Hilaria, 246
Thompson, Ben, 357
Thompson, Christian, 357
Thoms, Tracie, 205–7, *206*, 213, *221*,
    222, 225, 226, 237–38, 322, 353
Thomson, Lynn M., 83, 96
Thoreau, Henry David, 251
Thornton, Oliver, *191*, 192, 193
Three Chris's, 104
Threepenny Opera, 106
Throne of Blood, 269
Thunderbirds, 301
Thurber Carnival, A, 111
Thursday's Child, 326
tick, tick... BOOM!, xxiii, 1, 9, 277,
    293–99, *294*, *297*, *298*, 309, 330,
    346
Tiffany & Co., 159

Tillman, Nicole, 328
Timberlake, Justin, 204
Time Café, 18
"Times They Are A-Changin', The,"
    257
Timon of Athens, 106
Tisch, Jonathan, 230
Tisch School of the Arts, 108, 201, 214,
    246, 331
[title of show], 61
To the Castle and Back, 264
Tobocman, Seth, 163
"Today 4 U," 55, 68, *103*, *124*, 124–25,
    138, 216, 217, 218, 231, 279–80,
    300, 336
Together Through Life, 258
Toklas, Alice B., 278–79
Tokyo Disneyland, 102
Tommasini, Anthony, 18, 92, 229–30
"Tomorrow Belongs to Me," 111
Tompkins Square Park, 44, 220, 283
Tony Awards, xii, 59, 61, 63, 64, 66, 67,
    86, *103*, 105, 109, 111, 115, 150,
    153–55, 170, 244, 262–63, 281,
    299, 303, 307
Too Fast to Live, Too Young to Die, 275
Too Many Clothes, 170
Tormé, Mel, 254
Tosca, 22
Toscanini, Arturo, 39
Town Hall Arts Center, 343
Towson University, 343–45
Trafalgar Theatre, 143
Tragedy of a Ridiculous Man, 248
Trance, 209
Trash & Vaudeville, 163, 168
Trask, Stephen, 102
Traveling Wilburys, The, 257
Travers, Henry, 267
Travolta, John, 109
Treadwell, Sophie, 63
Treasure Island, 210
Triad, The, 300
Tribeca Films, 198, 200
Tribeca Performing Arts Center, 66
Tribes, 311
Trinity Repertory Company, 63
Triptych, 170

Trombino, Julius, 336
Troubled Island, 266
True Blood, 117
Truly Blessed, 116
Trumbly, Derrick, 312
Trumbull High School, 345–46
Trumbull Youth Association, 346
Trump, Donald, 56, 246, 260
Trungpa, Venerable Chögyam, 261
Trybe, 209
Tse-tung, Mao, 273
Tsui, Sam, 350
Tudor, David, 255
"Tune Up # 1," 120, 203
"Tune Up # 2," 121
"Tune Up # 3," 122
Turandot, 22
Turn of the Screw, The, 110
Turner, Tina, 189
Tveit, Aaron, 321–22, *322*, *323*
Twelfth Night, 3, 166
Twentieth Anniversary Tour (U.S.), 66,
    68, *169*, 171, *182*, *185*, 185–86,
    357
Twentieth Anniversary Tour (UK)
    194–95
Twenty Love Poems and a Song of Despair,
    273
Twilight: Los Angeles, 1992, 61, 209
Twitchell, Audrey, 339
Two Gentlemen of Verona, xix, 209

U2, 87
Ubu Repertory, 105
Unbreakable, 112
Uncompromising Artistry, 316
Under Hellgate Bridge, 105
Underwood, Blair, 115
Underwood, Todd, 325
Union Square, 115
Universal Studios, 198, 199
University of Bologna, 245
University of California, San Diego,
    62, 63
University of Chicago, 277
University of Cincinnati College-
    Conservatory of Music, 60
University of Freiburg, 264

University of Michigan, 60, 100–101,
    257, 347
University of Notre Dame, 160
University of Southern California, 60,
    198
Unky's Music, Ltd., 306
Ursino, Alex, 336
Usher, 204
Utley, Byron, 81, *90*, 117, 354

Vagina Monologues, The, 105, 109
Vallotton, Félix, 278
Van Dyke, Will, 283
van Hove, Ivo, 48
Van Outen, Denise, 191, *191*, 192
Vance, Brent Davin, 355
Varhola, Kim, 354
Variety Arts Theatre, 142
Varvatos, John, 253–54
Vedder, Eddie, 77
Velez, Loraine, 354
Veness, Adam, 341
Venice Film Festival, 245, 248, 268
Via Galactica, xix
Via Theatre, 105
Vicious, Sid, 275
Victor/Victoria, 153–54, 300
Vida, Bruno, 337
Vietnam War, xvii, xviii, 262, 268
Village Gate, 8, 9, 293, *294*, 309
Village Theatre, 105
Village Vanguard, 253
Village Voice, The, 111, 280–81
Villazón, Rolando, 40
Vineyard Theatre, 61, 104
Visconti, Luchino, 248
Vivian, John, 233–34
Vizzini, Ned, 202
Vogel, Susanna, 334
"Voice Mail # 1," 120, 203
"Voice Mail # 2," 123–24
"Voice Mail # 3," 134–35
"Voice Mail # 4," 137
"Voice Mail # 5," 81, 140
Voidoids, 253
Volcano Lover, The, 277
Volpe, Skyler, *169*, 357
von Karajan, Herbert, 39

Wade, Cory, 336
Wagner College, 347–48
Waits, Tom, 54, 85
Waldman, Anne, 261
Walker, Alice, 266
Walker, Nik, 319, 333–34
Walker-Browne, Fredi, 70, 91, *98*, 116, 117–18, 204, 207, 232, 353
"Walking in Memphis," 296
Wall Street, 117
Wallace, Marisha, 314
Walsh, Casey, 346
Walsh, Kate, 102
Walters, Barbara, 147
War Paint, 64
Ward, Pat, 338
Warhol, Andy, 253, 255
Warner Brothers, 198, 199, 200, 201, 211, 212
Warren, Michael John, 238, 240
Wartella, M., 280
Wartella, Michael, 357
Warwick, Dionne, 255
Washington Post, 46
Washington, Denzel, 270
Washington, Krystal L., 184, 354, 357
Washington, Zuri, *31*, 321
Wasser, Martha Marie, 337
Watergate, xvii
Watermark Theatre, 105
Watson-Davis, Myiia, 353
"We Are Family," 225
"We're Okay," 37, 56, 70, 128–29, 135, 211, 238, 322
Weaver, Sigourney, 147
Weavers, The, 1
Webb, Jay, *191*, 193
Weed, Morgan, 357
Weil, Tim, 51, 54, 65, 83, 89, 96–97, 116, 185, 210, 308, 321
Weinstein, Bob, 198, 200
Weinstein, Harvey, 198, 199–200, 201
Weinstein, Scott, 341
Weiss, Adrienne, 166
Weiss, Daniel A., 65, 195
Weitzman, Ira, 13, 42–44, 45
Well Hungarians, The, 9

Welles, Orson, 143
Wells, Kaleb, 357
Wells, Robert, 254
Wenders, Wim, 245
Wendland, Mark, 283
Wendt, Angela, 54–55, 166–69, 186, 283, 285, 321, 340
West Boca High School, 337
West Side Story, xvii, 2, 40, 53, 61, 188, 196, 276, 285, 347
West Wing, The, 102
West, Brit, 313, 326
West, Kalyn, 315
Westbeth Community Performance Space, 12
Westchester Broadway Theatre, 347, 348–49
Wester, Wayne, 332
Westminster Theatre, 194
Westphal, Cynthia Kortman, 347
Westrich, Mike, 337
"What You Own," xi, 16, 39, 56, 72, 89, 95, 139–40, 184, 192, 223, 283, 289, 315
What's Wrong with This Picture?, 61
Wheeler, Hugh, 276
"White Christmas," 254
White, Sue, 92
Whitman, Walt, 266
Whitten, Mark, 327
Whitty, Jeff, 240
Who, The, 1
Who's Afraid of Virginia Woolf?, 143, 263
Who's Tommy, The, xx, 109–10
"Why," 295–96, 309
Wicked, xix, 102, 108, 109, 110, 281, 313
Wiegert, Marcy, 330
Wilcock, John, 280
Wilcox, Patricia, 348–49
Wilcox, Wayne, 209–10
Wild About Harry, 112
Wild Party, The, 60, 102, 109
Wild Things, 115
Wilder, Thornton, 278
Wildhorn, Frank, 101
Wilke, Alex, *335*, 336
Wilkison, Jay, 354, 357

Will and Grace, 102
"Will I?" 55, 81, 91, 100, 127, 141, 203, 318
Williams, Cindy, 340
Williams, Gregory L., 334
Williams, Layton, *193*, 195
Williams, Robin, 61
Williams, Tennessee, 48, 115, 198
Williams, William Carlos, 260
Williamstown Theatre Festival, 63, 106, 117
Wilson Jr., Bruce, 357
Wilson, Maia Nkenge, 354
Window on the Nether Sea, A, 160
Winfrey, Oprah, 244
Winspear Opera House, 186
Winter's Tale, The, 64, 106
Without a Trace, 104
"Without You," 38, 55, 77, 94, 137, 141, 162, 179, 192, 205, 222, 232
Wiz, The, 116, 196
Wizard of Oz, The, 2, 256
Wolf, Dan, 280
Women on the Verge of a Nervous Breakdown, 340
Wonder, Stevie, 151
Wonder Boys, 258
Wonderful Wizard of Oz, The, 256, 281
Wonderworks, 117
Wontorek, Paul, 203
Wood, 102
Wood, Haneefah, 357
Wooten, Jason, 315
Work Light Productions, 185
Working Girl, 246
World Trade Center, 199
World War II, 245, 249, 252, 258, 268, 270, 279
Worthington, Andrew, 345

Wright, Anthony, 318–19
Wright, Doug, 48, 64, 170, 240

X, Malcolm, 244
X-Files, The, 114

Yale Dramatic Association, 349–50
Yale School of Drama, 349, 350
Yearby, Marlies, 65–66, 89–90, 153, 174, 185, 186, 230
"Yellow Bird," 1
York, Michael, 113
York Theatre, 12, 65, 101
Yorke, Thom, 251
Yorkey, Brian, xxiii, 63, 114
"You Okay, Honey?" 122, *335*
"You'll Get Over It," 57
"You'll See," xxi, 56, 69, 125–26, 215, 267
You're a Good Man, Charlie Brown, 113
You're the Top," xxi
Young Frankenstein, 7
Young, Eric Jordan, 319
Young, Keith, 66, 220
Young, Steven, 327
Young, Tricia, 355
Youngblood, Shay, 66
"Your Eyes," 39, 56, 87, 97–99, 141, 315

Zabriskie Point, 245
ZAG Animation Studios, 202
Zanna, Don't!, 319
Zappa, Frank, 251
Zara, 168
Zayas, Jose, 313
Zeffirelli, Franco, 40, 334, 335
Zia, 317
Zidan, James, 332, 333
Zirilli, Jared, 319

THE FAQ SERIES

AC/DC FAQ
by Susan Masino
Backbeat Books
9781480394506................$24.99

Armageddon Films FAQ
by Dale Sherman
Applause Books
9781617131196.................$24.99

The Band FAQ
by Peter Aaron
Backbeat Books
9781617136139 ....$19.99

Baseball FAQ
by Tom DeMichael
Backbeat Books
9781617136061....................$24.99

The Beach Boys FAQ
by Jon Stebbins
Backbeat Books
9780879309879.................$22.99

The Beat Generation FAQ
by Rich Weidman
Backbeat Books
9781617136016 ....$19.99

Beer FAQ
by Jeff Cioletti
Backbeat Books
9781617136115 ....$24.99

Black Sabbath FAQ
by Martin Popoff
Backbeat Books
9780879309572...................$19.99

Bob Dylan FAQ
by Bruce Pollock
Backbeat Books
9781617136078 ....$19.99

Britcoms FAQ
by Dave Thompson
Applause Books
9781495018992 ....$19.99

Bruce Springsteen FAQ
by John D. Luerssen
Backbeat Books
9781617130939....................$22.99

A Chorus Line FAQ
by Tom Rowan
Applause Books
9781480367548 ....$19.99

The Clash FAQ
by Gary J. Jucha
Backbeat Books
9781480364509 ....$19.99

Doctor Who FAQ
by Dave Thompson
Applause Books
9781557838544....................$22.99

The Doors FAQ
by Rich Weidman
Backbeat Books
9781617130175 ....$24.99

Dracula FAQ
by Bruce Scivally
Backbeat Books
9781617136009 ....$19.99

The Eagles FAQ
by Andrew Vaughan
Backbeat Books
9781480385412...................$24.99

Elvis Films FAQ
by Paul Simpson
Applause Books
9781557838582...................$24.99

Elvis Music FAQ
by Mike Eder
Backbeat Books
9781617130496......................$24.99

Eric Clapton FAQ
by David Bowling
Backbeat Books
9781617134548 ....$22.99

Fab Four FAQ
by Stuart Shea and Robert Rodriguez
Hal Leonard Books
9781423421382.......................$19.99

Fab Four FAQ 2.0
by Robert Rodriguez
Backbeat Books
9780879309688...................$19.99

Film Noir FAQ
by David J. Hogan
Applause Books
9781557838551.....................$22.99

Football FAQ
by Dave Thompson
Backbeat Books
9781495007484 ....$24.99

Frank Zappa FAQ
by John Corcelli
Backbeat Books
9781617136030.....................$19.99

Godzilla FAQ
by Brian Solomon
Applause Books
9781495045684 ....$19.99

The Grateful Dead FAQ
by Tony Sclafani
Backbeat Books
9781617130861.....................$24.99

Guns N' Roses FAQ
by Rich Weidman
Backbeat Books
9781495025884 ....$19.99

Haunted America FAQ
by Dave Thompson
Backbeat Books
9781480392625......................$19.99

Horror Films FAQ
by John Kenneth Muir
Applause Books
9781557839503 ....$22.99

James Bond FAQ
by Tom DeMichael
Applause Books
9781557838568......................$22.99

Jimi Hendrix FAQ
by Gary J. Jucha
Backbeat Books
9781617130953......................$22.99

Prices, contents, and availability
subject to change without notice.

ohnny Cash FAQ
by C. Eric Banister
Backbeat Books
9781480385405 .... $24.99

ISS FAQ
by Dale Sherman
Backbeat Books
9781617130915 .... $24.99

ed Zeppelin FAQ
by George Case
Backbeat Books
9781617130250 ....$22.99

ucille Ball FAQ
*by James Sheridan
and Barry Monush*
Applause Books
9781617740824 ....$19.99

M.A.S.H. FAQ
by Dale Sherman
Applause Books
9781480355897 ....$19.99

Michael Jackson FAQ
by Kit O'Toole
Backbeat Books
9781480371064 ....$19.99

Modern Sci-Fi Films FAQ
by Tom DeMichael
Applause Books
9781480350618 .... $24.99

Monty Python FAQ
*by Chris Barsanti, Brian Cogan,
and Jeff Massey*
Applause Books
9781495049439 .... $19.99

Morrissey FAQ
by D. McKinney
Backbeat Books
9781480394483 .... $24.99

Neil Young FAQ
by Glen Boyd
Backbeat Books
9781617130373 ....$19.99

Nirvana FAQ
by John D. Luerssen
Backbeat Books
9781617134500 .... $24.99

Pearl Jam FAQ
*by Bernard M. Corbett and
Thomas Edward Harkins*
Backbeat Books
9781617136122 .... $19.99

Pink Floyd FAQ
by Stuart Shea
Backbeat Books
9780879309503 ....$19.99

Pro Wrestling FAQ
by Brian Solomon
Backbeat Books
9781617135996 .... $29.99

Prog Rock FAQ
by Will Romano
Backbeat Books
9781617135873 .... $24.99

Quentin Tarantino FAQ
by Dale Sherman
Applause Books
9781480355880 .... $24.99

Robin Hood FAQ
by Dave Thompson
Applause Books
9781495048227 ....$19.99

**The Rocky Horror
Picture Show FAQ**
by Dave Thompson
Applause Books
9781495007477 .... $19.99

Rush FAQ
by Max Mobley
Backbeat Books
9781617134517 ....$19.99

Saturday Night Live FAQ
by Stephen Tropiano
Applause Books
9781557839510 .... $24.99

Seinfeld FAQ
by Nicholas Nigro
Applause Books
9781557838575 .... $24.99

Sherlock Holmes FAQ
by Dave Thompson
Applause Books
9781480331495 .... $24.99

The Smiths FAQ
by John D. Luerssen
Backbeat Books
9781480394490 .... $24.99

Soccer FAQ
by Dave Thompson
Backbeat Books
9781617135989 .... $24.99

The Sound of Music FAQ
by Barry Monush
Applause Books
9781480360433 .... $27.99

South Park FAQ
by Dave Thompson
Applause Books
9781480350649 .... $24.99

Star Trek FAQ
(Unofficial and Unauthorized)
by Mark Clark
Applause Books
9781557837929 ....$19.99

Star Trek FAQ 2.0
(Unofficial and Unauthorized)
by Mark Clark
Applause Books
9781557837936 ....$22.99

Star Wars FAQ
by Mark Clark
Applause Books
9781480360181 .... $24.99

Steely Dan FAQ
by Anthony Robustelli
Backbeat Books
9781495025129 .... $19.99

Stephen King Films FAQ
by Scott Von Doviak
Applause Books
9781480355514 .... $24.99

Three Stooges FAQ
by David J. Hogan
Applause Books
9781557837882 ....$22.99

TV Finales FAQ
*by Stephen Tropiano and
Holly Van Buren*
Applause Books
9781480391444 .... $19.99

The Twilight Zone FAQ
by Dave Thompson
Applause Books
9781480396180 .... $19.99

Twin Peaks FAQ
*by David Bushman and
Arthur Smith*
Applause Books
9781495015861 ....$19.99

UFO FAQ
by David J. Hogan
Backbeat Books
9781480393851 .... $19.99

Video Games FAQ
by Mark J.P. Wolf
Backbeat Books
9781617136306 ....$19.99

The Who FAQ
by Mike Segretto
Backbeat Books
9781480361034 .... $24.99

The Wizard of Oz FAQ
by David J. Hogan
Applause Books
9781480350625 .... $24.99

The X-Files FAQ
by John Kenneth Muir
Applause Books
9781480369740 .... $24.99

HAL•LEONARD®
PERFORMING ARTS
PUBLISHING GROUP